D1199154

THE MYSTERY OF
HAMLET
KING OF DENMARK
OR
WHAT WE WILL

AMONG THE AUTHOR'S PREVIOUSLY PUBLISHED WORKS:

THE CANTERBURY PILGRIMS · JEANNE D'ARC · SAPPHO AND PHAON · THE SCARECROW · THE PLAYHOUSE AND THE PLAY · A GARLAND TO SYLVIA · THE CIVIC THEATRE · SANCTUARY · SAINT LOUIS · A THOUSAND YEARS AGO · THE MODERN READER'S CHAUCER [with Prof. J. S. P. Tatlock] · CALIBAN · COMMUNITY DRAMA · THIS FINE PRETTY WORLD · TALL TALES OF THE KENTUCKY MOUNTAINS · EPOCH: THE LIFE OF STEELE MACKAYE [2 vols.] · THE GOBBLER OF GOD · WEATHERGOOSE-WOO! · ANNALS OF AN ERA: 1826–1932 · THE FAR FAMILIAR · MY LADY DEAR, ARISE!

A COMPLETE BIBLIOGRAPHY OF PERCY MACKAYE'S WORKS
WILL BE FOUND IN THE LIMITED EDITION
OF THE TETRALOGY.

THE MYSTERY OF HAMLET KING OF DENMARK

OR

WHAT WE WILL

A TETRALOGY

BY PERCY MACKAYE

IN PROLOGUE TO

The Tragicall Historie of HAMLET, Prince of Denmarke

BY WILLIAM SHAKESPEARE

First Play: THE GHOST OF ELSINORE
Second Play: THE FOOL IN EDEN GARDEN
Third Play: ODIN AGAINST CHRISTUS
Fourth Play: THE SERPENT IN THE ORCHARD

PUBLISHED BY THE BOND WHEELWRIGHT COMPANY · NEW YORK · MCML

THE BOND WHEELWRIGHT COMPANY · PUBLISHERS
145 EAST 63RD STREET, NEW YORK 21, NEW YORK

PRINTED IN THE UNITED STATES OF AMERICA

IN CANADA
BURNS & MACEACHERN
TORONTO

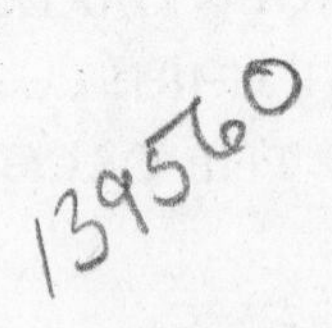

To Marion this her Garland

To

MARION-SYLVIA *

Can mind recapture the spirit? Can the mind,
Patching a poem, a latchet of literature,
Cut through to the quick, draw cobbler's blood, and find
The artery of the seer — the divinely pure

Ichor of life, that pours through sense-flusht veins
From out the fountains of the All-Profusion
That links the dead-quick with the quickening skeins
Of vaulting love — can it thus perform transfusion

Of earth-blood with heaven-springs? Was all our youth —
Love of my life, life of our love! — the darkling
Presage of an after-age — a young dawn of truth
Outsplendoring in vision all our sparkling

Poem-fancies with the ardorous triumph of POESIA? —
SYLVIA-Marion, ever MORE my Marion-SYLVIA!

*MY LADY DEAR, ARISE! Poems to Marion Morse MacKaye. Sonnet XLviii.

To

W. S.*

Shakespeare, whose clasping spirit entwined us two
  Into thy song, that garlands beauty and kindness
With the excelling ring of wreathéd tears, whose dew
  Is love! Spirit of undarkened blindness,

Who openest wide the shuttered walls of sense
  Into the windowless pasturings, where Nature
Consorts with Over-Nature, to experience
  Conception and birth of the heavenly forms which enfeature

Them both! Secret-teller and keeper! Whisper to her
  This untold secret, hidden-told: The play—thy play
And mine—youth-begotten, age-born, forever newer
  For ripening knowledge,—whisper near, and say

  This, from her cobbler-king: 'OUR play 's the scene
  Wherein I'll match the conscience of my Queen!'

*MY LADY DEAR, ARISE! Sonnet XLix: "SECRET UNTOLD": Now here told

KEY TO MARGINAL SYMBOLS

[USED THROUGHOUT THE TETRALOGY]

The Crescent Moon:—*marks the passing from the visible to the invisible world*

The Crescent and Star with Cock:—*appearances of* GALLUCINIUS: *inward communion of the character with himself*

The Ram's Horns:—*token of* YORICK *in his moments of second sight*

W S with Bodonian Dash:—*direct quotations from Shakespeare's* HAMLET

NOTE: The designer, in collaboration with the author, has evolved these symbols as a means of bringing the theatre to the printed page. Each of these symbols takes the place of lighting effects through which a separate plane of action and thought is suggested to the audience. A wavy line dropping from the first three of these symbols indicates the extent of that particular action and thought.

PUBLISHER'S FOREWORD

WE OFTEN speak of the "magic of the Tetralogy," for it would be nearly impossible to explain the circumstances behind these printed pages in any other way. The story of its publication has the elements of a fairy tale. To begin with, we became publishers in order to do this book. Bolstered by the author's faith in our venture, we decided to obtain funds to print a brochure which would describe the beautiful volume we visualized, bring us enough subscribers to pay for printing the book itself, and make a modest but comprehensive popular edition possible. Even this proved difficult. But in the meantime, my wife, having complete confidence in the outcome, went on editing the Tetralogy; Raymond Da Boll went on making sketches for the brochure and various pages of the book itself; and I succeeded in starting a list of subscribers for the limited hundred-dollar edition. Finally, we decided to see whether the printers we had chosen would be willing to work with us on a credit basis, on the strength of our growing list of subscribers and the cooperation and enthusiasm of such individuals as William Rose Benét, Professor Henry W. Wells, Gilmor Brown of the Pasadena Playhouse, and many others.

Perhaps it was our faith that set the magic to work at that point, for it was on the morning before my first interview with R. R. Donnelley & Sons that a call from Texas caught up with me. James Ross Boothe, a young poet who had spent months of tireless effort working for Percy MacKaye on the manuscript, believed in the Tetralogy, too. His first thought when he inherited some money was to help us, for he knew of our project and its problems in detail. It was his voice that came over the wires offering a sufficient sum for us not only to start printing the brochure, but to go ahead on the book without waiting for more subscribers. From then on, there was still another year's work ahead of us, but the project moved forward steadily.

Those responsible for the production of the book at the Lakeside Press put their hearts into it, determined to make it the most beautiful example of bookmaking ever issued from their plant. The purpose of printing the de luxe edition, as we have said, was to pay for the composition and printing in order that this and subsequent printings by offset in reduced format could become available at a moderate price. But it was impossible to include the four scenes of the Prelude to the Tetralogy, and certain of the notes and records appearing in the Limited Edition. These are in the nature of source material and therefore of primary interest to students of the drama and English literature. We shall be glad to refer any interested reader to the libraries where a copy of the Limited Edition may be read. Most of the copies were subscribed to before publication; however, at this printing there are still a few copies available.

Our list of original subscribers ranges all over the literary and economic scale. Significant in the thoroughly heterogeneous list are people in the retail book trade who bought the book for their own libraries; contemporary publishers; at least three employees of the printer, and the designer himself, who sent us a check for his early numbered copy at a time when his hundred dollars brought our bank balance up to two hundred dollars—long before our Texas call.

The literary aspect of this work we leave to the reader's judgment, but if in these few words we have been able to give some insight into the faith and devotion behind this publication, then we have succeeded in conveying an idea of the powerful effect the Tetralogy has had upon all those who have come under its spell.

Some day the remarkable saga of the creation and publication of this work may be written, but perhaps from this fragment can be gleaned a little of what we mean by "the magic of the Tetralogy."

BOND WHEELWRIGHT

CONTENTS

THE GHOST
OF ELSINORE

THE GHOST OF ELSINORE

BEING
THE FIRST PLAY
OF THE TETRALOGY
THE MYSTERY OF HAMLET
KING OF DENMARK, OR
WHAT WE WILL ✢ BY
PERCY MACKAYE

THE GHOST OF ELSINORE

DRAMATIS PERSONAE

[*In the order of their first appearance.*]

VOLTIMAND, *Danish soldier, a guard*
GERTRUDE, *bride of Hamlet, King of Denmark*
HAMLET, *King of Denmark*
YORICK, *court fool*
ANGELA, *daughter of Yorick*
POLONIUS, *secretary to the Lord Chamberlain*
CLAUDIUS, *brother of King Hamlet*
CORNELIA, *wife of Polonius*
FIRST *Danish soldier*
SECOND *Danish soldier*
MOLL COWSLIP, *midwife*
APOTHECARY

Assembled Danes; Voices of Soldiers outside the Castle.

PRESENCES:
Voices of the Invisible
VOICE OF THE COCK
WRAITH OF GERTRUDE
GALLUCINIUS
Processional Figures

PERSONAE: [*Of Inner Scenes from Shakespeare's "Hamlet, Prince of Denmark"*]:—*Prince Hamlet, Horatio, Marcellus, Ghost of King Hamlet.*

SCENES

PROLOGUE:—Elsinore. Ramparts of the Castle.
Moonlight, just before dawn.

ACT FIRST:—Anteroom to the Bedchamber of King Hamlet and Queen Gertrude.
Sunrise of the same day.

ACT SECOND:—Same Scene as Act First. Bright candlelight.
Seven months later.

SCENES

[*Continued*]

ACT THIRD:—Interior of a War-Tent. Stormy night.
Two months later.

ACT FOURTH:—Throne Hall of Elsinore.
Evening of Prince Hamlet's birth.

Note. Stage-right and stage-left are from the actor's point of view.

PROLOGUE

ELSINORE. RAMPARTS OF THE CASTLE. *Moonlight, just before dawn.*
A GUARD, *at his post. A clock's bell is striking three.*

GUARD

Stand, there! What 's stirring?—Who is this that comes
Without the countersign? What man 's in the wind
Yonder?

VOICE

No man.

GUARD

What!—Is the wind a woman
To moan so wild?—Your name?

VOICE

Gertrude, the Queen.

GUARD

Madam, your pardon!

GERTRUDE
[*Appearing, shadowly.*]

Hush!—Where is the King?

GUARD

Madam——

GERTRUDE

The King—Hamlet, my husband—where
Is he?

GUARD

Lady——

GERTRUDE

He is not there, in bed.
I fear that he has walked forth in his sleep
Into the raw air.

GUARD

In his sleep!—*Walked* forth?

GERTRUDE

Even in his slumber. 'Tis a trick of nature
Sometimes that snaggles him, when he will seize
A dark, unlighted torch and hold it high,
Staring at the heaven through unlifted lids,
And reach to ignite the dead wick of Arcturus
With his own fire, or blaze Orion's Belt
With spirit alchemy.—Ah, from this height
If he should reach, and fall in the dark!—Which way
Went he?

GUARD

Madam——

GERTRUDE

To-morrow—see, it dawns now.
Already the awful morrow! This very day
He 's sworn to answer Norway's battle-challenge,
Leave me—go forth to fight with Fortinbras—
Unless my love can hold him. Still—he wavers.
Even in his dreams I heard him cry: "No, no!
Never from *her!*"—But then I winked, and when
I wakened, he was gone.—What shadow-priest
Art thou, for whom I make this castle wall
Of Elsinore the pale confession-crypt
Of a wailing heart?

GUARD

A poor guard, at his post;

No priest, your Majesty, but Voltimand,
Your servant.

GERTRUDE

Hamlet's guard. Then guard him well,
Your king, and bring me to his face.

VOLTIMAND

Where, lady?

GERTRUDE

Where last you saw him on this battlement.

VOLTIMAND
[*Slowly—in awesome tone.*]

I have seen no one on this battlement,
All night.

GERTRUDE

Then guide me round this jettied tower
Till we have circled the dawn, and found him.

VOLTIMAND

Madam,
I will.

GERTRUDE

Your hand! Lead carefully my feet,
For they bear more to Hamlet than his queen.
[*Exeunt, lower left.*]

PAUSE.

The dawn reddens palely, and the CRY OF A COCK *lifts along the light, with eerie echo. Enter slowly, from upper left,* KING HAMLET, *with closed eyes, holding an unlit torch. Coming to a stand, with back turned, he raises it high above his head against the dawn. From far below, there rises a deep, tumultuous murmur of enmingled* VOICES.

VOICES

Hamlet!—Hamlet!—Hamlet!

KING HAMLET

Who calls?

VOICES

Yourself,

Dan-e-mark! Dan-e-mark! Dan-e-mark!

KING HAMLET

Why do ye call?

VOICES

Hamlet! Dan-e-mark! Save us from Fortinbras!

[*Upon a rampart, left centre, in the dawn, appears the* WRAITH OF GERTRUDE, *reaching towards him.*]

WRAITH

Hamlet!

Save us!

KING HAMLET

Gertrude!—Whom must I save?

WRAITH

Ourselves:

Hamlet, thy soul; Hamlet, our son; and Gertrude—
All three in one: our love.—Save us from Denmark!

VOICES

Dan-e-mark! Dan-e-mark! Dan-e-mark! Save us from Norway!
Fortinbras! Kill him!

WRAITH

Hamlet, be kind to Hamlet!

KING HAMLET

Ah, me!

VOICES

Kill, kill!

WRAITH

Be kind!

VOICES

Go forth!

WRAITH

Remain!

VOICES

Kill, kill! Go forth! Go!

WRAITH

Stay! Be kind!

KING HAMLET

Ah, me!

O miserable all! Mad world, be mute!
Radiant love—go black! Blot out! Be dumb!

[*He drops his unlit torch.*
The Wraith of Gertrude vanishes.
Out of the dimness, sing Voices of the Invisible.]

THE VOICES

Hark
How now the shrill dawn-fires
Riddle
The hilly dark:
Now, how
The tone-tauten'd fiddle
Twangs, and the roan-comb'd choirs
Cry: Cockadiddle-diddle-diddle-
Dow!

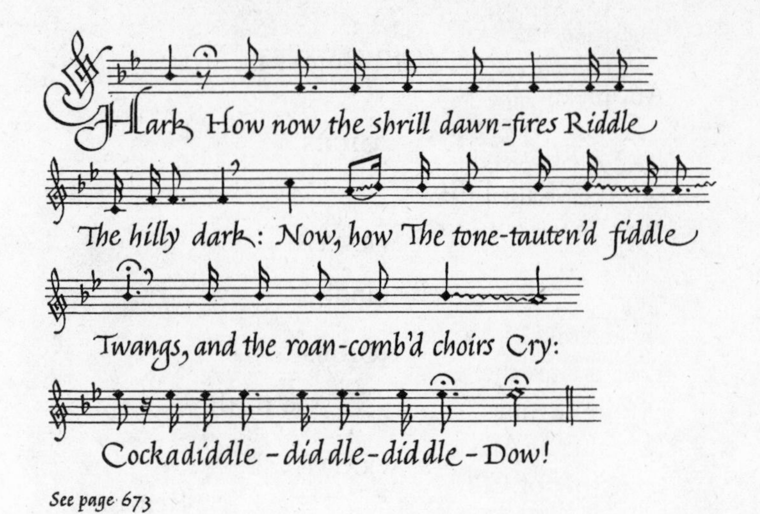

See page 673

[*In the background sky, ridges of coral light flare like the comb of a Cock, and a far-resounding* VOICE *chants, like a deep, clear bell.*]

THE VOICE OF THE COCK

I perched on Pharaoh's tomb.
I crew beyond the Pyramids.
Peter heard me—and cowered.
My trumpet shook the tent of Alexander
till he shattered the banquet-cups
and his lips foamed.
In the straw of a stable at Nazareth
I flapped my wings
and a cradle was rocked.
On a hill of Golgotha, between two thieves,
I rose:
I wrenched the bleeding nails from the wood.
My *Cockadiddle!* sang high over the Cross
till the shanks were shrunken
and the neck-bone drooped the slant head.—
At the third dawn
my clarion cleaved the cave-rock
and rolled it away.

[*At a bend of the upper platform, an eerie Pageant is seen entering: nine* FORMS, *clad piedly, with heads in masks, crested with cocks' combs. Eight of these Forms, with coral crests, are small and slim-legged, four of them bearing, and four accompanying, a wattled litter, from the centre of which looms a great shining Crystal, shaped like an egg. The* LEADER, *who is larger and taller than the others, has a ridged crest of deep scarlet, and is gowned in rainbow colours. Pacing with silent dignity, he comes downward with the Pageant, which pauses close to where King Hamlet stands and speaks during its approach.*]

KING HAMLET

What voice?—What dawn-processional is this
That makes the scallop'd east a battlement
Of bloodstones, and the cry of Chanticleer
To vaunt of Alexander's foaming lips
And crow of Christ the Lord, in Elsinore?
And thou, that broodest with thy cockerel's crest
This luminous egg—what spectral thing art thou?

THE LEADER
[*Removing the mask with his head-crest.*]

My name is Gallucinius—mine art
Erosophy. Novitiate I am
To Gallus, the Cock Eternal, in whose van
Mine is the eerie, transubstantiating
Cry of the primal energy—to warn
And waken all drowsy earth-dwellers to insight
Of their solar birth. My aim, at Elsinore,
King Hamlet, is to show thee to thyself.

KING HAMLET

Me! Show *me* to myself?

GALLUCINIUS

Thy very ghost:
Thy double-ganger: Hamlet, the King and lover;
Hamlet, the State; Hamlet, the seed and flower
Of love, the murdered and self-murderer
Of passion.

KING HAMLET

Murdered—I!

GALLUCINIUS

In imagination
Realized; and still immortally reborn
To expiation and to innocence.

KING HAMLET

You breathe enigmas. In what mirror, then,
Will you englass this image of myself?

GALLUCINIUS

Even in this crystal egg, gotten of the Cock
And hatch'd of the Hen of Destiny. Gaze inward
There, where the white of ever-future Now
Circles the yolk of all-recurring Past.
Focus thine eyes in the *I* of Consciousness,
Charted in stars, whose constellations rise
And set in thine own eternal firmament.
Fathom thine Ego there. Behold—and harken!

[*King Hamlet gazes in the Crystal, which grows more luminous, as slowly the dawn-light darkens, and a deep-toned bell tolls twelve.*—]

WS ———

Enter [Prince] *Hamlet, Horatio and Marcellus.*

Hamlet. The air bites shrewdly. It is very cold.
Horatio. It is a nipping and an eager air.
Hamlet. What hour now?
Horatio. I think, it lacks of twelve.
Marcellus. No, it is struck.
Horatio. Indeed? I heard it not;
Then it draws near the season wherein the spirit
Held his wont to walk.

[*A flourish of trumpets, and ordnance shot off, within.*]

What does this mean, my lord?

Hamlet. The king doth wake to-night, and takes his rouse,
Keeps wassels, and the swaggering up-spring reels;
And, as he drains his draughts of Rhenish down,
The kettle-drum and trumpet thus bray out
The triumph of his pledge. . . .

[*Enter the* GHOST *of King Hamlet.*]

Horatio. Look, my lord, it comes!

Hamlet. Angels and ministers of grace defend us!—
Be thou a spirit of health, or goblin damn'd,
Bring with thee airs from heaven, or blasts from hell,
Be thy intents wicked, or charitable,
Thou comest in such questionable shape,
That I will speak to thee; I 'll call thee, Hamlet,
King, father, royal Dane: O, answer me.
Let me not burst in ignorance! but tell,
Why thy canóniz'd bones, hearséd in death,
Have burst their cerements! why the sepulchre,
Wherein we saw thee quietly in-urn'd,
Hath op'd his ponderous and marble jaws,
To cast thee up again! What may this mean,
That thou, dead corse, again, in complete steel,
Revisit'st thus the glimpses of the moon,
Making night hideous; and we fools of nature,
So horridly to shake our disposition,
With thoughts beyond the reaches of our souls?
Say, why is this? wherefore? what should we do?

Horatio. It beckons you to go away with it,
As if it some impartment did desire
To you alone.

Marcellus. Look, with what courteous action
It wafts you to a more removéd ground:
But do not go with it.

Horatio. No, by no means.

Hamlet. It will not speak; then will I follow it.

Horatio. Do not, my lord.

Hamlet. Why, what should be the fear?
I do not set my life at a pin's fee;
And, for my soul, what can it do to that,
Being a thing immortal as itself?
It waves me forth again;—I 'll follow it.

Horatio. What, if it tempt you toward the flood, my lord,
Or to the dreadful summit of the cliff,
That beetles o'er his base into the sea,
And there assume some other horrible form,
Which might deprive your sovereignty of reason,
And draw you into madness? . . .

Hamlet. It wafts me still:—
Go on, I 'll follow thee.

Marcellus. You shall not go, my lord.

Hamlet. Hold off your hand.

Horatio. Be rul'd, you shall not go.

Hamlet. My fate cries out,
And makes each petty artery in this body
As hardy as the Nemean lion's nerve.—

[*Ghost beckons.*]

Still am I call'd;—unhand me, gentlemen;

[*Breaking from them.*]

By heaven, I 'll make a ghost of him that lets me:—
I say, away:—Go on, I 'll follow thee.[1]

[*Exeunt Ghost and* (Prince) *Hamlet.*]

——— WS

[*King Hamlet, whose staring gaze has been riveted upon the Crystal, lifts his head and starts forward, with a cry.*

As he does so, the reddening dawn-light returns, and the WRAITH OF GERTRUDE *re-appears on the parapet.*]

KING HAMLET

Come back!—I 'll follow both!—O wondrous night,
That flickers from moonshine into flares of dawn,
Revealing metamorphoses of me—
My limber youth wax'd old, mine age waned young—
In very deed my ghost and double-ganger:

My silent armour stalks with visor'd helm,
Wafting dumb gesture to mine eloquent larva
Slough'd back from grizzled chrysalis.—What are they?
What else than them am I?

GALLUCINIUS

Hamlet, the King,
Of them the self-creating instrument,
Forger of metal molten of stellar fires:
Royal artificer of state and scion.

THE WRAITH OF GERTRUDE

Father of him, incarnate through my womb
To be thine avenger—Hamlet, *Prince* of Denmark.

KING HAMLET

Avenger!——
Gertrude!—What word of prescience, born of night
And sleep conceptual, dost thou deliver
Now to thy lover?

WRAITH

Consummatus est!
Our spark is quickened. In the beginning is the Word
That uttereth life everlasting, and hath spoken
Him, who now is, and ever shall be, Hamlet—
Our son!

KING HAMLET

Our son!
[*After a gasped pause, in fierce gladness.*]
So Fortinbras shall die,
And Denmark reign perpetual.

WRAITH

No, no, no!
Still alter that inevitable!—Woe is me,
Who shall be, what I will not—thy betrayer!

KING HAMLET

Betrayer—thou!

WRAITH

And he—thine avenging angel
To purge my shame.

GALLUCINIUS

Gaze in the crystal.—Listen!

[*As Hamlet once more turns his eyes to the Crystal, the dawn-light resolves into shadowy moonshine, wherein again Voices of the Invisible are heard singing.*]

VOICES

Gaze
There, where the moon's white beams
Wander
The mind's amaze!
Keep sleep
Enworlded in yonder
Orb, where the soul-stoled dreams
Lead Death to ponder, ponder, ponder
Deep.

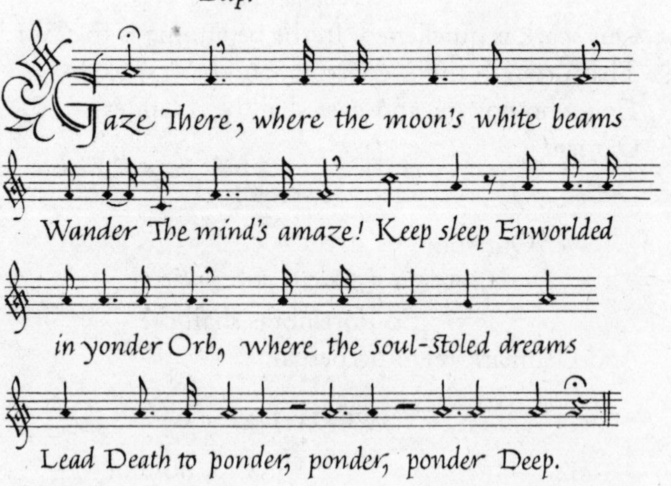

See page 673

WS

Re-enter Ghost and [Prince] *Hamlet.*

Hamlet. Where wilt thou lead me? speak, I 'll go no further.

Ghost. Mark me.

Hamlet. I will.

Ghost. My hour is almost come,
When I to sulphurous and tormenting flames
Must render up myself.

Hamlet. Alas, poor ghost!

Ghost. Pity me not, but lend thy serious hearing
To what I shall unfold.

Hamlet. Speak, I am bound to hear.

Ghost. So art thou to revenge, when thou shalt hear.

Hamlet. What?

Ghost. I am thy father's spirit;
Doom'd for a certain term to walk the night;
And, for the day, confin'd to fast in fires,
Till the foul crimes, done in my days of nature,
Are burnt and purg'd away. But that I am forbid
To tell the secrets of my prison-house,
I could a tale unfold, whose lightest word
Would harrow up thy soul; freeze thy young blood;
Make thy two eyes, like stars, start from their spheres;
Thy knotted and combinéd locks to part,
And each particular hair to stand an end,
Like quills upon the fretful porpentine:
But this eternal blazon must not be
To ears of flesh and blood: —List, Hamlet, O list!—
If thou didst ever thy dear father love,—

Hamlet. O heaven!

Ghost. Revenge his foul and most unnatural murther.

Hamlet. Murther?

Ghost. Murther most foul, as in the best it is;
But this most foul, strange, and unnatural.

Hamlet. Haste me to know it; that I, with wings as swift
As meditation, or the thoughts of love,
May sweep to my revenge.

Ghost. I find thee apt;
And duller shouldst thou be than the fat weed
That rots itself in ease on Lethe wharf,
Wouldst thou not stir in this. Now, Hamlet, hear:
'Tis given out, that sleeping in mine orchard,
A serpent stung me; so the whole ear of Denmark
Is by a forgéd process of my death
Rankly abus'd; but know, thou noble youth,
The serpent that did sting thy father's life
Now wears his crown.

Hamlet. O my prophetic soul!
Mine uncle!

Ghost. Ay, that incestuous, that adulterate beast,
With witchcraft of his wit, with traitorous gifts,
(O wicked wit, and gifts, that have the power
So to seduce!) won to his shameful lust
The will of my most seeming virtuous queen:
O, Hamlet, what a falling-off was there!
From me, whose love was of that dignity,
That it went hand in hand even with the vow
I made to her in marriage; and to decline
Upon a wretch, whose natural gifts were poor
To those of mine!
But virtue, as it never will be mov'd
Though lewdness court it in a shape of heaven,
So lust, though to a radiant angel link'd,
Will sate itself in a celestial bed,
And prey on garbage.
But soft! methinks, I scent the morning's air:
Brief let me be:—Sleeping within mine orchard,
My custom always in the afternoon,
Upon my secure hour thy uncle stole,
With juice of cursed hebenon in a vial,

And in the porches of mine ears did pour
The leperous distilment; whose effect
Holds such an enmity with blood of man,
That, swift as quicksilver, it courses through
The natural gates and alleys of the body;
And, with a sudden vigour, it doth posset
And curd, like aigre droppings into milk,
The thin and wholesome blood: so did it mine;
And a most instant tetter bark'd about,
Most lazar-like, with vile and loathsome crust,
All my smooth body.
Thus was I, sleeping, by a brother's hand,
Of life, of crown, and queen, at once despatch'd;
Cut off even in the blossoms of my sin,
Unhousel'd, disappointed, unanel'd;
No reckoning made, but sent to my account
With all my imperfections on my head.

Hamlet. O, horrible! O, horrible! most horrible!

Ghost. If thou hast nature in thee, bear it not;
Let not the royal bed of Denmark be
A couch for luxury and damnéd incest.
But, howsoever thou pursu'st this act,
Taint not thy mind, nor let thy soul contrive
Against thy mother aught; leave her to heaven,
And to those thorns that in her bosom lodge,
To prick and sting her. Fare thee well at once!
The glow-worm shows the matin to be near,
And 'gins to pale his uneffectual fire:
Adieu, adieu, Hamlet! Remember me! [*Exit.*]

Hamlet. O all you host of heaven! O earth! What else?
And shall I couple hell?—O fie!—Hold, my heart;
And you, my sinews, grow not instant old,
But bear me stiffly up!—Remember thee?
Ay, thou poor ghost, while memory holds a seat
In this distracted globe. . . .[2]

——— WS

[*Starting back from the Crystal—which disappears, with Gallucinius and the Pageant, together with Prince Hamlet—King Hamlet cries aloud.*]

KING HAMLET

O all you host of heaven! O earth! What else?
And shall I couple hell?—Who cried those words?
Who cries them through my throat?—What blasphemy
Of man, or nature, prongs me with this pang
Of purgatory, doom'd before the deed
Of malice, to suffer crimes vicarious
Even in myself—my ghostly voice petitioning
Vengeance—of whom? Of him, this youth, whose heart
Cries: *Hold, my sinews, grow not instant old!*—
Old as mine own wann'd image? Vengeance—*on* whom?
O my prophetic soul! mine uncle!—Nay,
My *brother!* Wherefore? How?—O thou cock-crested
Astrologer, tell me *wherefore?*—Blotted out!
All blotted—gone! The crystal egg hath hatch'd
In the dawn's nest, and loos'd a brood of midnight
To plague till doomsday *this distracted globe*—
Ay, thou poor ghost!—*thy* globe of destiny
Where thou shalt breed divine anticipations
Blasted with hellish memory.

[*Staring upward toward the* WRAITH OF GERTRUDE, *who has reappeared on the parapet, against the brightening dawn.*]

Gertrude!—Love!—
Nay, lewd betrayer—canker'd flower of our morning,
Flaunting the perfume of incestuous sheets!—
Why?—Wherefore? Tell me, *thou!*—Love—Gertrude!

[*Climbing towards her, he stumbles, and rises again.*]

Gertrude!

[*Still climbing, as the Wraith fades away.*]

—Gertrude!

VOLTIMAND

[*Appearing below, left, at a bend of the platform.*]

My liege! My lord, the King!

[*Calling back to Gertrude, who enters below, as he rushes up the steps of the parapet.*]

Hasten, my lady!—My liege, you 'll fall.—There 's death.

[*On the verge of the parapet, he clasps the King, who falls back in his arms.*]

GERTRUDE

[*From below, calling upward.*]

Death?—Hamlet! Hamlet!—Voltimand, speak: Is he dead?

VOLTIMAND

Lady, he sleeps.

CURTAIN.

ACT FIRST

ANTEROOM TO BEDCHAMBER OF KING HAMLET AND QUEEN GERTRUDE, *the walls of stone, with tapestries.*

In background, an arras, closed.

At stage left, an oaken door to a stairway, also closed.

At right, a stone Gothic window, opening upon a vista of Elsinore: a turret, touched by the sunrise. Upper right, a small door. In foreground, right, a cushioned bench.

Seated on the bench, YORICK *is discovered. He wears a fool's-cap with bells, and is thrumming a small psaltery, as he lilts, in a low pitch:*

YORICK

My Sorrow is gone,
And my Joy 's gone with her.
How shall I live
Without my dear cronies,
Joy, bonny Joy,
Sorrow, sweet Sorrow!

[*Enter a girl,* ANGELA, *from behind the arras.*]

ANGELA

The King hath waked.

YORICK

Aye, so hath the King's cockerel,
Daughter. He clapp'd it like the chapel chimes
At Candlemas, when Voltimand bore hither
The King to his chamber.

ANGELA

Think it !Almost he toppled
Into the tide. 'Tis awful to go awalking
And still asleep.

YORICK

Almost as awful, lass,
As go adreaming, and still awake.

ANGELA

The Queen
Was weeping, till he waked. But now I saw her
Smiling—O Sir, so joyful!

YORICK
[*Strumming.*]

Joy, bonny Joy! . . .
How shall I live?

ANGELA
[*Peering through the arras-slit.*]

He 's risen. They 're coming now.

YORICK
[*Thrumming, as he lilts.*]

Without my dear cronies,
Joy, bonny Joy,
Sorrow, sweet Sorrow!

Come back to me, Joy,
Bringing our Sorrow!
How shall we live
Unless all together—
Sorrow's brave Joy,
Joy's lovely Sorrow,
And I![3]

[*While he has lilted, the arras curtains have parted, and* KING HAMLET, *with* QUEEN GERTRUDE, *enters, coming forward to Yorick.*]

KING HAMLET

And *I* ?—How shall we live?

YORICK

All together, my liege!

KING HAMLET

How comes it, Yorick, that thou, my jester, croonest
Of "lovely Sorrow"?

YORICK

How comes it, Sire, that lovely
Sorrow crooneth of Joy—when Love, the midwife,
Delivereth Death?

GERTRUDE
[*Touching Hamlet's sleeve.*]

His song remembers still
On his dear bride—dead, when this lass was born.

YORICK

Is not that a jest, my lord, for the digestion
Of fools—like us, who ask: "How shall we live?"
Waking, on the brink of dreams, when the cock laughs
In the King Sun's face?

KING HAMLET
[*With look dazed and far-off.*]

King's son!—the King's son's face—
On the brink of dreams——?

GERTRUDE
[*With solicitude.*]

Hamlet!

KING HAMLET

All blotted now—
Dark—[*Gazing in her eyes, as she takes his hand.*]
thanks to this sunrise! Night-walkers are worms
That gather wings in the dawn's gaze.

GERTRUDE

Day is come.

KING HAMLET

[*Starting.*]

The day that I must go.

GERTRUDE

Must go?

KING HAMLET

Yorick! Take word
To the Duke Claudius that we await
Here his dear presence.

GERTRUDE

Is he so very dear
That he needs enter, at this votive moment,
Between us and farewell?

KING HAMLET

He is very dear.
He is my brother.

YORICK

[*Lilts.*]

No brother deer but scorns
To shed his velvet horns
The shell,
When Spring takes breath
And Winter saith
Farewell![3]

KING HAMLET

What 's that, sirrah?

YORICK

Sire, a snatch Cain sang, lang syne,
To Abel, in the apple-orchard. The tune 's antique,
For brotherhood 's a close-fit shift, needs darning
In a patch'd-up world.

KING HAMLET

Fool, are you on your way?

YORICK

I am, Fool; and my way 's a maiden's milk-path[4]
In a droughty midnight. Angela, bear this
Behind the arras, and turn the tight screws loose.

[*He hands her the psaltery, and bows deferentially to Hamlet.*]

*L*oose, *l*ady, *l*ord, *l*ove, *l*echery: all 's spelled
With *ell,* each over.—Exit poor Yorick, the Fool!

[*He goes out, left. As Angela stands hesitant, Gertrude points to within the arrased room, whither she disappears.*]

GERTRUDE

There, Angela.

[*To Hamlet, who stands staring at the closed door.*]

Poor Yorick, indeed! What pity
That birth of her, and death of his dear lady,
Should so contort his spirit in a knot
Of tunes and discords, that his mirth is gutted
With rue—himself, like his instrument,
Tauted, or loose, in tones and flats.

KING HAMLET

Yes, Gertrude,
This inch between ourselves and the unknown
Is thin as knife-edge, when our reason whets
The thumb upon it, at the testing second
Of execution. Now is the all-enacting
Second.—Sweet wife! Is love the deed, or dream?

GERTRUDE

Love is the deed that dreams, the dream that acts.
Love is the all-begetting, all-conceiving
Executive and servant. There 's none other
Than love.

KING HAMLET

There 's war.

GERTRUDE

Begotten in love's womb.

KING HAMLET

Philosophy.

GERTRUDE

Love's mate.

KING HAMLET

Nay, mentor, who
Guides metaphysic to exhort the stars
To unveil man's destiny.

GERTRUDE

The stars are infinite,
And all are satellites of Venus' smile.
The stars are master-magi in her sphere
Of heart; man 's but a darkling amateur
In his of mind.

KING HAMLET

You are a woman, Gertrude,
And woman's mind is frail.

GERTRUDE

I said so, Hamlet.
'Twas not my mind that spoke, but something far

More tenuously strong, more eloquent
In power: a sense less sick than metaphysic.
Nothing is more unwholesome to my mind
Than amateur philosophy.

KING HAMLET

[*Smiling, he sits beside her on the bench.*]

Your mind:
Still, still, your woman's mind!

GERTRUDE

Woman, or man,
Are we not proud of each? And I so proud
To be your lady, as to serve my lord
In Love's obedience! Let us both obey
Our Greater Lord of Love.—Go not to war!

KING HAMLET

My sweet girl, what am I to do? I 'm torn—
Torn by a surging conflict of desires
And duties. Gertrude—Hamlet—Fortinbras:
I rise between you, like a wavering shield
Flung from the arm that holds it fast—an arm
Tactless to attack, defenceless to defend,
Defiant to free, renunciant to be freed.
My consort, country, and mine enemy
Wait on the word of Love, or gauge of War,
Whilst I—a moon-path-stumbling sleep-walker,
Verging another world at red of cock-crow,
Am fallen amort, and lean to stare, as now,
In your eyes, your all-engulfing eyes, and know not
Whether I wake, or wink.

GERTRUDE

You wake in them
To the only world: *our* world—the world of being

Ourselves, for whom all else is Lethe,
But this god-pulse of passion, lull'd by love,
That goads our lips to twin, and utter—life.

KING HAMLET

All else—even as now?

GERTRUDE

Now, with no morrow,
And morrow, with no yesterday for pawn,
But only—now.

KING HAMLET

All else, but now!
[*They kiss. He droops to her, with deep breath.*]
All else!
[*She holds him, fast clung, and smiles: her look, far-off; her utterance soft, but vibrant clear.*]

GERTRUDE

Now, Fortinbras, knock on the gates of Denmark!
Hamlet, my love, hears not. He sleeps—at home.
[*A low knocking sounds on the door, as from far off.*]

A VOICE
[*Muffled, without.*]

Hamlet!

GERTRUDE
[*In wondering whisper.*]

Who calls?—Who bore my secret thought
Across the world?

THE VOICE

My liege, the King!

GERTRUDE
[*In startled murmur.*]

Who heard me?

[*Hamlet, with eyes closed, pays no heed to the low knocking, but droops, half swooned, against the cushions.*
Stealing from beside him, Gertrude treads softly to the door, and speaks low.]

Who 's there?

[*The door is opened, and an elderly-faced* YOUNG MAN, *lightly bearded, enters, fidgeting.*]

—Polonius?

POLONIUS

Do I intrude,
Madam? Intrusion is a brusque *faux pas*
In bridal chambers, as it were; but *brusque*
Is *brisk* as 't is, and brisk must be the message
I bear, as 't were, ambassadorial,
In loco ambassadoris, to his majesty.

GERTRUDE

His majesty is sore fatigued. His malady
Stole on him in the night. He 's sleeping.

POLONIUS

Ah!
Malade, indeed, my lady, is the malady
That stealeth sleep from sight, by day; but sightless
Slumber, that 's stolen from benighted legs,
Set into motion, as 't would seem—nay, doubtless,
Must *be*—sans all diurnal senses—
Dumb-blind—

GERTRUDE

Whist, crow,—God's name! Thy chatter-caw
Hath crackt thy master's rest.—He 's risen.—Ah!

KING HAMLET
[*In loud, hoarse voice.*]

What shatters all else, and trips it, clattering,
Heels up, to doomsday?—Who 's here?—yonder?

POLONIUS

Sire,

Polonius is here, *in propria*
Persona, properly; but yonder, most
Improperly, all unimpersonated
By Justice, Valour, or Civility,
Stands Fortinbras—a bog-strewn journey hence—
With the whole might of Norway in his glaive,
And hurls, by courier, this lance of challenge
Again—a third time hurl'd—at Hamlet, King
[Forsooth!] of Denmark, damn'd in these three words:
Denmark, or Death!

KING HAMLET

Then here we hurl him back
These two:—*Die, Fortinbras!*

POLONIUS

My liege, the challenge—

KING HAMLET

What challenge?—*Denmark, or Death?*—Nay, Fortinbras,
Not either, but both: not *Or,* but *And,* shall answer thee:
Denmark AND Death! For *we,* the answerer,
Are *Denmark,* and we 'll forge thee death, hot-haste;
Run forkéd lightnings down thy boastful gorge
To spit thy vitals, till the roasted gizzard
Sings, and the loins sizzle.

GERTRUDE

Hamlet!

KING HAMLET

So
Thy vaunted invasion itself shall be invaded
With counterpoint—tooth for a tooth, and tongue

For tongue, split even, like a jackdaw's beak,
Gaping for worms.

POLONIUS

Yea, worms for worms!

KING HAMLET

How, jackdaw!
Wilt swallow offal, to vomit echo? Nay, then,
Ambassadorial bird, transform those worms
Of Norway's belch to wriggling boa-constrictors
Back to his weasand.

POLONIUS

Constrictors?—

KING HAMLET

Such foul snakes
As strangle infants for their mother's milk
And spet it, to feed their spat.

GERTRUDE

Hamlet!

KING HAMLET

Speed hence
His courier! Clap the door behind thy breech!

POLONIUS

Briskly, in time, my liege: in tempo, brusquely! [*Exit.*]

GERTRUDE

Hamlet, my husband!

KING HAMLET

Wife, my Gertrude! Woman—
Eve—Angel!

GERTRUDE

What poison-adder of the night,
When thou didst wander blind in Elsinore,
Hath stung thee to this frenzy?

KING HAMLET

That same dragon
Which coils the scaly links of Fortinbras
And spets his challenge. Woman, this is *War*.
Mortals must feed on mortals, till the residue
Is dung, for states to bloom in. I am the State
Of Denmark, sprung from murk of rottenness
To clamber, like a vine of morning-glory,
To wreathe your love-suckt lips, and shrivel in dust.
To die, is to be born again—to die.

GERTRUDE

To die, is to be born again—to live.
You live again within me, and your scion
Demands his father living, in the glory
Of morning—not a corpse, for guttering candles
To weep with wax-dew.

KING HAMLET

Father?—Gertrude!

GERTRUDE

Yes,
Hamlet. We die, indeed, who, lip to lip,
Droop to each other's hearts, and vision there
Eternity—incarnate of the source
Which makes us one.

KING HAMLET

We two, in one.

GERTRUDE

We *three*,
Unseparate. The third—

KING HAMLET

What of the third?

GERTRUDE

Thou art the King of Denmark; I am the Queen;
The other—

KING HAMLET
[*With joyous cry.*]

Ha!—O, *Prince* of Denmark! Welcome
Home, to our throne of Love, in thy to-morrows!

[*He embraces her with ardour.*
On the door, thrice repeated, resounds a rippling knock, in three rapid raps, with slow intervals. They turn, listening.]

GERTRUDE

Again? [*As they move apart.*]
—What knocks?

KING HAMLET

Doubtless 't is my brother,
Claudius: I know his knock: a knuckled rap
I taught him in our boyhood, when we played
Together, with shields. He 'd tap it on the rims
For countersign of loyalty, in play-war.

GERTRUDE

In play?—I 'll teach our prince to rap more soft
On his shield, when he 's behind it. But perchance
'T will prove to be a princess, and learn naught
But stuff a poppet's head with lamb's wool, lest
Its woman's mind turn frail, and crack, in war-play.

KING HAMLET
[*With fond smile.*]

Tush mothering *it,* afore 't is ripe. Love *me,*
Whilst I am green—with envy.
[*The rapping begins again, less loud.*]
Quick! This secret 's
Not yet for him, nor any but Angela. Go
To her, and in this play-wrought war, remember,
Let it be only Hide and Seek, in whispers.
[*To her gesture of appeal, for him to accompany her.*]
No.—Go.
[*As she disappears behind the arras.*]
Come in!
[*Enter* CLAUDIUS. *Hamlet goes to meet him.*]
Claudio, my brother dear!

CLAUDIUS

Amleto!
[*They clasp gladly, with both hands.*]

KING HAMLET

So!—As we piled the wooden blocks
Of childhood's Rome, and castled them, with towers
To build another Elsinore—so now
We stand, as then, together, glaive in glaive;
And so we 'll hunt again for Hannibal
In Fortinbras, and pitch our tent together.

CLAUDIUS

God save the King! And may his gracious queen,
Who waits for him, behind, be saved to us—
And him, to her!

KING HAMLET

Be saved!—the Queen? What, think you
That Fortinbras himself shall fail to fall

By Hamlet's hand, even at the bourn of Denmark,
When we have sped to gauge him there?—How, brother!
What are you dreaming on?

CLAUDIUS

I 'm dreaming on
One, who—in dreams of her beloved lord—
Shall start from sleep, and ope a lonely casement
Towards a pale face in heaven—the lovely face
Of the Lady in the Moon—even paler than
Her own, in endless gazings on the dead,
And wonder, with that other lady's eyes,
Whose cardiac blood, upwelling from below,
Reddens those spurting streaks of ghostly gules
In the northern lights!

KING HAMLET

Have done! Look not like that
Towards yonder arras. 'T is no casement curtain
To ope towards inward midnight here. And yet
It opens, in my mind, towards that same moon
I had not dreamed on. How, then, brother,—how
Shouldst *thou* have dreamed it?

CLAUDIUS

Is a brother's love
Less dreamful than a husband's, when the doubt
Hovers 'twixt life and death?

KING HAMLET

Doth she peer forth
There, even now—even so—so pale as that—
On such a dreamless lover as *me?* What! Leave her
Behind, lonely—alone? No guardian lord
But—who? Polonius—him?—A bearded
Baby, beswaddled in law and rhetoric,

Crying on poppinjay to shake his rattle!
He 'd tiding Gertrude with echoes of disaster
Bawl'd from his parchment-cradle.—Yorick?—Aye,
There 's Yorick, the Fool,—and me, a madder one
To name him guardian of my noble girl!—
Roguish, and good, and soundly wise-of-heart,
But witless to ward mine own quick-witted queen
And sweetheart. Fie! By my soul, Claudius,
In all of Elsinore, when we are gone,
Is there none other, quick of wit and kinship,
To guard the Queen—me, absent? None: none other?

CLAUDIUS

Thee, absent—there is Claudius, thy brother,
If the King grant my presence—here, behind.

KING HAMLET

Thyself—*behind!* My Claudius, who always
Hath twinn'd me in the van of battle—here,
A chamberlain?

CLAUDIUS

Who keeps in better charge
The keys of a brother's chamber, than a brother?
Here 's home, where we were born, and bred together;
Coupled our boyish games; shared our one youth;
Rode forth, twin-bridled, for the hunted stag;
And when thou rodest, with thy pommell'd lady
Fresh from her wooing, to the chapel-step,
'T was here, in Elsinore, beside the altar,
I gave thy bride the brother-kiss of welcome
Home to our castle-kindred.

KING HAMLET

Claudio,
My noble brother! Thou alone canst know

The bitterness I bear, in being sunder'd
From her, to clinch with Fortinbras.

CLAUDIUS

I know;
And, knowing, share thy need of victory
For Denmark; though the bitterness of parting
For such a goal of joy, is only equalled—
Nay, acerbated—by the bitterness
Of staying behind. To go is glorious.
To stay were ignominious, except
To serve my brother-king and sister-queen
Were glory enough, to one who loves them both—
Albeit with a difference, of course.

KING HAMLET

The difference is nothing. All is love
To the loving. Now the night of dawdling doubts,
Toppling from moony ramparts, is dissolved
In morning action.
[*He strides to the oak door, flinging it open, and calls downward.*]
Yorick, ho! Mine armour!
Fetch forth mine armour, slough'd in maudlin sleep,
And clamp mine ankles with Apollo's spurs
To sting my champing horse to Norway's doom!
[*Going to the window, he leans out and calls down.*]
Ho, Voltimand!—The riding-horn: blow, blow!
To horse! Time 's up. To arms!
[*From below, the blast of a bugle resounds, responded to by* SHOUTS OF MEN.]

THE SHOUTS

To arms! To arms!

KING HAMLET
[*Going to the arras.*]

Gertrude, come forth! The sleep-walker hath waked
And sees the stars, beyond these vaulted beams,

Blazing a million suns of victory
To jewel Denmark's crown. Come forth, and wear it,
My own, and queen!

[GERTRUDE *comes forth, with face white. He embraces her, and—turning upward her face—points above, toward the vaulted roof.*]

Look there—thy crown! It burns
With destiny of all our proud to-morrows:

[*Then pointing toward Claudius.*]

And there—our pledge: thy brother-keeper—

[*Kissing the jewelled ring on her finger.*]

guardian
Of this our opal gem of trothal-fire,
Which glows in answering glory here.

[*Showing his own finger-ring; then kissing her lips.*]

—Adieu!

GERTRUDE

No, no!

KING HAMLET

[*Striding to the open door.*]

What, Yorick! Art thou mad-asleep?
Mine armour, here!—Nay, then, I 'll fetch it *for* me!

[*Exit.*]

GERTRUDE

[*Crying after him, poignantly.*]

No, no, no!

[*Then slowly fixing her stare upon Claudius, she speaks in dull, raw tone.*]

No.

CLAUDIUS

[*Kneeling to her.*]

My Queen!

CURTAIN.

ACT SECOND

THE SAME SCENE AS ACT FIRST. *But now, bright candlelight. At right, near the narrow turret-door, there stands a tapestry-frame; beside it, a carven chair, and a table, with skeins of vari-coloured silks upon it.*

Opposite these, at left, not far from the great oak-door, is a spinning-wheel, at which a young girl, with light braided hair, sits spinning. The girl is ANGELA.

Beside her, on the stone floor, under the glow of candles, is a little heap of carded white wool. As she spins, she sings a song, with sweet, clear voice, whose tones in the couplets quaver with stressed retards, but run more quickly in the hummed refrains.

ANGELA

Shepherd, call the sheep home!
Cradle, cross: cross, cradle.
Shear the wool and shine the comb.
Cross, cradle: cradle, cradle, cross.

Who 's asleep in our stall?
Cradle, cross: cross, cradle.
Ox and ass, and that is all.
Cross, cradle: cradle, cradle, cross.

Hark, how croweth the manger-hay:
Cradle, cross: cross, cradle.
"Mary, Mother, let me play!"
Cross, cradle: cradle, cradle, cross.

[*She pauses, to gather up some wool from beside her; then goes on singing. While she does so, a* HUMAN SHAPE *appears in the doorway, for a moment, then vanishes.*]

What shall warm the cold night?
Cradle, cross: cross, cradle.
Woolly cloutings, cuddled bright.
Cross, cradle: cradle, cradle, cross.

How shall we the work begin?
Cradle, cross: cross, cradle.
First we 'll card, and then we 'll spin.
Cross, cradle: cradle, cradle——

[*She stops suddenly, as she sees the* QUEEN *entering from behind the arras; rises, makes curtsey, and speaks low.*]

Madam!

Refrain one
SHEPHERD, call the sheep home! Cradle, cross:
cross, cradle. Shear the wool and shine the comb.
Refrain two
Cross, cradle: cradle, cradle, cross:
Who's asleep in our stall? Cradle, cross: ... etc.
Ox and ass, and that is all. Cross, cradle: ... etc.
slow
Hark, how croweth the manger-hay: Cradle, cross: ... etc.
"Mary, Mother, let me play!" Cross, cradle: ... etc.
What shall warm the cold night? Cradle, cross: ... etc.
Woolly cloutings, cuddled bright. Cross, cradle: ... etc.
How shall we the work begin? Cradle, cross: ... etc.
slower
First we'll card, and then we'll spin. Cross, cradle: ... etc.

See page 673

[*Scarcely noticing her, Queen Gertrude goes slowly to the carven chair, and sits, with deep-drawn breath.*]

GERTRUDE

One week of months, and seven months of years
Since his farewell. Yet, gossips say, a week
Hath seven days. They say, too, heaven help them
In their ignorance, that days of miracle
Have ceased, while, even as they speak, the moon
Stands still in the heavens, and the night refuses
To shed her ghostly shadows.

[*Looking toward the spinning-wheel.*]

Little spinster,
How old art thou?

ANGELA

Fourteen.

GERTRUDE

Twice seven: just
A fortnight: twice as old as he 's away
And I 'm a-widow'd; yet thy fern-hid eyes
Still hold their bright brooks brimm'd, and thy smooth cheek
Is gullied not with salt rucks of old age,
Like mine.—What art thou spinning there?

ANGELA

Lamb's wool.

GERTRUDE

Lamb's wool—that once the star-led shepherds fetcht
To cuddle a little babe! What faery stuff
Fate spins, for mortal swaddling-cloth—or shroud—
To wrap our babies round with mystery,
Even as, this hour, thou spinn'st, sweet Agnes!

ANGELA

Madam,
My name is Angela. Why do you call me Agnes?

GERTRUDE

Both suit thee well, dear saint of angel-gifts
For new-born babes; for this is thine own eve—
St. Agnes' Eve.

ANGELA

Oh!

GERTRUDE

Tilt thy curls this way,
That I may see thy halo in the candle:
So,—ah! So once, before my bridal-day,
When I made virgin pilgrimage to Rome,
In *Sant' Agnese fuore delle Mure,*
I saw thee—crusted all with altar-gold—
Gleam in the candles' shine, 'midst bluebell flowers
And primrose-colour'd glow of holy tapers;
And where I knelt, beside a pillar's base,
I watched the singing priests bear, in their wattled
Baskets, the baby lambs, for thee to bless
In the bright *Bambino's* smile.

ANGELA

Oh! Was I there?
I can't remember it.

GERTRUDE

The saints remember
Before, not *after,* little Angela.
So be again, what thou art still, her angel,
And bear from me, to Agnes, on her eve,
My prayer to her—for Hamlet!

[*She kneels in the candlelight, with clasped hands lifted towards* ANGELA.]

Virgin flower,
Who gavest thy tender pap-buds to be burnt
By the upscorching flames of ragéd blindness,
For vision of the Invisible beyond
Those murky fires, and saw'st there, clear, thy Bridegroom-
Lord, with the welcoming, victorious eyes!
O, grant to me—to *me,* in those same fires—
Thy sure insight, to see my earthly lord
Beloved—through the levin'd battle-dark
Of blinding war—victorious in welcome
Of me, his yearning welcomer!—Amen!

ANGELA

Amen!

A MAN'S VOICE

[*Intones deeply.*]

Ah . . men!

[YORICK, *who has entered, unseen of them, comes forward, continuing.*]

So endeth the chapel-master,
And eke, anon, beginneth a new beseechment
Unto sinners all: "Ah,—men of little faith,
Yea, women, ye, of lesser!"—May the fool
Make emulation of the master?

GERTRUDE

Yorick!
What tidings of thy master?

YORICK

Ancient tidings, Madam,
Fresh from the prayer-book: Test thou thy Lord's savour,
And sip his cellar'd wine, tang'd with tart root
Of righteousness, bitter'd with humour's gall,
Most excellently mixt, to potion thee courage
Incorrigible!

GERTRUDE

Courage for the bleak-of-heart,
Whose prayers ring only echoes?

YORICK

Echo answereth
Herself: *Ah!* unto *Ah-ah-ah!* and *Ho!*
Unto *Ho, hilly-ho!—Bleak* wooeth *Black,* but *Bonny*
Winneth *Hey, nonny-nonny!*— Here 's a prayer
For groomless brides to call their bridegrooms home
With the echo on 't, and daughter, Angie, here,
To lull her daddy-fool by, o' St. Agnes' Eve:

[*He lilts, with toning lilt.*]

Our Father dear, which art
In every foolish heart
To make it heaven,
Whenas Thy living bread
Riseth from heart, in head,
On hallow'd leaven!

Let no man's foot trespass
Thy kingdom in the grass
His fellow's to gain,
But haste, on every hill,
To do Thy holy will.
Amen! Amen!

See page 673

GERTRUDE

Thy foolish heart hath hallow'd mine, good Yorick,
With wiser rede than weeping after echoes.
Here 's work at hand. Quick, Angela: my needles
And silks! Till Hamlet come, with fallen stars
From Norway's night, to gem our morrow's crown,
I 'll broider it here, in prophecy.

ANGELA
[*Fetching some materials.*]

These, Madam?

GERTRUDE
[*Pointing.*]

Yonder—those silks!

YORICK
[*Pointing.*]

Yonder—those sow's ears, Angie!

GERTRUDE

Sow's ears?

YORICK

For prophecy, my lady liege:

For crowns be coined for purses, and silk purses
Crafted o' sow's ears—leastwise, when the purser-
Steward o' the Crown hath craft to learn the art on 't,
By whispering in a lady's lug, the while
He puts it in his poke.

GERTRUDE

Thy prattle, Fool,
May serve for the pig-larder, but 't is nothing
Which hath consortment with the gentle wisdom
Of thy prayer-song—here, on this saintly eve.

YORICK

True, Madam. Here is your Royal Majesty's
Dream-sanctuary, arras'd from the ears
And tongues of publicans; and here, to oust
All gabble of prophetic fools, cometh now
Your noble lord-protector.
[*Suddenly, to* CLAUDIUS, *who has entered, on tiptoe.*]
Pox, Claudio!
Your pigskin is not greased. Your princely boots
Squeaked, but now, on the stairway.—Angela,
Tend to thy wool, when thou hast skeined the silks. [*Exit.*]

CLAUDIUS
[*Staring after him.*]

What aileth Yorick?—"Claudio!"—"Pox!"—Well, well!
He hath not named me so, nor eyed me so,
Since once we were boys, a-wrestling, when I tripp'd
Hamlet, and sudden he ducked between our legs
And downed me.—Well, well!

GERTRUDE

He doth all in jest,
Hunting for jests, as beagles are trained to hunt,
In puppyhood, for hares.

CLAUDIUS

In jest—hunt hairs—
To split them?—Well, he 's gone. You are going, too,
Your Majesty?

GERTRUDE

A moment—to my closet,
For needles.

CLAUDIUS

Needles?

GERTRUDE

For my tapestry.
Angela is at your service.

[*Exit, behind the arras.*]

CLAUDIUS

At my service—
Angela?

ANGELA

My lord?

CLAUDIUS

Thou 'rt busy?

ANGELA

Aye, my lord.

CLAUDIUS

But not *too* busy—*not* to be at service
To one, inquisitive?

ANGELA

Not? Aye, Sir. Nay.
Oh, yes, my lord.—I do not understand.

CLAUDIUS

What 't is, to spin?

ANGELA

Oh, yes.

CLAUDIUS

And what 't is *for,*
Being spun?

ANGELA

My lord—?

CLAUDIUS

Methinks that one, who tempereth
The tempest to shorn lambkins, would gather wool
For naked *princelings,* when the winter howleth
Too loud from Norway, on the blast of war.
What thinkest thou, Angela?

ANGELA

My lord, the song
Saith: "*First we 'll card, and then we 'll spin.*"

CLAUDIUS

Saith it so?

[*Picking up an object, from out the wool-heap.*]

What 's this?

ANGELA

A carding-comb, Sir.

CLAUDIUS

What 's it for?

ANGELA

To comb the wool.

CLAUDIUS
[*Playfully.*]

Over my eyes—or thine?

[*He makes an airy snatch, with the comb, from his own forehead to hers.*]

ANGELA
[*Starting back.*]

Sir, —Sir!

CLAUDIUS

Thy wool is curlier than mine,
And spinneth prettier in the candlelight.—
Doth never thy royal mistress play at cards,
Softly, with this same comb—hearing thee sing:
Cradle, cradle?

ANGELA

My lord—my mistress—the Queen—

GERTRUDE
[*Entering quickly, from behind the arras, goes to the tapestry-frame.*]

The needles are ready. But first, to thread them.

CLAUDIUS

Ah?

GERTRUDE

Then all 't would lack, to instrument the stars
In my crown's velvet headband, were deft fingers.
Mine are too numb, with waiting in the cold,
I fear, and clumsy.

CLAUDIUS

Mine are warm, dear sister,
Gertrude, and readier than the needles are
To hasten thy broidery. Feel them! May not I
Help thee to thread?

[*He grasps her hands.*]

GERTRUDE
[*Withdrawing hers from his.*]

Nay, brother; the only hands
Can help me here—wear glaives: and *they* are elsewhere.
I pray they be not cold!

CLAUDIUS

Be sure, they 're hot
In clutch of Fortinbras, to bear his heart
Out of his breastplate, home, in victory here.

GERTRUDE
[*Shuddering.*]

Peace, peace!—Let there be peace in Elsinore,
This night. This is St. Agnes' Eve,
When white wool needs be cradled.

CLAUDIUS
[*Under his breath.*]

Cradled!

GERTRUDE

Angela, spin!
I 'll stitch.

CLAUDIUS

Then may, at worst, these useless hands
Hold the silk skeins, for choice?
[*He lifts one of the skeins.*]
To hold fast, were
To help, in choosing *which?*

GERTRUDE

To stitch withal?
Perhaps. But not too fast. 'T would break the threads.

CLAUDIUS

Nay, truly: not *too* fast! That would be bungling.
Threads must be needled first, before the scissors
Snip them: or, is it—after? Will you pardon
A poor man-novice his want of subtlety
In woman's art?

GERTRUDE

Man served his novitiate
In woman's art, when he helped Eve appraise
The ripeness of the apple.

CLAUDIUS

Adam, methinks,
Was colour-blind. 'Twas Eve, who chose what stripe
To pick.

GERTRUDE

And picked it! So will I—this stripe
Of mine eye's apple, to be my prime crown-jewel:
This beryl, here. How think you, Adam-Claudius?

[*He holds the various skeins for her to choose, as they stand close to each other.*]

CLAUDIUS

Nay, beryl 's too envious green. Let not your crown
Show envy of *any* another's. 'Tis, itself,
Imperial. This puce were better: purple 's
The stripe of royalty.

GERTRUDE

For velvet,—true:
That 's for the headband,—look! But purple needeth
Brighter, to set it off. This stripe is redder.

[*Smiling.*]

Ruby shall be my star.

CLAUDIUS

The eye of Mars
In Venus' brow? Nay, lapis lazuli:
Sapphire is heaven's own hue.

GERTRUDE

I 'll brede them all
Into my broidery: beryl, ruby, sapphire:
A girdle of Pleiads for my morrow's crown
To glitter, with Norway's ravisht meteors,
In Hamlet's eyes, when he returns.

[*She claps her hands, laughing.*]

CLAUDIUS

Fair sister,
Remind him then, at least, when he shall turn
From armour'd trophies to thy silk-heap'd arms,
How that thine artful brother-chamberlain
Hath turned thy pallid lips to ruby laughter,
In bright anticipation of his welcome
Home.

GERTRUDE

I 'll remind him, and I don't forget
All, but his being home.

[*Enter, in haste, a* GENTLEWOMAN.]

What now, Cornelia?

CORNELIA

Madam, Polonius hath sped me here
To beg your Majesty, command your maid
Climb to the turret-window, towards the north,
And look down at the postern-gate.

GERTRUDE

[*Pointing to the narrow door, right.*]

Up, Angela!

Up, to the turret!

[*Staring at Cornelia, as Angela makes exit there.*]

What, are you dumb with speeding,

Woman?—What 's there, at the postern?

CORNELIA

Madam,

A rider.

GERTRUDE

From the north!—O, Claudius,

Can laughter shake the stars with prophecy

And fetch heaven home?

[*At the turret-door, calling upward.*]

What, Angela! O, Angela!

What seest thou there?

ANGELA'S VOICE

[*From above.*]

The moon.

GERTRUDE

The moon!—Look down

Below: below, thou babe! The Man-in-the-moon 's

Tumbled. What 's there, *below?*

ANGELA'S VOICE

Moonshine.

GERTRUDE

What?—What?

Louder!

ANGELA'S VOICE

All 's mist below.

GERTRUDE

Mist, mist! What 's all
This cold plum porritch?—Claudius, hast thou
A mouth to catch it, and to call for more,
That 's hotter?

CLAUDIUS

[*Smiling, goes to the turret-door, and calls upward.*]

Sister Anne! O, Sister Anne!
What seest thou?

ANGELA'S VOICE

Naught, my lord. Only mist.

CLAUDIUS

O, Sister,
Insist not upon only mist and moonshine,
For this is Bluebeard's captive-chamber, where
The only message of deliverance
Is tidings of the dawn.

[*He turns away, in laughter.*]

GERTRUDE

I 'll stop that laugh
With weeping, and scrabble all thy blue beard red
With bloody nails, unless thou wilt unhorse
Yon misty rider here, in this chamber, now,
And let me clamp him in my gyves.—Cornelia,
What trickery 's this of Polonius? Where stays
Your ambassadorial husband?

CORNELIA

Madam, he stays not.
He 's on the stairway—here, now—
[*Enter, hurriedly,* POLONIUS.]

POLONIUS

Gracious Queen,
The rider is stalled below, inside the postern,
And from his hand I fetch this letter here
Unto your Majesty.

GERTRUDE

For me—a letter?
[*Snatching it.*]
From—*him!*—Hamlet: yea, 't is his seal. I 'll read it
Alone.—Nay, Claudius, you—aloud, here. I 'm
Gone blind. All 's mist, indeed!

CORNELIA
[*As Gertrude leans against her shoulder.*]

Madam, you—

GERTRUDE

Hush!
[*To Claudius.*]
Read. Break the seal.

CLAUDIUS
[*Breaks it, opens the parchment, and reads aloud.*]

To our most radiant Love and Queen,
Gertrude, of Denmark—
Greetings in joy—

POLONIUS

"Joy," note!

CLAUDIUS
[*Reads.*]

—and great necessity: My own!—The battle is won—

GERTRUDE

Ah, heaven!—Won!

CLAUDIUS
[*Reads.*]

—and lost.

GERTRUDE

Lost!

CLAUDIUS
[*Reads.*]

Won—for as much as Fortinbras is hurl'd reeling to eastward,
fled to the wild swamps, whither we pursue him.
Lost—for as more, that I am wounded.

GERTRUDE

Wounded!—Hamlet!—O, let me—

CLAUDIUS
[*Reads.*]

Wounded not unto death—
but delay. Mine acheful hurt burns less deep than mine anger.
That shall kindle the rotted swamp to Norway's funeral pyre
and singe his ashes black, in the smoking urn
I'll bear thee homeward, soon, with victory.

POLONIUS

Note—"victory"!

CLAUDIUS
[*Glowering at him.*]

Tush!

[*To the Queen.*]

Gentle sister, listen:

[*Reads again.*]

Gertrude,

to-day my Queen of Love, mine Empress of all our to-morrows!
Kiss, on thy finger-ring, our fiery opal-stone—
there, as here my lips touch it, twinn'd with thine own;
and let no severance part it from there, but with thy life-blood.
—Hail with love our loyal brother, watchman of thee for me—
thy wounded only by hate, but ever healéd by loving—
Hamlet.

[*Gertrude, starting forward, reaches for the letter, but sways, reeling.*]

POLONIUS

Quick!—The Queen!

[*She faints, as Claudius catches her in his arms.*]

CLAUDIUS

[*Gazing swiftly around, lifts her, and speaks to Cornelia.*]

Draw back the arras, yonder!

[*Cornelia does so, partly revealing, within, the royal bed, towards which Claudius bears Gertrude, and, passing inward, speaks to Angela.*]

Angela, hurry: come to thy mistress' help.
The couch—there!

ANGELA

[*Breathlessly.*]

Oh!

[*She darts ahead of him.*
Cornelia, letting go of the arras, is just starting to follow, when Polonius hastens to her.]

POLONIUS

Wife, wife, shall I come, too?
No?—Where, then?

CORNELIA

[*Pointing to the great door.*]

Down—to the lobby. Fetch him here.

POLONIUS

Who—here?

CORNELIA

The leech. Fetch here the doctor. Haste!

[*Cornelia disappears within, as the arras closes.*]

Polonius, pausing, picks up and examines the parchment letter, dropped by Claudius, and mutters aloud, as he reads it.

POLONIUS

Lost—wounded—won: —*our fiery opal-stone*—
Funeral urns—Fortinbras fled to flaming
Of rotted swamps: *thy wounded only by hate,*
But ever healéd by loving—*Hamlet.*—"Fetch
The leech"—to heal the breach of wounded parchment
And mend the royal wax!

[*He hurries to the doorway, where he collides with* YORICK, *who is just entering.*]

How 's this! What 's here?

YORICK

Here 's exigency, Sir: the more of it,
The less of exit-way. Haste hot, speed cold.

POLONIUS

Hush, Fool! The Queen 's fainted. The King 's wounded.

YORICK

Fainted—the King?

POLONIUS

Nay, nay, the Queen. The King 's
Far off. The Queen lies in her chamber.

YORICK

Lies?

POLONIUS

Yonder—with the Duke Claudius.

YORICK

So, in bad sooth,
The King 's far off: as far—as far—as far
As sooth from forsooth, and saint from sanctimony.
And this, sir, is the Eve o' St. Agnes. Canst
Thou hear the bleating of lambs, in the Mass-bells?

POLONIUS

Nay:
Naught but the tinkle of bells in a fool's cap. Come!
Come away from here, with hasting wisdom.

[*Exit Polonius, hastily.*]

YORICK

Wisdom!

[*Tarrying, he moves slowly to the spinning-wheel, and blows out the lighted candles, there; then to the tapestry-table, doing the same; then to the Gothic-arched window, where the entering moonlight silvers the room's dimness.*

There, gazing out, he looks upward, and lilts, deeply.]

Our Father dear, which art
In every foolish heart
To make it heaven——

[CLAUDIUS *comes through the arras-slit, and gropes forward.*]

CLAUDIUS

Who 's there? Is it the leech?

YORICK
[*Turning.*]

Aye, aye, Sir: I,
The sucker. Is it *bleed,* or *bleat,* my lord?
All 's blood o' the lamb, *in mundo medicale,*
Being leechcraft terrestrial: in the art celestial,
All 's silver fleecing.

CLAUDIUS

Yorick!—What moon-mumbling
Is this? What art thou doing at the window?

YORICK

Counting of crowns, my lord, to fill the cup
Of wisdom. The wise old moon 's scoop'd hollow
I' the pate-top, and the ripe stars are thick
As mulberry-crowns at Michaelmas, to pick
And brim the silver skullpiece—pardon, my lord!—
Casket were a prettier word, and cunninger
For wisdom to pronounce.

CLAUDIUS

Yorick,—good night!

YORICK

Yea, verily, the night is good indeed
For wisdom, in spite of fools—mumbling, or mute.
So *good* night, Claudio,—the wise Chamberlain!
[*He moves past Claudius, towards the door, lilting again, as he goes.*]

Let no man's foot trespass
Thy kingdom in the grass
His fellow's to gain— [*Exit.*]

[*Claudius gazes after him, with squinted eyes; then, moving to the arras, peers through, within; then, turning, looks, for a moment, at the spinning-wheel, then far away.*]

CLAUDIUS

There is a door, that opens into life
And shuts again, without a sound, if push'd
Gently—if *gently* push'd—with fingers light
As lamb's wool, and as agile—as innocence
At work. This little Angela hath fingers
Skilled to effectuate her song—her pretty
Ballad of *Cross* and *Cradle: How shall we*
The work begin?—By waiting?—Time can check,
Or ease, eternity. After the wool 's
Been shear'd, the wheel is placed, for turning. Mere
Waiting stalls all. To wait, is not to win.
Nay, first we learn to card, and then—to spin!

CURTAIN.

ACT THIRD

INTERIOR OF A WAR-TENT, *dimly lit by two torches, flickered by gusts, blown through the porch-slit, partly opened by the entrance there of* TWO DANISH SOLDIERS, *in semi-armour, who glance backward, as they come in and approach a bench, near an empty bed, where—chafing their hands—they stare at each other weirdly, as one sits on the bench, while the other stands beside it.*

FIRST SOLDIER

How wild the night is!

SECOND SOLDIER

None ever have I known
Wilder—more blent with all the elements,
Benign and terrible.

FIRST SOLDIER

Yea, heaven commingles
All, only to sunder them. Cold stings us hot
With freezing whips. The lightning's snaky flares
Coil the crackt thunder's rumbling cannon-wheels
And split the spokes with fire. Snow, slusht with hail,
Hath glazed the mounded sands, whereon the boreal
Dawnlights glister in patches, when the howling
Mob-winds tear gashes in the sky's black arras
For the wan moon's white gaze.

SECOND SOLDIER

Once, when it parted,
I saw her smile—that Lady, whose lovely profile
With the upcurving throat and cloudy hair
Our waiting mothers watch, on the ninth-month tally.[5]
What blessing could it bode for this raw battle,
Wherein our king hath wrung the victory
From Fortinbras, and torn the heart of Norway
Out of his armour'd breast?

FIRST SOLDIER

[*Gazing toward a corner of the tent, where the torch-flare gleams upon armour.*]

Yonder it lies—
The gore-sprent breastplate, flung there heavily
By Hamlet, in the first rage of his ecstasy
After that last blood-bout. But now all 's quencht
To a sullen sorrow of piqued loneliness,
Pining his love-queen, far in Elsinore
Pent from his yearn'd embrace, yet yearning birthwards
For another's cuddling arms.

SECOND SOLDIER

The babe, who cometh
In the ninth moon! Ha, *that* must the blessing bode
Of the Moon-Lady's smile, that broodeth worldward
So wanly tender, on these dead beneath,
Whose ghosts shall hail the infant heir of Denmark
With victory, in his father's house.

FIRST SOLDIER

Heaven will it!
Yet, comrade, much there is to daunt our hope,
In this uncouth sleep-malady, which leads
Our king to walk out of his tent, alone,
Into this night of omens, braceless gear'd
In his bed-clout, stark March-harish.

SECOND SOLDIER

When I followed
To ward his steps of pitfalls, he struck at me
With outzagg'd elbows, like a ruffled owl,
Beaking his blind eyes towards me.

FIRST SOLDIER

How he scents
The trail in the dark, troth, 't is half owlish, yet

Half houndish, too, when he stands, stark as a pointer
Nosing a grouse, through brambles.

SECOND SOLDIER

Hush! He 's coming.

[*Enter* KING HAMLET, *with closed eyes. He passes them, with no notice, and pauses near the bed, with face upturned.*]

KING HAMLET

Dark Sorrow, holy ark on stormy dooms
Loos'd by the levin'd flood, that damn'd the world
With Judgement's fury, bear me starkly up,
Till the slant dove-wings dartle thee with rays
Of love's deliverance.—Gertrude!—Ah,
Fortinbras!

[*He droops his head, shuddering.*]

FIRST SOLDIER
[*Starts towards him.*]

My dear liege—

SECOND SOLDIER
[*Holding the other back.*]

His ears are blind
As his eyes.

FIRST SOLDIER

But shall we not dry-gear him now
For bed, or else enarmour him, for the morrow?
The Norway eagles are nested, for to-night,
But they will swoop in the thunder's face, at sunrise.
They are no crows, to caw in parliament
For stolen corn, and when the game-cock cries
Kickereekoo!—fly from the field. The breed of Norse
Will avenge their king. We Danes are their own breed,
Though we be king'd, praise God! and they be kingless,
To-night.[6]

SECOND SOLDIER

Nay; kingless, they 're wingless and beakless,
To fly, or strike. They 're vanquish'd. 'Tis ours, the victors',
To ordain *Death to all Vengeance!* on both sides.

FIRST SOLDIER

Look there!—He lies in his bed.

SECOND SOLDIER

There let him rest
From his unwakeful draggling through the dark,
Till sun-bright dreams, to-morrow. Snuff the torches!
He recks them not. Come, cloak with me, in the porch-flap,
Where we will double-sentinel his watch.
Come!

FIRST SOLDIER
[*Snuffing the torch-flares.*]

That one 's out. Now, this!
[*Exeunt.*]

DARKNESS

Thunder rolls far off.

Then silence, out of which, suddenly, resounds the loud-vaunting cry of a CROWING COCK. *Simultaneously, the air is filled with a purple light, emanating from a luminous Crystal, in the glow of which stands* GALLUCINIUS, *gowned in scarlet, with forked head-dress of blood-hued crimson.*

GALLUCINIUS

Hamlet!

[*On his bed,* KING HAMLET *starts up to a sitting posture, staring at the Crystal.*]

Hamlet, the King! Fathom thy mind—
The crystal egg, which hatcheth hell and heaven:
Ovum of conceptual thought—fathom, and choose
Thy soul.

KING HAMLET

And art thou Gallucinius,
Come to me now, once more, in midnight!—Wherefore?
What bodeth that forkéd gule, in thy forehead, there?
That bloody *V*—what doth it signify?

GALLUCINIUS

Victory for Vengeance on the Vanquished.

KING HAMLET

And there! What 's there, whereon thou sett'st thy heel,
So proudly, in purple splendour—that waxy block
Of pallid chalcedony?—What is that?

GALLUCINIUS

The footstool to thy throne.

KING HAMLET

Footstool! What is 't?

GALLUCINIUS

The urn of Fortinbras. 'Tis filled with ember'd
Ashes of blood; for it holdeth his heart, which thou
Torest from out the breast of a kindred folk,

To furbish thy shield-of-arms. Its prison'd ash
Is bravely inurn'd, and seal'd with size so hard
No mortal hand can wrench it; but hands immortal
Can open it with an infant's touch—a babe's.
Hark, now! Stoop forth thine ear, with trembling finger,
And listen, within: Within—within—within—
What 's throbbing, there? Is it the unwinding clock
Of ticking Time? Or, is it the throbbing drum
Of Eternity, beating for Fortinbras
Heart-beats of *Vengeance! Vengeance on Hamlet's throne!*
Till all of Elsinore is dumb—and all
The rest is silence?

KING HAMLET

[*Groans.*]

Ah!—O, hideous,
Horrible victory!

[*DARKNESS*
again, and silence.
Then, once more, COCK-CROW—*but now, of an eerie cadence, far off—and out of a cowslip-coloured glow, reappears* GALLUCINIUS, *gowned now in blue, and garlanded.*]

GALLUCINIUS

[*Gently.*]

Hamlet!—Lift up thine eyes. The egg of night
Hath cast its shelly hate, and the milky lymph
Of heaven's love pours, luminous with peace,
Around thy globéd spirit. Quicken thy soul in 't.
Peer in the crystal wonder!

KING HAMLET

O, flower-gownéd
Peace! Say: What olive sprangle, notcht to weld
Two parted links in union, prongs the blossomy
Chaplet, that brows thy gaze? What meaneth *that V?*

GALLUCINIUS

Victoria—of Vision *for* the Vanquished.

KING HAMLET
[*Pointing nearby.*]

Oh, there!—What secret crib of innocence,
All wattled with wildflowers and daffodillies,
Hides there, in the hedgéd green?

GALLUCINIUS

A kinglet's nest,
Laurell'd too freshly yet, to crown with ruby:
The cradle of thy son.

KING HAMLET

My son!

GALLUCINIUS

Thy princeling,
Hamlet of Denmark, heir of Elsinore.

KING HAMLET

Ah, Queen of our To-morrows, thou hast won
World-victory, in him!—Gertrude, none else—
None else!

[*He kisses the ring-stone on his finger.*]

GALLUCINIUS

Yonder—the urn: the cradle—here:
Hamlet, which heart-shield wilt thou choose?

KING HAMLET
[*Reaching his clasped hands towards it.*]

The cradle!
O, wonderful—O, stingless victory:
Victoria, in excelsis Caritati!

DARKNESS
through which chords of far thunder roll their deep organ-tones.

CURTAIN.

ACT FOURTH

THE THRONE HALL OF ELSINORE.

At upper left, on dais, with several steps of approach to an upper landing, stands the lofty Double-Throne.

At upper right, a great fireplace.

Between these, at back, the high, wide entrance, galleried, with walled approaches, beyond, behind curtains [visible only when the curtains are drawn back].

At lower right and left, smaller entrances, curtained. POLONIUS *and* CORNELIA *discovered.*

POLONIUS

Tears, tears! Why, why?

CORNELIA

They are for her, poor queen!

POLONIUS

Poor, poor—the Queen? Our majesty of Denmark,
Whose scope of envied splendour may claim riches
Would beggar Midas!—Poor?

CORNELIA

O, Polonius,
Would *she* and *we* were beggars, whose unenvied
Bairnlings might claim only their mothers' smiles,
Not pearléd tears, to dower them!

POLONIUS

Pearléd tears:
A pretty metaphor!—But why, why, why?

CORNELIA

Our little Laertes, when he grows to lisp
The songs of Yorick, will better language it
Than I can now, thinking on Hamlet's bride,

Whose bairn, so yearn'd for, many these wintry months,
Pries even now the primrosed latch of heaven,
To peep at her, for welcome—*how,* dear God!—
Fatherless?

POLONIUS

So, so, so!—And yet, perchance,
Not so! *Less,* 't were, indeed, lacking a father
Merely: but *more,* lacking a kingly sire,
Whose lack would dower with royal attribute
Him, or, *videlicet,* her, the princeling-princess,
Whose loyal-royal uncle, in the meanwhile—
What!—Whither, now?

CORNELIA

What sayst thou?

POLONIUS

What, said I,
But *whither?* What 's that saw, which Yorick sings:

"Whither dost thou wander?
Upstairs, downstairs,
To my lady's chamber:
There I met——"

Art thou the *Goosey-goosey,* and I the *Gander,*
To tangle our beaks, in nab of a *left leg,*
And all because the encountered might n't *say*
His prayers?

CORNELIA

Prayers?—May I pray *thee,* tell me, what 's
All this about?

POLONIUS

About our all in life:
Our checks and balances; our salary;

My humble promotion, and thy gentlewoman's
High perquisites of millinery: all dependent
On whether my lord Claudius will keep
A goose-garden, and we the guardian-keepers,
Or the kept tenants. Terse: terse, now, I 'll be,
If terser wax not worser, in the telling.

CORNELIA
[*Wearily.*]

O, husband dear—

POLONIUS

"Husband thy words," wouldst say?
So will I—store the sheaf, for winnowing,
And thou shalt munch the kernel, I the chaff
Fann'd from the harvest. Mark me, how I say,
So *will* I, will *he,* nill *he:* "he" implying,
Of course, my lord, Claudius, *and* King Hamlet,
Brothers, in separation, but united
In separate homage to the sister-queen
To whom we vow allegiance.

CORNELIA

So we do,
In deepest loyalty. So, what, again,
Is all this?

POLONIUS

'T is the aiming-mark of terseness,
Which oft, too oft, the arrow, Eloquence,
Doth miss; but sometimes, slanting off oblique,
May hit, in the very mouth of reasoning,
An idea—gaped for utterance. I know,
Thou knowest, too, these dragging months
Since the King's letter—his *first* letter, for
Others have later followed, till latterly

All 's silence—how the tidings of his wound
And Fortinbras' besetment in the swamps
Have waned from bad to better—*better,* meaning
Not *badder,* heaven forfend!—construe me not
Amiss, for all 's in the connotation of
The listener!—till now——whither, now? Why, even
To Claudius: He hath invited me
To parley with him, anent the consequences
Provisional, always provisional, if—
If—mind you well!—if Hamlet's wound shall prove
Mortal.

CORNELIA

Mortal!—And if that thought should bring
Mortality to *her,* who lieth yonder
In birth-pangs, even now!

POLONIUS

So imminent?
Even now?

CORNELIA

The midwife waits with her.
Oh, dear one, cease! Cease casuistry of words,
And face the primal Word. Let calculation
Of great, or small, of bad or better things,
Ply its own death, and come with me to the door
Of life, where on its threshold we will pray
Together, for the bringer of all greatness—
The little child, who comes.

[*Enter, left,* CLAUDIUS, *and a* WOMAN.]

POLONIUS

Whisht! Who, that comes
Yonder, with Claudius, is *she?*

CORNELIA

Moll Cowslip,
The midwife! Heavens! Then I will take her place.
Oh, parley not too long—but pray!

POLONIUS
[*Catching at her sleeve.*]

Cornelia!

[*She hurries off, left.*]

CLAUDIUS
[*To the Woman.*]

Upon the dug, thou sayst?

MOLL COWSLIP

Aye, Sir, the nipple.
A dab o' wormwood—six or seven dabs,
'T will serve—rubb'd round wi' thumb and finger—
To harden the teat. "Run, run!" saith I, to Angie,
"Fetch me the 'pothecary. Now is now,
And late 's too last, to medicine the Madam,
And prime the little suckling, when 't arrives."

CLAUDIUS

So that 's what thou wast saying to Angela?

MOLL

Aye, Angie, Sir: I borned the little thing
Myself. Alack, the mother were a prettier,
But weak i' the wing, to nestle her chick. Poor Yorick!
'A made a sorry face for a fool, that drizzly
Dawn o' St. Luke's Little Summer, she gave up ghost.
Angie 's her twin-apple, now, in her daddy's eye.

CLAUDIUS

And the apothecary?

MOLL

Oh, aye, aye:
The wormwood! Tetchy-bitter 't is, to suck,
But soon swabbed off. I come o' Dansker folk,
And they be n't raised o' Guernsey stock, to milch
For butter. Nay, Sir. Wormwood hardens the gums
O' Danish bairns, for teeth to bite the arms
O' Fortinbras. And him, the bairn I 'll born
For Elsinore, the bairnling boy—aye, sooth,
'A 'll be a *boy,* the babe, your nephew, Sir,—
I 'll warrant 'a 'll sprout him even so a set
O' birthday teeth, to welcome his father home
From Norway's bout.

CLAUDIUS

And the apothecary?
"Now 's *now,*" thou saidst to Angela.

MOLL

True as true!
And I must hurry back to the Queen's bed.—
But there 's the wormwood!

CLAUDIUS

I will have it fetcht.
Send Angela to me. I 'll give it her
For you.—"Now, *now!*"

MOLL

I 'll send her, straight.
Aye, aye: wormwood 's the word for Elsinore!
[*She hurries off.*]

CLAUDIUS

I know a better bitters.—Polonius!

POLONIUS

My gracious lord!

CLAUDIUS

What are those flaps you wear?

POLONIUS

Flaps! Wear, my lord?

CLAUDIUS

As blinders to your eyes,
Twin-swivell'd to your cheeks?

POLONIUS

[*Feeling of his own face.*]

These? Ears, my lord.

CLAUDIUS

Ass's, or unicorn's?

POLONIUS

Or unicorn's?

CLAUDIUS

Which shields armorial wear.—Wilt emulate
Aesop, to carry thine ass upon thy back
To pitch in the river, for taking poor advice,
Or saddle an unicorn, and ride at ease
Into a rich device of princely arms?

POLONIUS

My lord, I do not ride. I serve on foot.

CLAUDIUS

I thought so: ever pedestrian. One ear,

Tilted, would reach to your foot; but your leaden sole
Won't kick to the height of your eyes, behind
The other ear. I see, you somewhat lack
Athletic ambition, and prefer to teeter
Between the princely-precarious, and the safely-
Asinine, rather than jump. Still, you have ears
To catch a midwife's gabble, and you have legs
To fetch an apothecary. Can you use them?

POLONIUS

I can, my lord, and will.

CLAUDIUS

Then quickly use them,
And fetch him here, from his shop.

POLONIUS

My lord, at once.

CLAUDIUS

Wait!—Tell him, bring wormwood, with that *swiftest* unguent
He wots of!

[*Eyeing him intensely.*]

You wot of it?

POLONIUS
[*Bewildered.*]

Soothly——

CLAUDIUS

In sooth!
Unguent of heaven, to *soothe* all knees that pray.
And "swiftest"—thou legs of Hermes, with the spavin
Of Vulcan!—thou wottest whereof *swiftness* is made;
So—swift, swift, swift! Twirl thy caduceus! Wing it!

[*He motions Polonius off. Then, seeing himself alone, turns dreamily, and sits on the first step of the throne-dais.*]

Claudio, thou wast a boy, once; and a babe
Before that; and before *then*—what? But now
A brother. And an hour, perchance, from now?—
An uncle. And a moment after that?—
The guardian-regent of a kingly scion,
Fatherless, or father'd still, perhaps, afar;
Or, else—bereavéd uncle of a babe
Still-born—royal brother of a childless queen,
Widow'd—or, *to be widow'd:* Which of these? . . .
Claudio, thou wast a boy, once; and a babe
Before that; and before *then*—what? Ah, yes:
That *then,* which tangles *now,* and *soon,* and *after!*
This eager mind, that stretches to leap *forward,*
Why does it fail to turn the stubborn neck
Over the shoulder, and look what lurks *behind,*
Which, following, *makes* what follows after?—"Look,
Before thou leapest!"—But which way, Claudio?
Shut tight thine eyes—to see; and close thine ears—
To listen.

[*Holding his hands over his ears, he closes his eyes.*]

The light in the room grows pale, and gradually darkens to

BLACKNESS

A VOICE
[*Speaking, quietly.*]

Claudio.

CLAUDIUS

Who art thou?

THE VOICE

Claudio,
Thyself.

CLAUDIUS

Let me see thee.

THE VOICE

Look!

The blackness duskens to a twilight, wherein stands GALLUCINIUS, *gowned in blue, holding in his arms a white lamb.*

CLAUDIUS

Thou—*me!* What holdest thou?

GALLUCINIUS

A white remembrance,
Sent thee by one who loves thee.

CLAUDIUS

Who of all earth
Loves *me?*

GALLUCINIUS

One of all heaven, thou wouldst hurt
The most, but canst not.

CLAUDIUS

Cannot! Why?

GALLUCINIUS

Because
Love is not hurt by hating, but healed with sorrow
For hatred. Bethink thee!

CLAUDIUS

How?

GALLUCINIUS

Which way to look:
Bethink thee—backward, to St. Agnes' Eve,
And keep her token.

CLAUDIUS

What token?

GALLUCINIUS

This wisp of white
Wool.

[*He plucks from the lamb's side a curly wisp, and holds it toward Claudius, who starts, and reaches for it, with his right hand.*]

CLAUDIUS

Lamb's wool—

[*As he grasps it, the air turns*
BLACK
again, while he gives a moaning cry.]

Ah,—the bairnling!

[*There is a sound as of harsh coughing, then silence, out of which* THE VOICE OF GALLUCINIUS *speaks, with acid tone.*]

THE VOICE

Claudius!

CLAUDIUS

Again?—What art thou now?

GALLUCINIUS

The same.

CLAUDIUS

No other?

GALLUCINIUS

Ever the same, and infinitely other:

[*The blackness reddens to a brilliant dusk, in which stands, with leering smile,* GALLUCINIUS, *gowned in pied grey, and masked in a peaked face, with pointed silvery beard, under a cap of black velvet, corded with scarlet tassels. One of his hands is gloved in black, the other in red, and—between both—his leather-covered fingers keep passing, restively, a small crystal object, which shines silverly. He speaks, with satiric lilt.*]

Thyself, Claudius.

CLAUDIUS

[*Still holding in his right hand the lamb's wool, stares at him.*]

The Devil, wouldst thou clepe me,
In such a habit?—I am no devil, I!
Thou speakest an outdated fashion, customary
To fools.

GALLUCINIUS

Why, even such a fool am I,
Being customer to an apothecary,
Whose token I present thee, as a gift—
Gift, being German, germane to the purpose—
A gift of love for—kinship, should I say?
Nay, kingship.

CLAUDIUS

Cease, thou punster!

GALLUCINIUS

Whose quintessence
Is stored in this crystal vial.

CLAUDIUS

What is there?

GALLUCINIUS

Reach out for it thine other hand—the left,
To balance with the right one. Which scale tips?

CLAUDIUS

[*Seizing it, with his left hand.*]

Ha!

[*Holding out both hands, tremblingly balanced, he glances from the wisp of wool to the vial.*]

Is 't the wormwood?

GALLUCINIUS

Nay, I 'll spell it:
It beginneth, as hell—aye, heaven itself—beginneth,
Achefully—with an *aitch*.

[*He whispers in the ear of Claudius, who screams aloud, as all again is blotted in BLACKNESS.*]

CLAUDIUS

Angela!

[*His scream is answered by* ANGELA'S VOICE, *calling, as the room leaps starkly into light.*]

ANGELA

My lord!

[*She runs in, from the left, to where Claudius has risen and stands, with opened eyes, staring before him. Seeing him, she starts back, pausing.*]

Oh!—Did you call me?—Are you ill, Sir?

CLAUDIUS

Ill?
Yes, yes: ill of an ail, for which I 've sent for unguent.

[*Feels of his side.*]

'Tis here.

ANGELA

Your heart?

CLAUDIUS

The rib, which, pluckt away,
First fashioned woman. Its lack hath left an ache,
That sighs for restoration of what 's gone—
Being alone in Eden, all alone;
Yet that were hell, without the knowledge of it;
So let us give thanks to Satan, for his cunning.—
Angela, knowest thou how to pray to him?

ANGELA

To Satan? Oh, Sir!

CLAUDIUS

'Tis very simple: sate him
With himself. Then he will howl for God, and cry:
"God bless me, I 'm made over. See! New-made,
Even in the very image of perfection,
To start all over!"—Wilt thou kneel with me,
Here, at foot of the throne-seat?

[*He kneels on the dais, and looks up, pointing upward his clasped hands toward the right throne, facing him.*]

He is seated
There. Look! And *She,* in the other. Look, look, how
She leans the other way, and beckons him
With hind-love. Dost thou know what hind-love is,
Angela?—'T is the hind, the hart will after,
When the love-bird sings to the plum-tree blossom, *Sweet!*
And the huntswoman calls *Harrow!* to the husbandman.
That 's why the coupled throne is double-saddled,
Till the girths break, and the honeymoon is ditch'd!—
But thou 'rt not kneeling, little one, to pray largess
Of *Him* and *Her,* there.

ANGELA

Sir, I see no one,
There.

CLAUDIUS

What! Not *Him* of the snaky lip, and *Her*
Of the ravish'd rib?

ANGELA

The thrones are empty, Sir;
Both of them.

CLAUDIUS

So are we, both,—of bootless prayers.
But thy prayer, Angela, fits thy soul's white slipper
Like foot of Cinderella in the prince's lure,
While mine goes bare as a friar's, excommunicate
For kissing Cupid.

[*Enter* POLONIUS, *puffing.*]

Ha, there 's the allusion
Brings Hermes back on the trail.
[*To Polonius.*] Where lags thy quarry,
Hunter with the snaky staff?

POLONIUS

Following, following,
Following—

[*Behind Polonius, there enters, gowned in grey, a* MAN, *leering a peaked face, with pointed silvery beard, under a cap of black velvet, corded with scarlet tassels, and wearing black gloves on his hands, between which his leather-covered fingers keep passing, restively, two capsule-shaped objects: one, of crystal, which shines silverly; the other, of an ochre hue.*]

CLAUDIUS

[*Covers his eyes, shuddering.*]

Face, face—beard, cap and tassels—all!
Begone, second sight of Satan!

[*Uncovering his eyes, he stares at the approaching Figure; then turns suddenly to Polonius, and motions him vehemently towards the central entrance, saying low.*]

Follow thy tail!
Follow off! Remember: *thou* didst fetch this,—*thou!*

POLONIUS
[*In great perturbation.*]

My lord!

CLAUDIUS

Lord, Lord, Lord of Sodom and Gomorrah!
Split thy legs, lackey-priest, and let them swing
His incense, elsewhere, elsewhere—else—!

POLONIUS

Oh, elsewhere!

[*Exit, at back, through the curtains.*]

CLAUDIUS
[*Turns to the grey-gowned Man, and speaks, very quietly.*]

Apothecary, hast thou brought the wormwood?

THE APOTHECARY
[*Handing the ochre-coloured object.*]

Here, my liege lord: in the *brown*.

CLAUDIUS

Oblige me, Sir:
No lordly-lieging! Is *there*—the unguent?

APOTHECARY

Here,
In the *crystal*.

CLAUDIUS
[*Handing him coin, from his purse.*]

Here 's gold for both. Good day.

APOTHECARY

Good day, Sir.

[*Exit, left, counting the coins.*]

CLAUDIUS

[*Looking closely at the crystal vial.*]

With *aitch*—as hell beginneth: *hebenon.*

[*Then turning to Angela, who has retired, at a distance.*]

Angela.

ANGELA

Sir?

CLAUDIUS

This ailing in my rib
Needeth my care. The brown capsule will ease it.
This crystal one shines bright for babe and mother.
Give this one to the midwife. 'Tis the wormwood—
She sent for.

[*Angela takes the crystal vial from his hand.*]

I will rest a while.

ANGELA

Good rest, Sir!

[*Claudius turns away toward the door, right.*

Angela starts for the door, left, where YORICK *is entering the room, just in time to see the departure of Claudius, who, in the doorway, glancing back towards Angela, sees Yorick, and pauses, hesitating.*]

YORICK

[*Singing.*]

And all the world were a green cheese,
And me a mouse, a wee, grey mouse—

What, Claudio, wilt thou sing the Cat, in the round:
Meow, meow? The Cat, 't was, killed the Rat,
That gnawed the rope, that hanged the butcher, that killed—

CLAUDIUS

Nay, Yorick!—I 'll bark the Dog, that worried the Cat,
That sings, *Meow, meow!*—Peace to all ribald
Foolery, in this house of birth, so near to death,
Where only sacramental prayers should rise
For the infant heir of Elsinore.—Farewell! [*Exit.*]

YORICK

Farewell, with *thee,* to Elsinore!—Now, Angie,
Whither away? What hast thou there, i' the vial?

ANGELA

'Tis wormwood, for the dug. The midwife waits for 't.

YORICK

The midwife waiteth for sweeter milk of promise
Than wormwood bitters.

ANGELA

Is 't bitter?

YORICK

So, so, bitter.
Tuck it away in thy sleeve. She needs it not.

ANGELA

I 'll taste it, first.
[*She uncorks the vial and tastes, making a wry face.*]
Ugh! Fearsome bitter. Agghh!

YORICK

What did I tell thee? Here, give here to me.
I 'll tuck it in my poke, and keep it for thee.
[*She gives him the vial, which he puts in his pocket.*]
Come with me to the firelog.

[*He takes her hand, and leads her to the ingle-bench, beside the burning wood, in the fireplace.*]

'Tis the only
Lover, whose heart laugheth itself to death
To warm its mate—save one: one only, Angie:
That was thy Momsy—Mariana mine!
She was my laughing heart—my brave firelog,
Wi' cricket and kettle singing—that now is dumb
Ash. Ay, but I can hark her yet, in the chimney,
When the wind 's north in the night, and the sparks wing up
To make the stars. But she laugheth lonesome a laugh,
Now, calling "Angela!" 'Twas herself that named thee,
That borning-night o' St. Luke's Eve. And she looked
Right in thy blue, wide eyes, and laughed—and left us,
Thy Momsy did—lonely-lone, but together still,
With her, here.—Dost thou slip my hand? For why?

[*Angela, who has drawn her hand from his, rises, and looks fondly in his face, hesitant.*]

ANGELA

Daddy—if I should be needed, yon?—the babe!

YORICK

[*Harshly, starting up.*]

Nay, there should be no more babes born to the world!
Once was enough. That once!—And plenty good
Enow!

[*Stifling a sob, he kisses her; then takes both her hands in his.*]

And must, let midwives ply their trade
For wailing kingdoms. Our trade 's for lilting fools
I' the fire-laughter. Lilt with me, Angie! Sooth,
Thy hands be hot, lass. Sit we farther off,
Out of the ingle, here, on the floor.

[*They sit, on the edge of the stone hearth, side by side.*]

Now, lilt it
Wi' me, together: *The Round o' the Mouse, Cat, Dog!*
It lacks a third; but follow, single. I 'll double
I' the *Wee-meow-bows.*

[*He sings, briskly, Angela joining in after him.*]

See page 673

[*Laughing loud, Yorick pats Angela on the back, and calls.*]

Now, lead, Mousie! Lead off, single! I 'll follow.

ANGELA

[*Begins in a blithe tone, which slowly trembles and huskens.*]

And all
The world were a green cheese,
And me, a mouse, a wee, grey mouse—
Mee-wee! mee-wee!
I 'd fall
Ne 'er down on my four knees
To pray for better house
Above,
To make . my . mansion . . of . . .

[*She sways, where she sits, and falls, sidelong.*
Yorick, lost in his lilting, waits for the second Mee-wee!, *knits his brows,*
turns, sees Angela prone, and, with a cry, reaches over, to lift her.]

YORICK

Ha! Angie, what aileth?

ANGELA

[*As he lifts her, with closed eyes, sings faintly.*]

Mee-wee . . .

[*Opening her eyes, gazes at him, anxiously.*]

Did n't I sing 't—

The mouse?

YORICK

[*Putting her hands against his face.*]

Thy hands are hotter still. Thy cheeks
Be red-blotcht. Yet the flame-log, 't is but embers
Now. What can ail? Thou shiverest—so hot?

ANGELA

Oh! [*Trying to rise.*]

Oh, I should ha' took it to her!

YORICK

Took it?

Took what?

ANGELA

The wormwood.

YORICK

Ha, the vial!

[*He seizes it from his pocket, uncorks it, and smells–groaning.*]

Worm's

Offal! Didst taste it?—Yea, I saw!—How much?

ANGELA

A little.

YORICK

Who gave it thee?

ANGELA

Duke Claudius.
'Twas bitterer than thou didst say.

YORICK

Ho, Claudio,
The Cat! *His* bitters! Yea, bitterer shall it be
For him, than—No, no, Angie! That would bite
Bitterer than life.

[*Stooping over her.*]

My Angie, Angie! Up!

[*He raises her.*]

Blink back i' my eyes—thy Daddy's eyes!

[*She droops, silent, against him.*]

All 's blind
And dumb.—Dear Mousie, never a word?

[*He lifts her in his arms.*]

—To bed, then!
But not to the Queen's bed, Claudius!

[*Tenderly, to Angela.*]

So, bairn!—Rest thee!

[*He carries her off, left.*]

For a moment, the room is empty and still, save for low sounds of the firelog embers, crackling.

Then, through curtains of the great entrance, at back, enters the tall figure of a SOLDIER, *in mud-sloughed armour and helm, the visor half-closed, followed by* POLONIUS, *holding a parchment, folded and sealed.*

POLONIUS
[*Fidgeting.*]

You came, by Norway road, bringing this letter?
[*The Soldier nods.*]
For whom?

THE SOLDIER

'Tis written there.

POLONIUS
[*Reading the superscripture.*]

To the Lord Chamberlain of the Queen
Elsinore
—*From* whom?

THE SOLDIER

The seal
Also is there.

POLONIUS
[*Turning the parchment.*]

True, true. The seal, Ah, 't is
The King's! 'Tis Hamlet's seal.

THE SOLDIER

'Tis from the King.—
And the Lord Chamberlain?

POLONIUS

I 'll find him, straight.
I am Polonius, the King's—my lord, the King's—
The King, my lord's—abstract in absence, look you,
As 't were, secretarial—*non jam in officio*—
Treasurer of the Royal Thesaurus, which
Dealeth, *in se,* with seals and superscriptures.—
I 'll find him, straight, and take it to him—*him*
Purporting the Lord Chamberlain, so termed,

Not of necessity, *per se,* yet of
Possibility—an *alias* of lordship.
But that can wait construing. I will wait
Upon him, in the mizzen. You can await him
There, in the stern

[*Pointing back to where they entered.*]

—yonder; that is, until
I fetch his answer and command, Sir.

THE SOLDIER

Thanks.

[*Exit, at back.*]

Polonius looks about in bewildered hesitation, and starts for the door, left, as CLAUDIUS *enters, from the right.*

CLAUDIUS

Polonius—?

POLONIUS

My lord! That is your Maj——

CLAUDIUS

Lord me what stripe you please: majestical,
Or otherwise.—A letter?—More good bad news?

POLONIUS

The seal, my lord,—that is, his majesty's
Seal—as you see—the crown, in red—is fixt
Too firm, for *inside* breakage of the news,
Whether bad-good, new-old, or otherwise.

CLAUDIUS

Give over, and give here.

[*Snatching the letter.*]

—I 'll break it for you.

[*Reading the superscripture.*]

To the Lord Chamberlain of the Queen
Elsinore

[*Breaking the seal, he glances through the sheet, with knit brows, then reads aloud.*]

Brother,

Didst ever thou dream?

My wound is dream-struck—mortal till doomsday, and if that dawn shall break ever.

I am here in the sands.

The meal was ground fine, the millstones groaning merrily to cast grout, and the sack stood gaped for the filling.[7] *Earth was mine own.*

But my malady o'ertook me—the night-walking, till crow of cock—at night-slip, mind you, in the very nick!—and the Cock—crew!

And now my wound hath crackt open.

Tell this to no one, but—and if ever thou hast dreamed—thyself, account for it.

Thine, healéd by death,

Hamlet.

What make you of *that* news, Nemo?

POLONIUS

Nemo?

CLAUDIUS

You,

No one, to whom my brother bids me tell it.

POLONIUS

Healéd by death, is 't writ?

CLAUDIUS

[*Showing the letter.*]

Look.

POLONIUS

[*After examining it.*]

Healéd by love,

'Twas writ, in his first letter, and *wounded by hate.*
But here: *healéd by death.* Thus note we here
A growth of difference. Love—death. What 's love,
But life? What 's death, but want of life and love
And all?

CLAUDIUS

Is it?

POLONIUS

What else?

CLAUDIUS

Aye, that 's the leak
I' the letter.

POLONIUS

"The letter killeth." The question is, then,
Killeth *whom*—the writer, the recipient, or
The letter-carrier? Thus are propounded,
Threefold, the *from,* the *to,* the *through,* whereby
And whether the letter carry, or miscarry,
The spirit, which saveth. Note that. 'Tis the spirit
We must construe, unto the very letter
Of the letter's spirit. As: Is 't a bloody spirit,
Or a blessed?—Let 's probe.

CLAUDIUS

Wilt thou stop letting blood
Out of this patient parchment, and let drop
Some lymph of pity, in the probing?

POLONIUS
[*Examines the parchment more closely.*]

Dream-struck—
Sands—and *the meal ground fine!* Aye, *sands,* as 't were,
Is *meal ground fine,* in a sort: a sort of meal—

CLAUDIUS

Hard swallowing, ha?

POLONIUS

And *millstones*—

CLAUDIUS

To hang around our necks, groaning so merrily
To cast the grout. Aye, that is coarser meal
And easier to spit. Let 's cast out all,
And start afresh.—No word of Fortinbras.
Yet, once sore hurt, methinks my brother's wound
Would worsen in the swamps, and waste in sands
The readier, for death to heal it.—So?
Thinkest thou so?

POLONIUS

Indubitably doubtless.

CLAUDIUS

Doubtless indubitable rings redundant—yet
We think, 't will serve: not so?

POLONIUS

Your humble servant
Craves but to serve.

CLAUDIUS

Then this sad news might serve
For thy promotion.

POLONIUS
[*Bowing low.*]

Sire!

CLAUDIUS

Tut! *Might* 's not *may*, yet,
Nor *may* 's not *shall*. 'Tis *if* comes first.

POLONIUS

If?—if?

CLAUDIUS

If thou rememberest, *thou* didst fetch that fellow
In the black cap, with scarlet tassels.—Ha!
"Didst ever thou dream?"—My dear, dead brother asks it.
Come!—Carding 's over. Now for the spinning! Come,
And watch us mount the spindle!—Lift our train,
And bear it after, to our footstool.—March!

[*Slowly, he paces toward the throne-dais, while Polonius follows him, in awe, lifting an imaginary train. At the foot of the throne-steps, Claudius motions Polonius to stay, and himself mounts to the right throne.*

As he stands there before it, with exultant, lifted gaze, a low MURMUR, *rising suddenly to a loud* TUMULT *of glad ringing cries, breaks forth from beyond the great, curtained entrance.*]

THE CRIES

Huzzah! Hail, hail, hail, hail! Long live the King!

CLAUDIUS
[*Staring toward the sound, in glad bewilderment.*]

"Didst ever thou dream?"—

POLONIUS

By night, never yet
By day, your Maj—

CLAUDIUS
[*Triumphantly.*]

Till *now!*

THE CRIES

Long live the King!
Hamlet! Hamlet! Welcome to Elsinore!

POLONIUS

That is—as 't were—his majesty—

CLAUDIUS

[*Harshly.*] *Returns!*

[*With hoarse, wild laughter, he leaps down the steps and seizes Polonius by the throat.*]

Ah-haha, Nemo! Thy millstone fits thy neck,
To hang, there—thee—
[*Flinging him off, clutches his own throat.*]
and mine—me! Ha, in truth,
Now are we *No One,* indeed! The grout is cast.
Spit, spit, loon! Spit!

POLONIUS

[*In terror.*]

My lord, my lord, my lord—!

[*Fanfare, and Cries, repeated, as the great-entrance curtains are thrown back, where—from amid a throng of Danes—comes forward, bare-headed, the Soldier in mud-sloughed armour, now bearing at one side his helm—*KING HAMLET, *who moves swiftly toward Claudius, who—outspreading both arms—springs to meet him, with a call, sweetly glad, which mocks the abject cry of the bewildered-shrinking Polonius.*]

CLAUDIUS

My lord, my lord and King!—Brother, welcome home!

KING HAMLET

[*Embracing him.*]

Home, Claudio! Back, in thine arms, at last,
Beacon, refuge, brother! [*Kisses him.*]
—This for my queen,
Till I can carry it to her! Where is she?
And how—how?—Well?

CLAUDIUS

Well may she be so, now,
At this thy glad return, unheralded
By none but him, who shines between the shadows
Of Faith and Love.

KING HAMLET

Who?

CLAUDIUS

Who but Hope, the shining
Herald!

KING HAMLET

Nay, but my letter, heralding
Myself, in person. Was it not delivered
To thee, in the mizzen, while I waited there
In the stern? [*Turning to Polonius.*]
What saith the King's "abstract-in-absence
Treasurer of the Royal Thesaurus?"—Ha? Aha!

POLONIUS

My liege, I—

KING HAMLET

Came I not "by Norway road,"
Bringing a letter?—Cryptogram, wouldst call it?
Was not *the meal ground fine?*
[*Bursting into laughter, as he turns to Voltimand and the others.*]
Ha, Voltimand,
Gaze here! Hath not my heart its yearned reward
In glad surprise? Full well have you, and these
My welcomers, kept my secret *dénouement*
To gladden Elsinore. Thanks for your welcome,
And yours, my Claudio!

CLAUDIUS
[*Smiling reproachfully.*]

"Healéd by death"
Had almost quench'd our hope.

KING HAMLET
[*His expression suddenly saddening, with a look dreamy and far off.*]

"Healéd by death"
Of Fortinbras! Yea, almost that had quench'd
My faith and love, till in the night I dreamed—
Dreamed what?—I only know—since then, my wound
Hath heal'd.

CLAUDIUS

Thy wound?

KING HAMLET

Of hate—here, in my heart,
Which now I 've changed for his, that sleepeth yonder
In peace.

CLAUDIUS

His—yonder?

KING HAMLET

Inurn'd in Norway's throne.

CLAUDIUS

You sent it back?

KING HAMLET

As a victor's offering
To his infant heir, his little Fortinbras,
Whose regent-uncle, loyal to his cause,
Shall treasure his rights of memory in my kingdom,[8]
Till it shall vantage him change love for love,
Instead of hate for hate, when he is crown'd.

CLAUDIUS

His infant son—

KING HAMLET

[*Starting.*]

Ah, where, then, is *mine own?*

Where?—Come yet? Come?

[*He turns eagerly toward the door, left, where* YORICK *has just entered, coming forward with a tiny crib, twined with blossoms, which he holds out to King Hamlet.*]

YORICK

'Tis here—your son.

[*He sets the cradle down before King Hamlet, who pauses, staring in utter silence, which pervades the great hall. Slowly then, bending over, he gazes down.*]

KING HAMLET

"All wattled with wildflowers and daffodillies" . . .
O, dream of night—O, little dream of love
And night! Let not the dragon shapes of dark
Nightshade thy slumber, but only dreams of angels—

YORICK

One sends you—this, in token of their dreams,
Which now they teach to her, being their namesake.

KING HAMLET

Who sendeth—what?

YORICK

[*Taking something from his pocket.*]

Angela sendeth—*this*
From heaven, bending over from there, with you,
To gaze on him.

KING HAMLET

Angela?

CLAUDIUS
[*Starting fearfully.*]

Yorick!
[*Controlling himself to smile, half ghastly.*]
—Yorick,
What is 't?

YORICK

Ah, smilest thou so, my lord?—Even so
Thou mayst well smile. It glinteth not, like crystal.
'Tis mere—a wisp of wool.
[*He hands it to the King.*]

KING HAMLET

Wool! Wisp of wool?

YORICK

Blest of St. Agnes, on her eve.—Saith Angie,
Ere she died:—

KING HAMLET

Died?

YORICK

"Say to my liege, I would ha' knit
The babe a snuggy shift, to keep him warm.
But now, his mother will do it purtier."

KING HAMLET

His mother!—O Gertrude, ere I haste to thee,
Mine arms about this, here, thou dear 'reaved fool
O' my heart, who feed'st it ever thine own brave wisdom!
[*He hugs Yorick, patting him fondly; then presses his own eyes.*]
Ha, dream! The dream hath blurr'd 'em!—Yea,
For here is wisdom doubled, now: aye, trebled

With mother, child, and fool.—Yorick, cradle-bearer,
Who comest from death to birth, and birth to life,
Bringing this brother of the daffodils
To greet his feud-worn father home from war,
Lift up again your blossomy burden, and bear it
Even to the throne-top, on the great right-hand,
And place him there, upon our kingdom's seat
Of power, prophetic of his own to-morrow.
Lift up, my Danes, your hearts, and trumpet the pledge:
Power and wisdom and love to the Prince of Denmark!

[FANFARE OF TRUMPETS, *and shouts of the assembled* DANES, *while Yorick, lifting the flowered cradle, bears it to the dais, and, mounting, places it on the right throne.*]

THE DANES

Power and wisdom and love to the Prince of Denmark!

[*From a corner of the scene, Claudius gazes at Yorick, fearfully. Then suddenly—as Yorick, on the throne, tosses some flower-buds from the cradle to the King—all but Claudius burst into joyous laughter, interrupted by Hamlet, who—lifting some of the flowers—kisses one, and shakes it aloft, in gesture of silence.*]

KING HAMLET

Hush!—
Seemeth our royal oak doth bud with daffodillies,
And the March Hare doth fling them at the Bear
Of Winter, to bid him change his burrow-fur
Of sallow, to match the blossoms.

[*Thrusting flowers in his hair.*]

So, he brightens
To win your laughter's blessing! For laughter springs
Of love, and love of sorrow, and sorrow of pride,
And pride is purg'd by prayer. So pray we now
Blessed St. Agnes, from whose holy eve
Her angel, Angela, pluckt this wisp of wool
To be a curl of candlelight in the brow
Of Caritas—pray we, in turn, her blessing
Of love, on him, our little Prince of Denmark,

And him, our Guardian-Jester on our throne,
And her, our Queen, to whom this heart, and all
Our hearts, hasten, to heal with victory:—these,
Love's bairn, and laughter's brother, and bravery's mother,
Kneel down to them, all thanes, we Danes, together!

[*Hamlet and All kneel, facing the throned cradle.*]

And yonder, beyond us all—beyond all princes
And kings, thanes, peoples, and love and laughter and pride—
Still, these all in us, within—within—within—
Now, bow we our hearts to the Heart of Victory,
Victoria, in excelsis, Caritati!
Amen!

ALL

Victoria, in excelsis, Caritati!
Amen!

[*Far off, as from supersensible Choirs, their earthly voices are echoed and answered by tones of* ETHEREAL VOICES, *in harmony.*]

THE VOICES

Victoria, in excelsis, Caritati!
Amen!

END OF "THE GHOST OF ELSINORE"

A PORTICO
IMAGINE

A PORTICO—On its lintel, upheld by ethereal columns, is written in gold the word IMAGINE!

Passing through, A READER *lifts his eyes to the golden inscription and pauses, murmuring to himself:* Strange!—Can a book be a temple, and a page—a portico? Apparently; for this book appears to be a group of shrines, built all of human speech, in structure fluently tetragonal. Already I 've explored its cloistral *Prelude,* and peered inwardly through the tiny *Open Window* that reveals, by ghostly moonlight, *the First* of the four play-temples, whence now I move on to *the Second.* Yet . . . just a moment!—In this quiet niche, here are scrolls of two poem-scripts:—One lingering moment, let me meditate these passages, and *imagine* the creative wonder of

LOVE—"THAT POWER WHICH WIELDS THE WORLD"

From THE EVE OF ST. AGNES *by* *KEATS*

[I]

St. Agnes' Eve—ah, bitter chill it was!
The owl, for all his feathers, was a-cold;
The hare limp'd trembling through the frozen grass,
And silent was the flock in woolly fold . . .

Ethereal, flush'd, and like a throbbing star
Seen through the sapphire heaven's deep repose,
Into her dream he melted, as the rose
Blendeth its odour with the violet—
. . . meantime the frost-wind blows
Like Love's alarum, pattering the sharp sleet
Against the window-panes; St. Agnes' moon hath set . . .

And they are gone: aye, ages long ago
These lovers fled away into the storm.

From ADONAIS: ELEGY ON THE DEATH OF KEATS *by* *SHELLEY*

[II]

He lives, he wakes—'tis Death is dead, not he;
Mourn not for Adonais.—Thou young Dawn,
Turn all thy dew to splendour, for from thee
The spirit thou lamentest is not gone . . .

He is made one with Nature: there is heard
His voice in all her music, from the moan
Of thunder to the song of night's sweet bird;
He is a presence to be felt and known
In darkness and in light, from herb and stone,
Spreading itself where'er that Power may move
Which has withdrawn his being to its own;
Which wields the world with never wearied love,
Sustains it from beneath, and kindles it above.

THE FOOL
IN EDEN GARDEN

THE FOOL IN EDEN GARDEN

[*Time: Seven years after the First Play*]

BEING THE SECOND PLAY
OF THE TETRALOGY
THE MYSTERY OF HAMLET
KING OF DENMARK, OR
WHAT WE WILL ✣ BY
PERCY MACKAYE

THE FOOL IN EDEN GARDEN

DRAMATIS PERSONAE

[*In the order of their appearance.*]

GERTRUDE, *Queen of Denmark*
HAMLET, *King of Denmark*
PADRE CELESTINO, *tutor of the Prince*
HORATIO, *comrade of the Prince, a few years his elder*
PRINCE HAMLET, *seven-year-old son of Gertrude and Hamlet*
YORICK, *court fool, crony of Prince Hamlet*
POLONIUS, *Lord Chamberlain*
CORNELIA, *wife of Polonius*
LAERTES, *their son, the Prince's playfellow*
CLAUDIUS, *brother of King Hamlet*
TOPAS, *grave-digger*
YAUGHAN, *gardener*
MOLL COWSLIP, *midwife*
RICHARD, *bell-ringer*
Cook, of Elsinore; Danish Guards, garbed as four-and-twenty Blackbirds; small Rabble of Children and Country Folk; Assemblage of Castle-Folk and Peasantry.

PERSONAE: [*Of Inner Scenes from Shakespeare's "Hamlet, Prince of Denmark"*]:—*Voice of Claudius; Prince Hamlet, grown; Laertes, grown; Voice of Gertrude; Voice of Osric.*

PERSONAE: [*Of the folk-drama: "The Grocers' Play of Norwich"*]:—*Prologus, Arbor* [*the Tree of Eden*]; *Serpens* [*the Snake*]; *Pater* [*God, the Father*]; *Adam; Eva; Aungel; Vita Arboris* [*the Holy Ghost*].

PRESENCE:—GALLUCINIUS, *as Voice of the Cock*

SCENES

ACT FIRST:—Elsinore. A Room in the Castle, used as a Play-Room for Children.

Night of Prince Hamlet's seventh birthday.

SCENES

[*Continued*]

ACT SECOND:—A Hall in the Castle, containing two Shrines.
Later, the same night.

ACT THIRD:—Hall of the Shrines.
The next morning.

ACT FOURTH:—A Walled Garden of the Castle.
Several weeks later. Hallowe'en.

ACT FIFTH:—Graveyard.
The following afternoon.

Note: Stage-right and stage-left are from the actor's point of view.

ACT FIRST

ELSINORE. A ROOM IN THE CASTLE, USED AS A PLAY-ROOM FOR CHILDREN.

At right, back and upper centre, on the floor, are building-blocks, in disorder; puppets; a closet, hung with wooden swords; and a wooden horse, on rollers, caparisoned in rich colours. In the stone wall at back, left of centre, rather high up, a niche. At left, upper stage, the corner of the room is diagonally cut off by curtains, stretched between, and rolled upon, two high poles, with a centre slit, closed by a flap. At lower left, a large doorway. In a wide jog of the right wall, a Gothic window, through which stars are visible. Within, the room is lit by many candles.

KING HAMLET *and* QUEEN GERTRUDE, *discovered.*

GERTRUDE

Hamlet, my own! What are you gazing on,
As if its fiery image would consume
The tinder of thine eyes, that touch it?

KING HAMLET

All—
All falsity, that fades in smoky air
Before that image.

GERTRUDE

Whose?—What image?

KING HAMLET

Thine:
Thou, Gertrude,—made of memory.

GERTRUDE

But I
Am here, beside thee!

KING HAMLET

Yes. So art thou there
Beside me.—Through the fragrant incense-smoke
That wafts the attar of our wedding-vows
The altar-bells are tinkling. Dost thou not
Sense them again, in memory?

GERTRUDE

Yet still
I say, I 'm here, not there.

KING HAMLET

Both there and here,
With Love, thine image.

GERTRUDE

Ah, that 's made of stuff
More tangible than memory: here [*Reaching her hand.*]
—touch!

KING HAMLET

[*Clasping her hand, as he looks into her face, lifted to his.*]

Oh, love, methinks, is memory on fire,
Leapt out of embers into sudden glory,
Revealing its own likeness by illuming
The eyes it smiles upon—uniting all
It was with what it is—to manifest
The invisible, even as it vanishes.

GERTRUDE

Vanishes?—Our love?

KING HAMLET

Into our own deep heaven,
And there swings forth our Seven Lamps of Promise
To star the birth-night of our kingdom's heir.

[*Still clasping her hand, he leads her to the arched Gothic window, and points outward into the night. As he does so,* YORICK *appears, in doorway, left, watches them a moment, then retires.*]

See, Gertrude! Yonder they are floating up
Over the gold hive of our heaven-stored years,
Like honey-bees out of the waxen comb—
The Seven Stars!

GERTRUDE
[*Gazing out.*]

Ye lovely Pleiades,
So may you ever rise, nor ever set
Under the seven seas!

KING HAMLET

Alcyone,
The brightest of their pollen'd swarm, hath tipt
The farthest wave with his fire-twinkling wing
Of spirit emerald.

GERTRUDE

That sprite is his,
Our little prince's birth-star, tangling the chain
Around the fleecy Ram's horn, for a bridle
To gallop the buck of Aries, straddle-back,
And chase the springtide Bull 'gainst summer's gate
To fling wide all heaven's kingdom for our throne.

KING HAMLET

Already he hath conquered heaven for us,
And what of earth remains, we 'll hold for him
As birthright—yonder! Seven years, together,
We 've watched the sap mount in our princely son,
Pricking the leafage of his sprite with buds
Of sprouting ardours; suppling his little limbs
With toughening fibre; glistening his eyes
To glow with love-fire; ruddying his cheeks
To flush with daring; yeasting his blood to daunt
The antagonists of play.

GERTRUDE

Perchance of play
More than of practice?

KING HAMLET

What! Impractical?
What wouldst thou of seven springtides—a full summer
And riping autumn? Nay, our sapling savours
Early of his oak—hardly of acorns yet.
But hast thou watched him, when the fit is on,
And he is plotting passions with his puppets,
How his rapt visions, struggling for their vent,
Flash the fine flectures of his knitted frown
And burst the impregnéd brain?

GERTRUDE

Too much from the brain
He waxeth, I fear, too little from the loins.

KING HAMLET

Too little?—Look there! See where his building-blocks
Lie rubbled in the ruin of Troy's towers!
Hast thou forgot his bout with Hector there:
How, yesteryear, when scarce he scored six Aprils,
He girt his loins with great Achilles' cuirass,
And miming his little crony, Laertes, up
To the chin in mighty Hector's armour, speared him,
And dragged him, by the heels, twice round the walls
Of fabled Ilion?

GERTRUDE
[*Smiling.*]

Ah, fabled, indeed!

KING HAMLET

And yonder, his Trojan Horse, within whose belly
He rolled his way into the doomèd city—
Himself, guised as Odysseus, with Laertes
As Diomede—and compassed the fall of Troy!

Where shalt thou find, my dear, a prince of prowess
So fettled with strategy as our little playboy?

GERTRUDE

All this—out of Homer's prompt-book!

KING HAMLET

'T is a prompter
Hath blazoned history's scroll.

GERTRUDE

And bloodied it, too.

KING HAMLET

What 's that? Thou shouldst be prouder than Hecuba,
Without her sorrows, and Achilles' mother,
Without her fear.

GERTRUDE

Ah, Hamlet, yet I hope
Our little prince have not Achilles' heel!
If that be fear, I share all mothers' fears,
And with them, a wife's—Andromache's—
For thee, my Hector, hero of my walléd heart.

KING HAMLET

I—Hector? And shall Elsinore, then, fall?

GERTRUDE

Who augurs the fall of man?—The falling stars?
Seven years have not yet blurred from memory
The ninth moon, when thou fought'st with Fortinbras;
Nay, nor that evening, when the heaven opened
And laid our prince in his cradle, and my pretty
Wool-spinner, Angela, in her grave.

KING HAMLET
[*Changing his look and tone.*]

'Twas strange,
Indeed, that twisted spinning of the Fates:
The daffodillies with the wisp of wool!
And stranger still, my brother's dumb departure
On pilgrimage to Rome—dear Claudio!

GERTRUDE

Why did he leave?

KING HAMLET

Still am I pondering—why.

GERTRUDE

And he went forth—?

KING HAMLET

The morning after, at dawn.

GERTRUDE

Without one word to thee?

KING HAMLET

Nay, more than one.
Ten words he spake to me: "I fare to Rome,
To *Santa Agnese Fuore delle Mure.*"

GERTRUDE

St. Agnes, Outside the Walls!—How passing strange!
I went there once. 'Twas just before thou brought'st me
Here, to our wedding. Dost remember?

KING HAMLET

How
Could I forget?—Surpassing strange, in truth!

GERTRUDE

And still no other word, in all these years!

KING HAMLET

In all these years, no word—whether he live,
Or else—

GERTRUDE
[*Quickly.*]

Not that!

KING HAMLET

Who knoweth?—Were there some pilgrim,
Whom we might send in quest of him, to find
And fathom his mystery—Ah, Celestino!
Come in, good Padre.

[*In the doorway, right, stands a* SERENE FIGURE, *whose alert presence seems to precede his motion, and to be conveyed by the loving smile from the lips of his lightly-bearded face. He is clad in a violet-blue cassock, with cowl thrown back. His first words, more chanted than spoken, in pure tones of their Italian tongue, are uttered low, but with a glad spontaneity of rhythm, as of far-chiming bells.*]

PADRE CELESTINO

Entra, O fidele, in questo asilo di pace,
Dove di Dio si parla, e poi si tace.[1]
[*He comes forward.*]
My dears, let us speak of God,
For that is ever good news and sociable;
Or let us be silent, for so He speaks to us.
All else is unimportant. Heaven in ourselves
Bring us all His starshine!

KING HAMLET

Such thy coming brings us.

GERTRUDE

Good evening, Father. Though I call thee so,
Thy youth shines such, despite thy wandering years
In many a land, I 'd liever call thee *Brother*.

CELESTINO

Then, father—brother—lover, call me, child,
All in His name, whose trinity is truth,
In this our natal ghost-land that surrounds us.

GERTRUDE

Ghost-land!—Wast thou born there?

CELESTINO

Oh, many times,
And, every morning dew-rise, ever the newer.

KING HAMLET

Methought thou saidst in Italy it was,
At Palestrina.

CELESTINO

True; my mortal dame
Mothered me there, in a little hostelry;
But our Immortal Lady cribbed me in a mansion
Under the evening star, in the same cradle
St. Agnes tucks her lambs.

KING HAMLET

St. Agnes! Then,
Perchance, thou knowest where her chapel lies,
In Rome, outside the city walls.

CELESTINO

Ah, often
Have I knelt there, with two eternal friends,

Having fresh come, together, from Frascati,
Where the live fountain of Aldobrandini leaps
Down from the Alban Mountains, to outpour
Her melodies through marble Orpheus' flute.

KING HAMLET

I see, 't is hard to lure thee from the bourn
Of thy bright ghost-land, here, back to the dusk
Of Elsinore. Yet tell us: knowest thou
Some pilgrim, who might bear a sealéd letter
Secretly to another pilgrim at
St. Agnes' shrine,. so as to reach him safely?

CELESTINO

I 'll be that pilgrim, son, and thou wilt trust me
With the hid secret underneath the seal;
For seals of earthly kingdoms are of wax,
But heavenly—of wisdom. Faith is the signet
Vouches the Great King's Word.

KING HAMLET
[*To Gertrude.*]

How thinkest thou?
Perhaps through him our seven-years' riddle were reded?

GERTRUDE

We 'll plan it, soon. Now comes another shepherd,
Led by our prince's star, to proffer gifts
Of festival.—Welcome, Horatio! Hast
Thou brought us tidings where our princeling tarries,
That he 's so late, to keep his birthday with us?

[*From the doorway, right, an* ERECT, HANDSOME YOUTH *comes forward quietly, and bows.*]

HORATIO

Madam, with Yorick.

GERTRUDE

Where?

HORATIO

In the scullery.

GERTRUDE

What, saidst thou? What word?

HORATIO

Scullery, my Queen.

GERTRUDE

What quip is this from Yorick's skull of jest?
He keepeth Prince Hamlet in the scullery!—Pray,
What doing, there?

HORATIO

Lardering, Madam.

GERTRUDE

Lardering?

HORATIO

Plying the cook for tarts and apple-dumplings,
And parsley sallet, to garnish his song withal.

KING HAMLET

His song! What song?

HORATIO

O' sixpence, your Majesty:
The one the blackbirds sang, when the bakéd pie
Was opened. And, my liege, he bade me tell you,
For sixpence, and for sake of our dear prince's
Birthday, he 'll sing you the very words of it:
"Is n't that a dainty dish to set before a king?"

KING HAMLET
[*Laughing.*]

Aha! What said our Hamlet to the song?

HORATIO

He said, he 'd rather hear the blackbirds sing it,
Than Yorick. But little Laertes, who was keeping
Close sentry guard by Yorick's breeches, said
He 'd rather have the pocketful of rye,
Than hear the singing—birds, or fool.

KING HAMLET

There, Gertrude!
Go put that to Polonius' wisdom: which
Of the bright sons of Gertrude and Cornelia,
By mother-wit, or father-geniture,
Hath won the blackbird-pie?

GERTRUDE

Horatio,
Thou art a sturdy lad, and staunch withal
As thy ready sword-blade, rustless in its sheath
To leap for action, yet as ponderable
As that great word, which bids the apple fall
Straight from its bough to earth. In all our kingdom
(I speak for both thy king and queen in this),
There is no youth of honesty and manners—
Nay, soldier, nor sage, elder in years—to whom
We would, in truth, more fondlier entrust
Our Prince of Denmark, to be bred in good
And guilelessness, than to Horatio.

HORATIO

Madam——

GERTRUDE

I say—this being so, not seeming,

Methought—and I 'd have laid a precious jewel
In pawn of that *methought*—that, when we bade thee
Fetch here young Hamlet from the clutches of Yorick,
Thou wouldst have brought him *straight,* not round a bush
Of singing blackbirds—baked, or otherwise.

HORATIO

Lady—

GERTRUDE

Speak up, not swallow down!

HORATIO

The truth is,
I bore your Majesty's command to Yorick,
And found *him* in the clutches of your child,
Not *vice versa.* Indeed, the boy was bent
To hug him so full of kisses—not of pie,
But of pure love—that the encaged court-fool,
To fend himself, must mount your royal heir
Pig-a-back, and go galloping for peace.

KING HAMLET
[*To Gertrude.*]

Ha, my dear, thou didst say it, he would ride
The Ram of Aries, for his birth-night steed!

HORATIO

My liege, in truth, how came you to guess *that?*
For, last I saw of them, the locks of Yorick
Were curled with double horns, which he had snatcht
From Dick the Shepherd's cupboard, thonged with hide,
And the wild princeling, 'straddle the fool's neck,
Was lifting aloft another crumpled horn,
Crookt like the cow's, that jumped the sickle-moon,
Waving it, like a huntsman.

[*The shrilly* BLOWING OF A HORN *is heard, from beyond the left entrance. Horatio turns toward it, exclaiming.*]

Lord of omens!
Yonder it bloweth—the horn of the Prince of Denmark,
Hailing your majesties—and hither cometh
His ram o' the scullery, rampant!

[*From the left—bursting in—enter* YORICK, *ram-horned, prancing with feet and hands in a galloping dance, with the child,* PRINCE HAMLET, *astride his shoulders, waving a horn, and calling.*]

PRINCE HAMLET

Yeigh-ho, tally-ho!

KING HAMLET
[*Calling back to him.*]

Tally-ho, tally-high, my huntsman!

GERTRUDE

Now, now, now,
Yorick, what 's this?

YORICK

The heir of Elsinore,
Your Majesty, come hither to kiss your hand,
Mounted on a crupper of the Zodiac,
Your ramshackle fool.—Hamlet, kiss the Queen's hand.

GERTRUDE
[*Smiling, reaches towards him.*]

My dear!

PRINCE HAMLET
[*Kissing her hand, with deference.*]

My mother!
[*Then tugging Yorick's hair.*]
Up, Aries!

[*Wincing, Yorick shakes his horns, and holds up his right forefinger, peering at the child.*]

YORICK

Alcyone,
Thy mother can tell thee, a Pleiad is placed on high
To twinkle, not to tug at bulbs of wisdom
Rooted in a fool's skull, nor to unhorn a creature
Heaven hath ordained to be thine oracle
And guardian of thy birthright. Pulling wool
Is work for shepherds, not for princes.

PRINCE HAMLET

Then
I 'll dig, instead, to make thee dance again.
[*With the narrow end of his hunting-horn, he pokes Yorick's scalp.*]

GERTRUDE
[*Chidingly.*]

Hamlet, the point is sharp!

YORICK

The point is blunt
That misses the point in question, and the question
Points upward, not down. The question is, Prince Hamlet,—
Since I am thine oracle, and shall appoint
Many pithy questions, yet, to be, or not be
Answered of thy conscience,—whether thou wilt descend,
Of thine own will, out of this airy region
Of Aries, unto earth, or be dismounted,
Against thy will, or ignorance. Which shall it
Be, or not be?

PRINCE HAMLET

Art thou done baaing, Ram?
Then, prance me again!

YORICK

So be it—on thine own head!

[*With sudden, bending shrug, he somersaults the boy, heels upward, onto his head, where he rolls over, and springs up again, rushing towards Yorick, who in turn flings himself down, stretched flat, calling, as he rolls over:*]

To earth! To earth, child! Earth is the All-Mother.—Suckle!

PRINCE HAMLET

So thou wilt suckle earth?—Not I! I 'll slay,
And conquer! What, do I bleed?—Brush off, ye red drops!—
Give here thy sword, Horatio,—and swiftly!

[*As Horatio hands it to him, he stands the sword, hilt upward, upon the prone body of Yorick, holding it at arm's length with his right hand, while with his left he raises his horn, in a triumphant posture, as he plants one foot on the body.*]

The kill! The kill! Look, angels! Here am I,
St. Michael,—lo, the Dragon, where he lieth!

KING HAMLET

[*Nudging Gertrude, as they look on, laughing.*]

"Too little from the loins?"

GERTRUDE

The blade is scabbarded.

YORICK

[*Turning his horned head to squint up at the posed St. Michael.*]

Art thou done baaing, Lamb?—Then lance me again
With thy reaping-hook, and I will bleed thee more
Bright ichor, from my veins of oracle.

[*Prince Hamlet, removing his foot, starts swinging the scabbarded sword into the ribs of Yorick.*]

PRINCE HAMLET

Tickle, tickle!
Sword, turn sickle:
Michael's reaping-hook is mickle!

[*At this, Yorick sits up, snatches away the sword, and hands it to Horatio. Thereupon, the child bursts out laughing, springs to Yorick's arms, where he hugs and kisses him, till Yorick, with changing look, holds him away, fondly gazing at him.*]

YORICK

Hang not upon my lips, sweet prince: the savour
Lingers, and saps the heart in after-time.
Other lips have hung here, and the mildew fusteth.

[*Moved by his sudden, changed expression of sadness, the child pats Yorick's head soothingly.*]

PRINCE HAMLET

Poor Yorick! I tickled too deep, and pulled thy hair!
I 'll cure thy head.

YORICK

Pat not this skull too near.
The earth is in 't, and the roil'd rain may run
Where I have suckled it. [*Murmuring.*]—Mariana—Angie—

PRINCE HAMLET

[*Softly.*]

Whom dost thou whisper to?

YORICK

The winds—the winds
I' the chimney flue.*

GERTRUDE

[*Approaching closer, with the King.*]

Well, princeling dear, and Yorick,
So endeth now the fooling?

YORICK

Nay, my lieges,
Fool's fooling hath no finity. Here, therefore,
Endeth the *Scherzo,* merely. Now beginneth
Il Misterioso.

*Cf. p. 90.

KING HAMLET

O, so! Must the merry
Become mysterious?—Why?

YORICK

Because—your pardons,
That I did overhear your royal communion
With bright Alcyone and the Pleiades
By yonder window, looking toward the tides
Of sea and heaven; for I have more to vision you
Of second sight, starring those awful tides,
Than Jason saw, seeking the Golden Fleece,
Whereof I wear these horns—from the scullery.
But first, touching upon our little Pleiad,
Hamlet-Alcyone, "brightest o' the pollen'd swarm,"
I 'll beg your moment's hearing; since this fool
Of Aries is divinator of the psyche
Of this, our prince, who shall be sometime king,
Unless . . .

[*He pauses, dreamily.*]

KING HAMLET

Unless?

YORICK

Once more, your pardons! You see
These horns I wear? They 're bone; but, just as we,
Of flesh and bone incarnate, still are made
In image of our psychic selves, unbodied
Of bone and flesh, so these zodiacal horns
Are imaged in the crookled trails of birth
That flex within the cusps of Hamlet's brain
To lead his intellect through their labyrinth
Unto his center'd will . . .

[*He pauses again, dreamily.*]

KING HAMLET

And then?

GERTRUDE

What so?

YORICK

So, then, I am his ramly image, yclept
In heaven—Aries, on earth—Irresolution.
Here, on my wobbling back, he wills to ride,
Huntsman and angler, both: to harry heaven,
Yet fish earth's silent pools: *tally-ho!* yet *hush!*
To sit the saddle, or dismount—still will-less
To shape the event; till, sudden, he 's somersaulted
By wilful destiny, heels over temples,
Where the dumb blood-drops trickle.

GERTRUDE

Doth he bleed?

Methought it a scratch.

[*Turning anxiously to the Prince, who is sitting on Horatio's knee.*]

Good darling, bleedst thou still?

PRINCE HAMLET

Mother, I hope so. But Horatio hath
Swabbed it away. Haply, 't will start afresh.

KING HAMLET

[*Touching Gertrude.*]

No mothering, now! Yorick, resume.

GERTRUDE

Say on.

YORICK

I say, my Queen, that being born in April,
Under the fool star, on the running Ram,
Your child were better born earlier, or more late.

For here, on my spine, peering across one horn,
He eyeth the Fish of Contemplation, tossing
A hookéd bait of wit to angle it;
Or, else, over this other horn, he taunteth
The pawing Bull of Action, who turneth rump
And kicks his hooves against the wit-hoop'd brain
Till it runs wine of blood—Nay, not this scratch
Of child's play, but the crash it bodes—of passions
Rampant on cloudy portents, whirling dark
Through arches of Elsinore, carmined with blood
Spilled by irresolution—that, it is,
Wrings my fool's withers. But enough of these!
Off, horns!—Hang up, my sign of oracle,
In the ram's stall! Back to the scullery,
Whence ye arose! My cap and bells, once more!
Your mercies, my lieges: Yorick 's your fool again.

[*Unhorning himself, Yorick takes from his pocket his belled fool's-cap, and puts it on. While he does so, Gertrude speaks aside to the King.*]

GERTRUDE

The daftness plagueth him.

KING HAMLET

Less as oracle
Than fool, perhaps.

GERTRUDE
[*To Yorick.*]

In troth, we do prefer
The bells' bleat, to the ram's.

PRINCE HAMLET
[*Springing from Horatio, towards them.*]

Give *me* the horns!
I 'll hang them on Polonius, and ride *him*,
To scare Laertes.

[*He snatches from Yorick the thong-looped horns, which he carries toward* POLONIUS, *who is just entering, left, with* CORNELIA, *and their son,* LAERTES, *a young boy of soldierly bearing.*]

POLONIUS

[*Bowing.*]

Greetings, my lord, Prince!
And gratulations on your festal birth-night!
May all its starry omens grace your forehead.

PRINCE HAMLET

They do, Sir. Here they are, to grace your own.

[*He presents the token.*]

POLONIUS

These—for my forehead?—Horns! The omen fits
But dubiously, my lord.

PRINCE HAMLET

Foreheads less bald
Have worn them gracefully, have not they, Yorick?

YORICK

Whom the cap fitteth, weareth it, methinks,
Honni soit, qui mal y pense. My cap doth bell
The wether, rain or shine, for ram, or sheep,
Or shepherd.

GERTRUDE

*Goat*herd rather! Savour thy jests
For churls, not children and gentles.—Welcome, Cornelia,
Polonius! Your little Laertes tops
Our Hamlet by an inch-height. Faith, he grows
Taller, each day.

CORNELIA

So he shall never o'ertop
His playfellow's heart, that grows in princeliness

More dear to him, each day, Laertes will
Rejoice; wilt not thou, laddie?

LAERTES

Hamlet can
Best me at battledore and shuttlecock,
But I can outreach him, with my lath, in fencing.

PRINCE HAMLET
[*Abruptly, tossing away the horns.*]

Prove it! I 'll lay, my reach is longest. Here!
I 'll fetch the foils.

[*From a cupboard, beside his blocks, he takes forth a pair of wooden swords, wrought of flat lath, with nubs of leather; eyes them over expertly, and steps forward with them, handing one to his boy-antagonist, with a flourish.*]

Come, crony! Touch, and go.

LAERTES

This is too heavy; let me see another.

PRINCE HAMLET

This likes me well. These laths have all a length,
Methinks; but hand him another, Horatio,
From the cupboard.

[*Horatio brings another.*]

LAERTES

This suits me better.

PRINCE HAMLET

Now, then!

KING HAMLET

First, let us lay our stakes upon this bout,
Polonius, father to father, for our sons'
Victory, or defeat. Capitulation
Is disruled, from the outset.

POLONIUS

Good my liege,
What favourence I hold as father, I
Would fain dispense withal, in favour of
My joy, as subject to your Majesty,
To see my son defeated, at the hands
Of this, his prince and playfellow.

PRINCE HAMLET

O, fudge!
Laertes is my fellow-cock, with spurs,
No chicken, to peep in the egg, for mush.

KING HAMLET

You hear,
Polonius, the Prince's proclamation?

POLONIUS

Which hath, perforce, my humble obedience.

KING HAMLET

Know, then, this being our prince's festival,
All handicap is waived. 'T is lad with lad,
Not prince with squire, shall cross these wooden swords,
As stern, as if their peril were of steel.
So grows their friendship in their foemancraft,
Forged by its testing, hand from claspéd hand
To hand on hilt. [*To the children.*]
—Grip hands!
[*They do so. The King points toward the wooden-horse.*]
Now be it published
To all, there stands the royal horse of Denmark,
Fresh from the fall of Troy, pawing to fell
More towering walls, and stable in loftier crofts.
Lo, then, our royal stake: that, hit for miss,

In blow and parry, the lad thrice hit shall fall,
Nor rise, except to offer gratulation
To his adversary, who straightway shall be
Led to the saddle, and be garlanded
By him he felled, whom he shall lift beside him
To gallop, together, toward new onsets.
[*Raising his hand, and dropping a kerchief.*]—Time!

[*The two small lads step back from their handclasp, stand facing each other, and prepare to fence with their wooden swords. While they do so, Yorick picks up the ram's horns, and, holding them lifted, gazes on them strangely, murmuring.*]

YORICK

Time!—Eternity!—Elsinore, Elsinore!

[*At his words, the scene suddenly darkens, all except a glow from the uplifted ram's horns, which throws upon the wall, high above the lads, a patch of palish light, where* SHADOWS OF TWO OTHER FENCING FIGURES *ply their foils at each other, with strokes and parryings strangely uniform with those of the two children beneath, but more disciplined in action. The Figures, maturely tall, vaguely resemble the dim, small forms of Prince Hamlet and Laertes, beneath them. Standing, at first, opposite each other, they commence their fencing only after a* DEEP VOICE *having spoken from the darkness, with clear resonance, has uttered the words: "Come, begin!"*]

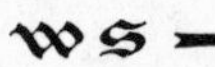

THE DEEP VOICE
[*In tones of the voice of Claudius.*]

Give me the cups;
And let the kettle to the trumpet speak,
The trumpet to the cannoneer without,
The cannons to the heavens, the heaven to earth,
Now the King drinks to Hamlet.—Come, begin;—
And you, the judges, bear a wary eye.

PRINCE HAMLET
[*Below, in child's voice.*]

Come on, Sir!

[*Above, in man's voice.*]

Come on, Sir.

LAERTES
[*Below, in child's voice.*]

Come on, Sir!

[*Above, in man's voice.*]

Come on, Sir.

VOICES OF THE SHADOWS ABOVE
[*In varying men-tones, with one exception—a woman's voice—from the dark, above.*]

HAMLET

One.

LAERTES

No.

HAMLET

Judgement.

A THINNISH, FALSETTO MAN'S-VOICE

A hit, a very palpable hit.

LAERTES

Well,—again.

THE DEEP VOICE
[*In tones of Claudius.*]

Stay, give me drink: Hamlet, this pearl is thine;
Here 's to thy health. Give him the cup.
[*Trumpets sound; and cannon shot off within.*]

HAMLET

I'll play this bout first, set it by awhile.
Come.—Another hit; What say you?
[*They play.*]

LAERTES

A touch, a touch, I do confess.

THE DEEP VOICE

Our son shall win.

THE WOMAN'S VOICE
[*In tones of Gertrude, from the upper dark.*]

He 's fat, and scant of breath.
Here, Hamlet, take my napkin, rub thy brows:
The queen carouses to thy fortune, Hamlet.

HAMLET

Good, Madam.

THE DEEP VOICE

Gertrude, do not drink.

THE WOMAN'S VOICE

I will, my lord;—I pray you, pardon me.

THE DEEP VOICE

It is the poison'd cup: it is too late.[2]

——— WS

[*From his lifted hands, Yorick drops the ram's horns, the hollow sound of whose falling on the stone floor dissipates the darkness.*]

YORICK

Once more, back to the scullery!
[*The Children are fencing alertly.*]

PRINCE HAMLET

One!

LAERTES

No!

PRINCE HAMLET

Judgement!

POLONIUS

A hit, a very palpable hit.

LAERTES

Well, again.

KING HAMLET

Stay, give me drink. Fetch yonder cup,
Voltimand;—first, to the Queen.

[VOLTIMAND, *who has entered, left, brings the cup, passes it, then turns to Polonius, speaks with him aside, and, at his gesture, makes exit, left.*]

YORICK

The cup, my Queen,
Is innocent.

GERTRUDE

The cup—is innocent—?

YORICK

Of oracle. But the horns—

GERTRUDE

The horns, again!
What of the horns?

YORICK

They spill a redder wine.

GERTRUDE
[*To the King.*]

Nay, he grows dafter.—Horns!—He looks mad.

KING HAMLET

Pshaw!
Now, children, back to the bout! Ye bear it deftlier
Than oft your elders do. We stand amazed
At childhood, primed so soon for manhood.

PRINCE HAMLET

Ha,
Horatio taught us practice. He is worth
A court of limping elders.—Now, Laertes?

LAERTES

Now!

[*They play. Prince Hamlet hits Laertes.*]

PRINCE HAMLET

One for me. That evens it.—Another?

HORATIO

No; that one missed. [*To the Queen.*]
This feud grows hot.

GERTRUDE

Too hot!
Stay, children. Catch your breaths, a little. Wait.
Here, Hamlet, take my napkin, rub thy brows.

[*Excited, Prince Hamlet waves her away, trying to parry a thrust of Laertes, which hits him, in consequence, to his angered chagrin.*]

LAERTES
[*As he hits Prince Hamlet.*]

Twice one is *two*. Ha!

PRINCE HAMLET

Ha! What of it, rooster?

[*Crowingly, flapping his arms, like a cock.*]

Thrice three is *diddle-diddle-diddle-dee!*

[*As he still flaps his arms, his crowing is echoed by the eerie* CRY OF A COCK, *while Yorick—having picked up the horns again—holds them toward the Queen, who steps back from him, with startled exclamation.*]

GERTRUDE

In the name of heaven—

YORICK

[*Shaking his head.*]

In the name of Elsinore!

[*As he holds the ram's horns still lifted, once more through sudden darkness, their glow illumines the wall, where the* SHADOW FORMS *of the mature Hamlet and Laertes stand confronting each other, and the* WOMAN'S VOICE, *in tones of Gertrude, speaks from the dark above, with anxious solicitude.*]

WS ————————————

THE WOMAN'S VOICE

Come, let me wipe thy face.

LAERTES

[*Above, in man's voice.*]

My lord, I'll hit him now.

THE DEEP VOICE

I do not think it.

LAERTES

And yet it is almost against my conscience.

HAMLET

[*Above, in man's voice.*]

Come, for the third, Laertes: You but dally:
I pray you, pass with your best violence;
I am afeard you make a wanton of me.[3]

———————————— WS

[*At hollow thud of the fallen ram's horns, the scene leaps once more into light, where Queen Gertrude, gazing at Yorick, nudges the King, and speaks low.*]

GERTRUDE

Stark daft, I say!

KING HAMLET
[*Smiling.*]

As always!

LAERTES
[*To Prince Hamlet.*]

Say you so, come on!
Have at you, now!—*Three!*
[*Laertes' sword hits Hamlet, and they scuffle.*]

KING HAMLET

Part them, they are incensed.

PRINCE HAMLET

Nay, come again!

POLONIUS

Look to the Queen, there, ho!

HORATIO
[*Laughing, as he parts the Children.*]

They 'd bleed on both sides, and their laths were mettle
As their steely wills.

POLONIUS
[*Touches him, pointing.*]

Methinks the Queen faints.

HORATIO

What!

[*He hastens to her.*]

KING HAMLET

Gertrude, what now?

HORATIO

Madam!—

GERTRUDE

[*Faintly, to Horatio, forcing a smile, and pointing to the ram's horns.*]

Bear them to the scullery.
The stars are falling, to behold this feud
Of childhood, on our prince's natal night,
And the shorn Ram hath shed his silver horns
In prancing with this fool.

YORICK

[*Lilting, as he moves away.*]

We cannot find
In human kind
The virtue that we wish we could.
Ah, never mind,
What 's that to thee, Sweet Solitude?*

[*Tinkling his cap-bells, he wanders toward the pole-hung curtains, at upper left, and disappears behind them, as Horatio, taking the horns, makes exit with them, at lower, left.*]

KING HAMLET

[*To Gertrude.*]

Thou heedest too much
The foolery of Yorick. Go fathom the dumbness
Of our dear Padre Celestino. There
Thou 'lt find the still pool of philosophy.

[*Queen Gertrude passes toward the right, where she rejoins Celestino, who, all the while, has been standing, by himself, lost in rapt contemplation.*]

Polonius, the stakes are thine. Laertes,

*See note 3 for *The Ghost of Elsinore*, page 671.

Come mount the Trojan horse, and Hamlet, hold
The halter, till the victor bids thee ride
The pommel behind him.—Mount!

[*Laertes holds back, shyly, with puzzled frown.*]

POLONIUS

Laertes, hear'st thou
The King's command?—What, what, what?—Have not I
Disciplined thee to obey thy mighty elders
And ever to hold thy humbleness before them?
And am not I thy father, who instructs thee?

LAERTES

Yes, Sir; but whom must I obey: my father,
Or Hamlet's?

POLONIUS

Why, both.

LAERTES

Sir, you have bidden me
Never to climb higher than my prince; but now
His father bids me mount above him.

KING HAMLET

Ha,
Polonius, I see thy child would barter
The button of my crown, for the crown-jewel
Of thy paternity, and thereby pose
Questions as old as Adam's, when he 'd got
His first two sons, and asked himself: "What now?
Is Adam king in my house, since this same love
Which queened mine Eve as mate, now makes her mother
To this seditious feud betwixt my realms
Of Royalty and Paternity?"

POLONIUS

The opposites
Of power and gentleness, of might and meekness,
Would seem, Sire, to converge, and poise their tensions
For union, only to explode.

KING HAMLET

Why, true: You saw
How here my cockling, Hamlet, flapped his winglets,
Venting his vaunt, to crow his childish ire;
Yet that same king-cock-cry wakes the world's dawn
To love and generation of the gods.—
What, then, is this cock, this king? What 's love? What 's life?
What are these lover-father, mother-mate,
Whose feudal offspring fence with foils of war
To spill the precious blood of brotherhood?
Yea, power to command, and patience to endure,
The poles of being, fixed in flesh and soul
To make the craven kingliness of man,—
What are all these, in that still-mask'd design
Which builds in love's sweet bower a slaughter-house,
Wherein, as Yorick saith, mid trophied spoils,
The Ram of Heaven hangs high his Golden Fleece?

POLONIUS

Questions all-pertinent, yet less to the law
Of Adam, than of angels, dear my liege.

KING HAMLET

We 'll put them, some or all, to the quiet Padre
And ask his taciturnity to tell
More than our tongue can sound.
[*To Celestino.*] Good Father, pray,
What is love? Hast thou a book on 't, to reveal?

CELESTINO

Yes, certainly. I keep it by me, always.

KING HAMLET

So close?—Within thy cassock?

CELESTINO

Next my heart.
'Tis writ on seven tables, and 't is named
The Book of Amor.

KING HAMLET

Faith, it doth not swell
Thy cassock's bosom. Is it, then, brief?

CELESTINO

As time,
And long as memory.

KING HAMLET

Are its leaves so many?

CELESTINO

The Book of Amor hath as many leaves
As teem the gales of autumn, when their winged
Tempest is loosed in glory; as many tongues
As beaks of springtime vowel in the vales
Of lone Parnassus' mountain; and its margins
Are all emblazoned with as varied blooms
As star the broidery of Flora's breasts,
Or tinge the lips of Galilean lilies
With gules of roses, pluckt from gory thorns
Of Golgotha.

[YORICK *re-enters from behind the poled curtains.*]

GERTRUDE

And is it writ therein
What paths of joy, or pain, our prince shall tread
Through those lone vales, that lead love's pilgrim on
To pluck the roses from the gory thorns?

CELESTINO

A shadow falleth across those paths.

GERTRUDE

A shadow!
Whose shadow?

CELESTINO
[*After a pause, quietly.*]

His mother's.

GERTRUDE

Mine!

YORICK
[*Who has approached.*]

Aye: and another's.

GERTRUDE

Whose, else?

YORICK

Another pilgrim's. The lone paths
Meet in the vale of Elsinore, where the sea
Moans on the beetling cliff's base, and the shadows
Mingle their darkness there.

GERTRUDE
[*Shrinking against the King, and pointing at Yorick.*]

Take him away.
He 's mad.

YORICK

Ah, mirth 's a madman, Madam,
And I am his pilgrim, who hath cast this shadow
Of a belled cap on my prince's path.—Your mercies,
Once more—and the gentle Padre's.

[*Re-enter* HORATIO, *who approaches.*]

CELESTINO

Pax
Omnibus vestris! The great *Book of Amor*
Is broidered, I said, with shine and shadow. How else
Could Love be blazoned? So I have brought our prince
One of its tablets, for a birthday gift.

[*Taking it from his cassock, he shows it to Prince Hamlet.*]

See, child: 't is of boxwood, dyed with berry-blue,
And hinged with dawn-gold. Look: the *laminae*
Are ivory, and waxed by honey-bees;
And here 's the stylus, to indite the wax
Anew, with all that 's writ here. Canst thou read it?

PRINCE HAMLET
[*Peering, eagerly.*]

Why, 't is all blank. The leaves are empty!

CELESTINO

Ah,
They are all filled with silences, for thee
To cipher. 'Tis the table of memory,
And there are more, six others, and each one dyed
A different hue; and they are named, the Seven:

Memory, Clarity,
Ardency, Serenity,
Mastery, Humility,
Verity.

I give thee, here, the first; for first and last
Include them all: *Remember only the true!*
Then thou 'lt be loving.
[*Handing the tablet.*] —There!

PRINCE HAMLET
[*Taking it.*]

But you will need it,
Yourself, to keep with the others.

CELESTINO

Nay, *there* 's only
Boxwood and ivory. The table itself
Is kept safe, here—
[*Touching his own left side, and then the child's.*]
where thou must keep it, too,
For 't is in both our hearts; and thou must write in 't,
When thou art grown a man, for meet it is
That thou shouldst set it down, anew, what 's writ
Already there, unseen, and wipe away
All trivial fond records, all forms and pressures
Past—all but love, and memory.

PRINCE HAMLET

Thanks, Padre.
I will remember.

KING HAMLET

Had we our sword at hand,
I 'd bid him swear upon 't, not to forget
So sacred a mandate. [*Looking around.*] Ah, Horatio—

HORATIO

I was about to offer mine, my liege,
As birth-gift, and my young lord will accept it,
Being the sword hath tutored his wooden lath.

KING HAMLET

We 're sure, he welcomes it. Here, Hamlet, press
Thy hand, with good Horatio's, on the hilt,
And swear, to the holy father, thy heart's vow:
Each, now, and both of you: *Love and Memory:*
Swear!

PRINCE HAMLET & HORATIO
[*Together, pressing their right hands on the sword-hilt.*]

Love and Memory!

CELESTINO

And *Verity:*
Remember only the true! The hilt is His,
Who is King of Fathers. Each shall wield its cross,
In battle 'gainst His foes—*His* hilt in hand.

PRINCE HAMLET & HORATIO
[*Together, pressing the sword-hilt.*]

And Verity!

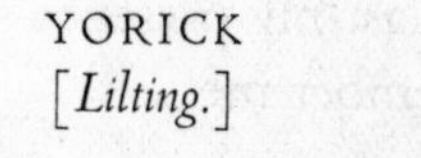

YORICK
[*Lilting.*]

And may this heart of fool make, also, gift
Of love, in the name of father, to this son
Of king?

*See page 47, *The Ghost of Elsinore.*

KING HAMLET

Good Yorick, what gift?

YORICK

[*Showing it.*] This tiny sprig
Of rosemary, for little Hamlet to place,
Instead of rue, in greater Hamlet's hand,
Which shall bestow it back, for remembrance' sake,
To his child's hand.

[*He gives the sprig to Prince Hamlet, with a smile and gesture towards the King.*]

Aye, reach it to thy father.

[*The child does so.*]

KING HAMLET

Thanks, Yorick. [*To Prince Hamlet.*]
From thy mother's heart and mine,
That all thy thoughts of us, through future lights
And darks, may guard our love, take now this sprig
Of fragrant rosemary, my little son,
Nor part with it to any, save for love;
And when at last my presence says, *adieu!*
Hamlet, remember me!

PRINCE HAMLET

[*Taking the sprig from the King, who hands it.*]

Remember thee,
Dear father?—Yea, here I have my tables ready,
And I will set it down, in wax, to-morrow.

KING HAMLET

To-morrow?—To-morrow's wax may melt. Then, write it
In love, to-day.

PRINCE HAMLET

I 'll do it, Sir.

[*He kisses the King, impulsively.*]

'Tis done!

[*Then, abashed, he turns suddenly to his boy-comrade.*]

Laertes, where 's my sword?

LAERTES

'Tis yonder—there,
Where thou didst throw it down. But here is mine,
To make thee birthday-gift. I 've nickt it, thrice,
So thou canst wear the winning-score.

PRINCE HAMLET

[*Taking the wooden sword, claps Laertes on the shoulder.*]

Crony-boy,
I 'll give thee my best battledore in place on 't,
And foil thee—so!—left-handed. Horatio
Shall hold the stakes. How sayest thou, Horatio?

HORATIO

I say, I know a secret, neither can guess.

PRINCE HAMLET

What?

LAERTES

What is 't?

PRINCE HAMLET

Tell us!

HORATIO

'Tis a riddle.

PRINCE HAMLET

Unriddle it!

HORATIO

There 's three: you can't guess 'em.

PRINCE HAMLET

Pop the first.

HORATIO

What will Laertes be, when he grows man?

PRINCE HAMLET

Court-minister, like his father.

LAERTES

Nay, I 'll be soldier.

HORATIO

Right. And what—Hamlet?

LAERTES

A king, of course, like *his*.

PRINCE HAMLET

Not so. I 'll be a player, and act kings,
To plague them. [*Pointing at the King.*]
—All but *him*, of course.

HORATIO

Of course!

Now, for the third.

BOTH LADS

What is 't?

HORATIO

Who 's hiding, yonder,

Behind that curtain with the poles?

PRINCE HAMLET

Why, that 's
Our stage-curtain. Beyond it, is the platform,
With exit-doors. Up yonder, in that wall-niche,
Is the prompter's box. The curtain hides our stage,
Where we play Troy, and Carthage, and old Egypt,
And mighty Rome, and Julius Caesar's death
Polonius taught us, because he acted it
At the university.—That riddle 's easy.

HORATIO

Wrong.

PRINCE HAMLET

I say, I 'm right. You know, yourself, right well,
That what I said is there—*is* there!

HORATIO

I said
Nothing of *what,* but *who: Who* is hiding, there?

PRINCE HAMLET

Oh!

LAERTES

Come, let 's see!

PRINCE HAMLET

Come on!

[*They start to run toward the curtain.*]

HORATIO

Stop!—Call you that
Guessing a riddle—to run it down, like puppies
After a rabbit?

[*They pause, then come slowly back.*]

PRINCE HAMLET

Hiding, quoth he!

LAERTES

[*Dubiously.*] Give it up?

PRINCE HAMLET

No, no; not I!
[*Suddenly, to Yorick, who has approached, looking on, with the King and others.*]
Is 't the cook, with the blackbird-pie?

YORICK

Dost hear it, singing?

PRINCE HAMLET

No.

YORICK

Then, 't is not opened.
The birds are hiding yet.

PRINCE HAMLET

Hiding! Where?

YORICK

In the pie,
Of course. But wait. They should be singing, soon.

LAERTES

Fiddle-diddle! [*To Prince Hamlet.*]
Give it up, and done.

PRINCE HAMLET

I 'll first be bakéd
In a pie, myself.

[*Suddenly, he makes a hushing gesture, and stands aghast, listening.*]

—Hark!

[*Mysterious sounds rise, from within.*]

—Hark, Horatio!

Listen, my lord, Father!

KING HAMLET

[*Who has been watching and overhearing.*]

Godamercy, Yorick!

What are these warblings and twitterings?

YORICK

The tuning,

My liege.

KING HAMLET

Tuning?

YORICK

The tune-up, to the song

I promised.

KING HAMLET

Song?

YORICK

O' sixpence, Sire. But first,

My lords and ladies, all, your places, pray!

[*At his gesture, they draw back.*]

The fool is master of the festival,

And sergeant to the song.—Be opened, Pie!

[*From within, the curtains are parted at a centre slit, through which emerges a black-and-white* PROCESSION, *headed by the* COOK *of Elsinore, dazzle-white. in his cap and tabard, bearing before him a huge round platter of gold, upon which is a great amber-brown* PIE, *with the crust opened in up-slanting triangles, followed—two abreast—by four-and-twenty tall,* DANISH GUARDS, *garbed as* BLACKBIRDS, *all of them singing.*]

ALL

Sing a song o' sixpence,
A pocketful of rye:
Four-and-twenty blackbirds,
Bakéd in a pie.
When the pie was opened,
They all began to sing:
"Is n't this a dainty dish
To set before a king?"

PRINCE HAMLET
[*Clapping.*]

I guessed it was the cook!

KING HAMLET

A dainty dish,
Indeed.

GERTRUDE

And daintier birds, withal.

LAERTES

But, Yorick,
How did you hide 'em in the pie?

YORICK

In the egg.
They hatched by singing, as all poets hatch,
That grow to pieman stature, to earn sixpence.
[*Waving his fool's-cap, for baton, and singing.*]
The king was in the counting-house—

THE BLACKBIRD GUARDS
[*Singing.*]

The king was in the counting-house,
Counting out his money:
The queen was in the kitchen,
Eating bread and honey:

The maid was in the garden,
Hanging out the clothes,
Along there came a pretty bird
And nippéd off her nose.

YORICK

[*Treading, bird-like, to Prince Hamlet.*]

And nippéd off her nose!

[*Nabbing the child's nose, with twist of thumb and fingers, he pulls from it a sixpenny coin, which he holds out on his palm.*]

PRINCE HAMLET

I 'm not the maid!

YORICK

Yet hast thou the maid's nostril
For a pretty bird, when along he comes, to tip her
On the nose-tip, for sixpence. Here it is.
Pray, hand it to your royal father, as
These minstrels' earnings, proffered by the fool
To enrich our prince's birthright.

KING HAMLET

[*As Prince Hamlet hands him the coin.*]

So it is
Received, and hoarded in the counting-house.

GERTRUDE

With bread and honey, of the Queen's thanksgiving
For the kitchen-feast of pie and song.

YORICK

The song
Being ended, now the feast beginneth—not
O' the pie, which, being oped up to the court,
Descendeth down once more unto the kitchen
With Master Cook—but now a feast of different

Serving, to whet your appetites for food
Baked for angels, in ancient time. But erst
Stand forward, Master Cook, divest thy platter,
And hand to Denmark's Minister of Rations
The Epistle from the Pie!

[*The Cook hands the platter to two of the Guards, who hold it, while he takes from inside the pie an emblazoned parchment, which, with a bow, he extends toward Polonius, who awaits it, officiously.*]

Polonius,
Receive the Epistle, prithee, and expound it.

[*Taking the parchment from the Cook, Polonius waves him back to the platter, which the Cook takes from the Guards and makes exit with, left, at gesture from Yorick.*]

POLONIUS
[*Bowing to each and all.*]

My lord, the King; your Majesty, the Queen;
My gracious prince; most reverential father;
Madam, my noble lady and gentle spouse;
My lords, ladies and gentlemen, *et omnes!*
The Epistle claimeth exposition; the exponent
Receiveth the claimant, will expound the claimed,
Punctilious to his plea—or, rather, *its*—
And, craving all your clemencies, shall now,
Without expostulation, or parenthesis,
Expose the points perpendent—or, as 't were,
More finely put, perpend*ing*—in five words,
Thus:— [*Reading from the parchment.*]

Now are the players arrived!

PRINCE HAMLET
[*Jumping up from his cushion.*]

The players, ho!
Where are they?

POLONIUS

In custody of the joint-conspirators:
Yorick and Horatio.

PRINCE HAMLET

[*Pointing to the closed curtain.*]

What, hiding there?
More riddles? Nay, I 'll join 'em. I 'm a player.

GERTRUDE

Hamlet, thy cushion!

[*He returns to it, frowning, excited.*]

Let not thy surprise
Make clown of thee. Thy place is prince, and manners
Thine art, not playing.

PRINCE HAMLET

Then playing is mine art,
For manners are merely playing. Polonius
He is a player, but a poor one, spite
Of his Julius Caesar. I 'll do him better than that.
When I 'm a man, if I must still be prince,
I 'll play I 'm player, and teach the players mine art
In learning theirs.—Manners!—Why come they not forth,
Or clear the curtain?

YORICK

They come, my lord, but first
'T is meet they should be introduced in state;
For, majesties, the platter of the pie,
Garnished with song terrestrial, must now
Give way unto the truncheon of the ram's head,
Choired with starry omens, and garlanded
With festal wreath of fadeless rosemary,
Sprung from the little sprig our princeling weareth.—
Horatio, fetch forth once more the horns
Of the Ram's Sign, that I again may hood
My fool's-cap with the mask of oracle;
Yea, from the kitchen—fetch it!

[*Exit Horatio, left.*] So shall it rise

Even from the scullery to the ebon skull
Of night, that domes with stars the mind of man,
To divinate these blackbirds.

KING HAMLET

[*At a perturbed touch, from the Queen.*]

Must the Ram
Resume his function?—Why?

YORICK

My liege, because
These players stem from immemorial days
When blackbirds sang in Eden, before their coats
Turned dark, for sorrow of this sinning world,
And put on mourning for Adam's fall. That awful
Event, it is, which they shall re-enact
In Elsinore, to show portents of times
Long gone, and still to come, entwisted round
The ring'd horns of the Ram. Wherefore, our play,
This night of royal sign, is a Mystery,
Mingled of elemental humours, born
Both of our genesis and destiny.

KING HAMLET

What is its name?

YORICK

The Grocers' Play of Norwich,
That little town of the great paradox,
Of porritch and cold plums, that burnt the mouth
Of the Man in the Moon, when he asked his way there,
Having come too soon—for caution.

KING HAMLET

Ah, that 's in Britain,
Where caution 's never practised—in moon-gazing,
Or plum-raising.

YORICK

Yes, as I ought to 've said
At first, our players are wandered hither from
The sweetly solemn, merry land of England—
That island stud of courage, wit and kindness,
Which breeds, from guilds of grocers and great earls,
Manstock for the world's freedom.—Ha, Horatio!

[*In the doorway, left,* HORATIO *is seen, holding on a silver salver, the head-mask of a black ram, the crookled horns garlanded with a misty wreath of silvery stars.*]

Bring hither the Ram's head, that his silver Sign
May mask me soon in Delphian silence; till when,
Lilt with me here his welcoming-song, and all
Ye royalties and blackbirds, sing refrain!
[*Lilting.*]—"The Ram's head in hand bring I—"

HORATIO

[*Bringing to Yorick the ram head-mask, on the salver, as they sing, together.*]

The Ram's head in hand bring I,
With garlands gay and rosemary.
I pray you all sing merrily,
Qui estis in convivio.[4]

ALL

Qui estis in convivio!

YORICK

Now, silence, all! Your seats.—Hark! The play knocks.
[*From behind the curtain, three slow knocks resound.*]
Now Yorick's feet shall mount the prompter's box,
Where the Ram's head, surveying all beneath,
Shall watch the Mystery, from his starry wreath;
And whoso deemeth to dub this merely quaint,
He knoweth not the picture from the paint.

[*Covering his own head with the head-mask of the ram, Yorick moves silently to the wall, at back, left of centre, and mounts steps to the stoned niche, wherein seated, with only his black-and-silver mask visible, he overlooks the audience and stage, below.*

While he is moving to do this, Queen Gertrude, in a low voice, calls softly to Prince Hamlet.]

GERTRUDE

Come hither, my sweet Hamlet, sit by me.

PRINCE HAMLET

Nay, Mother, here 't is cosier, by my crony.
[*He places his cushion next Laertes.*]

POLONIUS
[*To the King.*]

O ho! do you mark that?—Our own choose their own,
My liege.

KING HAMLET

Aye, the good foilsman chooseth his foil.
Feudists may quarrel, but friendship keeps the goal.

[*Enter, through the curtain slit, a* PLAYER, *gowned in brownish grey, wearing a green garland.—Seeing him, Laertes nudges Prince Hamlet, and points.*]

LAERTES

Who 's that?

PRINCE HAMLET

It must be the Prologus. Listen!

PROLOGUS

Your majesties and lordings, I am Tree,
Alias, Arbor Parva, Tree, the Little,
Sprout of *Arbor Magna,* Tree, the Eternal.
There is none but God, the Father, the Great Tree
Of Kenning and Cunning and Loving Infinite:
Pater, Arbor Vitae, Infinitissimus.
Dramatis Personae in this Mystery,
I, *Arbor,* have sap of Kenning, to know myself;
Serpens, the Snake, whose hole is in my trunk,
Coileth from roots of Cunning, to hate himself;

Pater, whose domèd brows overarch my branches,
Hath eyes of stars, to understand Himselves:
Kenner of Cunning and Kenning, he loveth Oureachothers.

So God, the Father, is *Arbor,* in earth's changing lights,
And *Serpens,* within his darkling hole of hell,
And *Pater,* in heaven's all-knowing, ever-shining stars.
There is none other than the Tree of Life,
Whereof the twig, that bendeth rib of *Adam*
To bud forth *Eva,* furnisheth eke the sword
Of *Aungel,* with flaming lymph of *Vita Arboris,*
Sap of the unseen, all-seeing Holy Ghost,
To cleanse their sin of ignorance with sorrow.

Thus Seven imperson this play, whose elements
Of playfulness are brewed of pity. They are thus:
Arbor, Pater, Adam, Eva, Serpens,
Aungel, Vita Arboris; and all are *ARBOR.*

Of these, in the Mystery which followeth,
I am mute, as meet is, for that world within,
Where I am green with knowledge, which turneth grey
In this outer world. Hence wan I stand before you,
Mere trunk, divested of my glistening verdure,
My visioning fruits, and listening silences,
Which overshadow the earliest speech of Eden,
Sibilant with amethystine surds of love,
Voluble with joy's engoldened vowelings.

That speech was primal: throbbing like the song
Which swells the thrush's throat before he sings,
It filled the heart, as fragrance fills a flower,
Withholden, even while floating heavenward.
Now—shook by the dumbing thud of Adam's fall—
'Tis sunk to this I utter, wherein all pent knowledge
Of pristine powers, which swelleth within me, pipeth
Thin as the thrush's, spiked upon a thorn.

That thorn is knowledge—stolen: knowledge, will-less
Of its own guidance: ignorantly stolen—
Like Adam's apple, which sticketh still in my throat—
Stolen from itself—yea, even from me, its Tree,
Not earned of freedom's choice; for there is none
Wins freedom, but by earning it, and least
By rifling his own treasure.

But suffice
These words of *this* time, shrivelled to thin tones
Of language fallen, withered of its birthright.
The olden speech within this Mystery,
Which ye shall hark, is not the primal Word
That quickened Adam from the dust, to utter
His wonder-love for her, and hers for him;
Yet holdeth it some inkling of that wonder;
And though it quaintly savoureth of a soil
More rude of tillage than the tongues of courtiers
Turn their curved lips to furrow, still its loam
Plumbs down to feeding rillets of old earth
Where the dung'd seed upshoots life to the sunbeam.—

Now, in that loam, I plant the rest of this,
My Prologue. Then am I Tree, the Mute,
Where only my free will shall eat my fruit.

[*Changing his bearing and gesture to a simple naïveté, he alters also his voice to the accent and tones of antique idiom.*]

This story is
Of the creacion of Eva, ywis,
With the Expellyng
Of Adam and Eva out of their dwellyng
In Paradyce,
Where in the Beginnyng
Was the Worde wys:
In principium erat Verbum Patris.
Finis.

[*Exit, within. Whereupon, after a moment, the curtain is rolled away, from within, till its two poles meet, at the upstage, outer side of an inner triangular platform, primitively set as* THE GARDEN OF EDEN, *with* ARBOR, *the Tree and* PATER, *God the Father, discovered—the latter seated above Tree's topmost, spreading branch.*]

PATER

Ego principium, Alpha et Omega, in altissimis habito;[5]
In the hevenly empery I am resydent.
Yt ys not semely for man, *sine adjutorio,*
To be allone, nor very convenyent.
I have plantyd an orcheyard most congruent
For hym to kepe and to tylle, by contemplacion.
Let us make an adjutory of our formacion
To hys symylatude, lyke in plasmacion.

PRINCE HAMLET

Who 's he, Horatio?

HORATIO

God, the Father. Hush!

PATER

In-to Paradyce I wyll nowe descende
With my mynysters angelicall of our creacion
To assyst us in ower worke that we intende,
A slepe in-to man be soporacion to sende.
A ribbe out of mannys syde I do here take;
Bothe flesche and bone I do thys creatur blysse;
And a woman I fourme, to be his make,
Semblable to man; beholde here she ys.

PRINCE HAMLET
[*Who has moved over next the Queen, whispers to her.*]

Look, Mother! He 's made the rib into a woman.

GERTRUDE

Yes, child; 't is Eve.

PRINCE HAMLET

Lady, shall I lie in your lap?

GERTRUDE

Nay, keep thy cushion!

ADAM

O my Lorde God, incomprehensyble, withoute mysse,
Ys thy hyghe excellent magnyfysens.
Thys creature to me ys *nunc ex ossibus meis,*
And *virago* I call hyr in thy presens,
Lyke on-to me in naturall preemynens.
Laude, honor and glory to the I make.
Bothe father and mother man shall for hyr forsake.

PATER

Than my garden of plesure kepe thou suer.
Of all fruts and trees shall thou ete and fede,
Except thys tre of connyng, whyle ye bothe indure;
Ye shall not touche yt, for that I forbede.

ADAM

Thy precept, Lorde, in will, worde and deede
Shall I observe, and thy request fulfyll
As thou hast commandyd, yt is reason and skyll.

PATER

Thys tre ys callyd of connyng good and yll;
That day that ye ete thereof shall ye dye,
Morte moriemini, yf that I do you aspye;
Showe thys to thy spowse now by and bye.
I shall me absent for a time and space;
A warned man may lyve; who can it denye?
I make the lord therof; kepe wyll my place;
If thou do thys, thou shall have my grace;

In-to mortalite shall thou elles falle.
Looke thow be obedyent whan I the calle.

ADAM

Omnipotent God and hygh Lord of all,
    I am thy servante, bownde onder thyn obedyens,
And thou my creatour, one God eternall;
    What thou commandest, I shall do my dylygens.

PATER

    Here I leve the, to have experyens,
To use thys place in vertuse occupacion,
For nowe I wyll retorne to myn habitacion. . . .
Se that ye have my wordes in most high estimacion.

ADAM & EVA

We thank the, mighty God, and gyve the honoracion.

ADAM

Oh bone of my bones and flesh of my flesh eke,
    Thou shalt be called Woman, by-caus thou art of me.
Oh gyfte of God most goodlye, that has us made so lyke,
    Most lovynge spowse I muche do here rejoyce of the.

EVA

    And I lykewyse, swete lover, do much rejoyce of the.
God therefore be praised, such comforte have us gyve
That ech of us with other thus pleasantly do lyve.

ADAM

To walke abowt this garden my fantasye me meve;
    I wyll the leave alone tyll that I turne ageyne;
    Farewell, myn owne swete spouse, I leave the to
        remayne.

EVA

    And farewell, my dere lover, whom my hart doth
        conteyn.

PRINCE HAMLET

Why doth he leave her alone?

KING HAMLET

Whisht!

PRINCE HAMLET

Mother, look!
See, there—behind the tree—the snake——oh!

GERTRUDE
[*With stilling gesture.*]

Hush!

SERPENS

Nowe, nowe, of my purpos I dowght nott to attayne;
I can yt nott abyde, in theis joyes they shulde be.
Naye! I wyll attempt them to syn unto theyr payne;
By subtylty to catch them the waye I do well se;
Unto this, angell of lyght I shew mysylfe to be,
With hyr for to dyscemble; I fear yt nott at all,
Butt that unto my haight some waye I shall hyr call.

Oh lady of felycyte, beholde my voice so small! . . .
Oh gemme of felycyte and femynyne love,
Why hathe God under precept prohybyte thys frute,
That ye shuld not ete therof to your behofe?
Thys tre ys plesant withouten refute.

EVA

Ne forte we shuld dye, and than be mortall;
We may not towche yt, by Godes commandement.

SERPENS

Ne-quaquam, ye shall not dye perpetuall,
But ye shuld be as godes resydent,

Knowyng good and yll spyrytuall;
No-thynge can dere you that ys carnall.

EVA

For us than now what hold you best,
That we do not ower God offende?

SERPENS

Eate of thys apple at my requeste.
To the, Almyhgty God dyd me sende.

EVA

Nowe wyll I take therof; and I intende,
To plese my spowse, therof to fede,
To know good and yll for ower mede.

PRINCE HAMLET

Ah, here comes Adam back! Good, good!

ADAM

I have walkyd abought for my solace;
My spowse, how do you? tell me.

EVA

An angell cam from Godes grace
And gaffe me an apple of thys tre.
Part therof I geffe to the;
Eate therof for thy pleasure,
For thys frute ys Godes own treasure.

PATER

Adam, Adam, wher art thou thys tyde?
Before my presens why dost thou not appere? . . .

ADAM

I herde thy voyce, oh Lorde, but yett I dyd me hide.
For that which I am naked I more greatly dyd feare.

PATER

Why art thou then nakyd? Who so hath cawsyd the?

ADAM

This woman, Lord and God, which thou hast gyven to me.

PATER

Hast thou eat of the frute that I forbyd yt the?
Thow Woman, why hast thou done unto him thys trespace?

EVA

The Serpente diseayvyd me with that his fayer face.

PATER

Thow Serpente, why dydst thou this wise prevente my grace,
My creatures and servantes in this maner to begyle?

SERPENS

My kynde is so, thou knowest, and that in every case,—
Clene oute of this place theis persons to exile.

PATER

Cursed art for causynge my commandement to defyle,
Above all cattell and beastes. Remayne thou in the fylde;
Crepe on thy bely and eate duste for this thy subtyll wyle;
The womans sede shall over-com the, thus yt have I wylde.
Thou, Woman, bryngyng chyldren with payne shall be dystylde,
And be subject to thy husbonde, and thy lust shall pertayne
To hym. I hav determynyd this ever to remayne.
And to the, Man, for that my voyce thou didst disdayne,
Cursed is the erth for ever for thy sake;
Thy lyvyng shall thou gett with swett unto thy payne. . . .

Myne angell, now cum furth and kepe the waye and porte,
Unto the tre of lyfe that they do nott resorte.

AUNGEL

Departe from hence at onys from this place of comforte,
No more to have axcesse or ells for to apere.
From this place I exile you, that you no more resorte,
Nor ever do presume ageyne for to come here. . . .

ADAM

O, with dolorows sorowe we may wayle and weepe!
Alas, alas, whye were we soo bolde?
Bye ower fowle presumpsyon we ar cast full depe,
Fro pleasur to payn, with carys manye-fold.

EVA

With wonderows woo, alas! it cane not be told;
Fro Paradyse to ponyschment and bondage full strong.
O wretchys that we are, so ever we shall be inrollyd;
Therfor ower handes we may wrynge with most dullfull song.

[*And so thei shall syng, walkyng together abowt the place, wryngyng ther hands.*]

ADAM & EVA

Wythe dolorous sorowe we may wayle and wepe
Bothe nyght and daye in sorowe, sythys full depe. . . .

[*N.B. These last two lines set to musick twice over and again, for a chorus of 4 pts.*]

VITA ARBORIS
[*The Holy Ghost.*]

Be of good cheare, Man, and sorowe no more;
This Dolor and Miserie that then thou hast taste
Is nott in respecte, layd up in store,
To the joyes for the that ever shall last.
Thy God doth not this the away to cast,

But to try the as gold is tryed in the fyer;
In the end, premonyshed, shalt have thy desire. . . .

ADAM

Oh! prayse to the, Most Holye, that hast with me abode,
In mysery premonyshynge by this thy Holy Spright.
Nowe fele I such great comforte, my syns they be unlode
And layd on Chrystes back, which is my joye and lyght.
This Dolor and this Mysery, I fele to me no wight;
No! Deth is overcum by fore predestinacion,
And we attayned wyth Chrystus in heavenly consolacion.

Therfor, myne owne swett spous, withouten cavylacion
Together lett us synge, and lett our hartes rejoyce,
And gloryfye ower God wyth mynde, powre and voyse.

Amen.

ALL THE PLAYERS
[*Old musick Triplex, Tenor, Medius, Bass:*]

With hart and voyce
Let us rejoyce
And prayse the Lord alwaye
For this our joyfull daye,
To se of this our God his maiestie,
Who hath given himsellfe over us to rayne and to governe us.
Lett all our hartes reioyce together,
And lett us all lifte up our voyce, on of us with another.

[*Lifting their voices in this song, all of the* Dramatis Personae *descend the steps of the stage-platform, marching in single file, and pass through and around their Elsinore audience, returning again to the stage (where, meanwhile, the curtains have been closed, all but the centre slit).*

There, just as the last of them, Serpens, *is about to disappear, dragging behind him his prodigiously long tail, which has just passed the cushion of Prince Hamlet and is now passing*

Laertes, Prince Hamlet—jumping up—calls out, and, joined by Laertes, leaps upon it with both feet, thus bringing Serpens *to abrupt standstill.*]

PRINCE HAMLET

Step on his tail, Laertes!—Ha, now I have thee,
Didst harm the woman.—Thou art the bad snake.

SERPENS
[*Removing his head-mask.*]

Nay, Hamlet dear. I am thine Uncle Claudius,
Returned from Rome, to keep thy seventh birthday,
And learn thee how to be a player.

[*Amid tremendous commotion of all, King Hamlet rises, exclaiming, and rushes forward to* CLAUDIUS.]

KING HAMLET

Claudio!

CLAUDIUS

Amleto—*ancora!*
[*They embrace.*] Was not "the meal ground fine,"
This time, to bake the crust o' the blackbird-pie?

KING HAMLET

Here—thy very self! Yea, finer hast thou ground
This meal for my surprise, than mine for thine
From sands of Norway, lang syne.*—What, Horatio!
Thou—play conspirator, *twice?*

HORATIO

Nay, Sire, but once
Guilty—in the pie-plot, not the play. I knew
The make-up, not the player, 'neath his mask.

*See page 96ff.

CLAUDIUS

[*Smiling, points at his serpent headpiece.*]

His mask alone is guilty—being its nature:
"*My kynde is so, thou knowest, and that in every case.*"

KING HAMLET

Great earth and heaven!—And so, Polonius,
For *this* thou didst expound the Mystery!

POLONIUS

The Epistle, only, Sire: in mere five words,
"Now are the players arrived!" The mystery
Remaineth for the wisdom of the serpent
To expound in his own dove-tones, secretly,
Unto your majesties. Myself am ignorant
Thereof, as Adam, in his innocency.

KING HAMLET

[*Laughing, as he embraces Claudius again, joyously.*]

Come, then, unto the dove-cote: to our chamber,
Dear *Serpens,* player of thy coiling role,
And shed thy scales, yea, and thy trampled tail,
And slough thy secrecy of seven long years,
Where thou hast slumbered, and whence slipt again
Home, to thy brother and thy sister-queen.—
Come, march thy sure-foot welcome, now. We 'll lead
The way, and thou, with Gertrude, fetch the rear;
And, all ye blackbirds, carry in your claws
The great snake's tail, and in your beaks—a new
Head, for the old song, *Qui estis in convivio!*
Horatio, here!—The Snake's head, for the Ram's!

[*Taking from Claudius his serpent-head-mask, he hands it to Horatio, who places it on the salver, as Claudius, unfastening his long tail, hands it to leaders of the Blackbird Guards, who go with it, singing—following Horatio, who steps backwards, bearing the salver before the King, who calls out the song's first words, as they march off, left.*]

"The Snake's head in hand bring I"—

ALL

The Snake's head in hand bring I,
With garlands gay and rosemary.
I pray you all sing merrily,
Qui estis in convivio!

[*As the refrain dies away beyond the edge of the scene, there—last in the procession—Claudius, with Gertrude, whom he is escorting, pauses, bows to her, and—taking from his garment a glistening object—offers it to her, with a bright smile.*]

CLAUDIUS

The apples of Eden are still red, my Queen,
And the bite still white.

GERTRUDE

[*Taking the apple, looks at it, an instant, as she holds it.*]

After seven years, my brother,
The taste, methinks, will still be sour.

[*Glancing up at him, she tosses it away, and goes quickly out, as Yorick, having descended from his niche in the wall, removes, but still holds, his ram head-mask, at the place where the apple rolls.—Seeing him there, Claudius, just starting to follow the Queen, stops suddenly, and stares.*]

CLAUDIUS

Yorick!
Art thou descended from heaven? Or dost thou doff
Yon head, in homage to One, who weareth horns?

YORICK

I remember but one, who weareth angel-wings.

CLAUDIUS

Still doth thy mind live only in remembrance?

YORICK

All is remembrance. There is nothing else,
My lord.

CLAUDIUS

Except—forgetfulness.

YORICK

And—apples!

[*Yorick picks up the apple, holding it toward Claudius. So they stand, looking at each other, as the curtain falls.*]

CURTAIN.

ACT SECOND

A HALL IN THE CASTLE. ELSINORE.

The same night as Act First: A little later. Against the wall, at back, TWO LOW SHRINES, *with cushions for kneeling. Between and above them, at centre, on the wall, a* CRUCIFIX.

At right of mid-centre, a table, with chairs, in one of which, at left of table, QUEEN GERTRUDE *is discovered, sitting, intent upon needlework in her lap, but at times turning to listen to the converse of* KING HAMLET *and* CLAUDIUS, *who are standing in front of the table.*

CLAUDIUS

The subtlest web is simple, when the weft
Is ravelled to its source. So is my secret,
Hamlet.

KING HAMLET

Then lead me to its source again—
A vision, thou didst say?

CLAUDIUS

A speaking vision.

KING HAMLET

Holy St. Agnes came to thee—herself?

CLAUDIUS

Herself, holding her lamb.

KING HAMLET

And spake to thee?
What words?—Once more recount them, for indeed
They cut to mine own heart's quick. What were her words?

CLAUDIUS

"Claudius," she asked me, "what is love?"—"Madonna,
I dread to know," I answered. Then she said:
"Knowest thou what it is, to burn alive?"
"Perhaps," said I. "Then follow me to Rome,
Unto my shrine, where I alive did burn

To ashes, learning what love's secret is,
Self-immolation, for another's need.
So wouldst thou learn past any peradventure,
Depart with me, at dawn." "I will, Madonna,"
I said.

KING HAMLET

When was this vision?

CLAUDIUS

'Twas at midnight
Of that same eve Hamlet, thy son, was born,
And, as thou knowest, in the dawn, I went.

KING HAMLET

But why? What other's need could speed thee forth
So swift, to be a seven years' wanderer,
Bereft of this thy home, and me, thy brother?

CLAUDIUS

My brother's need—thine own.

KING HAMLET

Mine—mine! How mine?
My dearest need was—is—thy presence here
Beside us, at our double-throne's right hand,
Mine own and Gertrude's.

CLAUDIUS

Nay, dear liege, mine absence.
Once, 't was my presence here in Elsinore
Did serve your need.—When you went forth to fight
With Fortinbras, gladly, albeit sadly,
I stayed behind, to serve my queen and you.
Even so, when you returned, I went away
To serve you—and your son.

KING HAMLET

Our son?

CLAUDIUS

The Prince
Of Denmark, Hamlet, heir of Elsinore.
Erstwhile, the nearest heir was Claudius.

KING HAMLET

Still
Duke Claudius, loyal uncle of his prince.

CLAUDIUS

Nay, brotherhood surpasseth unclehood
In loving loyalty. No shade of duke,
Nor shadow of uncle, shall bemist the sunrise
Of this new-risen nephew-prince, nor obscure
The morning-gladness of my brother-king
And sister-queen, with fetid exhalations
From gossipt rumours of a regent's eye
Fixt on futurity, and an uncle's ear
Itched by the tattled rumblings of a crumbling
Double-throne, in the dank corridors of statecraft.

KING HAMLET

Your words are misty, and their meaning altogether
Missed. What *is* all this, my Claudio?

CLAUDIUS

All this is but to say, Amleto mine,
I cannot dub thee *liege* and *majesty*
When thou dost sit thy throne, even as a milkmaid
Her stool, plucking the teats of innocence
To fill her taintless pail with morning milk.
So milk-white is thy mind; but mine is dark

As a thatcht byre with goblin bugaboos.
Thou art a puss in pattens, and I am—lo,
My snake's head on the salver! Shall we laugh,
Or cry, at this, seeing the gossip world
Hath made us mummers in this masque of state,
Wherein thy part is scrolled as King-that-*is*,
And mine, as King-that-*would-be?*

KING HAMLET

Would be—king?

CLAUDIUS

Consult Polonius: hath he not a sleek
Chameleon-skin, to catch the lights and darks
Of court-shine? Or, perchance, these seven years,
Hath he outworn his *as it were's* and *if so's?*
'Twas he, announced: "The *players* are arrived."

KING HAMLET

The players are departed, Claudio;
And there, discarded on the salver, droops
The serpent's face; and here the soul, that sloughed it,
Stands gazing in these eyes of *welcome-home!*—
Your brother's eyes of wonder and of pride
That you, who love me, left me, even because
You loved me, lest your presence should o'ershadow
My little son, his heirdom—*our* dear son,
Gertrude. Thou hast not spoken yet, but now
Thy voice with mine: Dear brother, not our thanks
We render you, but both our hearts, in one,
With all our wondering love.

GERTRUDE
[*Looking up from her needlework.*]

Our wondering——

KING HAMLET
[*Embracing Claudius, breaks into laughter.*]

Aha, but thou—not I, 't is thou, that art
The milkmaid innocent, to dark thy mind
With goblin bugaboos and gossip tales
Of dire futurity. Polonius,
Even he, shall learn to laugh with us at this.
He hath grown solemn, since he hath, himself,
A son and heir, and stuffs for him his bag
Of saws with treasured plums of statecraft.—Ah,
But crafts of state and craftiness of war
Are blotted, like a fading winter's dream,
Upon the springtide margent of the vellum
Wherein is writ our book of life—*Amor,*
The Logos of the secret: *What is love?*
Yea, brother, thou hast entered here a new
Schoolroom, for elder children, where a master,
Who is himself Love's pupil, reads to us
From out its sacred pages, and illumines
The ancient script with inward light.—Wait here,
And I will bring him, for 't is now his hour
Of coming, and perchance he tarries, fearing
To intrude. Not so; for thou shalt share with us
His sweet communion, and relate to him
The vision.—Gertrude, make our brother welcome,
Till I return with Celestino. [*Exit.*]

[*Alone with Gertrude, Claudius approaches her quietly, where she has laid her needlework on the table.*]

CLAUDIUS

Still
I await the ending of your sentence, sister.

GERTRUDE

Sentence?

CLAUDIUS

"Our wondering"—? Hamlet ended his own
With—"love."

GERTRUDE

Should love pass sentence—leaving no gap
To fill—before the end?

CLAUDIUS

You give me leave
To fill it, then, with—

GERTRUDE

Wondering.

CLAUDIUS

At what?

GERTRUDE

Your vision of St. Agnes.

CLAUDIUS

Am I so
Incapable of vision?

GERTRUDE

[*Dreamily.*] Said I so?
I thought not so. I thought of Angela,
My little spinster of the lamb's wool.

CLAUDIUS

So
Did I.

GERTRUDE

And wondered, doth she spin in heaven
The soft fleece of St. Agnes' lamb.

CLAUDIUS

Even so
Did I.

GERTRUDE

And sing her pretty wheel-song, there.*

CLAUDIUS

Cross-cradle: Even so.

GERTRUDE

You know her song?

CLAUDIUS

The cross, methinks, beginneth in the cradle,
And marks the meeting of two pathways, there.
Else, *"how shall we the work begin?"*

GERTRUDE

Those are
Some words of it. How strange is memory!
Methinks, I hear her sing it.

CLAUDIUS
[*Turning away, with a low moan.*]

So do I!

GERTRUDE

And was it that, perchance, which brought to you
St. Agnes from Angie's grave, in vision?

CLAUDIUS

Perchance.

GERTRUDE

Yet wherefore unto you?

*See *The Ghost of Elsinore,* page 42f.

CLAUDIUS

The fool, her father,
Is dear to Hamlet and to me, since we
Were lads together. Sorrow for Yorick's loss
Touched us, twofold. So was it, when I heard
That Hamlet had lost Yorick.

GERTRUDE

Had lost Yorick!
How?

CLAUDIUS

Even so—by death. *How,* was not stated
Clearly. But rumour clouded it with poison,
Or some obscurer cause. So, when I heard it,
Some months ago, I vowed my home-returning,
To make my consolations to the King
For our dear fool's demise.

GERTRUDE

What foolish rumours
Float on the winds, world-wide, like thistle-seeds
To sow their thorns! 'Tis true, Yorick was sick
O' fever; nothing more. Where heard you such false tidings?

CLAUDIUS

In England, from a strolling player, who
Had thither lately come from Denmark. So,
With an embarking troupe of Norwich Guildsmen,
I took my passage, understudying
The role of one, who quit the troupe, *en route:*
My role of *Serpens,* in the Garden of Eden,
My home of yearning, where here, in this bower,
I enter now, to find, in their innocence,
Even as of old, before the Expelling Angel,
Adam with *Eva*—and my head on a salver!

GERTRUDE

Poor Claudio! How many weary journeys
Must thou have wandered, over this great world,
From that sweet shrine outside the walls of Rome,
I, too, once kenned—even as our own dear Padre
Celestino, whom thou soon shalt learn to love
The more, for sharing memories of far exile.

CLAUDIUS
[*Drawing closer.*]

Ah, what is exile?—'Tis the hopeless nearness
Of eyes, to eyes that see not; of hands, to hands
That touch not; lips, to breathing lips, that part
Only to bid departure.

GERTRUDE

What strange nearness
Could so exile a brother from his welcome
Home?

CLAUDIUS

Is this home, indeed? Methinks, long since,
I heard a song, sung by a home-sick beggar,
Outside a door, latcht by a half-pusht bolt:

"Ah, home is where the heart is,
Not where the broken part is!"

[*From beyond the door, a* VOICE *is heard singing, as—listening—they look from there toward each other.*]

THE VOICE

Give me thy heart—all, or not at all!
The half-heart shrinks, to shrivel
Where sap of April-tide shall drivel
Amber-gum, in the fall.

But the whole heart—ah, the whole heart!
Thine with mine, and no reasons,
Shall keep as sound as the world is round
And savour all the seasons.

CLAUDIUS

Outside a door, I said. Is the bolt pushed tight?

GERTRUDE

Why, that was Yorick's voice, was 't not?

CLAUDIUS

The tune
Toned deeper than the voice. Didst hear the words:
"Give me thy heart—all, or not at all!
The half-heart shrinks——"

GERTRUDE

He 's ever lilting,
Dear fool!

CLAUDIUS

His lilt shall *savour all the seasons,*
If—but the door-bolt: is it pushed?

GERTRUDE

The door?
There is no bolt.

CLAUDIUS
[*Leaning nearer.*]

None, Gertrude?

GERTRUDE

Nay, what need?
This is the schoolroom for the elder children,
Ourselves, as Hamlet said, where the wise Padre
Reads us the *Book of Amor.*

CLAUDIUS

[*His cheek close to hers, speaks in a half-whisper.*]

Amor is—Love.

GERTRUDE

Who teacheth himself to know what *Amor* is;
And here, behold, cometh the Padre.

[*Enter* PADRE CELESTINO, *with* KING HAMLET, *followed by* YORICK.]

Welcome,
Father!

KING HAMLET

I found him, acting chamberlain
To our princeling, tending him to bed.

CELESTINO

To tuck
Another birth-night token 'neath his pillow,
To sleep upon: *Clarity,* for clear dreams.
This night, methought, your majesties, my children,
Might better dispense with Father Celestino
Than Brother Claudius, here returned to you.

KING HAMLET

With neither shall we now dispense, but in both
Delight, bidding you share each other
In our affection. We, as lovers, freed
From the high throne of Elsinore, here lowly
Will sit beside your lectern, whilst you quote
Some further passage from that love-wrought poem,
You read us yesternight, by the great lover-
Bard of your own land, Dante Alighieri,
His *Comedy Divine.*

CLAUDIUS

A comedy?

CELESTINO

La Divina Commedia, dark comedy
Of that illuminating death, wherein
We mortals gulp our rhythmic breaths, *Signore,*
As gold-fish pulse their gills, in a black pool
Where, sudden, Apollo's shaft plunges his sun-dart,
And, lo, the murky waters are alive
With ruby angel-lights and flashing forms
Of wonder. See! They float around us now—
Ah, nay! We see naught, for the gloried shaft
Is hooded in ourselves. We are our own
Cloud-banks of cowardice, fearing the wind
Of inspiration, whose wild gust would rend us
And sere our blindness with the clear sun-gaze
Of our dearest lover,—Death. But wait: let us peer
Behind these claspéd covers.

[*He steps to the lectern, where he unclasps a dark-bound volume.*]

Here is hid
Lightning, yea, pealing thunder of that gust,
Whereof I now will render you a murmur
From that dark passage where, beyond the portal
Of death, the Ghost of Virgil makes reply
To Dante, who, in dread of three lewd beasts
Of hell, still hesitates to climb the dark
And savage way, to claim his lady in heaven.

KING HAMLET

[*With gesture to Claudius and Yorick.*]

Be seated with us, brother. Yorick, listen.

CELESTINO

[*Reads from the volume.*]

And then the ghost of the great-hearted answered:
"If rightly I understand what evil hath cumber'd
Thy soul, 't is this: that cowardice hath cancer'd

Thy courage, so no longer thou art number'd
'Mongst honourable men, but art as a beast
That starteth backward, raised from where he slumbered."

CLAUDIUS

"Backward—from where he slumbered": who saith that?

CELESTINO

Virgil, to his friend, Dante, who is afeard
To press on to his goal; and he continueth:

"*Therefore, in order that thou shouldst desist*
From evil fear of evil, I will leaven
Thy pain, and tell who bade me be thy priest.—
I was amid those neither of hell nor heaven,
And there a lady called me, a lady, so
Blessed, that by her beauty I was shriven.
And when she spoke, her eyes began to glow
Like morning stars, and like an angel's bell,
In her own tongue, her voice rung sweet and low:
'O thou, who once in Mantua didst dwell,
Whose fame of courtesy throughout all time
Shall live as long as kindness casts its spell!
One dear to me, but not to fate, doth climb
The desert hillside, and is so impeded
That he for fear forsakes the path sublime;
And, from the tidings I in heaven have heeded,
I am afraid lest, in his great mischance,
Already too late I may have interceded.
Ah, go! and with your gracious speech and glance
Aid him—and me, as well, who yearn to sleek
His sorrow—ah, bring his soul deliverance!
I am Beatrice, who thus bid thee seek
His good. I come whence I would fain return.
Love moved me, and 't is love that makes me speak.' "[6]

CLAUDIUS

Pardon, good Padre! I am a novice here.
But may I question: is it permissible
To ask elucidation of this text?

CELESTINO

My son, this mighty *Comedy Divine*
Is but a note in the margin of *Amor*.
We are all novices and must eagerly
Ask of each other help and hope of learning.

CLAUDIUS

Then, who is this lady, Beatrice, whom
Love moves to save one dear to her, but not
To fate?

GERTRUDE

She is the one who, even in her bower
Of Paradise, could not be glad, for pity
Of him who had lost his way, alone, and wandered
Within the bourn of hell.

CLAUDIUS

For pity of him?
Do they, who pity,—love?

CELESTINO

Love pities all
Who fear the pangs of hell.

KING HAMLET

Hell hath no pangs
Except for cowards.

CLAUDIUS

Why, then, pity cowards,

Who lose their way? This lady, Beatrice,
Methinks, hath something of a mother's sorrow
For her wandered child's mishap.
[*To Gertrude.*] Or dost thou deem
'Tis more, my sister?

YORICK

'Tis a purring sorrow, Sir.
[*Lilting.*]

The mother cat will purr
And lick her kitten's fur
To clean the stain on his spotted silk
From the murdered mouse, that makes his milk.

CLAUDIUS

Have fools novitiate here, as well as exiles?—
What know you of this lectern's lofty theme,
That climbs from Adam's fall to kiss the stars?

YORICK
[*Lilts again.*]

What I know is all I know,
And all I know is this:
That many 's the fall is ta'en by all
Who clamber for a kiss—
And miss.
That 's all, ywis!

HAMLET

Yorick, thy quips are for the little folk,
Are gone to bed. The stars that shine above
Our Padre's lectern are an elder folk
Whose converse is in wiser parables
Than waggeries.—Brother, you boldly say
Our heavenly theme is knowledge.

CLAUDIUS

Nay, I make bolder:
Since all man knows is as a mustard seed
To that immensity he doth not know,
And is itself a mighty mountain range
To mine own mustard seed of knowledge, then
Why may not I render my tiny world
A realm unto itself, a walléd Eden
Whereof I am God, the Father, and the Master-
Maker of mine own law?

CELESTINO

So you may, *Signore.*
And as the morning lark doth fill his crop
With mustard seeds, so may your tiny world
Be swallowed, to make heaven-song for *Amor.*
For Love is all-consuming, and devours
Terror, in his tenderness, and egoism
In his All-Ego.

GERTRUDE

Is he, then, so great,
Father? If so, almost you make me fear him.—
We have never feared him, Hamlet, have we?

KING HAMLET

Feared?
We have never asked the question, which to ask
Were to make mere negation of ourselves,
Beyond all scope of pity. Claudius
Asked me: Why pity cowards? Why, indeed!
Corruption is the twin of cowardice,
And purity of courage. Each crawls, or stands,
With the other. Is there any name more valid
For love, than courage, Padre?

CELESTINO

Ah, my dears,
How many courages the valiant name
Of *courage* vaunts: the coward's hot bravado;
The sage's cool insistence of the truth;
The soldier's gay *coraggio;* the clown's bluff;
The statesman's scorning of the mob's applause;
The maiden's parry of the satyr's leer;
The old wife's humour at the kiss of death;
The lover's curb of lust; the saint's shy laughter;
The poet's torment for the perfect word:
All these, corrupt or pure, are vestiges
Of that unconquerable will for love
Which stirs the flutterings of an infant's eyes
To open, in its mother's raptured gaze,
And answer: "This is I, *Amor,* the Invincible!"

CLAUDIUS

So, even from a corrupted courage, think you,
Some balm may spring, can heal the wound of yearning?

YORICK
[*Lilts, as he goes to the doorway.*]

Lovers, would ye learn
Nevermore to languish
Yearningly—
Turn, turn
All of ogre anguish
To elfin ecstasy.
Leave life's dull play of school
For love's dear school of play,
And follow the fool,
Follow the fool—away!*

*Regarding this and preceding lilts, see note 3, *The Ghost of Elsinore.*

KING HAMLET

Whither biddest us follow thee, Fool?

YORICK

To dreams, a-bed,
Where little folk play *hoodman-blind* wi' the dead. [*Exit.*]

GERTRUDE

Ever his lilting harps on his one theme,
Love's treasure lost—his Angela, whose end
Unites us all with him, mad though he be.

CLAUDIUS

Is he deemed mad, indeed?

KING HAMLET

His counsel oft
Spurreth our laggard minds to follow it;
And so, methinks, under our little son's star,
We 'll follow now to bed, where *hoodman, blind*
Shall teach us *goodman, find*—all treasure lost,
Whereof, dear Padre, you 've revealed to us
The secret lurking-places in our hearts,
Lit by a ray of the *Comedy Divine.*
But first, our hearts in hush, while here, within
Their still confessionals, beneath the Cross,
Which throbs its quivering passion on the air,
We join our orisons of memory
For Yorick's Angela and his lost love,
In silence, to St. Agnes.

[*While Celestino and Claudius stand, with heads bowed, the King and Queen—on the two cushions, facing the shrines, at back—kneel for a hushed moment, then rise.*]

So, good night,
Our Celestino!

CELESTINO

Pax, in Caritate!

KING HAMLET

Claudio mine, here in our Virgil's care,
We leave thee, till to-morrow, our good night.

CLAUDIUS

Good night, Amleto!

GERTRUDE
[*To Celestino.*]

Peace to thee, Padre dear!

[*To Claudius.*]

Brother, good night of peace!

CLAUDIUS
[*In low voice, kissing her hand.*]

Good night,—*Beatrice!*

[*Exeunt Hamlet and Gertrude.*
Where Claudius stands gazing after them, Celestino, who has watched quietly, approaches, with a smile of sweet sadness.]

CELESTINO

The heart's confessional of silence speaketh
Soft as the kisséd hand.

CLAUDIUS
[*Turns, with bewildered start.*]

What—what?

CELESTINO

Amor
Is gentle, as well as terrible.

CLAUDIUS

Holy father,
How cometh it that thou, an anchorite,
Discoursest of love, whose very seed is forged

Of 'getting and conception? What knowest thou
Of the wild pastures in the lover's brain,
Where pawing winds pant with the burst of Junetide
And mad joys wallow in mire? Wast thou begotten,
As I, by the tingling loins of Taurus' Bull?
And hast thou harkt, across musk-smelling brakes,
The bruiting of the herd of Helios' kine,
And snufft the prickling foison of that belling?
Or hast thou lasht, as I, from off thy spirit's
Haunches, the swarming hornets of desire?

CELESTINO
[*Quietly.*]

Yes, I, as thou, was loined of Taurus' Bull;
As thou, have harkt, through the musk-smelling brakes,
The belling of the herds of Helios;
And borne, as thou, upon my self-lasht soul
The rabid burning of those hornet-pangs.

CLAUDIUS

What, thou?—Impossible! Or, if it were not,
What healing herb canst thou prescribe for what,
Even by thy vow, thy practice cannot test,
Nor ever prove what 't is to be in love?

CELESTINO

Ah, but I am, and vowedly, forever.

CLAUDIUS

In love!—With whom?

CELESTINO

With one divinely dear,
Who is the enamouring source of all our natures,—
Nature, herself.

CLAUDIUS

Divine, you mean, not human.

CELESTINO

There's nothing human that is not divinely
Engendered,—even brutes that prey on saints in prayer.

CLAUDIUS

Ha, if the brutes preyed only on their own kind,
The gentle breeds would wax, and lure the saints
From heaven, to seek beatitude on earth;
But malice is carnivorous of kindness,
And rancour sucks the marrow of meditation,
And grossness gorges on the delicate
Tissue of modesty, till the world bloats
With beauty's carrion. So do our natures
Make of their own defects their deities
And build them altars, where they sacrifice
Straight naked truth to coiling Sophistry,
Love's virgin candour to the Moloch, Lust,
The lamb, Compassion, to the Tiger-tooth
Of Hate, and all their inborn angel-beings
To monstrous idols of their egoism.—
Think you I know not this?—So, like all others,
I bow to Nature.

CELESTINO

How?

CLAUDIUS

Even as we all must.

CELESTINO

Yea, even to ourselves—for *we* are Nature! We
Are not the serfs but masters of our errors
To make our passions slaves to truth!

CLAUDIUS

Ha, truth!
All 's carrion, I say!

CELESTINO

How comes it, then,
The delicate fare is never exhausted, but
The carrion quickens with ambrosial blossoms
That feed celestial senses?—Nay, my son,
All breeds of earth and hell are heaven-born:
Apollyon is kin-cousin to Apollo,
And dumb Tom Noddy is Plato's poor relation.
Hyperion sired them all, and Hyperion
Is but a golden spore of pollen, wafted
From Christus' Lily of Eternal Life.

CLAUDIUS
[*Gazing up at the Crucifix on the wall.*]

Christus, his lily!—Are the dews of pain,
That drip from off his petalled lips—blood-drops
Of balm, or cellules of poison? . . . Listen, Padre!
Far in the faeried heaths of Eire's isle,
In the eighth century after Christus' woe,
There lived a holy sect of saintly friars,
Who wandered forth out of their cloisters, over
The known world, even to the icéd Alps
And valleys of the fabled Rhine, where—near
St. Gallen—in St. Constance Lake, they reared
An altar, on the island of Reichenau,
In a walled chapel.

CELESTINO

Ah, I once was there,
On pilgrimage, to seek the sacred relic
Of His blood, there.

CLAUDIUS

Wast thou, truly! I, also,
During my after-wanderings from Rome,

Went there, with two dream-fellows—so I call them,
With whom I only meet and part in dreams.

CELESTINO

'Tis strange: I, too!—By what names dost thou call them?

CLAUDIUS

Felix and Sylvia—who call me Sandrac.*

CELESTINO

More strange! They are mine own eternal friends,
With whom I, oft, in sweet St. Agnes' chapel,
Outside the walls of Rome, still kneel in dreams
Beside a pillar's base, 'midst bluebell flowers
And glow of holy tapers, where the singing
Priests bear the wattled lambs, for her to bless.

CLAUDIUS

Ah, then, methinks, there is no world but dream-world!
For in the chapel at Reichenau, where I
Stood staring at the relict drop of blood
From Christus' spikéd heart, sudden, the drop
Boiled up in bleeding froth, and filled a vial
In my hand—with *hebenon*. . . What said I?—what?

CELESTINO

Thou saidst, what the kist hand of the Queen, to-night,
Heard not, but felt, and what I hear, but hark not.

CLAUDIUS

Art thou, then, an arch-genius of confession,
Whose ears are dumb, and mind is mute?—To what
Order of holiness doth this thy cassock
Belong?

*Cf. page 123.

CELESTINO

'Tis the cassock of Caritas.

CLAUDIUS

Methought it
A Capuchin's.

CELESTINO

Yes, that is the lesser order.
But both of us belong unto the Greater:
Thou, in thy tabard; I, in my cassock.

CLAUDIUS

I—?

CELESTINO

Truly. I observed it, at once. Thou wilt progress
Far in that Order, if—

CLAUDIUS

If what?

CELESTINO

If thou
First wilt confess thyself.

CLAUDIUS

So, then, thou hearest
Confession?

CELESTINO

Oh, yes: each hour, almost each minute.

CLAUDIUS

So oft? How canst thou? Whom dost thou hear?

CELESTINO

Myself.

CLAUDIUS

Thyself—confess thyself!

CELESTINO

In whom, more secret,
Can I confide? Where else can I find God,
To whom, in whom, is all confession? Each
Is his own priest, in Caritas, for I
Am my own brother, even as well as thine.
We are each other's brother, both of us
Being His children.

CLAUDIUS

Much, methinks, thou sharest
Of Yorick's madness.

CELESTINO

Much, for that, I thank thee.
I hope so. Pray thee, kneel; and then will I.

CLAUDIUS

Kneel unto whom?—to thee?

CELESTINO

No, no: to thyself
Unseen, save only of our all-seeing Brother,
The Son of Man, from whose thorn-hedgéd temple
The blood-dews fall. For He hath said: "Be perfect,
Even as my Father in heaven"; and only His dews
Rise on our orisons to lift ourselves
Unto His own perfection. Kneel; for I
Am gone outside, to be with thee, within. [*Exit.*]

[*Left alone, Claudius gazes where Celestino has departed.*]

CLAUDIUS

Who is this olden youth, with name celestial,

Who brings me unto Christ? Is he, in sooth,
One of His angels, masked in a cassock, here,
To do His mission, even as I, an earthworm,
Was masked as *Serpens,* for His secret purpose?
What *is* His purpose—and mine? Are both at odds
Inexorably? . . Here I, now Duke of Denmark,
Stand fusted, between a cassock and a fool's-cap,
To wrest my anonymous kingship from the heart
Of my dreaming brother's half-awakening queen;
And what do I, now?—Kneel to the King of Kings
For heaven's pardon, and permission to keep
My boiling secret lockt in a bursting will.—
Ah, there is more than that! My hand is empty
Of a certain crystal vial, which to clasp
Again, and stopple the spilling hebenon
Before it dribbles death, I 'd cut the hand off,
That clasps it.—Clasps it *not!*—Yet, if it did,
The dribble 's out—the death is spilled. Ah, no,
'Tis thou, Angela! Thou, little Angie, thou,
Carding thy lamb's wool in the candlelight—
Not cassock'd priest, nor lilting fool, thy father,—
Who standest there, between me and my kingdom.
Nay, Christus of the thornéd crown, I know not
Thee, nor Thy kingdom, nor Thy heavenly Father,
His far perfection. But I know a child,
A budding elf, with hair of candleshine,
Whose flame of life I quenched, and snuffed in darkness—
Darkness, where now I groan, and grope to feel
The gentle love-light of her wondering smile
Glow on the lambs around St. Agnes' altar.
To *her* I 'll kneel, and, through the intercession
Of her dear saint, pray her forgiveness.—Down!

[*He kneels, facing the right-hand shrine, at back.*]

Shine up, my sin! Keep down, my kingdom,—dark!

[*As he ceases, the room dims into*

DARKNESS

and silence, through which is heard, faintly, a far COCK-CRY.]

After a moment, as the darkness pales into half-light, there is revealed—facing the left-hand shrine—another KNEELING FIGURE, *garbed like Claudius, but in blue, who—as Claudius, without turning, rises—rises with him, and turns toward him, only as Claudius speaks, with low moan.*

My words fly up, my thoughts remain below:

THE FIGURE

Words, without thoughts, never to heaven go.[7]

CLAUDIUS
[*Turning quickly, stares.*]

Thou,—Gallucinius?

GALLUCINIUS

Thyself—Claudius!

[*Again, more loud, rises the far* CRY OF THE COCK.]

CURTAIN.

ACT THIRD

THE SCENE IS THE SAME: THE HALL OF THE TWO SHRINES.

GERTRUDE *and* CORNELIA, *discovered, by the table, the one seated, the other standing, near.*

GERTRUDE

Most dear Cornelia mine!

CORNELIA

More dear my Queen,
If dearness may be measured!

GERTRUDE

On that eve
When the hornéd star signalled with heavenly lantern
Unto the angel, who should lead from there
My baby to his birth-bed, where I lay,
While still the furtive tuning of his heart
Timed with the throbbing welcome of my own,
It was thy gaze of love I gazed within
For succour of my pain, and certitude
He would be *he*. "Ah, *fiat filius!*"
Chanted my heart. "Let it be Hamlet's—*Hamlet!*"

CORNELIA

So was it—and your prayer made perfect.

GERTRUDE

Even
As soon thine own shall be, in consummation
Answering *thy* heart's: *"Fiat, O, filia!"*
"Let it be *she—Ophelia!"*

CORNELIA

What, so quick
To guess my secret hope, aye, even to give it
Girl-christening!

GERTRUDE

Godmothering is easier
Than mothering, and quicker than the moon's
Slow calendar.—*Ophelia.*—Dost thou like
The name?

CORNELIA

I *love* it!—'Tis a maiden's sigh,
All made of filial gentleness, with *O!*
To catch the wonder's breath, before the sigh
Beginneth. And yet—

GERTRUDE

And yet?

CORNELIA

And yet I pray
The sigh be not the ending of the wonder,
But only the feeling of it.

GERTRUDE

Oh, *feel* is the fondness
That fills its very heart, to overflow
Its font, midway. Her christening font it is.
So now she hath her name, ere thou hast asked me
Where first I heard it uttered.

CORNELIA

Where?

GERTRUDE

In a dream.
Last night, I dreamed I saw my little princeling
Grown stately prince. Alone he stood, beneath
A balcony, within a high-walled garden,

Green with verdure, and very beautiful
With yellow and pink flowering, of lilacs,
Rose-hawthorn and laburnum-bloom. All there
Breathed tranquil, as made of thought. The still prince stood
Eyeing a snail on a thorn, and listening
To a nightingale, that sang so clearly, he seemed
To catch from its wildly-wisely-twittering word
Some inward rhapsody, for from his poke
He drew a ring, whose emerald jewel-stone
Gleamed, in its circlet gold, green as a mosséd
Isle in that twining burn along whose shell-bright
Shallows, two gliding brook-elves swam, forever
Seeking to clasp each other.

CORNELIA

This—you dreamed?

GERTRUDE

And more!—Still gazing raptly at the ring,
The prince takes forth a tablet, with a stylus,
And thereon writes, as he were passion-tied,
A poem, whose rhyming thought he 's scarce begun
To carve in chaséd verse, Cellini-like,
Congruent to the ring, ere suddenly
Across the balcony's sun-window'd sill
Glitters a shape of golden girlhood. Bright
As through the shaft of risen morning shines
Upcurling dew-mist, round about her maiden
Sky-lifted face, so floats her hair, in ringlets
Like lupine-buds uprankt on fleur-de-lys
In curvèd petals, blent with elder-flower
Trailing melliferous fragrance.[8] The dazzled prince
Stared where he stood; then down he knelt, with eyes
Upyearning; and with reachéd hands, that clasp'd
The ring, spake from white lips, in quivering rhyme—
Which partly, even yet, I do remember:

"Ophelia, of faeries
Fairest symphony!
O filia Veneris
Pulcherrima! Tibi,
To thee, of thee, my prayer is
Wrought in this ring-rhyme.—Wear this!"

His muted voice poured, through imploring eyes,
The rest. And from her own, in fluttering wonder,
There floated down a roseate sigh—a scarf
Of rainbow love-light, 'neath whose vaulted arch
He vanished, with her.

CORNELIA

Vanished? Ah, in your dream!
Methought, it all was real, and we were near them,
Watching.

GERTRUDE

So are we, in our faith and hope
And love for one, unborn—and one, that 'waits her.

CORNELIA

O, Madam! Put no dream within my hope
Beyond the scope of dreaming.

GERTRUDE

'Twas my heart
Of nature wrought this mother-dreaming, not
My brain of queenly policy, wherein
My mately king, his stately majesty,
Might school me otherwise; even as thy lord,
Polonius, might politize such love
With stately diffidences of his own,
Touching too-royal ambition.

CORNELIA

[*Smiling.*] Ah, Polonius!

He hath already laid a quintuple crown
Upon a son, and christened him: Agamemnon-
Alexander-Julius-Caesar-Pompey-Augustus!

GERTRUDE

And little Laertes?—How shall he outlord
Such younger brother?

CORNELIA

Oh, he shall be Pope,
And crown his brother, thrice: in Rome, in Athens
And Constantinople.

GERTRUDE

How much cosier,
And nearer home, 't will be, then, when he greets
His loving sister—*Princess,* in Elsinore!

CORNELIA

Far nearer the home of my heart, dear Queen.

GERTRUDE

And mine,
Cornelia. So, between us now, henceforward,
To pledge this sacred secret of our hope
And token our sweet sharing of babe-born dreams,
Prithee, *Queen* me not, and *Madam* me no more,
But *woman* me with my girl-name, Gertrude.

CORNELIA
[*Reaching her hand, in shy affection.*]

Gertrude!

GERTRUDE
[*Smiling, bends and kisses Cornelia's hand.*]

Madam!

[*Then embracing her, impulsively.*]

My sister!

[*Then, with sweet solemnity, kissing her on the cheek.*]

Ophelia's queen!

CORNELIA

That kiss
Shall be my baby's coronal.

GERTRUDE

Nay, coronet.
Come! Here 's her coronal. See: 't is platted
Already.

CORNELIA

Where?

GERTRUDE

Here, on her coronet weeds;
I 've wove it with needles.

[*From a reticule bag, which hangs from the table's edge, she draws forth and unrolls some tied-up material, which she lays, spread-out, on the table.*]

Look! Here 's gowning stuff
Of princess' weeds, she 'll wear, that happy dream-day
We wot of.

CORNELIA

Fashion'd already?

GERTRUDE

Out of dream-stuff
To substance even as silken.

CORNELIA

But here 's two!

GERTRUDE

Aye, twain. This little head-coif, soft as bluets

On a moss-bank, is to wimple her in heaven-hue
Fresh as she cometh. This gown, greenly slender
As bough of willow, that doth bend aslant
A brook, wherein its hoary leaves are glass'd,
Is silvery-leaféd likewise; and mid-tween
The breasts, just verging where her heart is hidden,
To twin the wreath shall be her coronet,
I 've breded a garland, plaited of folk-flowers
Loved, or bewondered, by the innocent.

CORNELIA

How colourly 't is needled! How call you the flowers?

GERTRUDE

Crow-flowers, nettles, daisies, and long-purples.

CORNELIA

And wherefore chose you these, from other blooms?

GERTRUDE

Crow-flowers, because what time the first-spied crow
Of springtide telleth with his flapping wings
For watchful maid, risen at dawn, to count—
Shall time her wedding-hour.

CORNELIA

But these: why nettles?

GERTRUDE

I know not why—unless it were, methought,
I saw them growing in a corner-nook
Of that same still dream-garden, where I saw
My grown prince, pondering alone; and so,
This very morn, waking, I rose and hastened
To needle the nettles, here amid the daisies.

CORNELIA

Doth folk-say hallow daisies?

GERTRUDE

They are the eyes
Of day, that close at eve their ferny lids
To dream upon the stars, which they 'll become
In another dawn.

CORNELIA

Fallen stars?

GERTRUDE

Aye, fallen
On graves, where they take flower, to sow their heaven-seed.

CORNELIA

And these long-purples?—They do seem, as both
To dream and droop, in passion. What do they
Betoken?

GERTRUDE

Oft shepherds name them by a word
Too gross for maiden ears; and oft cold virgins
Do call them dead men's fingers.

CORNELIA
[*With a shudder.*]

'T is a meaning
Too shiversome, 't would seem, to broider in weeds
Of flowering girlhood.

GERTRUDE

Ah, my fond one!
Shall we, once girls, whose lives, mating with love,
Draw newly unto birth, so near to death,

Shiver for being new-born? Both of its namings—
Male-hot with pollen'd passion, and cold-calyx'd;
Purple with life in bloom, and paling death—
Whereby this flower is token'd by simple folk,
Symbol our flowering natures. Thou shouldst ha' been
Beside me here, even in this room, to learn
With me, from our wise Padre's smile, how sweet
And strong a power death is, that moveth love
For pity of a soul in pangs of hell,
To speak beyond where dead men's fingers clutch.

CORNELIA

Would I were ever beside thee, dear my——

GERTRUDE

Say it!
Our secret 's ever with us.

CORNELIA

Dear my—Gertrude!

GERTRUDE
[*Kissing her lovingly.*]

Ophelia's gown—how likes it thee?

CORNELIA

Past liking—
Too deep in yearning. But these tears are drops
Shining in daisies' eyes, and dangle no more
From lashes of long-purples, to fall in the dark.—
Ha! Through their misting, now, what 's this I see
Swimming beneath the garland, there—a mermaid?

GERTRUDE
[*Smiling, as Cornelia—with cry of wonder—gazes at the gown on the table.*]

Well, in strange truth, it is a kind of brook-elf
I could not deftly catch with a needle-hook.

CORNELIA

One arm is reaching upwards, toward the garland,
Is 't not?

GERTRUDE

Ah, then, I needled it well!—'T is so,
It reacheth up. Yet with no needle's eye
Could I have caught the finger-clutch I saw
In dream—a clambering reach, as if beseeching
Some broken sliver, pendant from a bough
Of the o'erbending willow, beyond grasp.[9]
And then, methought, still dreaming, that I heard,
As blown from out the floating mermaid's mouth,
The snatch of an old song, the air of which
Cometh back to me, even yet.

[*She sings, in low voice:*]

To-morrow is Saint Valentine's day
All in the morning betime . . .[10]

More of the words
Are lost to me—but so echoes the tune of it.

[*Pensively, she hums on, till her far-off gaze catches glimpse of something beyond the doorway, and—starting—she touches Cornelia's arm, speaking in a whisper.*]

Ah, quick!—Here—stand between!

CORNELIA

What is it?

GERTRUDE

Hush!
Where eyes have ears and lungs,
Secrets should tie their tongues!

'T is the fool's adage. Closer!—while I tie up these.

[*Snatching the materials from off the table-top, she bundles them swiftly into the reticule, which she is just closing, as* POLONIUS *and* CLAUDIUS *enter, in conversation.*]

POLONIUS

Indeed, my lord Duke, it was in the passage
Coming from the King's chamber, that I saw her—
But soft! You see, 't is so.

CLAUDIUS

Yes, yes. Enough!

GERTRUDE

Polonius,—is 't thou?

POLONIUS

Your Majesty,
'T is I, indeed, in person, but imperson'd
By greater presence than my humble self
May dare, as ablegate, to take precedence
In speaking before your Majesty, before
He deigneth himself to speak.

CLAUDIUS

He deigneth not
To speak thy tortuous dialect of Dane
For the Queen's torture.—Gertrude, good morrow!

GERTRUDE

Claudius,
Good morning! And may good morrows follow it
To gladden you in Elsinore. But how
Comes it you trace the morning's trail so early
To find me, where I left you, yesternight?

CLAUDIUS

To find where midnight hides his dawn-gold, and
Retrieve some shining ounce of it. But, pray,
Pardon me [*Bowing to Cornelia.*]
—you, as well, my lady!—for

Intruding, I fear, upon some closeted
Business between yourselves, here.

GERTRUDE

Nay, we 've none,
But seeking something lost.

CLAUDIUS

Something you 've lost?

GERTRUDE

Last night—a little book: methought, perchance,
I left it behind here, when I went to bed;
But, likely, 't is otherwise.

CLAUDIUS

A little book?
What kind?

GERTRUDE

A prayer-book.

CLAUDIUS

May not I assist you
In seeking it? Often, I 'm not unapt
At catching cues for clues.

GERTRUDE

Thanks; but we 've searched
All crannies hereabouts.—Cornelia,
Look if it may not be in thine own bower,
Where thou perhaps didst lay it by, unwitting
'Twas mine, in place of thine.

CORNELIA
[*Mystified.*]

Unwitting, 't would be,
Madam, and I will look for 't; yet I doubt—

GERTRUDE

Polonius will help thee, without doubt.
Will not you, Sir?

POLONIUS

Doubtless, indeed! I know not
Dubiety in my queen's service, nor
My king's, nay, nor my duke's. In Elsinore,
Such goeth unquestioned by Polonius,
Even unto the questionable, as,
To wit, the unwitted presence of the prayer-book
In my lady's bower.

GERTRUDE

Au revoir, Cornelia!
There beats no thought within thy heart, but claps
A bell that echoes in mine own, to summon me,
Whene'er thou wilt, to service in that chapel.

CORNELIA

'Tis there I 'm sure to find the lost prayer-book
And fetch it to you, my Queen.

GERTRUDE

Nay, keep it, thyself,
And treasure it fondly there, for the dear sake
Of our St. Agnes, who doth cherish all
Our prayers. *Addio! Pax tibi, O filia*
Veneris!

CORNELIA

Vobis pax, Regina amica!
[*Exeunt Cornelia and Polonius.*]

CLAUDIUS

Methinks, my sister, that the Latin tongue

Telleth of more than little prayer-books lost.
Do I deem true?

GERTRUDE

Why, nay and yea, my brother.
'T is true Cornelia's heart is a pure chapel
Where bells of love do tinkle secret prayers,
And the lost little book holds one of them
That 's hidden from all listeners but myself.
But 't is not true—indeed, I fibbed to say so—
That I did seek it hereabouts.

CLAUDIUS

You might
Have sought it hereabouts, and found it.

GERTRUDE

Where?

CLAUDIUS

Nay, in no chapel, but a prison-chamber.

GERTRUDE

A prison-chamber?

CLAUDIUS

Here—my heart, wherein
The lost prayer it doth hold is dungeoned, far
Too deep and close, for its enclampéd wings
To flutter 'gainst the barréd door and burst
The heart itself, for utterance, unless—

GERTRUDE

Unless—?

CLAUDIUS

Unless some hand of grace would reach
To unclasp the bar and free the clampéd wings.

GERTRUDE

Every heart of yearning prayer hath such a door,
Methinks, to baffle it. The hand of grace
Is God's.

CLAUDIUS

He hath not reached it down, to raise
The heavy iron from mine.

GERTRUDE

He entereth *through*
The iron, not *under,* and needeth not to unhinge it.
Prayers need no lips for gateway unto Him,
Who readeth them, unuttered. So reads He my own;
Yes, even as I—by grace of that same power
Which once moved Beatrice to speak pity
To one in hell—read yours.

CLAUDIUS

Beatrice!—Ah,
Thou readest *mine*—and answerest my prayer?

GERTRUDE

Nay, Claudio, not thine. Thy prayer is uttered
In every glance, thou lookest—aye, leerest—at me.
I pity thee but half. I pity wholly
The one whose prayer, unuttered and unguessed
By himself, or by any else but God and me,
Still holdeth him in hell before his time,
Smiling, for love of me.

CLAUDIUS

Ah,—*him!*

GERTRUDE

Yea, Hamlet.
Whom else?

CLAUDIUS

Pitiest—thy king and husband?

GERTRUDE

Him,
Thy "milkmaid innocent," thy "puss in pattens,"
Who smiles to greet thy grin of mockery
With guileless trust, all witless of his doom,
Were I, with *reaching hand of grace,* to unclasp
My barréd door, and let thy clampéd wings,
Scaled with the skin of *Serpens,* coil my heart,
While, like constricting boa, thy maskéd yawn
Swalloweth thy brother puss-in-boots, ere he
Can doff his pattens, and cry *meow!* for mercy.

CLAUDIUS

Demons of love, and angels of delusion!
What vision of hell is this, thou conjurest—
Beatrice, the Blest?

GERTRUDE

The secret of thy heart,
Made manifest. Thy pardon, brother mine—
Yea, brother still, for welcome, wilt thou yet
Confess 't was *that,* thy secret lust of me,
Made thee obey thy midnight visitant
Of vision, St. Agnes, and go forth to seek
Her shrine, for transformation of thyself
And purgement of thy sinning?

CLAUDIUS
[*Sinking before her.*]

That! Yea, that!
Forgive, O *Hamlet's* Beatrice! Let me
Kneel, till thou bid me rise, my Hamlet's brother,
Damned by myself, to be his penitent,

Without his knowing and with your forgiving,
Purgéd at last of all but brotherhood,
And keep this vow, even as thine anchorite.

GERTRUDE
[*After a pause.*]

Poor Claudio,—rise, and take this hand of sister.
Like murder, mildewed love must *out,* and breathe
Its own pure element again, to shed
Contagion, in fresh sun of kindness.

CLAUDIUS
[*Rising, kisses her hand.*]

Kindness:
How shall I name thee else for ever more,
From whom all curing breathes? Yet how to say so
In service, tell me, pray!

GERTRUDE

'Tis simple telling.
Dost thou remember how, even here, last night,
Communing of Dante's pain on his lost way,
Thou saidst, turning to me thy gaze—and still
I 've kept thy words: "This lady Beatrice,
Methinks, hath something of a mother's sorrow
For her wandering child's mishap: or, dost thou deem
'Tis more, my sister?"

CLAUDIUS

Yes, ah, yes; but then
I was interrupted. What would you have answered?

GERTRUDE

I 'll answer now. 'Tis more than mother's sorrow,
'Tis mother's joy—of love's anticipation
For what may come of love, that 's overshadowed
By fear of itself—a dreadful joy.

CLAUDIUS

I fear
I do not catch the dread import. For what
Should mother's joy take sorrow, in this case?

GERTRUDE

For Hamlet's little Hamlet—my own princeling.
Ah, there you pierced me to my mother's quick.
And now you have made your vow of penitence,
I pity no more my king; but I do dread
Something, I know not what, which shall befall
My joy in him, our waxing Prince of Denmark,
Unless we guard him well.—You ask to serve me.
Serve *him,* in me, whose womb of love's possession
Shelters him still, reluctant to release
His winging heart of innocence to the world's
Sharp archery. So, even of thee, purged *Serpens,*
Who knowest the juices of the jungle, I ask
The wisdom of the serpent, to protect
My dove from the poisoned dart.

CLAUDIUS

Aye, so: 't is *Dyaksh,**
Squeezed from wild crabs of Borneo, to spittle
The forkéd tongues of thorns, which pigmies poison
To stab the hearts of giants in their sleep—
Yes, yes, I know it: Suchlike is the world's venom
For dreaming innocence. Ought not I, *Serpens,*
To know, who here am risen from Eden's root
To pay thee service of redemption?

GERTRUDE

I
Will trust thy truth of guilt redeemed, as thou

*Pronounce *di-āk-sh.*

Must trust my muteness of all knowledge on 't
Whispered in Hamlet's ear.

CLAUDIUS

Thy dumbness is
Reward enough to me for my redeeming;
So trust in me henceforth, as penitent
Unto the King, and guardian of the Prince.

[*In a* LONG STILL PAUSE, *they stand looking at each other.*]

GERTRUDE

Look not so pale!

CLAUDIUS

Gaze not so dawningly!

[*They draw back and away from each other, as* KING HAMLET *and* YORICK *enter, the latter in high, chuckling laughter, holding his right hand flattened over his face, and peering between the fingers towards Claudius and Gertrude.*]

KING HAMLET

Why makest thou to stopple so thy mouth
And gag thy laughter, Fool?

YORICK

I 'll do 't no more!

[*Swivelling his hand swiftly, so that the end of his thumb touches the tip of his nose and the flanging fingers extend toward Claudius, for an instant, he then removes his hand from his face.*]

For why should there be anything but laughter
In all the world, seeing—

KING HAMLET

Ah, seeing—what?

YORICK

How there is nothing but happiness on earth,
And all is Eden again, where even the Snake,

Looping the Angel's sword, makes joy to slough
His skin, and each who lives possesses
What most he loves, and would not part with it
For all he loathes.

KING HAMLET

How prove you that?

YORICK

Doth not
The wise man love his wisdom? Would he part with 't
For the fool's wit?

CLAUDIUS
[*Approaching.*]

You mean, for Yorick's wit?

YORICK

Nay, that were hand for glove! Doth not the saint
Hug sainthood? Would he swap his heaven for
The murderer's hell?

CLAUDIUS

Perchance the murderer
Would toss him coins for it.

YORICK

Nay, love is the luck
He lots on, and his own black lot of loving
He would not change for any other bliss
Than love of murdering. No misanthrope
Who rots in bogs of hypochondria
But lilts his bog-groans as the lark his sky-song.
The cynic laughs to make the lover wince,
And the fond lover laughs because he fails to.
The bad are glad of badness, and the good
Of sadness for the bad. So both are merry,

And Yorick laughs for all, whichever lilts,
And is as happy as a wooing lover
Whose passion is returned, or a murderer
Whose life is forfeit.

KING HAMLET

Then we 'll also laugh
To share the world with Yorick's laughter.

YORICK

Catch, then,
I laugh not *at* the world, but *for* it. 'Tis a tender,
A good, good world! It devoureth gentle lambs
With such a relish of their tenderloins
As sweetens its wolf-smile. That 's why I pay good coin
To attend horrible tragedies and weep
Buckets, to purge my belly of all badness;
Yet 't would take Aristotle to construe my tears
Whether they *purge* me, or not. So I quote Scripture:
Let us learn to laugh humbly before God.
Saith not the Good Book so?

GERTRUDE

Yorick, that once
I spoke such folly as to call thee mad,
I ask now thy fool's pardon.

YORICK

Pardon, liege lady?
That you should find in me what all men seek
To cherish in themselves, and castigate
In others?

GERTRUDE

What 's that?

YORICK

Why, madness.

GERTRUDE

What mean you?

YORICK

Ah, mean! For me to report what madness means,
Your Majesty must needs ship me away
To the universities: at Basel, on Rhine,
To ask of the learnéd Doctor Paracelsus
Theophrastus, Bombast von Hohenheim, who 's burned
The books of Galen and Avicennae, to learn it;
Or else to Wittenberg, where the illustrious
Magister Georgius Sabellicus Faustus Junior,
Magus Secundus, philosophus philosophorum,
Fons necromanticorum, chiromanticus,
Agromanticus, pyromanticus, in hydra arte secundus,"[11]
Revealeth cabalisticly the meaning
Of madness, fools misname philosophy.
Ah, then, my liege, when I return to you,
Gown me in grey, and I will found in fustian
The University of Elsinore,
And wear the mortar of my cap and bells
To crown my Doctorate with royal degree
Of *A.M., Asinus Maximus,* which rendered
In vulgate readeth—*Aristotle, the Mighty.*

KING HAMLET
[*Laughing.*]

Madcap, pack with us to the dining-hall,
Where we will fully digest thy Great Foundation
With corollaries of thy blackbird-pie.—
Come, Gertrude. Claudio, come. Canter before us,
Asinus Maximus!

YORICK

Nay, majesties,
After!—I canter no more. Mine asinine parts
Are thwacked too sore with brain-cudgels. I amble
With [*Lilting:*] *Pacey goes the countryman, heigh-ho!*

KING HAMLET

Now, Claudio, wilt thou turn and follow us?
[*Exeunt all but Claudius, who pauses.*]

CLAUDIUS

Follow—follow—follow where? . . Who followeth
That is not *led* by beckonings of hands
Unseen? O night in day! Who leadeth me
Toward day in night? Ah, mist of madness, what
Lantern of foxfire leadeth the little foxes
To scorch the mountain with their burning brushes
And parch the mildew'd tarn? . . "Look not so pale,"
She said; and I—"Gaze not so dawningly!" . .
The Lord is my Shepherd. I shall not want. He leadeth me
Beside the still waters—reflecting *what?*
Her gaze of dawn through Hamlet's glowering stare?
Or gleam of Angela's curl by St. Agnes' candle?
Her gaze of dawning—*what?* Desire, or suspicion? . .
The lost prayer-book—the sheltering mother-sorrow,
Praying: "Protect my dove from the poison'd dart—"
The *poison'd* dart!—*How* poisoned?—By wild spittle
Of Borneo's *Dyaksh,* or Elsinore's
Home-*hebenon?*—And Yorick's laughing code
Of love and happiness: the murderer's bliss
In his black lot of murdering . . Ha, is 't *double?*
Can it be, her gleam of suspicion catcheth glow
Of knowledge, from his eyes between his fingers
Flatted across his mouth for muteness?—*Whose*
Muteness?—his own, or hers, or both? And, again,

Of *what?*—Their guess or knowledge of my guilt,
Halved between them? Which knoweth what, how much,
Or nothing?—"Trust my muteness of all knowledge on 't,
Whispered in Hamlet's ear," she said, and I:
"Thy dumbness rewardeth me for my redeeming."—
But *I?*—Am I myself indeed redeemed,
Who now do split redemption's hairs, to weave 'em
Into a slip-cord's noose, wherewith to strangle
Mine own deliverance from evil, coiling
Such knotted doubts of good and ill as *these?*
What, are we liars, *all,* groping alone
For touch of some near hand to fetch us forth
Out of this guileful mist, that mocketh all
Who yearn to follow innocence?

[*Enter* YORICK, *holding a napkin.*]

YORICK

My lord,
Supper is served.

CLAUDIUS

Ha, what?

YORICK

Supper. 'T is served.

CLAUDIUS

Is night, then, come so soon?

YORICK

For some, it cometh
Early; for others, late; but, to-night,
The dew is something overdue, and supper
Awaits the thirsty: so, to serve on time,
I 've fetched to you an earthy substitute
For heaven's tears, long cellared, once distilled
By an apothecary.

CLAUDIUS

Fetched me—*what?*

YORICK

[*Taking it from the napkin.*]

This, Claudio. Art not thou thirsty for 't?
The vial is unstoppled.

CLAUDIUS

[*Seizing it, with a shrill cry.*]

Ah, the vial!

YORICK

Thou seest, 't is almost full. The lacking drops
Were sipped, to test their tang of bitterness,
By Angie's lips.

CLAUDIUS

[*In stifled voice.*]

Angie—the hebenon—

YORICK

At last, *'t is out*—between us?

CLAUDIUS

[*Thrusting the vial within his garment.*]

What 's between us?

YORICK

Naught, now. 'T is in thy pocket, in mine no more.

CLAUDIUS

For what canst thou have fetched this unto *me,*
Of all men else?

YORICK

For love.

CLAUDIUS

Love! Thou speak'st simply—
Or subtly.

YORICK

Aye. Love 's simple for simpletons,
And subtle for the over-wise. We 're both.

CLAUDIUS

And liars, both?

YORICK

Unwittingly, let 's pray.

CLAUDIUS

Why didst thou lie, to instil the strolling player
With rumour of thy death? Was that unwitting?

YORICK

Ah, *that!* Nay, that was witting. I ask pardon.
E'en fools may lose their wits, for love.

CLAUDIUS

For love!

YORICK

And so, for losing what they lack most, find
Redemption, more replete than murderers gain
By keeping what they have.

CLAUDIUS

Once more, I ask thee:
Why didst thou lie thus?

YORICK

And once more I answer:
For love.

CLAUDIUS

Of whom?

YORICK

Of thee.

CLAUDIUS

By what mad antic
Couldst thou love *me?*

YORICK

A wily one. I wanted thee
At home. I missed thee, much. So did thy brother.

CLAUDIUS

And sister?

YORICK

She will tell thee, when thou askest
How much.

CLAUDIUS

Thou *knowest,* then?

YORICK

God knoweth,
And will inform her, in good time, or bad.
But I was telling thee about my love
For thee.

CLAUDIUS

Ah, yes; go on.

YORICK

I wanted thee
Here, to restore to thee what thou hadst lost:
Thy soul, stoppled in a vial.

CLAUDIUS

My *prisoned* soul,
Ha?

YORICK

Yes. To unstopple it.

CLAUDIUS

And drink the bane
In toast to a heavenward journey? Thanks. I 'm earth-bound
By more enticing, heavenlier bitters
Than lure to suicide.

YORICK

Nay, to pour it
Forth on the spongy earth, in sweet libation
To lovelier goddess than an earthly queen.

CLAUDIUS

As—who?

YORICK

Claudia, the soul of Claudius,
That so thyself may intercede to win thee.
A crownéd sister.

CLAUDIUS

Grazie, ancora!
I yearn me not to win a crown of thorns
For woman, nor man, neither.

YORICK

Dear my Duke,
Such thorns are thistles and yield silk. Think gladlier,
And empty the vial out.

CLAUDIUS

Only as lice-bane.
I itch, and there are lice in Elsinore.
I need this liquor for 'em; till which time,
I 'll keep it corked, *Yoricus Asinus,*
Unless thou 'lt borrow some, to keep the rats
From gnawing oats in thine own crib. I see,
Thou feelest thine ass's oats, since thou didst jog
With *Pacey goes the countryman, heigh-ho!*

YORICK

Well, as you will, and I will jog once more.
The stolid ass, even as the racing stallion,
Feeleth his rider's oats more than his own,
And as his mount hath fed, so stirs his mettle.
Thus am I rid by the wild jockey, Joy,
And, for the gracious guerdon of love's gauntlet,
We take our hurdles toward the heavenly goal
With *Up, up, up,—and over!—Addio, addio,*
Claudio carissime!

[*Exit, with an upward gesture.*]

CLAUDIUS

Addio, addio!—
Which is to say: *To God, to God! Farewell!*
To God, then, *go!* And I will aid thee go . . .

[*Taking forth the vial and gazing at it.*]

But not with this. This holds too hellish woe.

CURTAIN.

ACT FOURTH

A WALLED GARDEN OF THE CASTLE. ELSINORE.

The high, angular wall of clay-set stones, clambered over by vines of bittersweet and climbing roses, turned to pale-red hips, meets, at lower left, the Castle building, into which a door leads. At upper left, the wall has a gate, giving toward alleys, overshaded by pine-boughs, visible beyond the wall-top, which elsewhere gives view of the sky. At right, centre, another garden gate gives exit towards a chapel, invisible, but indicated by tonings of its bell.

The garden plot is crossed by gravel walks, from gate to gate, and from the Castle door to a smaller door in the wall, at back, left of centre. The plot itself is grassed to the wall, which [at back, a little to stage-right of the door] is scarred by a GREAT CRACK, *whose jagged fissure has been newly stoned-in and clayed-over, more than half way to the top. There it is being mended by two peasant-clad, sturdy* YOUNG FELLOWS, *one lank, the other stocky, half hid in the wall's shadow, beside some buckets with clay and a shovel, as they stand leaning against the wall, listening to a* VOICE, *from behind it, heard singing there, in sad rhythms.*

From the sky beyond the wall-top, in glimmer of early evening, a slender new moon shines frostily down.

At slow-timed intervals, A CLEAR BELL *is heard tolling, through cadences of the Singer's voice.*[12]

THE VOICE

Sing, Sorrow, Sorrow!
Where the cold bittersweet
Is clambering—
O, sing
To the numbing winter sleet!
For O—for O—for O,
Sorrow,
Unless you sing, all melody
Of dear, lost June will die.—
Ah, would so could I!

THE STOCKY FELLOW
[*With mysterious gesture.*]

'T is Yorick, the fool!

THE LANK FELLOW

Why singeth he so sadsome,
Topas? Methought, 'a were a merry fool.

TOPAS

Art more a fool, thyself, Yaughan, for the axing.
A fool is a mender of wisdom. God is wise,
And He 's the master musicianer. When the merry
Need patching, He sendeth a fool with a lilt
To skein up the ravellments o' their sorrow. So
Mend thou thy wall, and patch its broken rib,
But half as well as Yorick mendeth hearts,
And thou 'lt please God.

YAUGHAN

I will! Please God, I will!

[*Lifting an enormous stone, he reaches it upward with both hands toward the top of the crevassed hole in the wall, but—staggering under the huge rock—lets it slip, falling, to the ground, where—with a grunt at its thud—he sits down on it.*]

Aggh! I ought a-climbed the bench. God 's too high up.

TOPAS
[*Mocking him.*]

Aggh! Uggh!—Thou 'rt too low down for mounting bench,
And mindest thine own breech more than the wall's,
To sit there, gapping at the Judgement Seat.
Where learnest thou thine art, from the under part,
Or the upper?

YAUGHAN

Mass! I 'm wondering why his lilt
Did toll so sad!

TOPAS

To match the chapel bell.
It tolleth for the Mass, and calleth to prayer
For one that died aborning. 'T is a lass.

YAUGHAN

So? 'T is *alas,* indeed, when mother loseth
Her babe.

TOPAS

'T is more, when babe loseth her mother,
For though she crieth unto heaven, "Alas!"
The mother cannot answer.

YAUGHAN

Mother, is it?

TOPAS

Aye, 't is the lady Cornelia. Her wee bird
Be hatcht out fine as chick outen the egg,
And peepeth glad to spy its pin-feathern,
So purty goldy-yellow they fuzz i' the dayshine.
And me, soon I must off to play the hussif
And ply my craft to make a bed i' the hoarfrost
For the good lady to lie in, whiles Moll Midwife
Loaneth her paps to wax the little suckling
Until the weaning-time.—Hist! Here she cometh,
And greatness with her. Tend thy trade. I 'll help thee.

[*They both turn to mending of the wall, as* GERTRUDE *and* MOLL COWSLIP *come forth from the Castle doorway.*]

MOLL

Aye, 't is an elf-child, kinned to faery folk,
And born'd o' Hallowe'en.—There, there, Ma'am, there!
Stint weeping. So, so,—there!

GERTRUDE

Cornelia,
Ah, my dear—dear—!

MOLL

And dearie, 't is, her babe,
An elf-bit-bodykins, as ever played
Ring-rosy round a toadstool. Heigh, did n't I

Thumb her betwixt two fingers o' one hand
And hold her up into her mother's eyes
Afore they darkled out!

GERTRUDE

What did she say,
Her mother? Tell me again.

MOLL

A faery word,
I trow, it were: "*O filia,*" quoth she,
"O daughter mine!" And seemed her eyes would eat
The darling up, for joy, so hungersome
They clutched the air between. "O daughter dear!"
Quoth she; and once more, soft—"Ophelia . ."
Then, like a candle in a sudden wind,
Out she winkt . . and—God's mother quit me blame!—
I washed the wee one's face wi' my own blub tears.

GERTRUDE

Mine still are fain to do the like.

MOLL

Stint, stint, Ma'am!
Here 's too much holy water for an elf-babe.
Aye, *elf!* I 'll say it on my ros'ry beads:
"Elf-babe—elf-child—elf-babe!" From Hallowe'en
Till Christmastide, I 'll babble it—but soft, though:
For, 'twixt us twain, this Sir, Polonius,
With all his agéd saws, and *he-haw-hums,*
And fidget winks, 'a 's fit to be her grandsir,
But—save the sweet soul of her blesséd dam!—
I 'll lay an acorn to a chinkapin,
The babe were sired by that unscotchnable
Elf, Oberon, who putteth his angel-ouphes
In the moon-cradle, for biggening brides to pick

Their wishéd girl-babes from, afore their cradling
In home-baskets.

GERTRUDE

Molly Midwife, what art saying!

MOLL

Troth, and what I should know, ha' plied my craft
These hunderd-fifty mother's moons, and more,
Sith first I suckled Yorick the Fool's babe,
And held that other angel-urchin up
In Mariana's eyes, for her to gaze
Into the wee blue stare of Angela,
Just ere *her* mother winked, e'en self the same
As this dear lady died.

GERTRUDE

Ah, God forbid
Little Ophelia shall berue her mother
As Angela did hers!

MOLL

The lucky-piece
O' love is chuckt to favour boy-babe mothers
More oft than girl-babe. So the coin was tosst
That lay your little princeling in his cradle,
Heads-up—his own, and yours, Ma'am.

GERTRUDE

Yes, my princeling!
How fond my dear Cornelia watched beside me,
To ease thy watchings, did she not, that night
Thou helpedst him be born!

MOLL

Nay, make us not
To swab our tears again, remembering all!

GERTRUDE

Yet—yet I cannot help it, but remember
Her sharing of our secret of the ring-rhyme,
Heard in my dream, and how—with catching breath
That half did stop my own—she said to me:
"O Madam! Put no dream within my hope
Beyond the scope of dreaming."

MOLL

Put no dream——?

GERTRUDE
[*With suddenness.*]

Molly!—for thou didst bring them both to the world—
This much I must—nay, now, this much I *will*—
Whisper to thee—and more, when time shall tide,—
But now, before they come—Dost hear them coming?—
This—*this:* My dream—our dream of hope—that hope
For her and me—Ophelia's and Hamlet's mothers—
Will be—*shall* be—*within* the scope of dreaming:
[*She whispers.*]
The babe just born shall be my Hamlet's bride.

MOLL
[*Whispering back.*]

The babes I borned ye?—
[*Bursting out.*] Mother o' God and Oberon,
But this for troth be Hallowe'en!

GERTRUDE

Whisht! Hush!

[*Enter, from the Castle,* KING HAMLET, CLAUDIUS, POLONIUS, PRINCE HAMLET, *and* LAERTES.]

KING HAMLET

The Mass-bell calleth still. Thy pardon, Gertrude!

We 'll on, together. But sorrow hath precedence
Of sorrow's sympathizers. Pray, go first,
Polonius.

POLONIUS

My lord King,—I!

KING HAMLET

Go first,
And with you, hand in brother-hand, our sons,
Twinned by this sudden grief.

GERTRUDE
[*With a start, clutching his hand.*]

Ah, Hamlet—thanks!

CLAUDIUS
[*Aside.*]

Thanks?

KING HAMLET
[*Fondly, to Gertrude.*]

Thanks for thine own hand.
[*To Polonius.*]
Lead! We, kith of kingdoms,
Will follow humbly in thy train of sadness.

POLONIUS
[*Pauses, bewildered, bowing, and speaks in broken tones.*]

Majesties; my lord, Duke; sweet my prince; and lastly—
If here it be permitted to convert
Last unto first, as Scripture giveth warrant
"First shall be last," and warranting, of course,
Right circumstances of precedence—lastly,
Laertes, my dear son! . . .
If, from within the vale of veiling death,—
I say not "valley of the shadow," for I would not
Suffer the shade of suffering to fall

Too sheer, or dark, upon the path of childhood
Where now you pace in mourning, all unwitting
What lieth beyond, in morn-breaks of far morrows
Wherein may hidden be (though God forbid!)
Heart-breaks more sudden-awful e'en than this
Which hath befallen us now—but if, I say,
Fro' the veil of death, which thy endearéd mother
Now weareth, with the wimple and the stole
Of silence, there, most like a sainted sister
In heaven's cloistral garden, walled around
Even so as this, yet with no fissured gap,
Such like as yon, for mending—if, say I
Once more, thy silent mother heareth from there
What here the majesty of Elsinore
Hath uttered to his most obsequious servant
Grief-tangled in these obsequies of tears,
To wit, Polonius, thy father, how
His majesty hath, in command, entreated,
As 't were, *thy father to go first,* whilst he
Will follow humbly—then, Laertes dear,
Then—then—oh, sure I am, that she, who ever
Harboureth the sense, and is—nay, was—no, *is*
Herself the soul of graciousness, will heed
And share with me my pride, that thy—that thy
Sweet mother's husband, even I, thy father,
Being honoured, so unworthy, yet so lifted
By majesty into majesty, as to be,
As 't were, her earthly king—that she, from thence,
Will say—will say—ah, come, little Laertes,
Thy hand in mine!—and thine, sweet Prince!—will say:
God bless him, Denmark's heart of graciousness,
Hamlet, King of compassion for us all!

[*Huskily.*]

Nay, come, come, come!

[*Seizing the children's hands, he hurries them forward with himself, his head bent over, in regardless groping towards the tolling bell, in precipitant exit, as the others look after him in astonishment.*]

KING HAMLET
[*Gently.*]

The pate of rhetoric
Cracks with grief's pain, to fill the rift with love.
God bless Cornelia's king!

GERTRUDE

Thy hand again,
Dear Hamlet mine! [*To Moll Cowslip.*]
Moll, whilst we kneel at Mass,
Within the chapel, prithee relieve Polonius
Of care for the two laddies. Give them range
Outdoors, for their young spirits to ponder
Thoughts lighter than this heavy loss. Await us.

MOLL

Madam, I will.

[*The King and Queen go out, together.*]

CLAUDIUS
[*To Moll, whom he accompanies.*]

Who mendeth the wall, there?

MOLL

'T is Yaughan, the gardener.

CLAUDIUS

And the other one?

MOLL

Topas, the grave-digger. 'A 's Yorick's crony.

CLAUDIUS

Yorick's?

[*He turns and looks back, as he makes exit with her, leaving Topas and Yaughan alone, together.*]

TOPAS

Yaughan, thou and I ha' both one trade.

YAUGHAN

How shall that be? Thou art a grave-digger.
I be a gardener, as mendeth my wall,
That God's great blow hath crackt wi' His hurricane.

TOPAS

Aye; so us both ply the same holy craft
His good Son plied, to heal His hurricanes.

YAUGHAN

What craft?

TOPAS

Christus his craft o' carpentry.
Thou workest in garden clay, and I in graveyard.
Behold, Heaven rendeth, and Yaughan righteth the rift.
Lo, Heaven raineth, and Topas roofeth the gulch.
The Lord Jehovah bloweth fro' His Castle;
Christus, 'a worketh in his shed, to build
Against the blows. God smiteth. Christus smileth.

YAUGHAN

Truly; yet 't is in Heaven they smite and smile.
Us be here. How can us mend their quarrel, far off?

TOPAS

'Tis no such quarrel, but a kind o' tangle
Which needeth the Holy Ghost to loose the knots.
Thou dost forget the Dove.

YAUGHAN

How, then, the Dove?

TOPAS

'A fetcheth a holly-sprig, to plant a tree
For Christus to make him planks to build a tower
For us to mount to Heaven and mend the matter
Betwixt 'em. So us make a berry-wreath
For God the Father to wear, and thus 'A smileth
As merry as Mary's child i' the manger-hay.

YAUGHAN

Aye, sooth: that same be so to Christmastide;
But now be Hallowe'en, when faeries steal
The berries, and pixies pinch our toes i' the frost.
How can us mend the matter, with them about,
To rumple us up?

TOPAS

Axe Yorick. 'A 's a whoreson rogue
As ever wheedled priest to dance hopscotch
At the devil's wedding, or devil to get drunk
With holy water, on a saint's eve.—Him?
'A 'll twiddle a psalm-tune on his funny-bone
Will make the pixies scamper to churn the cream
They 's come to steal. 'A kenneth the little folk
I' the Elf-king's bower, and great folk i' the Castle;
And 'a 's court-fool to both their kingdoms, and tinkleth
His cap o' bells for laughter and for prayer.
Aye, Yorick, his heart 's the home o' Hallowe'en
Where man and fay forgather, and all this lore
O' 'tarnal things that leaketh from Topas' mouth,
'T is larned of his liltings.

YAUGHAN

'A larneth more than us.
Yestreen, whiles I were swabbing clay, like now,
To patch this hole i' the wall, here cometh Yorick
Foreby, wi' the little Prince, and stayed to watch.

"Hamlet," quoth 'a, "see there!" And then 'a lilted:
"Imperious Caesar, dead, and turned to clay,
Might stop a hole to keep the wind away—[13]
E'en so as yonder mud in Yaughan's fist, there."
"How mean you?" saith our princeling. Then, quoth
Yorick:
"We all be clay in the Great Sculptor's hand,
And Yaughan 's His right-hand man." And so 'a smiled
Kindsome a smile at me, as made me laugh,
But Princey laughed not. "Yaughan 's His right-hand man,"
Quoth 'a. And, Mass! I know not why I laughed,
Nor why the Prince laughed not.—What think'st thou,
Topas?

TOPAS

Methinks——

[*Topas pauses—his glance being suddenly focussed upon something on the edge of the scene, and—pointing left—he pitches his voice low.*]

Methinks we 'll stop this swabbing tongues
With clay, and stoop to greater task.

YAUGHAN

What spyest?

TOPAS

More greatness, coming to watch. Raise up thy buttocks
And mount the bench. Belive! I 'll heft this rock
For thee to hold, till I take stand beside thee;
So then we 'll heave together, and place it back
Up yon, atop the gap, where it belongeth.
Great folk ha' scorn of idleness—in others.
Whisht!—List me thieve a lilt from Yorick's pouch.

[*As Topas makes a gesture that pushes Yaughan to mount the bench,* CLAUDIUS *appears, left, and comes slowly towards them, while Topas—with assaying gaze at the great stone—stands peering down at it, and up at the wall, resting his right foot on the spade which he holds with his right hand, as he lilts, to an old folk-tune.*[14]]

A spade—a spade—is foot and hand.
A hand 's but half a spade.
Ten foot below 's full low to stand
For to heft a stone so laid.

CLAUDIUS

Methinks, one spade were less than half a hand
In such a game of euchre.

TOPAS
[*Doffing his cap.*]

Euchred I be not, Sir.
'T is a dark Jack holdeth his brother spade
In hand; and here 's two Jacks, within an ace
Of a King—craving your pardon!—ought win the stakes.
[*He bows, with his left hand held clutching his cap against his side.*]

CLAUDIUS

Aha, I see, thou holdest in thy sleeve
A joker, with thy double-bower. That
Should win thee the wall-prize. But, good fellow, why
This grubbing tool, to lift so great a stone?
Methinks, thou errest. Thou dost need a hawser
To raise it.

TOPAS

Haw, Sir! 'Twould be a grave error
To raise a tombstone to a grave-digger
In his lifetime, by lifting such a load
To crack his skull, if be the noose did slip.
[*Setting his spade against the wall, he grabs Yaughan by the leg, to divert his look to the stone, around which he treads slowly and dubiously, as he lilts again.*]

Ten foot by hand is high—is high—
Ten stone of stone to heave,
But twenty stone of man cometh nigh
To heaving this 'n, believe.

[*Spitting on his palms, he rubs them in the dirt, grasps hold of the rock, lifts it to Yaughan's reach, and staggers up beside him on the bench, where together they raise the stone and shove it part way into the gap at the top of the wall, during which Topas sings hoarsely, with pauses of grunted puffs, to his lilting.*]

So heave, Topas—to pass—to pass
This—ah—stone—ah!—to ten-stone Yaughan.
Four foot on bench—ha!—ten foot from grass—
Heave, ho!—Ho, heave!—up, yon!

CLAUDIUS

Brave hove, Sir Topas! Thou shouldst wear knight's gauntlets
On those braw hands, were I within another
Ace nigher King; aye, and a laureate wreath
Of hips, from off these climbing wall-roses,
To garland thee withal. The State of Denmark
Needs never dread crackt wall, with such stout Danskers
To mason it with music, mixt with brawn.
Methinks, thy lilting hath had tutelage
From Master Yorick.

TOPAS

[*Stepping down from the bench, with Yaughan.*]

Aye, Master Fool hath bred me
Up from the cow-byre, till now I can yield
Court-songs for cream and country-lilts for butter
To slick the gentry's ears. I sweat his wit
Outen my pores, like whey from cottage cheese,
E'en, Sir, as you may watch it oozing now
For elf-buzzers to sip, o' Hallowe'en.

[*Brushing away the sweat from his face with his forearm, he slaps at some hovering gnats in the air.*]

CLAUDIUS

Ah, Hallowe'en!—So 't is!

[*Broodingly, he turns to the bench, and sits there.*]

And I 've refrained

From Holy Mass for the dead mother's soul
To witch mine own, upon this elvish eve,
With strange discoursements here, in cow-byre jests
For knighting clowns, with grave-spades in their hands,
And tombstones toppling overhead. Yet thoughts
Of death breathe easier out of doors than in,
If be such thoughts can breathe, and not garrotte
The thinker.

TOPAS

For to crave your pardon, Sir,
And if your Greatness will look straightaway up,
'A 'll see how a plumb-lead down from yonder stone
Would part your Highness' hairs in the middle. Eke, Sir,
The stone itself, 't is yet but halvely put
In place, and topplesome; be not it, Yaughan?

YAUGHAN

Na, na! 'Tis solid. Nary a wind can blow
Yon stone away, let be 't were the great blow
Of God again. 'Twould take His hand to push it,
And 'A 's not here, to Hallowe'en. No pixy
Will try to topple it, up yon, I guess.
Haw, haw! Us hove it purty.

TOPAS

Laughter lilteth
Merry in the mouth, but sorry in the windpipe;
And *Building wall bodeth fall,* 't was writ
On Eden Garden gate. And *Mending gap*
Hinteth mishap, folk say. *But Hand of man*
May ease the Hand of God.—'Twas Yorick said it,
Helping me dig his Angie's grave.—Go fetch
A ladder, and let us set yon stone aright
Afore it breaketh the bench beneath his lordship.

CLAUDIUS

[*Rising warily, moves away from the bench, and looks up at the top-stone.*]

Thanks, Topas, for thy hint, and Yorick's with it:
The hand of man may ease the Hand of God!

YAUGHAN

Ah, then, well be it, Topas. But the ladder
It leaneth agen the wall on t'other side;
So come wi' me along, now, and hold fast
The bottom rungs, the whiles I climb up top
Wi' the clay-bucket, and mortise the rock safe.

TOPAS

So said,—ahead! [*They start toward the door in the wall.*]

CLAUDIUS

Well, go your ways. Good night!
Don't slip. New moon sheddeth more shade than light.
[*He goes into the Castle.*]

YAUGHAN

[*Pausing.*]

Aye, new moon, 't is. Yon hangeth her sickle. Na, na!
I 'll get me a ground lantern. It groweth darkish.
[*He starts away.*]

TOPAS

Come on! Thy sight will grow to it.

A LOW HOOTING CRY

[*Sounds from behind the wall.*]

To wit—
To wit—to wit—

YAUGHAN

[*Pausing.*]

Hist! Heard'st thou?

TOPAS

Aye; but who—?

THE HOOTING CRY

[*More deep.*]

Hoo-hoo—hoo-hoo?

YAUGHAN

[*Aghast.*]

Ha! It did axe thee—*who?*

[*Pointing to the top of the wall.*]

O, Topas, look what sitteth on the stone:
'A winketh moons, for eyes.

TOPAS

'Tis a horny owl.

YAUGHAN

His head 's a bushel big. 'A winketh *green* moons!

THE OWL

Thing seen
Glistereth green.

YAUGHAN

Mass! 'Tis a bird, can talk.

THE OWL

[*As its eyes change to a bluish gleam.*]

Thing true
Gloweth blue.

YAUGHAN

Can 'a see us, Topas?

THE OWL

See-er by day
Hath eyes of clay.

Seer in the night
Hath second sight.

YAUGHAN

I 'll not go where 'a 'll spy me. I 'll make home.

TOPAS

Stick still! I guess him; but I 'll axe.—Who be ye?

THE OWL

I be the baker's daughter,[15]
Born over water
To rest under, in sorrow,
To-morrow—to-morrow.

YAUGHAN

I 'm off!

TOPAS

[*Holding Yaughan.*]

I know him. Stay. Quake not thy wit.

THE OWL

Wit—wit—to wit:
Who-who?
Eyes, out!
Hell's doubt
All Heaven will flout.
Nicker in, nicker in![16]
Cometh man kin!
Adieu!
Oo-oo-oo!—Oo-oo . . . !

YAUGHAN

'A 's blinkt—'a 's gone!

TOPAS

'A 's Yorick's owl. Nary's else
Could toot his hoots in rhyme, to Hallowe'en.

YAUGHAN

Can 'a larn owls to rhyme?

TOPAS

Come, climb the ladder
And find the owl's nest.

[*Pulling Yaughan along with him, Topas flings open the wall-door, but starts back aghast, as there—in the dim light—the* OWL *comes swooping towards them, blinking green and blue eyes, from the end of a long pole, held in the hand of* YORICK, *who enters from behind the wall, holding in his other hand a flagon.*]

YORICK
[*To Topas.*]

His nest is in thine hairs,
Where the wild grapes tangle, Sir Bacchus.

YAUGHAN
[*Kneeling, with a cry.*]

Help!

TOPAS
[*In scared laughter.*]

Oh-ho!
Yorick, thou whoreson rogue!

YORICK
[*Holding the poled Owl as a staff.*]

Yea, kneel with Yaughan,
And ope thy drouthy mouth for draught of owl-wine,
Olden with wisdom. 'T is Minerva's bird
Hath prest it from the vineyard of thy locks
To store in vats of Rhineland, and borne hither
To sate thy thirst, o' Hallowe'en.

[*He holds the flagon above Topas, who has knelt beside Yaughan, and is staring up at it, with open mouth and eager eyes.*]

TOPAS

Ha, cellar-drink!

YORICK

Aye, cellared by the monks of Wittenberg
And stoppled in the casks of Necromancy:
Ope wider! Gape!—Nay, bow thee first, and pray.
'T is Rhenish. Replenish!

[*He empties the full flagon, with a great splash, down Topas' back.*]

TOPAS

[*Leaping up.*]

Ho—hah! Thou spilladregs!
My mouth 's not down my neck.

YORICK

It leadeth down.
I took short cut, to reach thy belly, Bacchus.

TOPAS

[*Shaking himself, in his soaked tabard.*]

Have at thine own, then, owl-bird! 'T is cram-stufft
With moley jokes, thou 's eat.

[*He makes a rush at Yorick, who darts backward and confronts him with the candle-eyes of the outreached owl-pole.*]

YORICK

'Ware! 'Ware my beak!
My jack-o'-lantern trumps thy double-jacks
I heard thee boasting, joker.

TOPAS

Ha, game 's up!
And me, I 's won a booby's skin, for stakes,
Soakéd with Rhenish. Well, I 'll suck the rags.
How said I, Yaughan, 'a were a whoreson rogue?

YAUGHAN

I 'll do with well-water.

YORICK

Aye, so wilt thou
Do well, Yaughan. Take this flagon and fill it,
And fetch a bowl, and apple-crabs for ducking.
[*He tosses the flagon to Yaughan, who catches it.*]
We 'll hallow this e'en with child-mirth. Here they come—
The children of Elsinore. Fetch eke thine own
Sistren and brother-laddies from thy garth.
We 'll lure the wee folk wi' wee apples, and make
Elf-cherries of 'em.

YAUGHAN

Aye, so will I, Master!

[*Exit, smiling, with flagon, through gate, right, as enter, left,* MOLL COWSLIP, *with* PRINCE HAMLET *and* LAERTES, *accompanied by a* LAD, *with a coiled rope in his hand. Yorick moves toward them, greeting Moll first.*]

YORICK

Moll, welcome!—Now the tolling bell hath ceased,
You all can hear the tinkle of my cap.
Welcome, crony-boys!—Here are Hallowe'en trophies
To trim your bonnets.
[*Plucking them from the wall and handing to each.*]
Hamlet, here 's bittersweet
To be thy crest, and hallow every bitter
With sweet o' thy Yorick's love. Laertes, wear
These frosty hips, for they are roses' helmets,
Fit for a hardy soldier-lad, to keep
Shining in his armoury.
[*To the third one.*]
—Ha, Richard Bell-Ringer,
Himself! So, Dick, I see thou bearest with thee
Thy wreath of office, e'en as I my staff.
What ropéd twist is this?

DICK, THE BELL-RINGER

Sir, 't is a tail
Of a chime's rope, got broken off. I be sent
To fetch a new piece.

YORICK

Couldst thou splice the old?

DICK

Aye, Sir.

YORICK

And canst thou play *Old Bob* on the chimes?

DICK

Aye, that I can, Sir, when the other lads
Jerk with me.

YORICK

Are the others handy now
By the chapel?

DICK

Aye; they 're in the belfry, Sir.

YORICK

Then haste thee back, and bid 'em play *Old Bob,*
To Hallowe'en, whiles here we bob in the bowl
For crabbies.

MOLL COWSLIP

Ha, but trothsake, Master Fool,
Shall *Old Bob* suit to play at Holy Mass?

YORICK

Old Bob is hallowéd, this thousand year,
For mirth of Mary's babe.

MOLL

Ah, well.

YORICK

[*To Dick.*]

So, haste thee,
And jerk the chimes a merry whirl.

DICK

Aye, aye, Sir. [*Exit.*]

PRINCE HAMLET

[*Who, with Laertes, having trimmed his bonnet, has been gazing up at the poled Owl.*]

Is this thy staff of office, Yorick? Methought,
Such be thy belled cap.

YORICK

Hast not watched me blink
Mine eyes before? Look! Blaze they not blue-green?

LAERTES

[*As Yorick widens his eyes at them.*]

Why, no. They 're hazel hue.

YORICK

Ah, but my pole-staff
Bespeaks mine owlish spirit, and that same
Is wove of hazel-boughs, with leaves in moonshine—
Earth-green with heaven-hue. Come! Help me place it
Now, i' this earth-patch. Here the Owl shall scan
Our merriment, and wisdom it with night-thoughts
Of the dear lady-mother dead, who 'd fain
Lift up her babe, that lieth in her blue basket,
To hark the joys of Hamlet and Laertes
Afore the far to-morrows dawn blood-red.
Here. Tip the pole straight. Steady! Scoop the loam
So—round it. Stamp it down. Soon cometh Yaughan

With crab-apples and bowls of well-water
For faery duckings.—First, though, whilst we 'wait 'em,
Yorick shall hold his goblin school; for hark! . .

[*Pausing, as the Children stare, he intones weirdly.*]

High on a hoar hillside of hardhack I hear
A hobgoblin hammering a horse-heel hoof!—[17]

'Ware! 'Ware!

For 'a holdeth the horseshoe horns-up'ards, like the owl's ears,
So they shall hold the hoary wisdom in,
And let none spill; for little folk must sip
Of ancient luck and lore, and let naught slip
'Twixt thumb and fingers from the supping lip;
For all of history, which time doth nick
On calendars of old arithmetic,
Is summed up, out of all earth understands,
In one face, thumbs twain, fingers of two hands.
Sit! To our tasks, lest goblins hobble round
To pick up answer-errors on the ground.
Now, to it! Hamlet, first, and count your gains:
Subtract thy nose from thy face, and what remains?

PRINCE HAMLET

I know! I watched thee do it afore.

[*He makes a twisting snatch with his hand at Yorick's nose, darting back the hand with thumb squeezed between fingers, and exclaims triumphantly.*]

A thumb!

YORICK

[*Drawing a long face.*]

Now am I noseless to smell peach or plum! [*Then quickly.*]
Divide all fingers by both thumbs.—Come, come,
Laertes, answer!

LAERTES

Four.

YORICK

[*Holds his hands, with thumbs touching each other, thus showing four fingers on each side of each thumb.*]

Two fours:—That 's *eight!*

[*The Children giggle.*]

Now, figure this—and keep your faces straight:
Add two lips to two lips. How many is
That sum of lips, good Moll?

MOLL

Four.

YORICK

Nay,

[*Suddenly smacking her lips with his.*]

—*one kiss!*

[*All roar with laughter, while Moll thwacks Yorick with her palms and fists till, dodging her, he holds up his finger, and goes on, turning toward Topas.*]

Multiply thy chin by thy crown. Answer!

TOPAS

[*Winking one eye at Yorick.*]

—*A beard!*

But, marry, mine 's a goat's, unripe to be sheared.

[*More laughter.*]

YORICK

Finis, mathematics! Now, for a riddle match.
Yoricus Asinus shall both toss and catch:
What spittal, spat in the ear, maketh eyes to shine? . .
I 'll answer that.—*A witty word.* That 's mine.
What small, clay pot holdeth the sun and moon? . .
None knoweth?—*The skull.* Now, for a final boon.
Tell me: *What seeth sans eyes, smelleth sans nose,*
Tasteth sans tongue? . . *Thought.* So, with thought, we close

These gates of sense. And now, in nonsense, snicker
This, if you can, in tempo quicker and quicker:

Was it Gilly, the goat heard, scraping steel
In the pitch-dark pit of the goat-herd,
Or the herd-scaped goat, stealing home to the herd,
Heard by Gilly, the goatherd?

Topas, herd thou thy goat, till I 've heard Gilly
Tune down this timing-rhyming see-saw-silly
To welcome Yaughan back, with his well-water
And ducking-bowls; for now I hear the stir
Of neighbour folk in the alleys.

YAUGHAN

[*Entering with a small rabble of children and country folk.*]

Hallowe'en!
Happy a Hallowe'en, my masters all!

ALL

Happy Hallowe'en!

YAUGHAN

Where shall I set the bowls?

YORICK

Here, round the Owl-lantern.

PRINCE HAMLET

I 'll show thee, Yaughan.

YORICK

Have welcome, hallowers of old Earth! Howe'er
Ancient a witch she seem, crutching her path
Betwixt Orion and the Milky Way,
With blinkings of her eyes in starry nooks,
She possums in her nods and winks, for she 's
A maskéd sprite, and weaves her wintry shrouds
Of daisy-chains, being—I tell you, secret—

The mother of Queen Mab, and twice hath twinned
An ogre with an elf, a giant ouphe
With Thumbling. Mistress Merryprank she 's, too,
And when folk sicken, she doseth buttermilk
To ailing grannies, and spiced rum-eggnog
To bawling babies. Most, she loves to sit
With sweethearts on a wild-rose bank, and feed 'em
Choke-cherry jam, until they die agiggling.
And so, my dears, she turneth to each of us
A cheek of laughter, with her lover's heart,
This old dear Earth, we hallow. Then let 's up
Belive with her, and give her tat for tit,
To prove our love. So pick we now our fellows,
And go find earth-friends on the grass; for he,
Who findeth friend and peereth in his eyes,
Peeps at himself there. Try it. Pick away, now!
But ye, who come with kobold clogs to dance it,
Or ye, with goblin grins to snuggle kisses,
Or ye, on gaffer crutches, come to o'ertop
New tricks with old—all ye!—hark the fool's preachment:
Friendship is born of difference. So, pick
Your opposites for cronies, and the world
Will weep glad tears. Belive, then! Pick your partners,
Jill with big Jack, faery with goblin-grinner,
And lumpkin-leg with pixy-on-tiptoe,
And Yorick, he 'll cry *Mum!* for his.

MOLL

[*As all scurry about for partners, taps Yorick under the chin.*]

'A *will* not!

Here 's *me.*

YORICK

[*Widening his eyes.*]

Thee?

MOLL

Aye, the one as borned thy Angie.

YORICK
[*Hugs her, weeping.*]

Angie!

MOLL

E'en let us dribble. *She* be glad
To swab thy tears, and wipe my nose of 'em.

YORICK

Moll,

Thou knewest her Momsy, too!

MOLL

I never knewed

A purtier.

YORICK
[*Kissing her.*]

Thanks.

PRINCE HAMLET
[*Who has drawn near, puzzled.*]

What, art thou weeping, Fool?

YORICK

Moon water.

[*Pointing up at the slim crescent.*]

See! The sickle 's slant. It spilled.

PRINCE HAMLET

And wilt thou kiss me, too?

YORICK

All thou 'lt gie me back!

[*They kiss and hug each other. From afar comes the sound of bells.*]

PRINCE HAMLET

Hark! Hark yonder, Yorick!

YORICK

Heigh, the chimes!
'Tis *Old Bob,* ringing: "Duck it!"—Duck I will,
Old Bob—to heaven at the bottom. Come
Away! Away to the bobbing!—Are the bowls filled?

YAUGHAN

Aye, Sir—brim-over. And bitefuls o' the big apples, bouncing.

TOPAS

And swallowfuls o' the wee wild crabbies, to tease 'em.

YORICK

Hoho! Halloa to Hallowe'en! Heigh-ho it!

ALL

Hoho! Halloa to Hallowe'en! Heigh-ho!

YORICK

Afore we duck, we 'll lift our lilt to the wee-apples,
The cherrycheekt, red-rosy crabbies, whiles Old Bob
Calleth from chapel and ringeth his bobbing chimes.
Ye ken the tune: *Wild Crabbies.* Together, all! Follow!
[*Singing.*]
Come, come, come, come!

[*Waving his hand, he leads them in the song, while they follow him, in an antique dance-step of ducking and bobbing, round and round the pole of the Owl-lantern, in and out among the apple-ducking bowls.*]

ALL

Come, come, come, come!
Duck, duck, my dearie,
Where the heart 's top-heady
And the water beats rum
I' the bobbing-bowl, that 's ready:

For hallow, hallow, hallow be your e'en
In the candle-sheen
Of stars that garland the pole
Standing steady
I' the bottom-top o' the bowl
Heady-ready.

YORICK

[*Pausing a moment, as he calls through the distant bell-chiming.*]

Hoho, Hallowe'en! Halloa! Hoho!

ALL

[*Calling, in answer, like a far echo.*]

Hoho, Hallowe'en! . Halloa! . . Hoho! . . .

YORICK

[*Singing again, both his arms uplifted.*]

Come, come, come, come!

ALL

[*Singing, as they follow again his leading in the dance.*]

Come, come, come, come!
Duck, duck, my dearie,
And bob for the blisses
O' the wee-apple kisses,
Crabbies that crinkle the smile of a cherry:
Bite the mad-merry
Cheeks o' the red-rosy cherry,
But spit out the stone—
Spit, spit, spit, spit,
Spit every spittal-bit,
Spit out the stone
That choketh the breath of your only own
Ducky-ducky-dearie:
Spit out the stone o' the rosy-red cherry!

YORICK

[*Calls, as the chimes are dying away.*]

Ho-ho-ho! . Ho-ho! . . Ho-halloa . . . Hallowe'en . . . . !

ALL
[*Calling, in echo.*]

Ho-ho-ho! . Ho-ho! . . Ho-halloa . . . Hallowe'en . . . . !

CLAUDIUS
[*Who has stridden from the Castle into their midst.*]

Yokels and yodellers from hell! What hoots
Of horny owls are these?—Unhallowed fool,
Yorick! How durst thou lead, in goblin dance,
This antick pandemonium of fiends
In sacred nearness to death and solemn prayers
Of Holy Mass?

YORICK
[*Lilts, quietly.*]

Let no man's foot trespass
Thy kingdom in the grass
His fellow's to gain . . .

You have His answer, Sir.

MOLL

And mine, to boot!

CLAUDIUS

What, wife! Thou, too? What, what!
Is 't so thou servest her majesty's command
To soothe this poor bereavéd child with thoughts
Of consolation for his mother's death?

MOLL

"Thoughts lighter than that heavy loss," she bid me
Fetch to the laddie. Lighter danceth life
Than death, methinketh; so, to follow fool
Leadeth him up the dale, not down the valley
To the shadow. Danskers aye be dancers, Sir,
And me, I be a Dansker, heel to headpiece.

TOPAS

Aye, that she be! I followed to her heel,
And nigh it hit my headpiece wi' her clog.

CLAUDIUS

[As stifled laughter breaks around him.]

Stop snickering, louts! Off to your alleys! Else—
What else, ye 'd best not stay, to stick in your bellies.
Be off!

PRINCE HAMLET

Good night, dear Yorick!

YORICK

Good night, sweet Prince!

[He kisses the hand of the child, who—turning with Laertes and Moll toward the Castle—looks back from the doorway, with frowning dignity, at Claudius, as the Others go off, with their gleaming jack-lights, leaving only the poled Owl-lantern and the sickle moon, beyond the garden wall, shining palely down upon Yorick and Claudius, facing each other on the sward.]

CLAUDIUS

"Dear Yorick!"—and "Good night, sweet Prince!"—
The Prince
Saith not unto the Duke: "Good night, sweet Uncle!"
Didst mark it, Master Fool?

YORICK

Yourself hath marked it
Past need for Yorick's commentary. Yet
One note I 'll jot in the margin of this moment:
Frowns of the child bode tempests in the man.—
O Claudius, why not rather be Claudio,
Sweet uncle and dear brother of Elsinore,
Than glowering Caligula, raper of Rome?[18]

CLAUDIUS

Raper and glowerer!—Thy commentary
Breeds compliments. Were not thy tinkling fool's-cap

Signpost of sanctuary, thou shouldst bleed
Red dews on this hoar garden-grass, instead
Of apple-juice, for these unduckéd bowls
Waiting for bitten fruit.

YORICK

Here 's one unbitten
As yet, for which you are not bidden to duck,
But, if bite you must, then bite it yourself, and not
Offer it to Eve again.

CLAUDIUS

Is this another
Riddle-match?

YORICK

Perhaps it is. 'T is certainly
[*Taking it from his pocket and showing.*]
An apple—pluckt from Eden, by thine advice,
Serpens.

CLAUDIUS
[*Glaring.*]

Ha!

YORICK

Tosst by the Queen—recall'st thou?—
Where the fool picked it up, that he might here
Return it to the apple-agent.

CLAUDIUS

Gratias!

[*Taking from Yorick the apple, Claudius puts it in his tabard pocket.*]

YORICK

The poke thou hidest it in, lurks near thy heart.
Let it not rot there, lest it sow infection

With its seed, and raise thee *rigor mortis.* 'Tis
A rosy apple, overripe with knowledge.
Bite it, thyself,—but spit, spit, spit out the core!

CLAUDIUS

I choose to digest it, ere it rot.

YORICK

'Tis well.
Digest, but not disgorge it, *Serpens* dear.
Skin, thou canst slough; and head, thou canst unmask—
To *be* the Angel thou didst emulate.
Oh, *be* him, then! Be not thy bellied self,
But wingéd. Choose thy real part—that 's royal
Beyond all theft of queens, to win a crown
That 's freely given thee, by merely willing it
To be thy self-gift.

CLAUDIUS

Merely willing it?

YORICK

Ha,
That *merely!* Yea, echo me that acid word—
Mere—mere. In that murk tarn of sucking quicksands
What millions are swallowed down to blinded gropings
Through mystery of weedy darkness!—*Will,*
And *choice,* and *freedom:* all "mere" words,
Till *will* is quickt, *choice* wrought, and *freedom* fought—
By *love.* Love, then, dear Claudio, thy self
Too dearly, ever to pawn it for another.

CLAUDIUS

What other?

YORICK

Thine other self: not Claudio,
But Claudius; not *Pater Coeli,* 't is,

But *Serpens.* Save thy life, by sacrifice
To Gertrude, not *of* Gertrude, and so save
Her life, and Hamlet's, with thine own.

CLAUDIUS

My life 's
Mine own. To save it—*I* 'll will how: not thou.

YORICK

And wisely said. We are well free of each other.
So, as you wish! This moment 's for free choice.
All lives are ours for choosing, only one
For willing. Good night,—Claudio!

[*He starts away, right.*]

CLAUDIUS

[*Suddenly changing to a suave tone.*]

Thou wilt
Return here?

YORICK

When their majesties return
From Mass.

CLAUDIUS

That will be soon. Why not
Await them here? And you may give them message
From me. Yonder 's a bench, where you can sit
And while the time with lilting, as you list
So fondly to do.

YORICK

Thanks. I 'll return to it
Before they come. The lilt 's still in my legs
And I must foot it off.

CLAUDIUS

Tell them, I 'm gone

Into the Castle, to my chamber—mine,
Not theirs, to 'wait them. This door leads me yonder.

YORICK

There is a door, that leads to doorlessness,
And I am that way headed—yea, and hearted,
For hallow, hallow, hallow is this e'en.

[*He moves slowly toward the garden gate, right, as Claudius pauses at the Castle door, hesitant.*]

CLAUDIUS

Hallowe'en!—In truth, this eve is elfin-strange;
And the new moon, beyond that hornéd lantern,
Curves glintier than the Owl's eyes—like a curl
Blown thither, perchance, out of that 'reaved babe's cradle,
New-born to this world of willing and unwilling
To 'scape its thraldom—even by a wisp in the air,
Breathed by pent winds of yearning! . . Art thou gone,
Yorick? Wilt not thou tarry yet—and I—
Perhaps—The door 's still wide.—

YORICK

Nay, doorlessness
Is wider still.— [*Lilting, as he wanders off.*]

So squanter, will I, by my lone,
Far from scan of proud and fickle,
To reap a love-sheaf of my own
With the moon sickle! [*Exit.*]

CLAUDIUS

[*Moves back upon the sward, and stands, pausing.*]

Doors!—Ever my haunted mind is hedged with doors. .
"A door, there is, that leads to doorlessness,"
Another, leading to a lady's chamber.
One leadeth to the other.—There 's a ladder . . .

[*Slowly, he moves toward the door, ajar in the dim garden wall, and passes inward, behind.*

While he is disappearing, there sounds—from far off—a drowsy calling of COCK-CROW.

After a long moment, there is a rustling, and the form of YORICK *shows again in the Owl-lantern's gleam, as he moves along the grass to the bench, where he sits, and strums low on his psaltery, which he has brought back with him.*

Pausing, he reaches one hand to the wall beside him, and fingers something on the climbing vine there.]

YORICK

The rose-hips, aye, and bittersweet—they twine
Together in seed-time. Truth is quick, not dead—
Froze solid forever. Nay, 't is seasonal,
And in dear springtide sweet doth shed its bitter,
And frore hips bud red roses in the vine.
Ah, newly, newly, newly, the red, red rose
Is June-sprung. The bleak mind blooms melody,
And in the heart, 't is Autumn-April, and October
Kisseth June's cheeks, till her love-tears rain laughter
Of linnets and wrenny-birds.—Mariana mine,
Our Angie's own Momsy, oureachother's own!
I 've reaped our love-sheaf with the moon's clean sickle
(For thou art the Unseen Lady in the orb it curveth!)
And all, 't is thine. And soon—soon—when the lark
Is ready, I will wattle a May-basket
Of red rose-hips and yellowy bittersweet
And rosemary, twined all with Marybuds,
Tangled so full of lilting laughter-tunes
That, when I tie it under his lifting wings,
The blue, blue skies o' thy witchling eyes shall spill it
In rillets of gladness.—Listen!—High o'er the mists—
Listen!—dost thou hear it—piercing, untouched, clear,
So sweet and fresh—our lark!—He sings and sings
To thee of me, of thee to me—he sings! . . . [19]
Ah, cease, cease, cease, sweet bird! O, love! Ah, pang,
Cease!—Hush, hush, hush!—For how else can I know
Thou hearest his song—my song, which is thee,
Heart of my sorrow?—Hush!

[*Softly, he sings, to his psaltery.*]

Hush, Gladness, Gladness!
Where the dumb rose-hips
So palely blush—
O, hush
Your song on those frozen lips!
For O, mad is—mad is this
Gladness,
Unless it cease where melody
And my lost love with dear June lie.—
Ah, would so could I!

See page 673

[*From behind the wall, above him, shadowed against the crescent moon, appear the head and shoulders of* CLAUDIUS, *who reaches his right hand to the great half-lodged top-stone.*]

CLAUDIUS

[*In low voice.*]

The hand of man shall ease the Hand of God.

[*He pushes the stone.*

DARKNESS

and a moaned cry . . . answered by the far COCK-CROW.]

*The darkness is broken by gleams of lanterns, held by Three Figures—*YAUGHAN, *at left, the* KING *and* QUEEN, *at right, staring down where, in the dimness,* YORICK *lies half prone, propped against the squatted figure of* TOPAS, *whose arms and gaze are fondling him.*

KING HAMLET

Speak, fellow!—Doth he live?

TOPAS

'A 's slipt away, Sir,
And curleth to me, clumpy as a kitten
Afore it hath its eyes. I ha' no dugs,
But, Mass! 'a pokes to feel 'em.

GERTRUDE

Breathes he still?

TOPAS

'A purreth, like.

KING HAMLET

How could it hap?

TOPAS

The rock, Sir,
It toppled down.

YAUGHAN

Aye, it were Hand o' God.
It crashed the bench's end, and mote ha' crumpled
Yorick, but mere it whanged his skull and rib.

KING HAMLET

Ah, God, my fool, my fool!—This elvish owl-light
Blinks darkness. Let me come close.—What 's here,
That tinkles?—Ha, his cap!—Is this blood on 't?

TOPAS

Blood, 't is, Sir. His head 's clouted wi' my sleeve.
I tore it off.

GERTRUDE

Poor blessed dear one!—Quick,
Send for the priest—the Padre.

YAUGHAN

'A cometh straight, Ma'am.
I 's been and told.

TOPAS
[*With a hushing gesture.*]

'A winketh open. Whisht! . .
[*A pause, of silence.*]

KING HAMLET
[*Softly.*]

Yorick!

YORICK
[*Stirring.*]

She saith, it is the moon-sickle;
But see,—'t is naught but my thumb-nail, broke off.

KING HAMLET

What?

YORICK

Nothing. 'T is nothing.

KING HAMLET

Who said it?

YORICK

Angie. But—
'T is nothing.

KING HAMLET

What did . . ?

TOPAS

Whisht, Sir. 'A 's slipt away
Again.

[*Enter, from the Castle,* PADRE CELESTINO *and* MOLL COWSLIP, *hastening.*]

CELESTINO

Ben'cite! All is well, I see.

MOLL COWSLIP

'A coloureth like the babe, in yon. 'A 'll live!

GERTRUDE

Oh, do you think it?

MOLL

Blush-rosy!

KING HAMLET

God, woman!
That blush is blood.

MOLL

Ha, blood or blush, 'a 'll fetch it.

[*Exclaiming, suddenly, to Yorick, loud and tart.*]

Fool!

[*Starting up, Yorick stares at her; then slowly winks one eye, crinkling a smile.*]

YORICK

Fisher! Angle thy hook lower.

[*He beckons with his forefinger, till Moll bends close over him.*]

So:
Smack hath it, again!

[*He gives her a loud-smacking kiss, and sinks back, breathing hard.*]

Two catches, in one night.

[*Yaughan and Topas stifle their mouths.*]

MOLL

Horn-pouter, I 'll gi'e thee double i' the gills.

[*She stoops again, and gives him two resounding kisses.*]

TOPAS

[*Bursting out.*]

Ah, haw! The whoresons, both!

KING HAMLET

Yorick!

GERTRUDE

Heaven's mercy!

What! Doth our fool play possum?

YORICK

Madam——

TOPAS

[*Choking, with aghast laughter.*]

Haw, Mass!

YORICK

Topas, methought I smelled it. Why saidest thou
"Dugs," ha? Thou meantest "bungs." Smell o' thy tabard.
Thou leakest Rhenish yet.

TOPAS

I 'll bleed to death with 't,

Afore thou dost.

[*He bursts out roaring.*]

KING HAMLET

Dearest fool, is all of this
Mere Hallowe'en madness?—Nay, for thou bleedest sore.
Great God!

YORICK

Aye, truly,—great is God, and good;

And—pardon, Madam,—gentle Lord He is
Of possums, as of priests—though I am neither.
Yet thou art one, good Padre: make my peace,
Prithee, *in veritate.*

CELESTINO

Verily
Our bleeding fool hath spoken it, dear Queen:
Our God is mirthful in His playful mercies,
And playeth possum to console His sorrows,
Not to irk His children, knowing He knoweth nothing
But His own good of any—even as Yorick,
His servant, knoweth it from Him.

GERTRUDE

Thanks, Padre.
Thy pardon, Fool deaı. Hamlet, we should dwell
With folk of simple faith and merry courage,
More in our garden and garth, less in our Castle
Of Elsinore.

KING HAMLET

True, Gertrude. Tell me, Yorick,
What can thy king still do to serve thee?

YORICK

Nothing—
And that is far too much. I 'd tell you more
Of that Great Nothing, but now——

TOPAS

Sst, sst! 'A 's slipping—

YORICK
[*Beckoning feebly to the King.*]

Where 's thy sweet kin?

KING HAMLET

Kin?

YORICK

Alcyone,
My Hamle'kins, my princey-pigaback?

GERTRUDE
[*To Moll.*]

Where tookest thou the child?

MOLL

To the Castle.

KING HAMLET

Fetch him,
In haste.

YORICK

Nay, let 'm ride softly, not a-gallop.
Tell him—go *pacey* in his uncle's path,
For *pacey goes the countryman* to quiet—
To quiet—up yon, where I 've a giftie for 'm—
A Hallowe'en giftie—up there! 'T is my curved nail;
And tell him, whene'er he spyeth it in his dreams,
To lilt this lilt to 't:

New Moon, New Moon, in my nap,
Merry thou dost sing:
"I am Yorick's nail-paring,
Flickt from off his big thumb's cap,
Telling all: I care not that—not *that*
Flick of a nail's tat-tat
For all earthy
Clutch of fingers for trouble:
But only for the mirthy
Bliss o' the unseen bubble
I hold in my arms, where it glistens the tress
Of the lovely trembling nothingness
And the nobody-can-see-me grace
Of my Lady's face. . . "

KING HAMLET

Of whose face doth he speak?

TOPAS

The Lady's, i' the moon.

KING HAMLET

But 't is the full moon only showeth a face.
The new moon holdeth nothing.

YORICK

Nothing: aye,
And Nobody can see it, for Nobody peereth
In the Padre's book, *Amor,* where her picture smileth,
Nor in *The Book of Job,* where she weepeth sore,
Nor yet in mine own, *The Book of Nob,* which Nobody
Hath writ and read, for 't is all lilted full
Of lovely Nothingness, which Nobody
Loveth so well as Yorick, and lilteth it with him—
Ah, yes, 't is nothing.

[*Starting up to a sitting posture, with sudden fierceness.*]

Yet Nobody hath a wit
To know—*Something!* Though the Word of it once scooped
A deeper pit in Nothingness—than this
Death-trap, dug in a crumbling garden-wall—
But the Word clave *Light!* And the dumb oceans roared
With Light, and the roaring blew a blast, that shuddered
The walls of Jericho, till the topmost stones
Came tumbling—not one, but wallfuls, and the shattered
Souls below awoke, and uprose, and *laughed*—
And all was wondering laughter . . .

[*He sinks back, with closed eyes, against Topas.*]

KING HAMLET

Ha, and what possum 's this! 'T is a lion, wounded,

And I will kneel, to touch his swathéd mane
In royal allegiance.

[*He kneels, and strokes very softly Yorick's bandaged head.*]

Gentle brother King,
What thou hast ruminated in the jungles
Of this fen world, and muted in thy roar
To lilts of mirth, and learned to clowns in courtyards,
And kings in castle-chambers—*this* shall outbrave
The blaring of scorn-bugles, and the piping
Of shrill politicos, and bring us heart-peace
For passion's rack, when the infected mists
Roll seaward, and we draw deep-lunged sun-breaths
Above this rock, fallen from its climbing roses,
Pitted in night,—aye, and we 'll laugh God's praise
With thee, our Yorick!—Alas, he heareth not.

YORICK

[*Faintly.*]

Ah, but he heareth.

[*Sitting up again.*]

And he would tell still more
How 't is, that 't is all—nothing, portion and all
Of the Great Nothingness, whither forever
The infected mists and deep sun-breaths
Roll seaward over this surge of time to His shore,
Where—hark!—the deep boom of the tidal breaker,
Near—nearer . . One more is rolling up the slopes
To that ultimate, heavenly ascension, when this initial
Phase is mingled with the passions of the ages
And—big with ardours—it rolls off into the Unknown . . .
Hark, Lady in the Moon! With thee, with thee, let me live—
Live a vibrating unison of harmonies
To the greatness of the spirit, to the melody
Of beauty—of blossoming flowers—glowing surges of
colour—
Immense visions, pulsing passions, exquisite fancies,

Delicate conceits of lacéd foam, sprinkling the edges
Of gracious reveries, and austere beatitudes—
There, there, forever, into eternity[20]
The miracle of thy comrade soul beside me,
Through lives to come, still to press on, as together
We face infinitude, heads up!—God's wind in our faces,
Blowing to us, from us—the love, love, love, that is pain . .
Ah, Lady in the new moon's nothingness—hearest thou?
Aye, and thou answerest: On with the new life,[21]
Good work, sweet play, serenity, joy to all men:
Ring out, ye bells—To-morrow—to-morrow is May Day!

[*Starting to his feet, his face still upward turned to the sickle moon, he sinks slantwise into the arms of Padre Celestino, who kneels to the ground with the weight of his body, which he lays stretched, listening at the heart for a long moment, while the others gaze down there. So, glancing near him, he lifts from the ground Yorick's psaltery, and looks up, with a smile.*]

CELESTINO

Now he lives in to-morrow. Kneel with me, friends,
Beside this brave, sweet instrument of gladness.
Yorick is gone.

[*Slowly, they all kneel. Celestino puts finger to his lip.*]

Silenzio! Let us pray—
And mirthfully!

[*All lift their faces toward the New Moon, while Celestino, thrumming the psaltery's strings, intones low, to the tune of Yorick's lilt, as the curtain falls.*]

Our Father dear, which art
In every foolish heart
To make it heaven . . .

CURTAIN.

ACT FIFTH

GRAVEYARD, ELSINORE.

Before the curtain rises, a bell is heard, tolling to another rhythm than its former cadences, accompanied by VOICES *of Men, Women and Children, singing, together, in mingled harmony.*

Dead, bow thy head
To dust, where the living start.
Lover, lift up thy heart
To the dead.

Ye, whose yearning after
Life, in the dust that lies,
Is the fool's learning, and laughter
Of the wise,

With the dead, out of dust,
Be your immortal trust
Born, to rise.

On lifting of the curtain, those who were singing are discovered gathered about two graves, near each other [upper left centre, and lower right centre]. Beside each, mounds of newly upshovelled earth are whitened over with light driftings of snow, under drooping boughs of ancient weeping-willows.

At the upper grave, YAUGHAN *is standing; in the lower grave, the form of* TOPAS *is sunken, his head and shoulders just visible above it.*

Besides these two, among the assemblage of castle-folk and peasantry, are KING HAMLET, GERTRUDE, CLAUDIUS, PRINCE HAMLET, POLONIUS, LAERTES, MOLL COWSLIP *and* PADRE CELESTINO.

KING HAMLET

Let rest our double burden! Lift we now
Ourselves from under it. Herewith we give
Back to old Earth these loanings from her hoard,
But keep the golden balance, earned of them,
Exceeding all earth-offerings, howsoe'er
Dear they erst were to us, and dearly treasured
Even to these bitter tears. Here, dumb and cold,
Have fallen in the cracking frost two brave abodes
Of goodliness, whose spirit-tenants speed now

To fresh embodiments of melody
And warmth within these houses, still left standing
Here at their graves—our hearts, which hold them
'Gainst dispossessing death, and give them home-come
Of housewarming so glad, that this white pall
Of pure snowdrift turns all to fine linen, cherished
In heaven's chambers, to heap 'em coverlids
Of stainless welcome, each in kind.—For these
So twain in semblance were in substance like.—
Cornelia, demure, of gentle ladies firmest;
Yorick, unconscionable, gentlest of fools:
The brackish rain that beat upon them both,
Crushing their fair birth-flowers, and saltening
Their garden soil with death, still failed to purge
Their staunchness of its savour, or unsweeten
The hardy roots of heavenliness they sprung from.
God's peace to them, within us!—Here, without,
To you, Polonius, sore-stricken man
Of this sweet wife,—our sorrowing love!

POLONIUS
[*Huskily.*]

Dear King,
My thanks,—and hers!

LAERTES

Father, don't weep,—prithee, prithee!
I won't—not even for her. Soldiers don't weep.
My lord, the King, look, Sir! This is my bonnet.
Here 's rose-hips on 't, that Yorick bid me wear
To prove I 'm soldier. I will give it back, now,
To him, and show I ha' not forgot. He 'll know,
And see, I love him more than all of you.

[*He throws the bonnet in the grave, and, flinging himself down on the heaped earth beside it, calls down from the edge.*]

Yorick, Yorick, Yorick!—Rose-hips—'T is Laertes!

PRINCE HAMLET

More, more, more! Ha, wilt love him more than me?
[*Throwing his own bonnet into the grave.*]
Yorick—bittersweet!—This is Hamlet, thy crony!

LAERTES
[*Leaping up.*]

The devil take thee! [*Grappling with him.*]
—So!

GERTRUDE
[*Crying out.*]

Child, child!

POLONIUS

Laertes!

KING HAMLET

Put them apart!

GERTRUDE

Hamlet!

MOLL COWSLIP

Good Puss, be quiet!

PRINCE HAMLET
[*To Laertes.*]

Take off thy hand! I love him more than any—

LAERTES

I tell 'ee, Yorick 's *mine,* not thine!

CELESTINO
[*Separating them.*]

Pax, pax!
[*With gentle, commanding gesture.*]

Yorick is calling us.—Hark!

[*The Children stare up at him bewilderedly.*]

LAERTES

Yorick?

CELESTINO

Listen.

PRINCE HAMLET

Where?

CELESTINO

[*As far-away chimes sound faintly.*]

Yonder! 'Tis Old Bob's voice. Can ye not hear
The words he 's lilting?

BOTH

[*Awesomely.*]

No.

CELESTINO

I hear them, as plainly
As I heard the tune, last night. I 'll lilt them soft:

[*He sings to the far bells.*]

Ring me Old Bob, *when I die,*
And let the chimes whirl away merry,
For I bobbed for a rosy wee crabbie, did I,
And spit out the stone o' the cherry.

And now, my dears, Old Bob is still, but Yorick
Hath had his wish, and we must *do* his wishing,
And spit out the stone of this hard quarrel within
The hearts of us, like Yorick, must n't we?
And that will prove who loves him more than any,
So who 'll spit out the stone?

[*He pauses, while the Children wince. Then slowly their faces reflect Celestino's gaze at them.*]

PRINCE HAMLET
[*Smiling back, spits softly.*]

'T is out. [*To Laertes.*] Thy hand!

LAERTES
[*Giving it.*]

Here 't is.

CELESTINO

Brave clasp! Now let your heads follow hands
And don your crests again, to wear as fellows
Not feudists of our dear fool's love.—Up, Topas!
Restore the bittersweet and roses' helmets
To these young masters of the guild of Yorick.

TOPAS
[*Handing them from the grave, as he climbs out of it.*]

Here, laddies: ha' your bonnets.

PRINCE HAMLET
[*Taking his, puts it on.*]

Thanks.

LAERTES
[*Doing the same with his.*]

We 'll wear 'em.

KING HAMLET

Methinks, our Padre holds the master-key
To this sweet sequel.—Father, lead us away
Now, from these dark and closing doors of clay.
Toward brighter vistas, opening before us.

CLAUDIUS
[*Glancing toward Gertrude, who returns his glance, half repellingly.*]

Yea,
Toward vistas opening brighter! Let us delay
No longer here.

KING HAMLET

[*Affectionately, to Gertrude and Claudius.*]

Come, wife, and brother dear!

[*Padre Celestino signals to the others and leads them from the scene. The last to disappear are Gertrude and Claudius, who pauses and sits on an upturned turf near the grave of Yorick, while those in procession are passing off, singing together.*]

ALL

Dead, bow thy head
To the dust, where thy shards dispart.
Living, lift up thy heart
To the dead.

Joy, pluck thy flower
From dust, in the dark of night.
Sorrower, suck all affright
From the dour.

Out of dust, with the dead,
Grievers, glad be your tread
Into light!

[*Meanwhile, standing in the graves, Topas and Yaughan turn to their work.*

Grasping a shovel, stuck upright in the mound of earth beside him, Topas pulls it out, and begins shovelling the snow-layered clay into Yorick's grave.]

CLAUDIUS

[*To himself, as he watches Topas at work.*]

The hand of God is eased,—so is my heart!
The clay that mends walls closeth lips. All 's dumb
Under the dirt. *There* is a muted kingdom,
Where court-fools fumble with their double meanings
And mumble secrets only to the worms.—
Now can I breathe free!

[*In his work, Topas accidentally dislodges some earth very near to him.*]

TOPAS

Begging my lord's pardon—

[*Begins singing.*]

In youth when I did love—did love——

CLAUDIUS

"Did love"!—Fellow, did'st not thou love him—Yorick,
The fool?

TOPAS

Aye, Sir.

CLAUDIUS

So why now dost thou sing
To bury him?

TOPAS

Why not? Love is the lilting
He larned me up on; burying be my trade;
I shovel dirt, Sir; you, my lord, sit on it.

Under shovel
All must hovel.

Sitter in the sun
Thinketh: Will be done!

CLAUDIUS

[*To himself.*]

True 't is! I am a sitter in the sun,
And so think I.—But *whose* will done? Now will I
Arise, and learn the willing of the thinking.

[*He rises, and moves slowly, left, towards where Gertrude stands hesitant, peering back towards him.*]

"A door that leads to doorlessness"?—Nay, Fool,
I knock on a door that opens a secret room.—

[*He approaches Gertrude.*]

TOPAS

[*Singing as he shovels.*]

In youth, when I did love—did love—
Methought, it was very sweet . . . [22]

[*While his voice is dying away in dusk, and the figures of Claudius and Gertrude, on the edge of the scene, stand, side by side, gazing at Yorick's grave, the dusk deepens into total dark.*]

Slowly from the dark emerges the luminous oblong of
A CLOSED DOOR,
with a KNOCKER *in the shape of* RAM'S HORNS.
Against its glow is standing
THE SHADOW OF CLAUDIUS,
who knocks once, emitting a low, verberating clang, through which is heard in higher pitch a poignant voice as of Gertrude speaking.

VOICE OF GERTRUDE

Who 's there?

SHADOW OF CLAUDIUS

I—and the air.

VOICE [*within*]—What will you, so?
SHADOW [*without*]—All we know.
VOICE—I know naught.
SHADOW—So I thought,
And I know.
VOICE—What?
SHADOW—Good is slow.
Swift is sin.
May I come in?
VOICE—No.
SHADOW—So!—
What then? [*He knocks, once.*]
VOICE—Again! [*He knocks, twice.*]
Thrice!
SHADOW—Why so nice?

[*He knocks three times. The door opens, inward. In the doorway appears* GALLUCINIUS, *clad as Claudius. He speaks low.*]

GALLUCINIUS—Amen!
CLAUDIUS—*Thou*—mockest her voice?
GALLUCINIUS—*Thou*—madest her choice,
Not she!
CLAUDIUS—I heard thy mockery!

GALLUCINIUS—Thine own thou heardest. We
Are one.
My voice is thine. It saith:
Have done!
CLAUDIUS—Yea, done!—Ha, swift is sin!
Stand back! I will go in
And lift her
Forth. What shall stay me!
GALLUCINIUS— One
Swifter!
CLAUDIUS—Who?

[*Beside Gallucinius appears* YORICK, *in shroud, with head bandaged. He speaks quietly.*]

YORICK— Death.

DARKNESS.

CURTAIN.

END OF "THE FOOL IN EDEN GARDEN"

SECOND PORTICO
CHOOSE

SECOND PORTICO—On its lintel is carved in carmine the word CHOOSE!

Re-entering, the READER *pauses, stares up at the burning inscription, and speaks broodingly:* Can Death allay the insatiate fire of Lust?—What sequel beyond? Pass on, to learn—or ponder, here? Again a quiet niche, for clues, holding two further scrolls: *Choose!* 't is carven, up there. And here again a silent moment, to ponder poem-passages and choose between

A TOOTH FOR A TOOTH, or BLESSEDNESS

A FROZEN CRATER

From Prologue to FENRIS, THE WOLF, *Tragic Drama by* PERCY MACKAYE

[I]

Odin. He sleeps, yet restive still; with eyelids squint
Through which his eyes, in dreams still shifting, flash
Like flame through knot-holes. Yet he sleeps; beside him
His wild pack, crouching, share his chain.—O thou
Dumb spirit of the mind! O mystery!
Were there a god whom Odin might invoke,
To thee would Odin sue for pity.—Ages,
A thousand ages, anguish;
Anguish, remorse, forgiveness, malediction,
Light into darkness, horror into hope,
Revolving evermore. O pain,—pain!
Sear not my spirit blind!—Thou, tameless wolf,
God of the void eternal retrograde,
Prone deity of self, by that thou art—
Illimitable passion, joyance mad
Of being, hate, brute-cunning, gnawing lust—
Fenris, I curse thee!
The Pack [*wildly*]:
Ulfr! Ulfr! vaknathi!—The wolf awakeneth!
Fenris [*barking*]:
Anarch! anarch! anarch!—All-Father, free me!

From THE SERMON ON THE MOUNT, *Matthew V*

[II]

And seeing the multitudes, he went up into a mountain:
and when he was set, his disciples came unto him:
And he opened his mouth, and taught them, saying,
Blessed are the poor in spirit:
for theirs is the kingdom of heaven.
Blessed are they that mourn: for they shall be comforted.
Blessed are the meek: for they shall inherit the earth . . .
Blessed are the pure in heart: for they shall see God.
Blessed are the peacemakers: for they shall be called
the children of God.

ODIN
AGAINST CHRISTUS

ODIN AGAINST ✠ CHRISTUS ✠

[*Time: Twenty-two years after the Second Play*]

BEING THE THIRD PLAY OF
THE TETRALOGY
THE MYSTERY OF HAMLET
KING OF DENMARK, OR
WHAT WE WILL ✠ BY
PERCY MACKAYE

ODIN AGAINST CHRISTUS

DRAMATIS PERSONAE

[*In the order of their appearance.*]

ERIK, *charcoal burner*
ISBEL, *his wife*
GAFFER, *Erik's father*
HAMLET, *King of Denmark*
HORATIO, *aide to the King and friend of Prince Hamlet*
VOLTIMAND, *Danish soldier*
GERTRUDE, *Queen of Denmark*
MOLL COWSLIP, *the Queen's attendant and flounced jester*
OSRIC, *courtier*
CLAUDIUS, *brother of King Hamlet*
OPHELIA, *daughter of Polonius*
KING'S CHORISTER
TOPAS, *grave-digger*
MARCELLUS, *Danish soldier*
POLONIUS, *Lord Chamberlain*
LAERTES, *his son*
YAUGHAN, *gardener*
PRINCE HAMLET, *son of King Hamlet and Queen Gertrude*
CORNELIUS, *courtier*
COURIER *from Norway*
COURIER *from England*
Courtiers and Ladies; Musicians; Servants; and Castle-Folk.

PRESENCE:—GALLUCINIUS, *as Cellarer of Elsinore*

SCENES

ACT FIRST:—*Scene One*

A Charcoal-Burner's Hut in a Forest, by the Baltic Sea.
At sun-up, early February.

Scene Two

Elsinore. The Queen's Boudoir. [*Followed by the Cellarage of Elsinore as visioned in Claudius' mind.*]
Valentine's Day.

SCENES

[*Continued*]

ACT SECOND:—*Scene One*

Elsinore. Ophelia's Bedchamber.

Valentine's Day, later in the day.

Scene Two

The Banquet-Hall.

Valentine's Day, at night.

ACT THIRD:—*Scene One*

Elsinore. A Corridor of the Castle.

The next day. Morning.

Scene Two

Anteroom to the Royal Bedchamber.

Later in the morning.

Scene Three

Hall of the Shrines.

Early in the afternoon.

Scene Four

A Room in the Castle.

Soon afterward.

ACT FOURTH:—*Scene One*

Elsinore. Shrubbery near the Castle.

Late Spring. Morning.

Scene Two

Ophelia's Bedchamber.

A few moments later.

ACT FIFTH:—*Scene One*

The Royal Library.

About a fortnight later.

Scene Two

Hall of the Shrines and Mirror.

Night. About two months later.

Note: Stage-right and stage-left are from the actor's point of view.

ACT FIRST

Scene One

A CHARCOAL-BURNER'S HUT, IN A FOREST, BY THE BALTIC SEA.

At left, in the doorway, ERIK, *the Charcoal-Burner, stands, looking out into the forest. Near him, at back—before a crude, wooden shrine, with Crucifix and carved image of the Virgin—his wife,* ISBEL, *is kneeling.*

ERIK

See, wife! 'Tis sun-up. The frore mist clings red
Round springtide's freezing heart. Our giant woods
Ha' donn'd the war-gear of us midget mortals.
Ice is their armour. Yon old oak 's a king,
Grizzled with hoarfrost, and his twiggéd beard
Is guled—each hair, a burning icicle.
The hollies be his henchmen, their thorny shields
Spatter'd wi' berry-blood. The spikéd tannen
Slant their glare spears around him, and the linden
Clink their encrusted swords.

ISBEL
[*At the shrine.*]

Ave, Maria!

ERIK

And us, that be the kith of olden kings,
Shunted and hunted through unnumber'd years
Under these forest boughs, with hungering folk
Harried by unending wars—us hath our weird
Shrunk to this starvéd pinch of charcoal-burning
In a poor wood-hut, whilst the war-lords stride
Their clanking pathway over us, and all
The frozen dead, out yonder.

ISBEL

Ave, Maria!

ERIK

And what be left, to spread our masters' board?
Can coals be gobbled? Can man-flesh be carved,
Salver'd on ice, and eat for venison?
'Fore yesterday, the cold thawed, and thou wottest
How keen the oozing corpses in their mail
Stank to our nostrils, ere we scooped the mire
To bury 'em deeper, where the slough'd horse-shanks
Mangled their riders' loins, in the blood-slather.
Welcome be frost, say I, to snaffle our noses!

ISBEL

Mother of mercies, Virgin dear, of pities!
Bring us thy peace, Maria! For thy babe's sake,
Thy peace on earth to us!

ERIK

"Maria!"—"Maria!"
Ever thy Maria! Wherefore prayest to her
For peace, whose weanéd babe hangs gutted, yonder,
On 's crucifix?

A HUSKY VOICE

[*Speaks from the sill of the inner door, right.*]

Aye, son: thou sayst—thou sayst it.

ERIK

Eh, Gaffer! Com'st thou gabbing from thy litter?
What, said I?

[*Tottering forward, the* OLD GAFFER *points to the Virgin's shrine.*]

GAFFER

True word. 'T is the woman, yon,
Hath wrought on us this world-woe. Long agone,
The sagas told 't would be.

[*He sinks down upon a rough stump-stool.*]

ISBEL

Gaffer, ha' done
Thine ancient sagas. They be sin-hatcht.

GAFFER

Ancient—
Aye, as the morning and the evening—old
As earth-word, and the Wise One—him, shall come
Again, after this eve of Ragnarok.

ERIK

Who?

GAFFER

Odin, the One-Eyed, the wise All-Father
Of battle-sons and breed o' master-men—
No brewer of virgin's milk, but victor's mead
In the tall tankards foaming; and, with him,
Loki, the Crafty One, who picketh the locks
Of wit, wi' his lightning key, and slicketh the hammer
Of Thor, the Thunderer. They three shall knot
The cords of Christus' strangling, and avenge
The poison o' the pap o' saintlihood
That suckles us wi' Christendom.

ISBEL

Stint! Stint!
No more, for Jesu's grace!

GAFFER

Erik, hast thou harkt
My word?

ERIK

Yea, harkt have I. What, then?

GAFFER

What, then!
Then, wilt thou cry with her, "Jesu, Maria!"
And bow thee to these idols of holy wood,
Carvéd to Christ and Virgin? Or wilt burn
The holly they be whittled on, to crackle
A cheery fire-flame in thy charcoal pan
In wassail to the One-Eyed, who shall come
Once more, to make us men?

ERIK

I 'll crackle it
Wi' splinters o' these false gods!

[*He starts toward the shrine, with fierce gestures.*]

ISBEL

[*Clinging to him.*]

Erik, Erik!
Hold back!

ERIK

Hold off! Unclutch me, Isbel!

ISBEL

Erik,
Oh, break 'em not! Thou 'lt break my heart, an thou do.

[*Screaming, as he grasps the Virgin's image, to break it.*]

Jesu, Maria!

A DEEP VOICE

[*From without.*]

Who cryeth, "Jesu, Maria"?

[*Enter, in armour, with battle-ax,* KING HAMLET, *followed by* HORATIO, *in semi-armour. Removing his helmet, to Horatio's holding, Hamlet reveals his face, grey-bearded, with a bandage across his left eye.*]

KING HAMLET

What quarrel 's here, in this hut?

GAFFER
[*Staring.*]

Ha, see! 'Tis *him*,
The One-Eyed!
[*Lurching forward, on his knees.*]
Hail, All-Father!

KING HAMLET

Father, I hope,
Of all who serve my realm, as ye, I trust,
Are fain to do, even in this smoky thatch.

GAFFER

And art not thou the Wise One, the One-Eyed,
Odin, the Old?

KING HAMLET
[*Removing his bandage.*]

Nay, gaffer. This swath'd eye
Was scotch'd by an arrow, but 't will heal, methinks,
To match the other. I am Hamlet, of Elsinore.

ISBEL
[*Kneeling, with Erik.*]

God save thee, O King!

KING HAMLET

God save *thee*, woman! Was 't
Thy voice, I heard, call on the holy names
Of Jesu and his mother?

ISBEL
[*Aghast.*]

Save us, King!

KING HAMLET

From what?—Well, wife, art dumb? And eke thy man?
Save you from what?

GAFFER
[*Rising.*]

From Jesu and his mother!
Aye, dumb these be, and crook their knee-knuckles
Unto thy kinghood. But I kneel to none
But Odin, the Wise, Father of Eld, who yet
Shall come again, to save us from him, yonder:
Yon cross-hung king, who counselleth: "Turn thy cheek
Unto thine enemy!"—Lo, where his cheek
Is turned, to kiss the cross, bidding us bleed
With him, for meekness' sake.

KING HAMLET

What words are these?

GAFFER

The words of Weird, from one, whose sires were kings
In Scyldingland, who eateth here this char-dust,
Sith that witcht night, when three kings from the east
Came following a star, to feed us dreams
Of loaves and fishes, falling from the skies
To fill our starvéd bellies wi' the glory
Of Christus' kingdom-come.—Ha, be they fill'd,
Or bloated wi' his wind o' will-be-done?
Aye, aye, his will be done, in sooth,—his will
To make us suck the spear-sores in our sides
Instead of wield the spears!

KING HAMLET

Were these the words
That made this poor wife scream to heaven?

GAFFER

Aye, were they,
And bade this charcoal-burning brat o' mine
Break up yon idol-trash for kindling-sticks
To warm us winter cheer.

KING HAMLET

Our Lady's shrine—
What! Burn our Lord his Crucifix—

GAFFER

To thaw
The numbing of our nails. The dawn 's death-cold.

ISBEL

Forgi'e him, King! Forgi'e his trespass! See,
The holy things be safe.

KING HAMLET

The holy things
Be safe, indeed, good wife. He hath not said
So ill, as seemeth. Icon is not the image
Which makes it visible, nor crown of thorns
The King, who wears it. Carven wood may feed
The char-fire: still the image doth remain
Unscotcht. The Lady of our prayers doth bend
Still to her babe, above the flames, and smiles
To watch the thawing of the numbéd feet
His burning mammets serve to warm. So safe
Be holy things from harm. 'T is Christus' will,
For thus he builds *His* kingdom. May mine own
Learn of his building-craft!

ISBEL

[*Gazes up at the shrine, murmuring.*]

Ave, Maria!

GAFFER

Learn well, O King of Elsinore! And when
Thou meetest the Other, wi' the One Eye, ask him
What craft he learned, at Mimir's fountain.
[*Beckoning to Erik.*] —Come!
[*He goes within, followed dumbly by Erik.*]

KING HAMLET
[*To Horatio.*]

At Mimir's fountain?

HORATIO

There, old sagas say,
Did Odin pawn his eye, for wisdom.

KING HAMLET

Wisdom!
His kingdom—and *mine!* What builder's craft hath wisdom
To plan their jointure? Or what architect
Hath magic, which can plumb the pillars of meekness
To uphold the lintel of power? Shall Denmark be
The macrocosm of this charcoal-hovel,
Charnell'd by dungeons of the frozen dead,
Rack'd by this ancient feud of Odin and Christus
To fall in a char-pit? Or shall it gird its groin
To stanchion arches of the Eternal House
Of Many Mansions, where the Son of Peace
Goeth to prepare his way unto the Father,
For weary folk to homestead, laden no more
With heavy sorrows?—Horatio!

HORATIO

My liege?

KING HAMLET
[*Laying off his gauntlets.*]

Here, for a moment, now, will I unglaive me.

See you this battle-ax? With my right hand
I grip its stubborn oak, studded with spikes
Of jaggéd flints and steely barbs—to deal
What, with it?

HORATIO

Death, in war, my liege.

KING HAMLET

And here,
Look you! With my left hand, I dip three fingers
At the Virgin's font, in this same holy water
Where new-born babes are christen'd, and here sprinkle
blessing
On this same dealer of death to babe-begetters.
Is this a circle of vice, or virtue?

HORATIO

'T is
The circle of the world, which we were born in.

KING HAMLET

Born in, for what?

HORATIO

For battle with ourselves,
To attain the stature of our babyhood—
The toppling height of innocence.

KING HAMLET

Aye, toppling
To indigence of power to poise ourselves
Above the battle.—Look you, again, fellow-warrior:
This right hand, clutching still this bloody emblem
Of self-expansion, is the State of Denmark,
Engined to weld the multitudinous
Scoriae of mothers' wombs into a crown

Of world-bedazzling glory, to be worn
By *whom?*

HORATIO

By you, yourself, my liege, in Denmark realm,
Where you are the State.

KING HAMLET

Ha, the State: an idiot, egoless
Ape-skull, empty of mind and all which makes
The master-soul it counterfeits: the State—
A poppet-giant, of brass and brainlessness!
Are we, then, Denmark, that official eunuch,
Which is not even an icon of ourselves,
Whom loins of love begot, but is a vacancy,
Sans vision, pulse and passion—an illusion,
Crested with real men's hearts, lustre-encrusted
With noble allegiances—itself unloyal,
Loveless, unliving, *nil,* yet fraught with illusion's
All-power to annihilate the real, that thinks it
Into its semblance of reality?

HORATIO

Therein, my liege, the battle lies, to gauge
And wrest the substance from the semblance.

KING HAMLET

Yea,
This meek left hand, feeling to touch its forehead
With heaven's clear dew, to wrest the victory
From the blind-bludgeoning right. Yet both these hands
Be gadgets of one body, with two arms.
Which, then, shall Hamlet battle with, and for:
His own unshielded arm, or the arméd shield
Of Elsinore?—His state of manhood, vow'd
To stablish Christus' Kingdom, or the State
Royal of Denmark?

HORATIO

Each, my liege, if both
Be fused in Hamlet's vow to stablish peace
In his own heart.

KING HAMLET

Why, thou didst watch, Horatio,
How, yesternight, stung by an angry parle,
I smote the sledded Polacks on the ice,[1]
For taunting of my dignity, as lord
Of Denmark. Well, was that my peace of heart,
To doubt mine own integrity, because
They dared to doubt it? Breeding, born of dignity,
Hath never need to take the dare of braggarts.
So, I misdoubt myself. Yet 't is a world
Where brutes are deaf, except to their own snarl,
And I must use their guttural, to twinge 'em
To know their master's tone. For we must on,
Horatio, with this war, to hold at bay
The Polack, pressing westward, ere from north
Young Fortinbras, forgetful of our pledge
Unto his father's urn, long years agone,
Of love between the Norse and Dane, come swooping
To force a peace of vengeance and disruption
On Denmark and our dreams of planting lilies
Of Christ, His Peace, within the walléd garden
Of Elsinore.

A VOICE

[*Calling, outside, distantly.*]

Ho,a! ho,a! ho,a!
Hamlet, the King!

KING HAMLET

Hark, there! Who calleth on us,
Yonder?—Go, find the cause, for 't is not known

We passed this way, to enter in this hut.
Fetch here the crier.

HORATIO

Straight, my liege.

[*Hamlet's gaze falls now upon the form of Isbel, who has been kneeling in utter stillness, her eyes fixed upon the King, in absorbed fascination. Gently, he speaks to her.*]

KING HAMLET

Shy bird,
That peerest at me, with such startled eyes
And knockings of thy nestled heart, atremble
With wonder at this steely thing's intrusion
Into thy thatchéd home,—sweet bird, poor throstle!
This armour'd beast, with bristling battle-tusks,
Shall not too long affray thee. Earth is quicker
With roses, than iron with rust. This icy dawn
Of frozen blood shall melt to crimsonings
Of petall'd blooms, and pollen thy smokéd wings
To dartle in sheen again, and whistle thy mate
Under the greenwood tree.—Poor birdling wife,
What is thy name?

ISBEL

Isbel.

KING HAMLET

Isbel, prithee,
What is thy fare, in this hut?

ISBEL

Acorns.

KING HAMLET

Naught else?

ISBEL

And hazelnuts. The mast is good with goat's milk,

But the King's soldiers took the nanny, to kill
For meat, afore the battle. Still, O King,
Though milk lack, I will fetch you mast, for breakfast.

KING HAMLET

Thanks, Isbel. I ate, ere dawn. But here 's a kind
Of nut, brings luck, in month of February.
Take it, in token of thy pretty offer
To share thy mast—which the King's soldiers spared thee.
[*He takes, from within his armour, and hands to her, something that glistens.*]

ISBEL

Ah, blue 't is, and bright! What is 't?

KING HAMLET

An amethyst.

ISBEL

How smooth it glistens! Is 't a lucky token?

KING HAMLET

It will be, and thou use it to buy goat's milk.
Take it in, to thy Gaffer. Tell him, 't is
The eye, that Odin pawned at Mimir's fountain.

ISBEL

Oh, Sir, I will. [*Exit, within.*]

KING HAMLET
[*Broodingly.*]

An eye for an eye—or wisdom!
[*Enter* HORATIO, *followed by* VOLTIMAND.]

HORATIO

'T is Voltimand, my liege, and brings a letter
Unto your Majesty.

KING HAMLET

A letter? Where is 't?

VOLTIMAND

[*Delivering it.*]

Here, my liege.

KING HAMLET

Ha, the Queen's hand!—Writ in red!
Why—red?

VOLTIMAND

I know not why, Sir.

KING HAMLET

We shall see.

[*Breaking the seal, he reads:*]

Hamlet—come home—Gertrude

[*Staring.*]

No more?—Nay, yes: ah, here, and underlined
In reddish rust:—*a kiss.*—God! Is this blood
For ink, turn'd brownish?—Look, Horatio.—What?

HORATIO

Methinks, my liege—— [*Pauses.*]

KING HAMLET

What?

HORATIO

'Tis.

KING HAMLET

What?

HORATIO

Blood.

KING HAMLET

Whose?—*Hers?*

HORATIO

'T would seem—

KING HAMLET

Not hers—*her own!*

HORATIO

Who knoweth?

KING HAMLET

Ha,

But this is nightmare! Voltimand, hark, sirrah!
Hath ink of Elsinore been foul'd, sith my
Departure thence? Ha' the quills been tinged
By scratch of hands, that sharpened 'em?—What, what?

VOLTIMAND

My liege, I know not.

KING HAMLET

Is the Queen ill?—Speak!

VOLTIMAND

My liege, I know not whether ill, or well.
She hath seemed much to miss you—oft, too sorely
For her to stay the lashes of her eyes
From dropping tears.

KING HAMLET

What, hath the Duke, my brother,
So let her pine, i' my absence? When I left,
And made him temporal regent of my realm,
I bade him, bid all statecraft lapse the while
Till my return, rather than let her pine,

Yea, fill the Castle with feasting, to divert her
From any pain of overthought on me.

VOLTIMAND

Oh, Sir, he hath obeyed you, to the letter.

KING HAMLET

That 's well, then. Ah, Prince Hamlet—stays he yet
At Wittenberg, in the university?

VOLTIMAND

Aye, Sir.

KING HAMLET

And no ill-tidings from him?

VOLTIMAND

None, Sir.

KING HAMLET

Polonius, keeps he well,—assiduous
In all things documental, appertaining
To daily business at the Castle?

VOLTIMAND

He doth, Sir,
And findeth occasion to philosophize
On all things else, to instruct our ignorances.

KING HAMLET

The folk and soldiery,—are there uprisings,
Or mutinies, to imperil our home realm,
For causes whatsoever?

VOLTIMAND

All is tranquil,
Save as the folk take joyance in their tankards,
When the good Duke whets 'em to share his rouses.

KING HAMLET

Then, in the name of Heaven—Heaven confirming
This be but brown ink, and not blood!—wherefore
These words: *Hamlet—come home—Gertrude—a kiss—?*
Is, then, a *kiss* the meaning of this blood?
Was there naught else—no further message, sent?

VOLTIMAND

Your Majesty, there was.

KING HAMLET

Ha, what? And how?

VOLTIMAND

My liege, the night I left, to bear that letter
Across the wintry waste—that selfsame night,
After supper-feast, the Queen led me apart,
And laid that secretly within my hand,
Whispering: "Take this to the King. Leave now,
By night. Say naught of this. Haste. God be with you!
And when you 've found the King, and he hath read
That first seal'd script, then hand to him—this other."

KING HAMLET

Another?——[*Snatching it.*]
What more of mystery is here?
[*Breaking the seal, reads:*]

Haste thee! Haste home, O, sever'd heart of mine!
The candle gutters on St. Agnes' shrine.
The cuckoo calleth from the Castle vine:
"Wild hawk doth pluck wings of St. Valentine!"

St. Valentine!—His feast day soon draws nigh,
When the first bluebird flashes: *Spring is here!*
This month, the fourteenth day. Now is the seventh.
One week, to plough the wilderness, and glean

Secrets, why saints of candles and of wings
Be harried by wild hawks.—Horatio,
This bolt hath hit its mark. What else is aiming?

HORATIO

What comes, comes. How 't is welcomed, when it comes,
Counts all, or nothing.

KING HAMLET

By my staggering soul,
Now am I cleft in twain! This one half me
Is Hamlet, mate of Gertrude, and this other
Is Denmark, mute of Hamlet. So the schism,
We spoke on, splits the crotch, and this one bulk
Is riven asunder. What doth wait behind
This cryptic kiss-word still is seal'd—love's secret.
What waits beyond, out there, on the bloodied ice,
Is open wide: 't is War. This ax must wage it
Even to the ghastly end, or Denmark crumbles.—
Share me, ye Kissing-Killing Powers!—Now
I go forth, east-west, *both* ways, from this thatch.
Voltimand, turn thy horse, outspeed our own
And bear this answer back unto the Queen:

War cries, *Go, kill!* and lips of home, *Come, kiss!*
Denmark kills on, and Hamlet comes with this.

On!—Up!—To horse!

CURTAIN.

ACT FIRST

Scene Two

ELSINORE. THE QUEEN'S BOUDOIR.

QUEEN GERTRUDE, *discovered, seated beside a table, whereon stands a mirror. She holds in her hand a book, with wooden binding.*

GERTRUDE

Aye, here 't is: boxwood, dyed with berry-blue,
And leaf'd with ivory, wax'd by honey-bees.[2]
"See, child!" saith our dear Padre, "Canst thou read it?"
Then my sweet princeling seven-year-old, he reaches,
Peers in it, eagerly, fingers the waxt leaves,
And murmurs—(Still I see his wond'ring stare!):
"Why, 't is all blank! The leaves are empty."—"Ah!"
Answereth Padre Celestino: "Ah,
They are all filled with silences, for thee
To cipher. 'T is the table of Memory—
From the great *Book of Amor.*"

[*She gazes before her, wistfully.*]

—Memory!
Silences!—*Amor!*—Two-and-twenty years,
Are ye, then, cipherable?—"What is love?"
Questioned our princeling's father. Quoth the Padre:
"The *Book of Amor* hath as many leaves
As teem the gales of autumn . . and its margins
Are all emblazoned with as varied blooms
As star the broidery of Flora's breasts,
Or tinge the lips of Galilean lilies . . ."
Lilies!—"as varied blooms . ."? Doth *Amor* tinge
The tiger-lily's cheek? Or dye the tuft
O' the princess-feather? Mutine the hot blood
O' the mulberry-bloom? Sallow the orange-blossom
Wi' the wilt lily's languor? Or doth love
Waft musk from the rank skunk-weed's wallow? . . Ah,
Sweet Celestino of the long ago,—

Whose lingering smile still floats here, like lost sunlight
On shadowy waters!—In thine exegesis
Of *Amor,* what omissions did thine own
Love of the beautiful leave in love's margin
To worm the hallow'd text with grainéd spots,
Flecking the broidery of Flora's breasts
With blotchéd canker-stains? . . O, Memory,
No more! Ye Silences, let me have done
With cipherings, which only in the end
Reach—cipher.

[*She lays the book down.*]

No! Let all my prayers be turn'd
Towards him, my princeling, grown,—my scholar-son,
Hamlet, now wand'ring far in Wittenberg,
At the great university, to find
Lost magic keys of learning, to unlock
This prison world.

[*Enter* MOLL COWSLIP, *bustling, with a hand-basket.*]

MOLL

Out, out, my lady-lorn!
Queen up your curls, and peep head out-o'-doors,
To smell and look and listen! Snails be opening
Their cabin windows, and crick out their necks
To sniff their neighbour gossips in the leek-bed.
Worm wriggles. Runnel tinkles. Blackbird twiddles
His beak, to cram his craw. Come, be about!

Hen sits sunning,
Rooster crows,
Sap is running—
And so 's my nose!

Abouts, fair Dame o' Doldrums! Up-a-daisy!

GERTRUDE

Why, Moll——

MOLL

Gird up! On, gown, and out o' town!

GERTRUDE

I 'm gowned, at home.

MOLL

But not your lord and master.
He 's gone agadding for wild Polack ducks,
The whilst his mourning dove doth tuck her neb
Under her wing, and ne'er will preen a feather.

GERTRUDE

Why should I preen, Moll?

MOLL

[*Mocking.*]

"Why should I preen, Moll?"—Mass!
Go axe the saint that painteth bluebird wings
The colour of his eyes, and daubeth a patch
O' dawn rose, for to dainty birdling's breast.

[*Singing.*]

To-morrow is Saint Valentine's day,
All in the morning, betime . . .

GERTRUDE

[*Staring.*]

What art thou singing! Where didst thou hear *that?*

MOLL

By Gis and by St. Charity, good sooth,
I heard it where the tumbling-master heard it,
When [*Singing.*] *. . . up he rose and donn'd his clothes,*
And dupp'd the chamber door,
Let in a maid, that out a maid
Never departed more.[3]

GERTRUDE
[*Absently.*]

Aye, so it was—the dream tune, when I sung it
To poor Cornelia, lang syne. . . What were the words?

MOLL

You 'll ha' no need to learn 'em to Lord Henhawk,
When he comes dupping the door.—What, did ye word
"Wild hawk," in your lord King's letter, like as Dame
Moll Chamberlain gave counsel?

GERTRUDE
[*Still dreamily.*]

Yes—yes—yes—

MOLL

And made it a red-letter valentine
Wi' thy quill-scratch?

GERTRUDE
[*Showing her left hand.*]

There.

MOLL
[*Looking.*]

The scab—'t is red, yet.
Aye, there 's a goose-peck shall draw gander's blood.
"Cuckoo!"—That pipeth horn, to blow him home
Afore the morrow!

GERTRUDE

To-morrow! Dost thou think it?
But what if Voltimand have lost the way
And failed to give the message? Still none cometh,
Master, nor messenger. Oh, what can speed him
Back to me faster, Moll?

MOLL

There clinks no spur,
Can gibe a pastured stallion in the loin
To jump the gates, and gallop to his mare,
Like pricking jealousy.—Who wotteth that
So well as me, as ha' been husbanded
A peck o' times, and harvested a bushel
Between kirk-chime and knolling!—My last man
Were Squire Paddock, master o' the manor,
And, sooth, I kept 'im jingling wi' his spurs
Until he lost his wind, jumping the lychgate.—
Dame Paddock: There 's a yardly name, for midwife
To swing the hutch-bar, and raise sucking calves!
Aye, bull-calves, kids and lambs, I ha' born'd 'em all,
Suckled 'em fat, and weaned 'em. But, God praise,
Now Moll's dugs be gone dry, and Molly Cowslip
Can gambol wi' her maidenhead afresh.
Yea, old be I in young experience,
And skill'd to chamberlain your Majesty
In all the lore and jigs o' jealousy.—
[*Showing her basket.*]
Look here, my sweeting Queen! I ha' fetcht thee posies
To plat a garland, for a valentine,
Shall preen thee for a kiss, what kind so be.
I puddled 'em behind the byre stack
In a sunny cove, to south, out o' the wind.
[*Lifting the basket-lid.*]
Look, la! The darlings: be n't they purty buds?
They be my christen-blooms and bear my font-name.

GERTRUDE

Cowslips!

MOLL

Green-gold, for Denmark's Queen o' May!

GERTRUDE

Of May? Ah, Molly! Two-and-twenty frosts
Of February, they have silted silver
Into these hairs, since that far Hallowe'en
Our dear fool, Yorick, died.

MOLL

Ho, Yorick, sayst thou!
He were a cowslip-platter, which could twist
A cow's tail wi' 'em, till the May-Queen's self
Could ride the rump in glory.

GERTRUDE

Moll dear, list!
Ever since he died, and strewed his path to heaven
With blossomy jests, thyself hast been for me
A kind of flounc'd court-fool; but thou dost wear
Thy cap-o'-bells too much on thy hip-flounce
Where thou sitt'st down, too little on thy forehead,
For me to catch the tinkle of thy jests.
They bumble too much.

MOLL

Nay, Yorick could outbumble
My lilts. He bumbled me a love-lay, once,
Which took the ram prize at the bussing bee.

GERTRUDE

The bussing bee? Prithee, what may that be?

MOLL

The kissing match, i' the kitchen.—Sidle, now:
Sit to the glass, the whiles I plat these buds
To crown thy braids. So will I lilt it for thee.
Ha, would I could as Yorick did, yon time,

Little and big, low-loud, sugar and sour!
But list: Now learn thee how the sow sips honey.

[*Singing, while she plaits the cowslips.*]

Night will glower.
Now, still, 't is sunny.
Ere the glowering hour,
Kiss me, Molly Cowslip,
Buss me, bunny!

Ere Forever
Creepeth to sever,
Let no sneaping mouse' lip,
Nibbling, make our Now *slip*
In Matrimony.

Nay,—but as clover cleaves the browsing cow's lip,
Like as the Yarmouth tide enyawns the tunny—
Buss me, prow,
And buss me, bow:
Learn, O learn me, Queen of Cowslips,
Learn me how
The sow sips
Honey!

[*Bursting into laughter.*]

Yorick!—Ha, but he were a whoreson rogue:
Topas, the grave-digger, he said it true,
When Fool he gi'ed me his death-smack on my mouth.
Oho!—Aha!

GERTRUDE

Hush, Moll! Hush. Look! What 's there,
Bobbing and cooing in the doorway, paunching
Its ruffle, like a pouter at his cote-hole,
Ere he ducks in?

MOLL

Faith, then, but you have named him
Afore I can. 'T is Milord Lahdidah.

GERTRUDE

Oh, Osric!

[*Appearing in the doorway,* OSRIC *makes secretive gestures to Moll, indicating the Queen.*]

OSRIC

Whist! . . Is 't?

[*Aping his gestures, Moll hollows one ear, like a deaf person.*]

MOLL

Is 't?

OSRIC

Is 't in the card
Of perquisites?—the calendar of permissions?—
The royal register of interviews?

GERTRUDE

Tell him, come in.

MOLL

My lord, the Queen hath nodded.

OSRIC

[*Coming forward.*]

The nod of royalty is, by impartment,
Both signet of obedience, and seal
Of obsequience, on part of the subserver.—
My gracious liege, may I, in turn, impart
The imputation of this entrance?

GERTRUDE

Sir,
You may.

OSRIC

The imputement hath a liberal

Connotement with this sealéd scroll, wherein
The encrypted conceit is hidden, yet whereof
The outward consignment is made manifest
By certain tokens—*si je puis me faire*
Conjecture, sans offense?—tokens, so imbued
With sense of the sweet saint, whose season now
We observe, that they are obvious to senses
Keen to the perfume of its import, as—*comme çi,*
Comme ça,—'t is written here, in gold:

[*He reads, aloud:*]

"UNTO THE ALL-EXCELLING, STILL-UNANSWERING:
R. S. V. P."

[*Bowing low, he presents the scroll to the Queen.*]

GERTRUDE
[*Taking it, hesitant.*]

Why deem you 't is for us?

OSRIC

"Unto the All-Excelling," it is written.

GERTRUDE

Who gave you this?

OSRIC

The saint, with azure wings,
Who dips his quill in dawn-gold, and ordaineth
Anonymity to his documents.

GERTRUDE

How came this to you?

OSRIC

A draft of Elsinore
Wafted it to me, down a corridor.

GERTRUDE

Methinks, we feel it blowing from the door
Behind you, still, my lord. Pray shut it tight
After you, as you leave, lest we catch cold.

OSRIC

Not for a draught of nectar, served by Hebe,
Would this your servant cause your Majesty
To catch cold, by the wafture of a feather
Blown from the blue, that blew him hither.
[*Stepping backwards, he bows himself to the entrance sill.*]
Adieu,
Chère Reine! [*Exit.*]

GERTRUDE

Puff!—Is the *rain*-shower over, Moll?

MOLL

There be no drafts fro' the crack. The door 's shut to.

GERTRUDE

Then open it again, and look if there be
Eaves' droppings, and the pouter sprinkling his feathers,
Or peaking for worms, to dangle in the beaks
O' the Castle doves, and make 'em coo with gossip.
[*Moll opens the door, looks out, pauses a moment, then speaks back to the Queen.*]

MOLL

Nary a drip, outside. He 's rounded the corner.

GERTRUDE

Come hither, then, and let us "sense," together,
The "encrypted imputement" of this "document."
"Unto the All-Excelling, Still-Unanswering"—
Hmm!—
[*Breaking its seal, she unrolls the scroll, and reads.*]

R. S. V. P.
Within this breath
I give thee what,
If thou again give not,
Withereth,
Unless thieving
All—which lips, forsaking,
Still keep—make bloom, retrieving
This
Breath-taking—
What? . . . . O, best
Kissworthiest
Unkissable,
Tell!
Say!—
Spell
Baiser:
Rhyme it with bliss!
Répondez, s' il vous plaît
And . . .

MOLL

Kiss!——
That ringeth the rhyme-bell.

A DEEP VOICE
[*From the doorway.*]

Oui!
[*Appearing,* CLAUDIUS *enters, continuing.*]
Et, je vous prie,
S' il ne vous plaît
Pas du tout
De répondre de voix,
Alors, un baiser
Pour moi!

GERTRUDE

Pour vous?—
De sœur?

CLAUDIUS

Du cœur
D'amour; mais, pourquoi
Dis tu: "Vous"?
Tutoyons-nous:
Dis: "Toi!"

GERTRUDE

Thee?

CLAUDIUS

Me.

GERTRUDE

"Vous"
Is "you,"
Not "thou,"
Or "thee."

CLAUDIUS

Then, vow
That *V*
To be
Thy *Valentine!*

GERTRUDE

Methinks, we 've Englished all the vows away,
St.Valentine would vent, *du cœur français!*

CLAUDIUS

Mean'st thou the kisses, which thy cowslipt hair
Hideth in braided coils, for lovers' lair?—
Ah, *they* need no translators, save the lips!
What kisses utter, hath in speech eclipse.

GERTRUDE

Well, Molly Cowslip, now thou seest the posies
Thy "christen-blooms" have scattered, turn to glozes,
That curl my ringlets all to rhymes, whose bells,
With double tongues, are rung in ding-dong knells.
How liketh thee Milord Duke's valentine
With my French lace, to frill it?

MOLL

Faith, all French
I ken 's in cookery. It lacketh me in the ear,
But liketh me on the tongue, tickleth i' the smell,
And smacketh on the lips. Yea, I can glint it
E'en in the eye—when Milord Duke doth wink it.

CLAUDIUS

What "Milord Duke" doth wink, shall be a trinket
To jewel that ear of Moll, which lacketh French,
And heareth no rain-drip, dropping from the eaves
Upon his ducal head, nor rustle of drafts
I' the door-crack.

MOLL

Jewels, they be purty favours
To folk as favour wearing 'em to bed,
For fear they mote be thieved; but Moll, she wanteth
No jewel to be guarded, save the one
Beshining gem she 's worn, wi' no disguise,
Through all the wane-wax moons o' womanhood,
In weather, foul, or fair.

CLAUDIUS

What jewel 's that?

MOLL

Odd zooks, my maiden jewel!

CLAUDIUS

Ah, sayst thou,
'T is *that,* thou hast the will to cherish, Moll?

MOLL

My lord, 't is not the will, it is the want.
I said I ha' the *want* of it, to cherish.
And who, that 's woman, would n't want it, sairly,
In these bad times o' war, when men o' greatness,
Aye, even kings, be rushing forth, by moon
And sun, by wind and rain, by snow and ice,—
Now here, now there, and every otherwhere,—
To carve their precious guts, and crack their crowns,
Wi' swords and battle-axes; and beslabber
Their skull-pans wi' their brains; and what, for all?—
All, for to gi'e God-glory to a Snow-man,
Will melt to mud! All, for to gear a Troll
In steel and brass, and kiss his bloody shield,
And lea'e the lily-white cheeks o' their lady-loves
To pine between their pillows, wi' nary chuck
To rosy 'em!—These man-lambs—these king-calflings—
These war-darlings! . . God bless the babes!

CLAUDIUS

Why, Molly,
What knowest thou of war?

MOLL

What wot I o' war?
What wot I o' the world o' Genesis
And Song o' Solomon, the mighty king,
Founded the midwives' craft?—Well, and you axe it,
My lord, I 'll gi'e ye the book.—In the beginning,
The World-Mother borned her babes, and they were triplets:
Noddle, Belly and Buttocks. And there beginneth
The Battle o' World-Babes—War. And Belly, he wins it,

Up-heads, or tails. The fight be all to fill Belly.
Fill him,—fight 's over; empty him,—bout begins again.
That 's what there be to war. Nurse babes, my lord,
And thou shalt know the book of history,
In-throughside-out.

CLAUDIUS

I see, thou art true Dansker,
And wagest battles even in baby-books.
I will bethink thy book of genesis
And song o' the wise king, who stablish'd midwives.
Meanwhile, methinks, thou art an eyewink-reader
And glintest this gleam, that wafts thee to the door,
Like my lord Osric, who was so complaisant
As shut it *after* him: *s' il vous plaît de comprendre?*

GERTRUDE

French leave doth not beseem true Dansker, Claudius.
Moll, thou mayst go—and leave the door ajar.

MOLL
[*Shrugging.*]

Jewel trinkets, ha!—My lord-babe Duke Royal,
Mind this: Moll Cowslip pimpeth for no master.
She platteth posies for the Queen o' Springtide
To preen her for the kiss of Oberon,
Whichsomever king be *him* in Denmark's Castle.
She mote be deaf-dumb-blind at door-cracks. Natheless,
She ranks more than *Dame Chamberlain*. Methinks,
'Tis Moll be *Regent*—here, in Elsinore! [*Exit.*]

CLAUDIUS

Regent?—Well, she is gone!—That 's something.
[*A pause.*
Claudius looks eloquently at Gertrude.]

Well?

GERTRUDE

Something—*well,* brother?

CLAUDIUS

Well,—something more than sister?

GERTRUDE

Nay,—nothing less than lecher,—do these raised
Inflections of ours ask something more, in answer,
Than still to be—dashes—between us?

CLAUDIUS

Dashes?

GERTRUDE

Dashes of all dear hopes of being well,
Ever beyond 'em. Ah, let 's make them bridges
To something better, higher, raising us
Out of this stench, reeking below, that poisons
Our wills, to deem it perfume.

CLAUDIUS

Ha, *moat*-bridges,
Thou meanest? Why, most queenly fortress
Of spousal faith, 't is thou, hast lowered such bridges—
In the long siege of my beseechments—even
Unto the slipping ledge of lifted lips,
Breath-toucht to span an instant's gulf, and mount
Into thy beck'ning ramparts, when—*flick-tick!*
Whip-whirl!—More wit-quick than the dizz'ning wings
Of humming-bird above a bloom of noon,
Petall'd to suck—thou hast withdrawn thy sightless
Bridgings, and plung'd the hovering portcullis
Of Hymen to its socket.

GERTRUDE

But—

CLAUDIUS

Bridges?—Nay,
'T is burning arrows, that must win my siege,
In storms from Cupid's quiver. *That* I carry
Upon my hip, and he shall pluck from there
The latest of ten thousand, now, this hour,
To sharp it with my pricking valentine
And flare the kiss, shall flame thy fortress—all!

GERTRUDE

Not till it be returnéd, can that fall.
Ah, well I know it, in my dizzy heart
That stoops to pick the flaming arrows up
And flare them back, but swoons—to smell the smudge.

CLAUDIUS

I 'll snuff the smudge, and lift thy swoonéd breasts
To feel the pressing cleavage of a rapture
Shall make the crumpling walls of Elsinore
To crumble in our union, where the wither'd
Garlands of Hymen shall crackle, in the bursts
Of Erebus' fire. 'T is lava of the gods
Which puny kinglets fear; but we shall wade in 't
Up to the thighs, yea, to the nipple-points,
And breathe the argon of its alkahest
Like incense, smoking from Apollo's altar,
Till we walk forth, immortal, in the naked
Splendour of Phoebus' porch, and seat us there,
As gods, together.

GERTRUDE

Claudio!—Claudio!
The walls of Elsinore crumple, indeed,
Here, in my woman's faintness. 'T is not fear
Of evil; not love, nor faith; nothing, there is,

That once was sanctity, can help me more
From toppling to the gulf, I gaze within.
Nay, 't is not even the witchcraft of thy wit
Can lure me there, by delicate gifts, that point
The arrow of a valentine, or powers
Of Erebus, that lead me to Apollo.

CLAUDIUS

Gertrude—

GERTRUDE

'T is naught of these, in thee—though, when
I look in lurings of thy wondrous eyes,
Meseems, I 'd follow them to any voids.

CLAUDIUS

Not voids—but vistas of enravishment,
Unveiling all which thou dost seek in me!

GERTRUDE

'T is naught at all in thee. 'T is everything
In me, myself, of all thou utterest,
Scorching within, which makes me now to stoop
At last, pick up the flaming arrow-heads
Shot by the singeing years, and choose this one
To pierce us both—

[*Leaning dizzily forward to meet his lips with hers.*]

Have *this—!*

A SHRILLING CRY

No, no! No, no, no!

GERTRUDE

[*Reeling back.*]

Ah!

[*The sudden, poignant cry, from without, is followed instantly by the entrance of a fair* GIRL, *with yellow hair, breathlessly covering her face with her hands, as she cries, again.*]

THE GIRL

Lady! O, dear my liege!

GERTRUDE
[*Gasping.*]

Ophelia!

OPHELIA

I cannot—cannot——

CLAUDIUS

Cannot—what?

OPHELIA

Sir, no,
I cannot listen it—

GERTRUDE
[*Staring at her.*]

Listen it, child?

OPHELIA
[*Pointing back.*]

There—there—

A VOICE
[*Singing, outside.*]

Let in a maid, that out a maid
Never departed more.

[*Enter* MOLL COWSLIP, *calling to Ophelia.*]

MOLL

Chucky, chucky!—What, o' God's world!—For to be
Weepy, all in the morning, betime!—Now, chuck,

[*Sings.*] *By Gis, and by St. Charity,*
Alack, and fie, for shame!

Ballet* it, wi' me, dearie! Himself, his highness,
Shall make us a third. Will not my lord Duke?—Now!

[*Singing, to a folk dance-step.*]

By Gis, and by St. Charity,
Alack, and fie, for shame!
Young men will do't, if they come to't;
By cock, they are to blame.

Quoth she, before you tumbled me,
You promis'd me to wed.
So would I ha' done, by yonder sun,
An thou hadst not come to my bed.[4]

CLAUDIUS

Get thee to the leek-bed, Moll, and lilt it louder
To the spring sparrows. They 're in the tumbling fit.

MOLL

The fit, quoth 'a! 'T is but a purty ballet,
Fit for a saint, on 's feast-day.

GERTRUDE

Pretty Ophelia,
Here, take my hand, dear. Come away with me.
We are not tuned to ballets, thou and I.

OPHELIA

Dear lady!—Ah, thy hand: 't is red. Is 't hurt?

GERTRUDE

A scratch.

MOLL

How 's here? La, sha' n't Moll tend her chick?
I would but lilt her merry; for I found her
Sucking her thumb, for somebody 's far off
In Wittenberg, methinketh.

*Pronounce the "t" in this word as used throughout.

GERTRUDE

No, Moll. Do
As the Duke biddeth. Get thee to the garden.

MOLL
[*Going.*]

Sparrows, quoth 'a!—And dearie chuck o' mine,
My purty hatchling bird, Ophelia,
She may n't pipe up a ballet roundelay
Wi' her old wilt cowslip nursie!—Sparrows, by cock!

[*Singing.*]

By Gis, and by St. Charity,
Alack, and fie, for shame! [*Exit.*]

CLAUDIUS
[*Reaching his hand to Gertrude.*]

Where are you going?

GERTRUDE

To Ophelia's chamber.
Her hair 's yellow as Angela's was.—Good holy day!
And may the blossoms of St.Valentine
Fall soft on bleeding arrow-heads.

CLAUDIUS
[*Taking her extended hand, looks at it.*]

What 's that,
So red, there?

GERTRUDE

This?—Oh, 't is a streak o' dawn,
Scratcht by a quill, pluckt from a wild hawk's wing,
To gash the dark, above a falconer's head.

CLAUDIUS

A falconer's,—ah? And why?

GERTRUDE

To token him,
Lift up his head to it, and follow it home.
See! 'T is a cross mark.

CLAUDIUS

So! And how must I
Unravel this subtlest of similitudes?

GERTRUDE

Even as I did, unravelling, but now,
Moll's ballet, with thread of Angie's spinning-song.[5]

CLAUDIUS

Cross-cradle, ah?

GERTRUDE

Yes, "by St. Charity,"—
Dear song—dear ballet—of salvation!—yes.
[*She takes off her wreath of cowslips, and drops it.*]
Come, sweet Ophelia! Come, child, and St. Agnes
Shall come along with us.

OPHELIA

Gramercy!

[*They go out, together.*
Claudius stares after them. Then, picking up the dropped cowslip-wreath, he fingers it.]

CLAUDIUS

Ha!
St. Agnes,—then; and now,—St. Valentine:
By Gis, I 'll blast 'em, both,—till she be mine!

He tears the wreath to pieces, and scatters it, staring at the pieces. As he does so, the room is filled with

DARKNESS.

Out of darkness: The glimmering of an oiled wick casts a smoky gleam, shadowly revealing TWO SHAPES, *against a half-seen background of vaulted walls, swelled with obtrusions, of differing sizes and forms.*
The nearer Shape is Claudius.

CLAUDIUS

Who 's here?—What!—Hast thou any face, to see,
Whom, facing, I discern not? Never, till now,
Since I remember, came I here before.

THE FURTHER SHAPE

Pardon, my lord, you have been here before.

CLAUDIUS

Can this be in the Castle?—Who art thou?

THE SHAPE

I am the Cellarer of Elsinore.
Nine fathoms underneath the kirkyard's floor
My home is cellar'd. Here, with the numb newt
And the blind mole, my lodging shares their mould.
The grave-pits are its eaves, but the slow seepage
Leaketh no patter through the noiseless walls.
My noon is glowworm-glory, and my midnight
Is darkness' nadir, where the neat's-foot oil
Flickers these shadings of its shadowy flares.
Here hath the toad no eyes, and the sallow cricket
No song. Here only are the squeaking bats
My starless nightingales.

CLAUDIUS

And art thou human,
Thus to consort with things o' the underslime?

CELLARER

Human.

CLAUDIUS

And dost thou never climb aloft,
To look on heavenly nature?

CELLARER

Once, I crept
Upward, beyond the crypt above, and peered
Out at the stars, since when their million eyes
Have seared mine own with balls of deathless fire
Beneath my shut lids, till I wink them open
And stare upon this place wherein I dwell,
To hold mine outward peace with it.

CLAUDIUS

Then, why
Dwell here?

CELLARER

Yea: why?

CLAUDIUS

What causeth thee to stay?

CELLARER

Custom.

CLAUDIUS

Custom?—Can custom tolerate
Toad-life, in a lordly castle?

CELLARER

Lordly castles
Must needs have cellars. Who shall keep the wines
For kin of royalty to hold their rouses,
Unless it be the cellarers of kings,
And o' them who would be kings, that aim so seldom
To explore their habitat of the underslime
And view the vicinage of their wine-vats?

CLAUDIUS

I cannot see plain, here. Are those the vat-skins,
Yonder,—those shadowy shapes upon the walls,
Bulging their paunches, like the bellied sides
Of courtiers in their cups?

CELLARER

They are the wineskins,
Fill'd with the ferment of that flatulence,
Your Highness' wit hath pour'd in metaphor
Before its bubbling source may reach the bellies.

CLAUDIUS

You twist my trope. The wine hath subtler goals:
Beauty of ensparkled eyes and laughing lips
Beyond the scope of bellies to envisage.

CELLARER

Why should it not? Love immemorial
For ancient soils, in hearts of simple folk
Tilling their vineyards under ruddying suns,
To madrigals of mirth, in old Provence,
On blossoming shores of legend by blue Rhone
And foaming Arno, have fill'd these treasured wineskins
With spirit honies, to enchant the tongues
Of lovers, in the after times, to taste
Their magic origins, and utter again
The love, that quickened them. That utterance
Is emulation—not of bellied trance,
But beauty, cull'd from heaven—as your Highness
Hath signified so subtly, in correction
Of my crude inference.—"Ensparkled eyes
And laughing lips," of course, can only utter
The love that shines in those, who "climb aloft
To look on heavenly nature."

CLAUDIUS

All 's too dark
Still, for my sense to pierce these contours. Yet
Now do I know, thou art he, whom I am seeking,
And here 's the destined place of my desire,
This very night, to mingle for one goblet
All of the magic spirits of these wines,
To win my goal. The Queen shall lift the goblet,
And quaff its keen quintessence, in carousal
Unto the wassail:—*To the King's return,*
This kiss of lips is cupp'd, in conjuring love!—
For, seest thou, Cellarer, 't is thus: Vowed, have I,
My brother, Hamlet, on my oath, to make
All Elsinore a feast-hall, till his coming
Home from the wars; that, so, oblivion
Of blood shall reign, in spirits blooming
With rose of wine, in place of pining's pallor;
With ruddy festival, in stead of rue,
Lest dooms of ruin fall upon this house
Of royalty, and crush it. Dost thou gauge
The source of my intent, and wilt thou aid it
To consummation?

CELLARER

Keenly I gauge your aim,
And will instruct your wishfulness to gain it,
Or not, as you, Sir, will, or nill. How may I serve you?

CLAUDIUS

Out of thy special craft and knowing. Tell me:
These wines of Elsinore, what are their kinds,
Their ages, and their vintages?

CELLARER

That were
To vivify a calendar of wisdom

Through vistas toward the birth of time, in shrines
Of saints and sages, who have tasted them
And given them sanctity.

CLAUDIUS

What! Wines of sanctity?

CELLARER

And sacrilege, my lord. They oft are mingled
To encharm our human sense. These shaggy hides
Of bull and goat and musk-ox, twinged by skill
O' the tanner's craft to wineskins, hold within 'em,
Even as our own, a blendure of strange bloods,
Prest from the primal grapes of white and purple,
To enamour, or enmadden. I could name you
Some samples, of both vintages.

CLAUDIUS

Pray, name them.

CELLARER

Yonder, within that farthest crypt, enswathéd
With spider-silks, dew-gemm'd with cellar-opals,
Is stored quintessence from the inverted bowl
Of Chuang Tzu, that knelled the heavenly death-gong
For his most dear belovéd, his soul's wife,
On her departure toward the spirit birth-realm.

CLAUDIUS

What words are these? Namest thou some ancient essence
Spirituous, or spiritual?

CELLARER

I said,
My lord, they oft are blent; but yon is pure,
Unmixt with our mortality.—Shall I
Go on?

CLAUDIUS

Go on.

CELLARER

Across the Himalayas,
By hinny-pack, hither borne through valley trails
And fords of centuries to yonder vault,
Still glimmers, concealed, the glow of inmost heaven,
Pour'd, to the King of Death, from the cupp'd lips
Of the acolyte, in the Rig Veda's song.—
Beside it, breathing yet with the sweet joy
Of young Akhnaton, moving to his tomb
In Egypt, sparkles inwardly the wine
Of bliss, outheld to him by the unseen hands
Of Ka, the conqueror of evil.—Near it,
Sail-borne across the blue Aegean, thence
And hither, in monkish crocks, a benison
Of bitterer tang lies stored for us: the sap
O' the hemlock bane, which Socrates, in Athens,
Quaffed to his dear disciples, Xenophon,
Plato, and Alcibiades.

CLAUDIUS

Incredible
Cellarer, wouldst thou mingle bliss and bane
To pledge self-murder, in the feasting-hall
Of Elsinore?

CELLARER

Patience, my startled lord:
I do but name these vintages, not pledge them
To any lip unwilling. They are silent.
The cobwebs cover them. 'T is you, must gauge
Their vantages, for feasting.—Shall I cease?

CLAUDIUS

Nay, tell the sequence.

CELLARER

Nearer where we are,
And ever more near where we shall be, in morrows
Less darkling, center'd for these mildew-vaults
In crimson at their heart, to make of them
A fane of spirit worship, yonder is stored
The Wine of Life. From water it was made,
By One, whose vintages are visionings
Of clear, still waters, turn'd to quickening wine
Within the grail He holdeth to the lips
Of all corruption, smiling its redemption.
The stretchéd fleeceling of a lamb doth hide
The dewfall from that grail, whose overflow
Hath fill'd the thirsting world, and still shall fill it
Beyond satiety.—Its quickening seep
Hath swell'd another form, of leathern strength,
With inner sweetness for its Stoic calm:
Yonder is vintage of the fortitude
Marcus Aurelius Antoninus sipped,
'Mid pausings in the marches of his legions,
Unknowing yet the Holder of the Grail,
Who poured it in his heart.

CLAUDIUS

Enough, enough!
What are these saps of sanctity to me,
Who seek a wine of witchery?—In all
Thy cellarage, hast thou no juice of joyance
To stir the quaffing lips to giddied mirth,
Blur the bright eyes with mistings of foxfire,
Jiggle the addled head to beckonings
And nods of luring; scarlet the slant cheeks
With pouting laughters, and emprickle the limbs
To darings of the dance?—This night of nights
Must blaze an orgic flame in Elsinore,
Shall singe the winglets of St. Valentine
To clap his shoulder-blades, like Chanticleer

At dawning, under hen-roost, and make peal
His clarion, with the wild cuckoo's call,
Throughout the feast-hall, fanning the red sparkles,
And spilling brandy-fire from banquet cups
To quench its own element.—Hast thou such wine?
I came for it! Where is it?

CELLARER

Ah, I see:
'T is the *other* vintages!—I had forgot
To name them. Many are they.—Here are these:
The rabid draught of raddled Alexander,
Bubbling hot carmine, prest from the burst brains
Of madness, in his stewing cups.—The negus
Of Nero, stirr'd with cinders of Rome's fire.—
The draught cerulean, which Antony
Poured in the Triton horn of weltering Neptune,
To potion wiles of Cleopatra's passion.—
But here, methinks, most witching-succulent
For orgy of Elsinore, 't were this old wine
Of Capri's isle, beglisten'd with aquamarine
Of the groinéd grotto, where the naked diver
Turns fish of silver, in the upslanting gold
Of liquid-burning sand-sun. Drunk with this,
Imperial Tiberius filled his beaker,
To lickerish squealings of his swineherd-pipes,
And plunged his foaming pearl, to kiss the scarlet
Lips o' the queen of his concubines.—Whoever
Shall swallow of this a thimbleful, shall quicken
Satyr, within the blood of Socrates,
Circe, beneath the bosom of St. Agnes,
And mingle both, to whirl in giddying dance
Before the shrine of Venus Pandemos,
And flaunt Delirium's limbs.

CLAUDIUS

No more! Give here!
Where is 't? I choose it—Tiberius' wine! To-night,

At feast, Marcellus shall come here to fetch it,
And, high in a beaten-silver pitcher borne,
Set it beside the Queen, for my right hand
To fill her goblet withal.—Where is 't, I say?
Snuff up yon smoking oil-wick, till I see it,
And thine own face, at last!

[*Bending over, the dusky form of the Cellarer snuffs the wick, which shoots upward a sudden flare, revealing his face—the face of* GALLUCINIUS.]

GALLUCINIUS

At last?

CLAUDIUS
[*Starting back.*]

Not *thou!*—
Gallucinius!—Again?

GALLUCINIUS

Again.

CLAUDIUS

Thy mouth
Hath spoke my choice—Tiberius!

GALLUCINIUS

Tiberius, be it!

DARKNESS

[*Out of the dark, returning light reveals again the contours of the Queen's boudoir and the form of Claudius—standing as before—staring at pieces of the torn cowslip-plaited wreath of Gertrude, on which he grinds his heel, harshly repeating his cry.*]

CLAUDIUS

St. Agnes,—then; and now,—St. Valentine:
Yea, God! I 'll blast 'em both—till she be mine!

CURTAIN.

ACT SECOND

Scene One

OPHELIA'S BEDCHAMBER. ELSINORE.

Between two Gothic windows, a canopied bedstead, at back. On the window-sills, in crocks, green plants, in bud, and vines, climbing slenderly the stone carvings of the windows. Near the left one, there hangs a wood-barred cage, with a BLACK BIRD*, perched still, within it. At lower right, near centre, a sewing-bench.*

Enter, left, QUEEN GERTRUDE *and* OPHELIA. *Together, they go toward the bench.*

GERTRUDE

[*Glancing at a script, held in her hand.*]

And thou, sweet one, wast reading this, when Moll
Burst out a-lilting, with her ballet?

OPHELIA

Madam,
She came so suddenly upon me, I—
I could not think, and then I cried to you.
I pray you, pardon it.

GERTRUDE

'T is nothing needful
Of pardon, rather of pity for poor Moll,
Whose love 's a hardy bludgeon, when 't should be
As pliant as witchhazel, to touch wound
Of bruiséd sense with solace. But so 't is:
The hoof of ploughmare is no delicate hand
To stroke a filly's side.

OPHELIA

Dear Moll is gentler
Than many be, and her big thumb and forefinger
Can thread a needle, quicker than I can.
Methinks I was at fault.

GERTRUDE

For what?

OPHELIA

For—for
Crying so sudden,—and I know not why.

GERTRUDE

Perhaps, for thinking on what 's written here?
Whence came this script?

OPHELIA

Madam, from far away.

GERTRUDE

Where, then?

OPHELIA

From Wittenberg. The messenger
Arrived 'fore yesterday, but said he was
To wait, and give it me for valentine.

GERTRUDE

From Wittenberg!—Ah, face of far-away
Looms near, when Now takes thought of Yesterday
And there is none to watch how showers fall
From eyes, in Elsinore. Princes afar
Ha' princedoms at home, and cast their shadows there
Across the seas, more darkly radiant
Than cloud-wracks, at sundown. Here are two Hamlets—
Who are not here! I dream on two of them,
And thou on one dreamest, dear child.—May I
Peep into this, and read aloud?

OPHELIA

Oh, yes!

GERTRUDE
[*Reading.*]

Thaw of ice,
Snow smell
Of the earliest bluebell—
Ignorance of artifice:

Bud, in blowing,
Dawn-wet
Touch o' the white violet—
Knowledge of the Ever-Knowing.

Maidenhair,
Breeze-swung
Blossom o' the bee-sung
Wisdom of the All-Aware:

They of thee, and theirs with thine,
Trance-entwine—thy Valentine.

Methinks, I hear the voice, within my own.
Know'st thou the hand?

OPHELIA
[*Looking.*]

'T is a clear, curving hand,
But there be slant strokes in 't.

GERTRUDE

'T was swiftly writ,
And the down-strokes are dark.

OPHELIA

I like the up ones.
They have a gallant curl, and dare the air.
The down, methinks, are jagged.

GERTRUDE

Methinks, not:
Raggled, a little, perhaps. But not the rhymes.

The verses grow, even as their virgin theme,
From nature's sweetness, ere the early scent
Is musted by enfouling emanations
From pools of stagnancy. Ah, yes, meseems,
From their fresh smell of unpolluted sense
I guess well where they grew.

OPHELIA

From where?

GERTRUDE

Suffice
To say: from "ignorance of artifice,"
Blended with "wisdom of the All-Aware,"
So artfully, their hiding origin
Is artlessness—revealed!

[*Kissing her quickly, she rises and turns away.*]

OPHELIA

Why do you kiss me,
So sudden, Madam?

GERTRUDE

For thou turnest me
A cheek, where even mine may savour lips
No pent breath can unfreshen by its passion,
Nor stale with stifled truth. Ophelia dear,
I love thee true. Dost thou believe it?

OPHELIA

Truly,
Madam. And you I love, as true--and more
Than I can say it.

GERTRUDE

And so we will not say it,
Who do not need to say it. Words enough

Are said of love—by love, without the knowing,
By hate, without the showing, true love lacks.
Yet love, true love: there 's not enough of it
Here, in this, is there? More, there must be, hidden
In other verses. Hath my Hamlet sent thee
More?

OPHELIA

Oh, many more.

GERTRUDE

All words?—No tokens
Else?

OPHELIA

One.

GERTRUDE

What token, more than word?

OPHELIA

A bird.

GERTRUDE

A bird?—Ah, yonder, in the cage!
[*Going to the cage.*] And when
Came here this Sir, of sombre plumes, to share
Your bedchamber?

OPHELIA

'Fore-yesterday, he came,
With the messenger.

GERTRUDE

[*In pensiveness, lit by a smile.*]

By trails of wilderness,
And weather-vanéd towns, through tidal storms,

And mists, and bright sun-bursts, to abide with thee,
Here, in thy maiden sanctuary!—O, Sir Silence!
Methinks, that you should ope that closéd neb,
The aureate dawns have kist to yellow-gold,
Gilding your black crest, and say: *Virgo, gratias!*

OPHELIA

Dear Madam, prithee, tremble not the bars
O' the cage, with your fingers; for, methinks, he sleeps.

GERTRUDE

Ah, soft, then; very softly! Yet may I
Enquire, in whisper, what his knightly name is?

OPHELIA

He 'll tell you, himself.

GERTRUDE
[*Laughing.*]

What, vocally,—in Latin?

[*Ophelia shakes her head, hushingly.*]

Etruscan?—French?—Nay, not in jackdaw! Not
In guttural,—in German?

OPHELIA

No, in our own tongue.

But he 'll not talk, nor sing. When first he came,
I fed him honey-cakes, in crumbs, but he 'd
Not touch 'em. So I talked to him, and sang
A little, but he would not answer me,
Except that, once, he turned, and pecked a bar,
To show me *that,* tied to it.

GERTRUDE

Ah, this token!

OPHELIA

'T is written there,—his name.

[*Gertrude examines a small, half-unrolled scroll, tied to the cage, and smiles.*]

GERTRUDE

In the same hand,
I see, as writ the valentine.—What 's here,
Sir Sombre?—Nay, do *you* write verses, too,
And share the same amanuensis?

OPHELIA

Madam,
Pray, don't untie it!

GERTRUDE

No!—But *read* it,—yes?

[*Ophelia nods. The Queen unrolls it, and reads aloud.*]

TO THE ENCAGING OPHELIA:

Lady!—I am Amsel.
Here, endearéd damsel,
From the enragéd
Realm of mortals, keep me cagéd,
Song-imprison'd, caught
In these
Bars of silences,
Where none may ever enter, but
Thee—and Thought.

Oh, let me steal away!—My dear, my dear,
My rude intrusion on this barréd silence
Hath led me to the inmost door of thought—
To darkness, where I dare not enter.

OPHELIA

Stay!
I prithee, tarry!—When you go away,

There will, indeed, be silence here, and only
My crocuses and wandering-Jew vines
For me to tend and water. Oft they smile,
But never speak, no more than doth my bird.
Tarry, and tell me of my mother, as
You wont to do, and I so glad to listen!

GERTRUDE

Cornelia!—My own Cornelia!

[*She sits on the bench, beside which, on the floor, Ophelia cuddles down, looking up at her.*]

OPHELIA

Was she like me?

GERTRUDE

As fleurdelys is like
To flowerdeluce, in gracileness of blossom,
But not in stalk and stature. She was taller
Than thee, and had no need to cusp her chin
Upward, with parted lips, to look i' my eyes,
As thou dost. She would prone her head, a little,
To make our gazes even.

OPHELIA

Was she light,
Or dark?

GERTRUDE

As I have told thee, more than Moll
Hath told thee pixy-tales, she was as light
As holly-shine, at evening, and as dark
As cypress, in the noontime.

OPHELIA

But they are
So different, each from other!

GERTRUDE

So was she
As different from *all* others. Light and dark
So mingled through the lashes of her eyes,
You could not guess them blue, or hazel, which,
And through her hair, which glittered fleurdelys
To float like tendrils of the morning-glory,
That whether she were amber, or were auburn,
I still am guessing it. Thou hast her hair
In radiance, but wash'd to cowslip-colour
In the new moon's cup, methinks.—Ah, me: ah, me!—
New Moon—and Molly's "christen-blooms": no, no!
Ask me no more, dear.

OPHELIA
[*Anxiously.*]

Have I hurt thee, Madam,
Telling me of my mother?

GERTRUDE

Only where hurting
Might probe the source of healing—if it would!
Ask me thy heartful.

OPHELIA

But perhaps—?

GERTRUDE

Ask on.

OPHELIA

When did she die?

GERTRUDE

When thou camest to this world,
As I have told thee.

OPHELIA

Yes, I know,—but yet:
How came I to this world, if she must leave it?

GERTRUDE

Ah, now thou 'rt asking Destiny, not me.

OPHELIA

I did n't know I was. Who 's Destiny,
I 've read about, in books?

GERTRUDE

There is one book,
And only one, can tell thee.

OPHELIA

What 's its name?

GERTRUDE

Amor.

OPHELIA

It is a lovely name.

GERTRUDE

And a lovely thing.

OPHELIA

Who wrote it?

GERTRUDE

The Moons and Stars.

OPHELIA

The moons and stars!
Why, there 's but one moon.

GERTRUDE

Thou mayst learn to count
Nine, in the heavens, some time. And the stars—
Look up, to-night, and thou shalt see their script
Writ all in myriad spangling valentines.
The moons of dark are Destiny's gestation.
The stars are pap-buds of unfurling night,
Who wraps her caul around infinitudes
Of infant worlds, that wait their suckling time,
As thou, bright world, Ophelia, didst await
Thy suckling and thy weaning, in this world
Of baby universes. Dost thou ask
A mother world to tell thee all she knoweth
From nine moons' knowledge of that Destiny
Which mothered her, and thee, and millions more,
Who live—to love, and die?

OPHELIA

What is it, to die?

GERTRUDE

To live, unknowing what it means to love.
That is one death. It is made all of shell.
The other, shell-less, is made all of life
Within, which moulds it. So there be two deaths.
And one is silent as hardness, and the other
Sings soft, and sweet as nightingale in spring.

[*Ophelia, who has listened breathlessly, starts, sudden, and, clutching her throat, stares at the cage.*]

OPHELIA

Ah!—Ah!

GERTRUDE

What is 't?

OPHELIA

And can it be—he 'll die?
He keeps so still.

GERTRUDE

Who?

OPHELIA

Amsel.

[*Springing up, and darting to the cage.*]

Oh,—not dead!
Can he be *dead?*

[*As she peers, with anguished look, into the cage, there is heard a* MELLOW VOICE, *singing—in soft, sweet baritones—distantly.*]

THE VOICE

Lily of the dell,
Ring, O, ring his passing bell!
Small birds, be his choir-boys!

[*Gertrude rises. Tensely, they look at each other.*]

GERTRUDE

What?—Listen!

THE VOICE

[*More near.*]

And sing, O, sing
An anthem to dear Spring
And her joys!

OPHELIA

Ah,—who is it?
Is 't the other Death, singing, as you told me, now,
So softly?

GERTRUDE

[*Who has listened, amazed.*]

It hath ceased.—Hath Destiny

A voice, perchance, as soft as Death's, to sing
A carol—of coincidence?—Ah, so!
Methought it so.—Wait not. Come in. Who 's there?

[*Enter a* MAN, *in white and purple vestments.*]

THE MAN

Your Majesty, 't is I—the King's Chorister—
Come bringing you a message, with this flower.

[*He presents a note, and a flower.*]

GERTRUDE

A tulip?—Ah!—Methinks, I know this hand.

[*Opening the note, she reads, aside.*]

Good holy day!—On bleeding arrow-heads
Have fallen blossoms of St. Valentine.
Here, pray accept this one. Sith Sorrow weds
Remorse, perchance Condonement's eyes shall shine
Forgiveness on two lips
Forever silent,
And one tulip's
Cup—hold return of tears, Compassion's sigh lent.

From "ignorance of artifice," to knowledge
Of its mastership, even to making rhymes sigh!
Ah, well. Who knows enough—*not* to forgive?

[*To the Chorister.*]

And, Sir, the message,—is 't by mouth?

CHORISTER

Mine own.

His highness, my lord Duke Claudius, entreateth
The Queen, your Majesty, to be so gracious
As to attend the high feast, in her honour,
Held at the banquet-hall, this evening,
In festal prayer for speedy home-coming
Of our most yearned-for, royal majesty,
King Hamlet, from the wars.

GERTRUDE

Sir, tell his highness . . .
The Queen will come.

CHORISTER
[*Bowing.*]

Her servant doth rejoice
To bear her message back unto the Duke.

GERTRUDE

Stay, yet. A song we heard, most gently soft,
Before your coming.—"Lily of the dell,"
It lilted, in sweet tones. Know you the singer?

CHORISTER

Ah, Majesty, your pardon! It was I.
The high feast hath rehearsals, and my lord,
The Duke, is most meticulous they shall
Be perfect. In them, I bear my humble part.
But had I deemed, at all, your Majesty
Could overhear me, in my undertones,
Bringing to voice and memory a portion
Of my small part, I would have checked—

GERTRUDE

Check naught.
But, as you go, recall again, we pray,
That same sweet strain, and tone it, as before,
That we may listen, the Lady Ophelia,
Here, with ourself, and echo inwardly
Its anthem to dear Spring.

CHORISTER
[*Bowing to each.*]

My gracious liege!
My lady!—Your servant. [*Exit.*]

GERTRUDE

So!—Coincidence
Hath share in destiny, and beareth his part
With gentle deference.—
[*To Ophelia.*] What, peeping yet
In Amsel's cage?

OPHELIA

He hath not stirr'd. He keeps
So still!

VOICE OF THE CHORISTER
[*Singing, without, close by.*]

Lily of the dell,
Ring, O, ring his passing bell!
Small birds, be his choir-boys!—

OPHELIA
[*Beckoning, eagerly, to the Queen.*]

He 's stirring, now! See, see! He turns
His pretty head, and shines his eyes to mine.
He 's not dead. He 's *alive!*
[*Clapping her hands, and dancing, she kisses the Queen.*]

GERTRUDE

My sweet Ophelia!

VOICE OF THE CHORISTER
[*Distantly.*]

And sing, O, sing
An anthem to dear Spring
And her joys! . . . . .

CURTAIN.

ACT SECOND

Scene Two

Reverberations of cannon, mingled with shouting and music of bagpipes and drums, precede the curtain's rise, which discloses

THE BANQUET-HALL, AT ELSINORE.

At back, a ramped dais, with long table, at which COURTIERS *and* LADIES *are seated. Below it, stools and benches, where* MUSICIANS, SERVANTS *and* FOLK *are grouped about an open front-space, in varied conditions of drunkenness. Among them are* TOPAS, YAUGHAN, MOLL COWSLIP, MARCELLUS [*sober*]. *At table are* POLONIUS, LAERTES, OSRIC, CHORISTER, *and* CLAUDIUS, *beside whom, at centre, is an empty seat.*

Led by the Chorister, amid clinking and clashing of drinking-goblets, cans and tankards, to squealing of bag-pipes, ALL *join in chorus to the Chorister's song.*

SONG

Who 's King? . . .
Who 's canniest
King o' the Castle of Elsinore?—
Who woul't be, O!
But 't is he, ho!—
Cannikin, Cannikin, Cannikin, the Canny,
Clink-can-clanniest
King o' the cups of Elsinore!
For . . . .
Who would pine with sighings more,
Can hail him, Cannikin, Cannikin, King Canny?

CLAUDIUS

[*Rising, with cup raised, in gesture for silence.*]

Ho, my lords, dames, gentlemen, and Dane-folk,
Long live King Cannikin, the Canny!—What can he *not?*
Yea, and what *can* he?—Can he not debouch
From glowering clouds of doubting on our dooms
This ambush'd band of joy, to storm redouts
Of war with wassail-beakers, and compel
Rebellious cares, by cannon of our rouses,
To own defeat of fear?—Aye, that he can;
And by his cunning can he coerce all
That carks our hearts, to choirs of carousal,

Singing: *Surrender, Gloom!*—So, beakers, up!
Wassail, the King of Elsinore,—King Cup!

ALL

Wassail! Wassail! Wassail!

[*Amid lessening shouts, Claudius beckons to his side the Chorister.*]

CLAUDIUS

Where stays the Queen?

CHORISTER

My lord, methinks, in the Lady Ophelia's chamber.

CLAUDIUS

Gave you to her our message, with the flower?

CHORISTER

I gave it, my lord.

CLAUDIUS

What said she?

CHORISTER

"Tell his highness,
The Queen will come."

CLAUDIUS

Ah!—But *will* she?—Your place!

[*The Chorister returns to his seat, as Claudius rises once more, to address the assemblage.*]

Lordings! Liegefolk!—*In officio*
Regis Vini Divini, in our office
As Regent of the Realm, and Vice-Dominioner
Of his divinest majesty, King Cup,
Welcome, once more, to Elsinore!

CRIES

Hail! Hail!

CLAUDIUS

Behold, now, in his reign, how he commingleth
Courtier and commoner in his swirléd praise,
Even as the wine and mead within our bellies,
Commingling, mount to bell-towers of our voices
In choirs, and to the watch-towers of our eyes
In sparkling bonfires, to his vernal feast-night—
This vine-feast of St. Valentine.

OSRIC

[*Rising, tipsily, kisses his hand to Claudius.*]

Perfection!

Past all penultimates, *pulcherrima!*
A most mellifluous similitude,
Parabolic of bells and bellies in metalepsis,
Venust with vernal collations of the Cup-King!
In vino—veritas: ex veritate—
Sanctus Valentinus!

[*He bows, right and left.*]

MOLL COWSLIP

[*Rising, curtsies, left and right.*]

Lahdidah to his lordship!

TOPAS

[*Pulling her flounce.*]

Down, Moll!

OSRIC

Naught, naught: a nothing! *Seulement un bon mot!*

[*He sits again, amid guffaws, and a glance of smiling annoyance from Claudius.*]

CLAUDIUS

So hath it seeméd, as "perfection's" part
Of this our feasting, that we summon, in sanction,
Down from the saintly watch-towers and choir-crofts,

Our royal Chorister, to join his praise
With ours, 'mid chimes of cannikins. Revellers,
The King's Chorister—and clink your rims!

CHORISTER
[*Rising, amid a tumult of tankards.*]

Your Highness, my lord Regent!—Word of royalty
Giveth, not asketh, sanction in Elsinore,
And vice-dominion is dominion's self,
In absence of the donor of all sanction
In Denmark realm, whom war and distant turmoil—
Long while for love, but little while in hope—
Hath sundered from our hearths, but not our hearts—
Hamlet, his kingly majesty.

CLAUDIUS

Amen!

CHORISTER

Thus, fellow-feasters, be it ever remember'd,
'T is Hamlet to serve—thereby our gracious queen
To solace, in his mournéd absence—hath
Our noble regent, lord Duke Claudius,
Commanded mirth and festival and music
For dousal of all dreads, and for upspringing
Sprigs of delight, to wreathe St. Valentine
In revels for the Queen, who cometh soon
To join our feasting. Therefore, do I humbly
Take part in this command; albeit more oft
The choirs of solemnities have claimed
My voice in leading. Yet if, as now, to mime
The chorus of King Cup, or, as othertime
To intone the King of Heaven, I be call'd,
I answer in allegiance—not to fear
Of Denmark's force, but faith in Denmark's love
For loyalty to regency.

CRIES

Hear! Hear!

OSRIC

[*Rising.*]

'Coutez! Regale, my lords! Loyalty to royalty—
'T is the inverse compression of the expression
Of regency.—*Voilà!*—There is my cup.
Voici!—Here is my lip.—The lip is to the cup
As loyalty to the King. Inverted,—lo!
The lip is unreplenisht—the cup is famisht.—

[*With sudden, explosive shout.*]

Long live surcease of famine in our fair land!
Regency forever!

[*Waving his cup, he topples, and slides off the dais, headlong to the floor.*]

CLAUDIUS

Marcellus!—Remove the cause
Of regency's eulogy.

MARCELLUS

At once, your Highness.

[*Marcellus lifts and carries off Osric, who, in process, kisses his fingers to Claudius and the laughing drinkers, as he calls out.*]

OSRIC

Rien, mes amis! Rien! Mere naught—a trifle—
Un bon mot pour la reine—a valentine! [*Exeunt.*]

CLAUDIUS

My lords, in Osric, delicate precision
Doth wax more voluble as his delicacy
Doth wane. The regency of Denmark needeth
No definition of its loyalty
To Denmark,—as our chancellor o' the realm,

Nestor of all our stately policies,
Polonius, I see, is even now
On point of rising, to attest.—Speak on,
Polonius! Your thoughts are for the world.

POLONIUS
[*Rising, flustered.*]

Indeed, your Greatness, 't is a spacious world
For thoughts to roam in, and perchance too roomy
To gather back my scatter'd ruminations
Into this room of mirth, where feast comes first,
And meditation follows after folly,
To check accounts.

CLAUDIUS
[*Startled.*]

With folly?

POLONIUS

With the exchequer,
Wherein—fear not, your Highness!—no folly entereth
Under Polonius' eye.

CLAUDIUS

Why, then, "accounts"?
What needeth accounting?

POLONIUS

Conscience. He, who fails
To check his conscience, loses his balance, even—
Pardon the allusion!—e'en as my lord Osric
Did put his foot, in place of his forefinger,
Before his lip, and so—per consequence
Of underchecking conscience in his action—
O'erdrew his balance, and held the floor no longer
Than, had he held his lip in hand, he might

Have held us all with his *bons mots.* Of such
Folly in action, needeth none, I hope,
Accuse Polonius. So, in perfect conscience,
Having thus regathered out of all the world
My thoughts, and uttered them in utter candour,
I let them roam again, and now resume
My humble seat of state—as 't were—in highest
Attestation of your Highness' regency.

MOLL

All hail *As-'Twere,* his seat of state! 'T is ample.
Edgy for to wedge all cracks, and wide enow—
As 't were—to buttock all the straddle-beams
I' the Castle.

TOPAS

[*Stifling her mouth with his hand.*]

Plug thy mouth! Wilt follow Osric
Into the hoist?

MOLL

Who 'll hoist me? Him as doth,
He 'll hug the heft of Elsinore in 's arms!

CLAUDIUS

King Cup, we see, hath got him a girl-bairn,
To bawl out in the Castle, when the mirth
Of menfolk lulls, to ponder stately matters.
Else, what were mirth, without a Molly Magpie
To peck—as 't were—the seat of polity
To echo noise of laughter, less politely
Than policy would counsel. We are here
For joyance, not analysis of joy:
Expression, not examination. So,
Bubble, cup! Foam, beaker!—But, our brave Laertes,
Prized son of cherish'd chancellor, what now?

The bubble lispeth in your cup. Pray, let it
Leap up, and out, and utter why it only
Lisps, and not trumpets, as beseems a soldier's
Spirit, on voyage to-morrow, for his earliest
Visit to Paris, the acropolis
Of martial wine-gods.

LAERTES
[*Rising.*]

Highness, I am devout
Disciple of those sparkling deities
Parisian. I abstain in Elsinore
From love, not lack, of that devotion. Now,
Ashore, to-night, I spare my lips, to stanchion
My sea-legs, on the morrow. For then I sail
Tides, whose rich foam along my vessel's rim
Shall be prophetic of a wilder foaming
In Paris, whirled from rims of spinning goblets,
Plunging to the bowl-bottom of a world
Where crafts of state, and freightages of war,
And gondoliering love, are suckt to deeps
Of swallowing oblivion, or left
To float among the wreckages of time
Under the starry spindrift.

CLAUDIUS

May your voyagings,
On both those wine-dark deeps, return you to us,
Convoy'd by *argosies* of foaming bowls,
Safe to home port! Meantime, ere you depart,
Now let your voice do what your lips abstain,
And drink, with draughts of joy, the source of wine—
The honey in the heart of youth, that lures
The bees of joy to swarm anew, and burst
Their hive, in blazing music.—Music, ho!
Now let the harp outpulse the kettle-drum

Till our own pulses catch the quivering beat,
Clutching our throats, to swarm the winging words
That sting our tongues to Roman resonance.
Chorister,—*Gaudeamus!*

CHORISTER
[*With gesture to the Musicians, sings, to harp-music.*]

Gaudeamus igitur,
Juvenes dum sumus:
Gaudeamus igitur,
Juvenes dum sumus!

Post jocundum, juventutem,
Post molestam, senectutem,
Nos habebit humus,
Nos habebit humus.

[*In the doorway, right, unobserved, appears* QUEEN GERTRUDE, *who looks on, listening.*]

CHORISTER
[*Solus.*]

Vita nostra brevis est . . .

ALL

Vita nostra brevis est,
Breve finietur.
Vita nostra brevis est,
Breve . . .

CLAUDIUS

Hold!—Cease!—The Queen! Your reverences—all!

ALL
[*Some rising, some scrambling to their knees.*]

Long live the Queen! The Queen! All hail! Wassail!
[*Going to meet her, Claudius escorts the Queen to the dais-table, at centre.*]

CLAUDIUS

Welcome, beloved Queen and sister! Now
Our joyance greets itself, to hail your presence
Amid your shining court and queendom.

GERTRUDE

Kingdom,
Our noble kinsman!—Denmark still, methinks,
Reaches to the darkling rims invisible
Where Hamlet stands, to greet us, from afar,
And bids you welcome to this seat beside us.
[*She sits, motioning him beside her, and the others to be seated.*]

CLAUDIUS
[*Still standing.*]

His seat awaits him, with our yearning hearts.—
You heard our welcoming song?

GERTRUDE

To this *brief life*
Of revelry? Yea, brother: *brevis est*
Vita nostra.

CLAUDIUS

Therefore, rejoice: *Gaudeamus,*
Igitur!

GERTRUDE

That so soon this earth shall hold us?—
Nos habebit humus!

CLAUDIUS

That this humus holds
Such humour still in us, to hold it jocund
As in the world's youth. Witness now its token

Of mirth perpetual.—Marcellus, fetch it
Here, to her majesty!

[*He beckons toward the doorway, left, where* MARCELLUS *stands, uplifting a silver pitcher, entwined and fringed with young vine leaves. At the Duke's gesture, he bears it to the dais, presenting it to the hand of Claudius, who speaks aside to him.*]

The watchword: speak it!

MARCELLUS
[*In low voice.*]

Tiberius.

[*He withdraws, among the folk.*]

CLAUDIUS

Here, royal sister mine,
High in this beaten-silver pitcher borne,
Bedraped with foldings of its living vine,
Far from the glowing zone of Capricorn,
Hath voyaged a mendicant from Venus' shrine,
Fraught with this message from St. Valentine:

Fill with this
Regina's glass,
That my bliss
To her may pass:
Sit vernalis
Aeternitas!

[*He fills the Queen's goblet, and proffers it to her.*]

GERTRUDE
[*Reaches to take it, but withdraws her hand.*]

Gramercy! But the only bliss, can beckon
To-night, must pass through listening ears, not lips,
For us to quaff the message it may bring
From that far zone, whence Hamlet wafts it, on winds
That freeze its wine of melting melody.

CLAUDIUS

[*With hushing gesture.*]

More music, then! But music, soft as sleeping
Memory, that wakens in her sleep,
To gaze on eyes, that hold her own enmirror'd,
Under dark brows, pall'd with wild roses blossoming.
Music—a single strain: all Elsinore
Be silent, else, as death!

[*With sign to the Chorister and the Harpist, he sits gently beside Gertrude, unobtrusively seeking her eyes with his own, while she listens pensively to the voice of the Chorister, who—having risen quietly—sings, to a single harp's tone, solemnly slow and soft.*]

SONG

Bind, bind with blossoms all
The bare year's boughs.
Wind, wind his poor black pall
With a rose wreath
And a green mantle, gayly.
For his cold brows
Twist a quaint coronal,
Every feat maiden, fayly.

Underneath, far underneath,
The dead year lies in funeral.
Lily of the dell,
Ring, O, ring his passing-bell!
Small birds, be his choir-boys,
And sing, O, sing
An anthem to dear Spring
And her joys!

And ever, at their antheming,
Fly, fly, thou raven, Doubt!
For earth is fair, without.
Fie, fie, thou cypress, Death!
The primrose blossometh,
And Spring—hey-day, the Spring!—
To her sweet maids' gathering
Cometh on the kine's breath.

Bind, bind with blossoms all The bare year's boughs.
Wind, wind his poor black pall With a rose wreath And a
green mantle, gayly. For his cold brows Twist a quaint
coronal, Every feat maiden, fayly.
Underneath, far underneath, The dead year lies in funeral.
Lily of the dell, Ring, O, ring his passing-bell!
Small birds, be his choir-boys, And sing, O, sing
An anthem to dear Spring And her joys!
And ever, at their antheming, Fly, fly, thou raven, Doubt!
For earth is fair, without. Fie, fie, thou cypress, Death!
The primrose blossometh, And Spring—hey-day, the Spring!—
To her sweet maids' gathering Cometh on the kine's breath.

See page 673

[*Having hearkened, with far-off gazing,—now, as the harp ceases,—Gertrude starts, and turns to Claudius.*]

GERTRUDE

Now will I drink!—Ah, reach me the goblet!—Danes,
Our loving Danes! Drink with me, now: *To Hamlet!*
Hamlet, his home-returning!

[*Taking from Claudius' hand the filled goblet, Gertrude drinks from it, while the others hail her, respondingly, and drink.*]

ALL

Hamlet! Hamlet!
Home to us! Hamlet! Return!

CLAUDIUS

[*Aside, as the shouting lessens.*]

Now, Cellarer,
Tiberius satyrs Socrates, and Circe
Holds cup to St. Agnes' lips, and Claudio
Reaps the rim-kiss!

[*To Gertrude.*]

A loving-cup, *To Hamlet!*
Sister and brother share the regency:—
Hamlet, his home-returning!

[*Reaching for the goblet, he takes it from Gertrude's hand, and, drinking, passes it between them, from lips to lips, till it is emptied; then, swiftly refilling, he reaches it again to the Queen.*]

More, to that wassail,
In bounty! Rebound it, music!—Let the bagpipes
Tweedle it to the kettles, and the cannon
Boom it from Elsinore to Poland's ice,
Cleaving the drifts, and thaw his homing-trail,
To join with us in Denmark's triumph-dance!
Marcellus,—out! Let cannon sound our rouses!

[*Exit Marcellus.—The bagpipes start playing a wild dance-tune, to the kettle-drums, punctuated soon by deep booms of cannon, as the Queen raises the goblet again, and drinks, to increasing applause of the Dane-folk.*]

GERTRUDE
[*Deliriously.*]

More!—More!—To Hamlet, life! Death to the Polacks!
To Denmark,—love!—love!—Claudio!
Is 't thou? What are thou?

CLAUDIUS
[*Swaying, with the drink.*]

Chorister o' the feast!
What, ho, lordings, Danes, and Romans!
[*Pointing at himself and the Chorister.*]
Deem ye
'T is Claudio be Chorister, or be Chorister—Claudio?
Lo, yonder vestment!—white-pure as leeks in lily-bed.
Mine 's peasecod-purple. Yet may double vestures
Be single-invested with truth. And hearts be trumps.
[*Embracing the Chorister.*]
Heart-brothers, both! Twin choristers! Or, deem ye
This bonny Rex—be I? Nay, song shall douse it:
Cannikins, chorus, now!—*Solus,* Claudio!
[*He sings forth, as the others chorus him, to the kettle-drums.*]

Who 's Rex? . . .
Who 's bonniest
Rex o' the Realm of Elsinore?—
Claudio, he, O?
How would he be, O,
Cannikin, Cannikin, Cannikin, the Canny,
Hey-nonny-nonniest
Rex o' the cups of Elsinore?
For . . . . .
Who needs buy, can borrow store
And—bail him, Cannikin, Cannikin, King Canny—

Nay, Cannikin 's no manikin to kings,
Rexes, nor regents. Cannikin remaineth Cannikin,
And Claudius—Claudio, and the Queen—

GERTRUDE

[*Rising, and moving to the music's rhythms.*[6]]

The Queen 's
Regina of the isle of roses.—Waves—
Waves o' the silvering wallows!—Wines—wines!
Burst, O bubble blueness! Rush—rushing
Rush the shallows . . . Hark! . . . Roar o' the shore-rocks!
Shallow is deep; shining the shallows—
Deep, deep let us dance,—for shallowly, shadowly
Slip the shores away . . . Claudio! . . . Claudio,
Come!

[*Taking his hand, she leads him from the dais to the centre open-space, oblivious of the on-staring folk and courtiers.*]

CLAUDIUS

Dusky the sands are.

GERTRUDE

Come!

CLAUDIUS

Dark—the cliffs—

GERTRUDE

Come!

CLAUDIUS

Why?

GERTRUDE

Dance!

CLAUDIUS

When?

GERTRUDE

Soon . . .

CLAUDIUS

Hark! . . .

GERTRUDE

Dance!

CLAUDIUS

Hark!—waves—cliffs.—Are they hissing?

GERTRUDE

Kissing . . Dance!

[*They dance, together.*
The music mounts, and the dancing with it.
The kettle-drums drown the harps.
The onlookers rise, leaning forward.

From the left, a clanging sound, from without, precedes a sudden, enlarged reverberation of the cannon's boom, which occasions, in the folk group, a bursting shout, from Yaughan, starting back from Moll Cowslip, who has hunched her shoulders, and is curving and flapping her arms, wildly, as she peers, squintingly, toward Claudius, in the dance.]

YAUGHAN

Whoop, Moll! Stint it!

MOLL
[*Screaming.*]

Wild hawk! Wild hawk!

[*Enter* MARCELLUS, *panting.*]

MARCELLUS

My lord,
Your Highness,—Voltimand!

[*Enter* VOLTIMAND, *in spattered saddle-gear. The music stops, suddenly.*]

VOLTIMAND
[*Calling to Claudius.*]

My lord Duke,—message!

CLAUDIUS
[*Staring.*]

Who—what—how!—Message for whom?

VOLTIMAND

The Queen.

GERTRUDE

Ah!—Ah,
Voltimand!—Speak! Speak it—the message.

VOLTIMAND

Hark it:
"War cries, *Go, kill!* and lips of love, *Come, kiss!*
Denmark kills on,—and Hamlet *comes* with this!"

[*Enter* KING HAMLET *in armoured riding-gear.*]

GERTRUDE
[*With shrill cry.*]

Hamlet!

KING HAMLET
[*Hastening toward her.*]

Ah,—dear, my own!—the kiss!

GERTRUDE
[*Starting to him, stops, as she sways.*]

Wings—wings!
No, no!

KING HAMLET
[*Close to her.*]

No?

GERTRUDE
[*Staring, points above him.*]

There!—Over thee—Wild Hawk!
Thy mouth: His beak is in thy face!

KING HAMLET

Beak!—*Beak?*

GERTRUDE

Pluck it from thy lips!

KING HAMLET

Pluck *what?*

GERTRUDE

[*Backing away from him.*]

The kiss—the kiss!

[*Turning, she rushes wildly from the hall, right.*]

KING HAMLET

[*Clenching his forehead, reaches one arm toward Claudius, with closed eyes.*]

Brother!

MOLL

[*Calls, with tipsy piping.*]

Cuckoo!—cuckoo!—cuckoo!

KING HAMLET

[*Squinting open his gaze.*]

Claudio!

CLAUDIUS

[*Sings, drunkenly.*]

Who's King? . . .
Who's canniest
King o' the Castle of Elsinore? . . .

[*The iron clang of a door resounds, within.*]

KING HAMLET

[*Glaring about.*]

Am I—in *Elsinore?*

[*Muffled boom of cannon.*]

CURTAIN.

ACT THIRD

Scene One

ELSINORE. A CORRIDOR OF THE CASTLE.
POLONIUS *and* VOLTIMAND, *discovered.*

POLONIUS

And so the Queen despatched you to the King
At war i' the wilderness; and secretly,
You say?

VOLTIMAND

Most secretly.

POLONIUS

When was this?

VOLTIMAND

Sir,
By night, a fortnight since.

POLONIUS

What said the King
To the Queen's message?

VOLTIMAND

I declared his answer,
Last night, aloud, in the banquet hall.

POLONIUS

I marked it:
"War cries, *Go, kill!* and lips of love, *Come, kiss!*
Denmark kills on, and Hamlet *comes* with this."

VOLTIMAND

'Twas so.

POLONIUS

But what *is* so, when contradiction
Cuts fact in two, like a dissever'd worm,
And the split halves go squirming to combine
Again, with naught to splice them—but a kiss?
What hath a kiss to do with Denmark's killing?

VOLTIMAND

Much had it, with the crashing of Troy's towers
When Helen toss'd hers there.

POLONIUS

Indeed, 't is true:
The breath of passion wreaks the death of reason
When lips of beauty pout it.—Here am I,
Lord Chamberlain, whose *raison d'être* of office
Is secrecy of state, whose daily bread
Is baked of cryptic messages, yet, look you!
Here must I beg of you, my messenger,—
Ostensibly mine—some crumbs of information
For my official belly, lest I lose
My paunch of public credit. Regency
May widen royal waistbands, but it wizens
Our own necessitous middles to a pinch
Of fashion resembling wasps. How think you?

VOLTIMAND

Sir,
Say, rather, bees, for both of us are buzzers
To furnish honey for our queen, who rules
This hive of Denmark.

POLONIUS

Ah, but doth she now?
The King 's at home again.

VOLTIMAND

At her behest,
Through wastes of storm and night.

POLONIUS

What, have you mark'd him
To-day, by morning light, wherein, methinks,
The storm still rumbles and the night yet darkles?—
The orgic climax of the weltering feast
Ruddled with witching wine and tankard rouse,
Amid which you did usher him to stare
Upon the dizzen'd partners in the dance
Encoiling Duke and Queen, now—like the blank
And sodden silence which doth follow flood-burst—
Hath left in all the crannies of the Castle
Tricklings of Rhenish and the stalish reek
Of ale-vomit. Drunk sleepers knuckle their eyeballs
To wink at noon-glare, weening it be moonshine.
Courtiers stretch legs and crawl upon their elbows
To douse their heads in rain-buckets. Glum clerks
Mumble their quills, and stick them in their ears
For ink-bottles. Night-glut doth make day-shambles.

VOLTIMAND

Shambles of guzzle so shameless have I ne'er
Beheld before, even at the Duke's gross bidding.

POLONIUS

Out of such havoc have I schooled my son,
Laertes, to take ship from regency's
Folk-feasting. Yet amid such reeky fust
Of after-feast must the great royal Dane,
Hamlet himself, pick warely his home-path
Of morning vigil.—Whist! He 's coming now,
Like the night's shadow. We were better shielded
Behind this jutty, while he passes by.

[*They withdraw quickly.*]

Enter, left, KING HAMLET.

Silent, he moves slowly forward; pauses, hesitant; turns; retraces his steps a little; turns again, moves forward; pauses again—feeling around him with his hands.

KING HAMLET

Mist . . mist . . here—yonder! Left and right, before
And after, all-enclosing mist! Down, either
Side—sheerness, shadow! All but *up:* there 's blue—
Pure blueness.—On what naked mountain ridge,
Narrow as grass-blade—nay, as cobweb-silk—
Must I now pace tight-rope, between the trembling
Points of remembrance and anticipation—
Alone?—How can it be that this, whereon
I stand—is love? And yet it bears me up—
Up to the blueness, yonder,—into the iris
Of pure St. Agnes' gazing, and of her
Who shared it with my own—in heaven, even
While gazing hence from earth. Matehood was ours,
Matehood, through love's own sainthood, burning to ashes
All earthy dross, in resurrection. Matehood
Was ours?—What mist of time invades these words
To numb their essence of infinity?
Was—will be: What is tense to lover's vow,
Which laid it on the altar of the Word:
"Ere Abraham was—*I am!*"?—No, Love immortal!
This narrow blade of thine, this tenuous silk
Whereon I walk tight-rope amid the mists,
Is mountain-firm, and poised resilient
Rock—over all abysses. Doubt is mist,
And truth the eternal blue. One stainless name
Hath matehood, and that goddess' name is—Gertrude!
[*Moving on, he starts at glimpse of the two Figures near him.*]
Ha, you—Polonius?—Voltimand?—Good morrow!

VOLTIMAND
[*Bowing.*]

My liege.

POLONIUS

Good morrow, gracious Majesty!
Yea, shining morrow now for Elsinore
After these nighty glooms of your long absence.

KING HAMLET

Such shadowy glooms as yesternight, you mean?
The mourning for my absence something relished
Of music, to give it solace, did it not?

POLONIUS

In sooth,—as 't were—

KING HAMLET

And somewhat of the cellarage
For savour in the cups, to drown the sorrow?

POLONIUS

'T would seem—as 't were—to drown it.

KING HAMLET

To the dregs.
So happily, the dregs being cast away,
Our Elsinore is purged of gloom to-day,
And all is fair.—How fare affairs of state?

POLONIUS

Auspiciously, my liege. The fatherland
Is safe and snug at home.

KING HAMLET

The fatherland?

POLONIUS

This beauteous state you father.

KING HAMLET

Once for all
Know this, O, learned minister of state:
Fatherhood breeds the quick and not the dead;
Statehood is no equivalent of manhood.

POLONIUS

Nay, as you say, my liege; of course, indeed:
Equivalence would be equivocal
And vocally devoid of verity.

KING HAMLET

'T is true, the state hath need of snuggery
And safety in the vaults, for in the vaults
It lies in state, august and catafalqued,
The dumb cadaver of a risen spirit.
So lies this thing, the state. Know you where lies
The fatherland?

POLONIUS

Out yonder—

KING HAMLET

Nay, in hither!
Here in the heart, which hymns the pulse of love;
Here in the loins, which sow the seed of man;
Here in the brow, which spans the arc of heaven.
The fatherland roots in that soil of song,
Flowers in beauty from that seed of passion,
Rounds in immensity that span of vision
Over the world, to image the goal of manhood.

POLONIUS

Methinks, I follow the trail—

KING HAMLET

To the fatherland?
Go on, then! Hark the herd-boy on the hill,
Calling his cattle home at milking hour
When the long shadows dusken. Hark, at dawn,
The braying of the bugles from the barracks
To the wild chargers' neighing, when the fighters
Leap saddle-back, yelling: *Yo-ho, the foe!*
Listen, at midnight, to the tolling knell
That parts the fallen soldier from his bride
Where sods are thudding on his sunken grave
And the green willow weeps to the white stars.—
Then sharp your quill of statecraft, dip it deep
In your heart's blood, and write, in neatest hand:
The soulless state is not the fatherland.

POLONIUS

In sooth, my King, sith all authority
Must emanate from your most royal self,
My own poor part—

KING HAMLET

Misunderstand us not,
Polonius. No portion of our wish
It is, to minimize your part in Denmark
As our Lord Chamberlain, whose office serves
The functions of the state. 'T is rich, not poor,
In service—be it merely understood
It is a sexton's part. The sepulchre
You serve must needs be duly minister'd,
Kept under key and lock and clean of vermin,
To guard the inmate of the catafalque
From any spot of obloquy, and make
A seemly monument for visitors
From other cenotaphs to gape in awe of.

Else could your king not draw his human breath
From healthful lungs, to hail this fatherland—
Which rises living from this deathly state—
With word of blessing, for its good allegiance
To one so grateful for it. Such shrewd service,
Therefore, as you have ever shown your king,
Is deeply welcome, as 't is dearly prized.

POLONIUS

Such praise, my liege, doth whelm me—even to dumbness.

KING HAMLET

Voltimand!

VOLTIMAND

My King.

KING HAMLET

To goad your horse's mettle,
Seven nights and days across the trackless wilds,
'Gainst lunge of wintry winds and lash of hail
Through cracking ice-gulch and hoof-sucking slough,
Even till his wheezing nostrils snorted blood,
To bear us our queen's tidings—think you, Sir,
You and your mount have slipt our memory
As swift as you, remounting, sped again
That arduous journey home?

VOLTIMAND

Your Majesty,
'Twas simply at command.

KING HAMLET

Command of yourself
Commends you to us, more than our commanding
Commends us to ourselves, in giving such.

Once, twice, would seem enough of commendation
In mere words, swapt for deeds. Yet thrice—once more—
It may be, we must put you to the test.

VOLTIMAND

My liege, the number boots not: 't is the need.

KING HAMLET

The need may press, or not. That is not ours,
But destiny's command. What the all-wise stars
May yet unlock within the cryptic message,
Utter'd by word of mouth through you, in the hut
Of a charcoal-burner by the Baltic Sea,
May wrench the beams of Elsinore, to tower
Heaven-high, or sink hell-deep. The secret key
To unriddle why saints of candles and of wings
Be harried by wild hawks, hath not been handed
Yet to our fingers' clutch. Perchance it dangles
Close. But meanwhile our captains in the east
Poise their war-spears, waiting our onward word
To rout the Polack hordes. So once again
Unbin the oats, staunch your intrepid horse
For seven nights' speed, fettle your own brave thews,
And stand taut-ready to take the King's word, yon,
Or else, companioning,—the King himself.

POLONIUS

My gracious lord! You—home, now—haste away?
Beseech you, no!

KING HAMLET

Not we—the stars will say.[7]

CURTAIN.

ACT THIRD

Scene Two

ELSINORE. ANTEROOM TO THE ROYAL BEDCHAMBER.
QUEEN GERTRUDE *and* MOLL COWSLIP, *discovered.*

MOLL

So, purty Queen! Now, one more dainty dab
O' rouge, and—for to rinse the night away—
Here 's sunny sip of elderberry wine!

GERTRUDE

Wine?—Ha, no more of what the witches still
To roil us with their murky draught! No, Moll:
Cold water—water from the icy floes
Of reason and of retribution—keen,
Cold clearness of the living well, where Ruth
Dips her clean pitcher; fetch me that, to purge
My lips of death.

MOLL

Death! Heigh, and well-a-day,
Here 's a fine morning purge, for a fair lady
To riddance her ails withal! Fro' death, is it?
And when did lady die?

GERTRUDE

Last night. What life
Is this, that doth survive the deathly message
'T was thou, thyself, didst urge me send?

MOLL

Aha,
"Cuckoo!"—My Lord Henhawk, methinks, did hearken
The echo, when my lady's royal falcon
Came swooping fro' the wars. Well, said I not
He 'd come at call?

GERTRUDE

He hath not come, all night.
Why should he come? Yet if he come, what morning
Oracle for the horrible night's enigma
Can I now utter for him? All my mind
Is midnight still, and my heart beats black blood
To deepen its darkness.

MOLL

Foldol! Doctor Cowslip
Shall be thy leech to draw the black blood out.
'T is jealousy doth heal love-lornity,
And Moll hath dealt o' that a double dose
Already, for to make thee rosy-red.

GERTRUDE

Moll, fool! Were not thy queen a greater fool
For having hark'd thy folly, she would answer
This: Jealousy is love's deformity
And strangles what it fouls. Ah, let me never
Cause that perversity! Too much I share
The wild hawk's luring wildness. Hold me in curb
To keep my love-nest clean, not whet me to tangle
Kissings of bloody beaks.—Nay, I am sick
Indeed, to crave thy succour. Go thy ways
Of happy foolishness, as I go mine
Of foolish misery.

MOLL

Not back to bed
By morning-shine?

GERTRUDE

I have not been to bed.
I go there, now—nay, not to sleep—to weep.
Good night! [*Exit, within, behind the arras.*]

MOLL

"Good night!"—while bright sun cryeth,
"Good day!"
Weep, wilt thou, dear? Then weep thy brains away.
Tut, what a suds o' tears these brainy folk
Churn fro' their wits, to wallow in the brine
Gaping their gills, and might be belly-merry
As bluefish in the billows, would they only
Wiggle for what they want. Scrape out all skull-pans
And fill 'em up with sweetbreads. Gi'e me a dish
O' calves' brains, fried in butter, and I 'll pour it
In the King's cranium.

[*In the doorway, left, she encounters* KING HAMLET, *entering.*]

KING HAMLET

Ah, Molly Cowslip!
Good day, mistress!

MOLL

God gi'e your Majesty
Good e'en, Sir!

KING HAMLET

Evening?

MOLL

Madam 's gone abed—
Soft, soft, Sir!—not to sleep, nay, but to weep.

KING HAMLET

To weep?

MOLL

"Good night!" quoth she, but now. Hush, Sir!
What frighted dove but would n't close the blind,
When the wild hawk be prowling at the chink

To pluck her purty winglets, for to feather
A fluttering valentine, and dangle it
High in the Castle vine, to hear it call
"Cuckoo!" to all the world?

KING HAMLET

What sayest thou?—
What words?—"Wild hawk—wild hawk," and "Castle vine!"
'Swounds, wife! What knowest thou of those—her words
Of secret message to thy lord and king?

MOLL

My king and lord—and craving heaven's grace
For an old hen, who hatched her chick and thine
From egg!—what knowest *thou* of thy home-pigeon
And all of heart-ache pining in her breast,
When thou be hunting on the Polack duck-pond,
Far off, in silly wars?

KING HAMLET

Those words, I say:
"The cuckoo calleth from the Castle vine,
Wild hawk doth pluck wings of Saint Valentine!"
'T was thou, last night—I saw thee flap, and cry:
"Cuckoo!"

MOLL

Unwelcome for a married ear
To hark at home-coming.

KING HAMLET

God's death, woman!
Art thou gone daft, in this unhallow'd rouse
Of drunkenness that reeks from Elsinore,
Or what of sacrilege is this, thy mouth
Utters to goad my quick?

MOLL

What gossips coo
I' the pigeon-loft—to catch the wind for Poland:
A little lilt, to drown the cannon's roar
In a king's ear, and if he 'll let the flea
Bite deep enough, and not scratch it away
Afore its blister warns his royalty
To prick up both ears, sharper than a donkey's,
And list what 's in the wind.

KING HAMLET

So it was thou
Had finger in that message sent to Poland,
Signed by the Queen in red.

MOLL

Aye, in her own blood,
Poor dearie.

KING HAMLET

What!

MOLL

Wi' the hawk's quill.

KING HAMLET

The hawk's!
What hawk's?

MOLL

The wild hawk, Scandal,—his
Who swoopeth in the wind for his dove-quarry,
When the King-Falcon flieth to the wars
And leaveth the castle cuckoo to cry forth
The word, which echo answereth with "cuckold."

KING HAMLET

Cut out thy tongue, which spits that scarlet word
Upon the whiteness of thy queen!

MOLL

My tongue!
My spittal! Think you, Molly Cowslip learneth
To ape the compliments of the court ladies,
Or my lord Osric's sallies, for the Queen
To catch their echoes in the corridors
O' the Castle?

KING HAMLET

Compliments—sallies—echoes!
Of what? Concerning whom?

MOLL
[*Imitatingly.*]

Your Majesty's
Concernment for the Queen: your Majesty's
Most exquisite, so liberal commands—
Fahlah!—for her most tender comfortings
In easement of your absence, as, *comme çi,*
Comme ça, resulting from your royal edict,
Conferring powers of regency upon
Your darling brother, the Duke Claudius.

KING HAMLET

Our brother! What of him? Dare they asperse
His honour, of neglecting our commands
For the Queen's comfort?

MOLL

Nay, nay; they applaud
The noble ardour of his constancy
In executing them.

KING HAMLET

Well, then? Well, then?

MOLL

Even to the least detail of love and duty
To win the dalliance of her majesty.

KING HAMLET

Dalliance?

MOLL

'T is the honiest word that sticks
On my lord Osric's tongue, like a dayfly's wing
On a toad's tongue-tip.—"Ah, *chères mesdames,* sweet ladies!
Did you but now observe the dalliance
Of our most gracious queen, in the archéd eye
Wherewith her grievéd spirit made acceptance
Of yonder wine-dark rose, the brave duke press'd
Into her lovely hand, to while away
One more disconsolate hour of separation
From her beloved lord, our war-torn king,
Hamlet, the Unhappy?—Have your gazes encounter'd
Ever such assiduity of duty
As gloweth there on the sad countenance
Of our enchanted regent, in responding
To the archéd eye-glint of the Queen's bereavement?"

KING HAMLET

What mimic drivel 's this?

MOLL

Moll Cowslip's role
Of my lord Osric, in the mystery
Of Hamlet, King of Denmark. Clap the curtain
Down on 't, and hark ye now, behind the scene,
To Molly Midwife's word for sovereign sucklings:

Be not the Dunce o' Denmark. Be thy dear's
Defender o' the Faith. She weepeth yonder—
Weepeth, feard o' the wild hawk's scandal beak.
Fetch her the kiss she craveth. Pluck the hawk,
And feed the feathers to the toad-frogs' tongues.
Clap thy duke-brother on the breech, and tell him
Thou comest fro' the wars, to bide at home
And make thine honour his, and his thine own,
As erst ye were lads together. Clean the Castle,
And make it merry, bed and bower, for hearts
In bellies, and for brains in noddles, sound
To hold their wits from leaking, and not crack
Fro' what creeps in their lugs.—So, Moll, quoth 'a!
Cards flat on table: will we this, or no?

[*Intensely absorbed in his own thoughts, the King seems but half to have heard her, and answers, absently.*]

KING HAMLET

Of course, we will it; but——

MOLL

But, but, but!

KING HAMLET
[*Dreamily.*]

If—

MOLL

If cracks the pot; *but* busts it. Nay, nay, nay,
Majesty, what we *will*, we *do!*

KING HAMLET

Even so,
We do.

MOLL
[*Pointing to within the arras.*]

Mum, then! She weepeth.

KING HAMLET

[*Sternly.*]

Moll, none other
But thee, durst say *mum* to thy master, by
This portal, sacred to thy sovereigns—
Our bedchamber. Yon arras is tight closed.
So let thy mouth be, to all else beyond
What sleeps, or weeps, within. This mystery
Is deeper than seems not, or seems, to be
To either of us, and what has left thy tongue
Has left it, never to be said, or sung.

[*He points to the door where Moll goes off in silence. Turning then to the arras hangings, King Hamlet parts them, and calls inward, tenderly.*]

Gertrude—my love!—

[*He goes within.*]

CURTAIN.

ACT THIRD

Scene Three

ELSINORE. HALL OF THE SHRINES, IN THE CASTLE.

At left, near the edge of the scene, a tall mirror.

Enter QUEEN GERTRUDE *and* KING HAMLET.

GERTRUDE

Entra, O fidele, in questo asilo di pace,
Dove di Dio si parla, e poi si tace.—
Here, Hamlet, at this shrine of long ago,
Take, love, my hand, and enter now once more
Where our dear Padre Celestino taught us:
"Enter, O faithful, here this asylum of peace!
Here, speak we only of God, else let us cease.—
The rest is unimportant."—Dost thou remember?

KING HAMLET

Yes, in this schoolroom of the elder children,
Here let us enter His heavenly silences,
Unenmesh'd by our faltering blunders, our stumbling
existence,
The turmoil and moil of our abortive and tangled
Efforts. Here 's God, my Gertrude, to whose altar
Of dear St. Agnes, long since, thou didst lead me
To know the bliss of matehood, through the fire
Which leaves all else but love in ashes.

GERTRUDE

Look!

Her candle shines clear, where I tended it
Last night, in mists of joy-enshrouding tears
At thy return. See, now it guttereth
No more, as in the crypt of my mad message
Sent to thee from my yearning perturbations.

KING HAMLET

Of them—no more! I 'm here. And here with thee
Is sanctuary for us both. Out there—
Out yonder, love, amid demonic wars,
I have beheld too crimson-clear what bodes
Our earth and all of beauty's sanctity
Which man himself hath direly self-attain'd,
When Odin copes with Christus. Now I know
The portent of those drops of pity's anguish
Yon thornéd brow upon His crucifix
Exudes, to make our own brows bleed with thoughts
Of what we are—and might be. How they gleam—
Those opal drops—and glitter envisionings
Of the All-Might-Be, the all-beckoning
World of redemption—there in the candle-glow!

GERTRUDE

Visions of all it means—to love!

KING HAMLET

Even so.
To love: 't is simple; and, by simply loving,
To be ourselves—our inner quickening flame,
Not shadows, cast from it by fitful breaths
Of murky other-beings, made of shadow
Wrought in our twisted flame's similitude.

GERTRUDE

Of murky other-beings—fitful breaths
From nostrils of the lewd beasts out of hell
Dante encountered, when the ghost of Virgil
Brought him the word of that transcendent lady
Whom pity moved to love, and love to pity
His mortal need.

KING HAMLET

The lady Beatrice?

GERTRUDE

She.—Was it because she knew what 't is to feel
The horror of the twisted flames of lewdness,
And yearned to fend away the scorching breath
Of her own knowledge on 't, in saving him
She loved? Or did she sense a mortal pang
Beyond her own imagining to share?

KING HAMLET

What, my own Gertrude! Why this anguish'd look?
The lady Beatrice bendeth from heaven
In the great lover Alighieri's dream
Of love and death—his *Comedy Divine,*
Our Padre Celestino long ago
Read to us from this lectern. Bendeth she
Here now so near us, that a poet's breath
Scorcheth my dear one's gaze, to glint these tears?

GERTRUDE

Is, then, a poet's breath so light a pulse
Of dream beneath the eyelid, that it makes
No tear to start, of memories that lie
Deep in the iris? Dost not thou remember
The Padre's burning lesson: *What is love?*
The ardour of his own eyes, when he told us
How love is all-consuming? And I said:
"Father, is love so great, then? Almost you
Make me to fear him." And I spake to thee:
"Hamlet, we 've never feared him, have we?"—"Feared!"
You said. "Fear love? Why, we have never ask'd
The question. Even to ask it were to end
Our power of loving, and to put ourselves
Beyond the scope of pity."[8]

KING HAMLET

I remember.

GERTRUDE

But Beatrice—in her blessed pity
For him who walked in hell—had she no fear
Lest all-consuming love should lacerate
The very texture of their spirit union?

KING HAMLET

Still Beatrice and her lover, Dante!
Cleave they so close to us?—Methinks they do,
Being immortal in that perfect confluence
Wrought by the forging fusion of their souls
Ordainéd by the stars for mated love.
Yet death had twain'd their flesh, when the sweet lady
Was moved of pity for her lover's plight
To send him message—not in questioning
But certitude of love. They knew wherefore
They loved. They loved, therefore they knew—
Even as we know.

GERTRUDE
[*Murmuring.*]

Even as we know.

KING HAMLET

Aye, even
As thou dost echo it. But for us, thank God,
Dear my own love, death hath not twain'd
This flesh divine, as nothing born of flesh
Can make us else than one. This fearless truth
We know. Its pulsing artery of knowledge
Putteth all fear to pallor. 'T is, itself,
The font of faith. Beyond, then, Beatrice
And Dante, sunder'd by the gulf of death,

Are we not blest, whose tingling hands can reach
To touch—and lips to kiss—this living, dreadless,
Questionless certitude!

GERTRUDE
[*As he kisses her.*]

Are we not blest—!

KING HAMLET

This sanctuary holds us. Here we have learn'd
The Padre's burning lesson: *What is Love?*
And here, heaven grant us, we will still impart it
To him, our son, forged of that quenchless fire
Wherein our hearts were welded.

GERTRUDE

Ah, yes,—him,
My Hamlet's waxing Hamlet,—our lithe prince,
Flower'd from our princeling bud, to be the proud
But unassuming crest of chivalry,
Petall'd with valorous charms, and golden pollen'd
With procreant spores of fecund intellect
To impregn the spirit quick of every land
With his soul essence, till all earth shall savour
Fragrance of Elsinore. Him—oh, heaven guard him!
Would he were home with us!

KING HAMLET

Aye, home!—Instead,
He wings forth, as youth will, from his familiar
Heaven of childhood and the cherishing
Arms of our schooling love, to seek far hostels
Of homeless learning, in the vexing lore
Of magic, and the erudite ignorances
Of the university. Godsooth, my dear!
As if there well'd not from his mother's eyes

More living springs of magic than he 'll quaff
From all the roiléd pools of Wittenberg;
Yea, even from his father's smiling scowl,
More savour'd sense of wit, than he might sup
From any other vintage—save it were
The laughter-bubbles in that old home-brew
He drank from Yorick's lips—rememberest thou?—
And he a laddie, riding our fool's crupper
Pig-a-back?

GERTRUDE

Blowing his crumpled horn, and thou
Hailing him huntsman!—Ah, those early days
When childhood clingeth to matehood, twining both
With their entangled joys! 'T is then earth's June-tide.
The mother-kinglet, by her green leaf-nest,
She knoweth not whether to heed the clear
Pellucid calling of her ruby-crownéd
Lord in the orchard, and to wing away
With him to evening ardours, or to heed
The tiny creakle of their fuzzy nestling
And fetch in beak the silly dangling worms
For sustenance, to make a sacrament
Unto her lord's heaven-song.

KING HAMLET

Our crown, indeed,
Is rubied with no glister, can outglow
That feather'd king's, in his orchard bravery.
Yea, let me live to die in an orchard, there
To sense what birds sing of! 'T is from their beaks,
Which dangle earthworms, we may sip quintessence,
In song, of our immortal nature, which
Our glut of earth both feeds and stifles. Birds
Are nature's words in flesh, on wing to utter
What bards imagine, and what fools of sense,

Callous to the supersensible, ignore—
All but our own dear fool, our Yorick's death-song:
On with the new life! Deathward, joyward climb:
Fate turns to freedom, when we vanquish time.
Yes, Gertrude: never did we feed our nestling-
Prince with diviner tutelage of heaven
Than when with Yorick's lilts we nursed his childhood.

GERTRUDE

Often, in sleep, I dream I hear him lilting:
Sun in the heart makes the mind on the bright.
Moon in the mind shows the soul infinite.
Love darkness, and all will be light.

KING HAMLET

His is the waking bird's creed: Love—more life—
Love-life: not love of life, but life of love—
Death's end, where birthward lives and deathward blend
In ever-renewing wedlock, to engender
Scions of consciousness, whose souls create
The goals they strive for—godhoods, for themselves
To serve the All-Self—Love.

GERTRUDE

Speak on, my Hamlet!
Think on, toward those high goals, far though they be,
Which show the boggy trails of our weak strivings
For what they are—dream-highways of the angels,
Sent us to make our stumblings in the ruck
Self-raising milestones. Oh, in thy black absence,
How have I fallen bruised here, lacking this
Thy voice, thy thinking glance, thy touch, to stay me!
Oh, never leave me more!
[*Clinging to him.*] What red mark 's that
Aslant thy brow?

KING HAMLET

The bruising of an arrow
On a boggy trail. What 's this, here on thy hand?

GERTRUDE

Scratch o' the quill, Moll told thee of.

KING HAMLET

The scabs
Of war without, and war within us, fall
Away. The living tissue is all love.
There shall be no more separation now,
Even to gall the surface.—

[*He takes her hand, and leads her before the mirror in the wall.*]

Look, my own!
How smooth is this calm mirror. There, reflected,
Is all we cherish here. Stand we together
Before it, link'd inseparable. Thou seest!
Its silence uttereth what our Padre said:
Enter, O faithful, here this asylum of peace.
Here, speak we only of God—else let us cease.
Else let us cease, indeed! So let our souls
Stand mirror'd in our own serenity,
Reflecting what we are—eternal mates,
Surface and spirit substance. Were we else,
The glass itself would crack in twain, and warp
Apart, in shiver'd splinters.

GERTRUDE

Hamlet,—love!
No earthy mirror of ourselves may glass
Perfection.

KING HAMLET

This, whereof I speak, is no
Mirror of outward form and fashion. 'T is
Our magic glass of truth.

A VOICE
[*As from behind the mirror.*]

Mais, s' il vous plaît,
Majestés gracieuses! Pardon, d'un cœur
Profond!

[*Enter, left,* OSRIC, *in soiled habiliments, dandling two sprigs. With smiling air of solemn dilapidation, he intersperses his bows and daintified gestures with vain attempts to stifle his hiccoughs.*]

KING HAMLET

What 's here?

OSRIC

If it may be permitted
So humble—*hic!*—servitor of courtesies
To utter felicitations from the Castle
Unto the aureate crowns of Elsinore,
Voicing this rich reunion of their jewels
By lips of their endazzled Osric—*hic!*

KING HAMLET

The scabs of castle courtesies, we see,
Fall off more easily than scars of war
To leave their tissue bare. What would your lordship
Anent the issue of this tissue?

OSRIC
[*Blankly.*]

Sir?

KING HAMLET

The sequel of this labyrinthic sequence?

OSRIC

Sir?—*hic!*——

KING HAMLET

Encoiling our "aureate crowns"?

OSRIC

Mais oui!

The *sequitur:* 't is thus. 'T is even that I,
Osric,—having been momently—*hic!*—amid
The risibilities of repercussions
Attendant on the buddings of mine own
Bons mots, absented from the Regent's banquet
Last night in prelude to your Majesty's
Royal arrival—may now, e'en in apparel
Still festal—*hic!*—albeit rouged i' the fustian
With wines of Chianti and of Muscadel—
May now enplume myself to be the first
To proffer laurel of felicitation
And rue of lamentation, both in one,
Unto your majesties—*hic!*

KING HAMLET

Both rue and laurel:
Why thus?

OSRIC
[*Proffering the sprigs in his hand.*]

This laurel—to your reunited
Loves i' the Castle, dear my King and Queen!
This rue—*hic!*—from all hearts of Elsinore
To you, sweet lady sovereign, that you
Once more must sadly seek the delicate
Solace of your dear kin in deep consolements,
For that our liege, so lately home to us,
Must now so imminently haste away
Again to war's invasions.

GERTRUDE

Haste away!

KING HAMLET

From whom, Sir,
Heard you these hasty tidings?

OSRIC

From Marcellus,
My liege, whilst he most love-tenaciously
Was tying of my taffeta—*hic!*—it being
Torn in the seam, by my last night's abrupt
Uphoisting to his arms. E'en so encurl'd
Is rumour's hatching.

KING HAMLET

Like the moth's egg, so
It seemeth—in the seams. And he, Marcellus,
From whom did he *un*curl this rumour?

OSRIC

From
The prest lips of Polonius, within
Whose ear 't was vocabled by Voltimand,
He having cull'd it from your gracious self,
Who now receive it from your humble Osric,
Whose breast hath been its pregnant chrysalid
Until this very birth-hour.

KING HAMLET

So! And, lo,
This splendid lunar-moth alighteth now
Upon our lips, whence we do puff it forth,
With spread wings, to your own, and bid you waft it
Back to Marcellus' tongue, which hatched the egg,
With our command that he attend us here
At once.

OSRIC

[*Bowing.*]

At once, your Graciousness!

KING HAMLET

And with you
Take here the Queen's rue. We will keep the laurel.

OSRIC

[*Taking the sprig of rue.*]

Long live the royal laurel! In the bosom
Of regency Osric will plant this rue. [*Exit, left.*]

KING HAMLET

These rumour-worms and scandal-chinches! They
Would gnaw the calyx of the Holy Grail
To spawn and hatch their grubs. But we, my dearest,
Are wise to 'em. Moll Cowslip lispeth well
The role of Osric, in this mystery
Of Elsinore, albeit she omitteth
His courtly hiccough.

GERTRUDE

How hath he contrived
To fetch so false a rumour of thy hasting
Away?

KING HAMLET

Contrived? His brain contriveth naught.
His mouth twirls on a smile-hinge, to gape open
And catch the spittal of others, for infecting
His own saliva to a like effusion
Of perfume for the Castle. Aye, they have it
Sprinkled, I see, on sprigs of rue and laurel
To scent our august persons—and our couch—
With attar of royal rose, adulterated
With oil of regency, to mix withal
A most seductive mildew, as cough-syrup
For cuckoos. Cowslip hath interpreted
The cryptics of thy message. Never fear,

Dear love, but I will hook the exuding worms
And squash 'em on the barb.

GERTRUDE

Ah, Hamlet, Hamlet,
My own! Let not my urgency of message,
Nay, nor poor Molly Cowslip's chatter-liltings
Of cuckoos and wild hawks, move thee to roil
Thy peace at Elsinore, for my sake.

KING HAMLET

For
Mine own, which is thy sake, I 'll cleanse the muddied
Waters, till they be settled pure and moteless,
And Elsinore be purged of Osric eggs,
Coddled of rouses like the revelry
Of last night's orgic feast. My brother whelms
Himself—and us and all—by such construing
Of my desire to embower my absence' bleakness
Yonder, with blooms of joyance here, for thy
Consolement.

GERTRUDE

'Twas his overzeal, to serve
Thy loving purpose, and to consummate
Thine own command to him.

KING HAMLET

And by such zeal
Excessive, to exceed it. So he makes
Rubbage for lies to squirm in, excrement
For Osric's lice to breed, till satin'd ladies
Flutter 'em from their fans in honest faces.

GERTRUDE

But Claudius——

KING HAMLET

Claudio must not belie
Himself, for sake of us, nor danger us
By whisper-tattle of his own dishonour
In honouring me by his obedience
To duty towards his sister-queen. But fear naught.
I 'll guard his honour as mine own and thine,
Spite of his blind devotion to our love,
Which blinks the scandal of it.

GERTRUDE

Let not such breath
Of murky guile invade our sanctuary.
See, love, how soft St. Agnes' candle glows!

KING HAMLET

Oh, you are right.
[*Nestling her to his heart, he points to the glass.*]
The world enmirror'd there
Is all we own to cherish.
[*In the doorway, left,* MARCELLUS *has appeared.*]
—What, Marcellus!

MARCELLUS
[*Saluting.*]

Majesty!

KING HAMLET

Osric hath but now informed us
You gave him tidings of our hasting forth
To Poland: tidings from whom, we ask.

MARCELLUS

The word
Came to me from Polonius, my liege;

And Voltimand standeth even now at stirrup
Below the postern, to companion you
Thither, he saith.

GERTRUDE
[*Exclaiming.*]

Hamlet!

KING HAMLET

And hath he said
Who his informant is?

MARCELLUS

He hath, my King:
Even your Majesty.

GERTRUDE

Ah! Is this more
Of murkiness?

KING HAMLET

Nay, Gertrude, 't is as clear
As yonder candle's beam, and leads to rays
More bright.

GERTRUDE

What!

KING HAMLET
[*To Marcellus.*]

And hath Voltimand said else:
Upon whose word his majesty doth wait
To send him message to set foot in stirrup?

MARCELLUS

He hath, my liege.

KING HAMLET

Whose word?

MARCELLUS

The all-wise stars',

He saith.

KING HAMLET

Why, right. He hath said true.

GERTRUDE

The stars!

KING HAMLET

Who else could utter the majestic Word
Which cleaveth Hamlet from the King of Denmark
And setteth him by the altar of Caritas
To keep his trothal vow here: purity
Of passion! War's arbitrament is obscure.
The candle, yon, shines clearer, and the eyes
Of Venus in the heaven clearer still,
And smile of Her, who bore the bridegroom, Christ,
Pellucid clear.—To candle-beam, to star-ray,
That lit the kneeling shepherds by the manger
To know at last the source of selfhood's freedom,
I vowed the vow of matehood—to defend
That fortress which to hold our wars are fought:
The home-rock of the sacred oath—the love
Inviolate of Love—the Son of Man,
Girder of mortal manhood to put on
Immortal arms, and vindicate his own
Even to death, the gauge of freedom's vow.

GERTRUDE

Hamlet—oh, Hamlet!

KING HAMLET

Gertrude—Venus—Mary—
Our life of love through Christus' death! Out yonder,
The hordes of Odin rage at Denmark's gate
To pillage all the swaddled cradle hides
Of heaven's pity for them, and again
Plunge in His flesh the acerbating spears
Which pierced the Crucified, to loose His spirit
For His unguess'd redemption of their hate.
The hordes of Odin plunge, and our brave Danes
Wrest from their hands the spears, to plunge—reversed—
Their barbs in the quick marrow, to empierce
Once more the groin of Christ. In His meek name,
War wars with war, to champion His peace
Of love. Dear God, is there none other way
Unto Thy kingdom? So it seemeth not,
Till man shall turn the love-light in the eyes
Of woman for her babe, to be the barb
Shall pierce his heart, and make its passion bleed
Hunger of milk to nurse it, not of blood
For sting of its renewal.

GERTRUDE

Oh, our son,
Who is not here! This love, that lights for his
Return to us, here in mine eyes, I turn
To thee, Hamlet,—'t is thine!

KING HAMLET

I feel, indeed,
Its limpid glow, its milk of kindness, yet
I am no man redeem'd, no father saved
By son-love, nay, nor hunger'd lover, nurst
At mother-breast for passion's sating. All
Of these I crave for my redemption. Still

My war-blood leaps for glory of our Danes
Battling at Denmark's gate 'gainst Odin's dark
Invasion of our home.

GERTRUDE

Ah, ride not forth
Again!

KING HAMLET

And so, Marcellus, cry this word
To Voltimand: "Up stirrup, on to Poland!
And bear with thee, companioning, this wraith
Of Hamlet, with the shield of Denmark, guled
With rubies of our crown, to glitter blood
Of Odin on the Baltic ice, and blazon
Victory for the arms of Christ, who bleeds
To shed his benison. Victorious
For Him who weeps the fallen on both sides
Be they, our captains and our valiant thanes,
To hedge our country with their barbéd spears
And make our garth the garden of His peace!"

MARCELLUS

Your message in mine ear, O King, my mouth
Shall speak again to Voltimand.

KING HAMLET

And this more:
"So rides with you the ghost of Hamlet, King
Of Denmark, whilst the father of your prince
And lover of your queen, Hamlet himself,
Abideth here, to rout the kin of Odin
With all the sly confederates *he* battens—
His cousin, Loki—imp of lies, and pixy
Of tricks incestuous—the lightning-bug
Of zigzag crawlings in the laps of ladies
To hang his scandal-jewels from their ear-lobes

For pawn with the bawd-baubles, kist from lips
Of whispering courtier-cozes. Him—him, Loki,—
Shall Hamlet nab by the lug, and twinge his nose
Until no more he smells the rats he breeds
In chambers of Elsinore. For there be wars
To wage with rats, at home, as well as rodents
Afield,—aye, revolutions in the cupboard
To purge the castle-feastings of the victors."—
These messages take hence to Voltimand,
Purporting why Hamlet may not companion
His ghost to Poland, but remaineth here.

GERTRUDE

Here! Here, with all our brave Danes champion—home!
Hamlet!

[*She moves to embrace him, but he withholds her momently by a gesture, turning to Marcellus.*]

KING HAMLET

One thing else bring to Voltimand
In mind and person. Bid him seek the thatch,
He wotteth of, where the poor charcoal-burner
Dwells with his mate, and give her this from us.—
Wait till I find it in my purse. Step here.

[*Standing by the mirror, he feels in his garb for his purse, opens it, and takes out something in his hand, to show Marcellus, who approaches.*]

Look!

[*While their heads are bending over it,* CLAUDIUS *appears, right, at edge of the scene, opposite, and is about to enter towards Gertrude, who—suddenly seeing him—puts finger quickly to her lip, with a look of anguished fear, glancing from him towards Hamlet, whose back is turned to them.*

As Claudius begins still to move towards her, she gives him a desperately commanding gesture, to which—smiling lewdly at her—he pays no heed, till she checks him to turn back, only by swiftly accompanying him off the scene.

Before and during this pantomime, Hamlet continues speaking to Marcellus.]

KING HAMLET

Know you what 't is?

MARCELLUS

A jewel-stone, my liege.

Red. Is 't a ruby?

KING HAMLET

Nay, a blood-stone. Say

To Voltimand——

[*Lifting his eyes from the jewel in his hand, Hamlet's gaze suddenly focuses in the mirror.*]

MARCELLUS

[*After a pause.*]

Say what, my liege?

KING HAMLET

Say—ah!—

Say——

MARCELLUS

Well, your Majesty?

KING HAMLET

Whether you see—

MARCELLUS

See what, my liege?

[*Exeunt Gertrude and Claudius.*]

KING HAMLET

A crack—a little rift—

Yon, in the glass—there!

MARCELLUS

In the mirror, Sir?

None, to my eye.

KING HAMLET

Not?—None, where my finger 's pointing?

MARCELLUS

None, Sir. All 's smooth. The glass is finely polish'd,
Methinks.

KING HAMLET

That 's not the spot—more to the middle:
Thin, thin—a tiny crack—a crookled cleft, that parts it—
Scarce visibly—in halves.

MARCELLUS

Nay.

KING HAMLET

Ah, that 's pity!

MARCELLUS

Pity, my liege?

KING HAMLET

'T is pity, when the unseen
Conforms not to the seen: and *vice versa.*
This glass, that holds the world we fumble in,
Should mirror our defects of vision—rifts
Within the seeing substance it reflects—
As well as our valid visions. So, 't is pity
The mirror is not crackt, to match its object—
Think you not?

MARCELLUS
[*Fingering his hair, bewildered.*]

Good my liege——

KING HAMLET

Aye, scratch the skull—
Right! For, 't is said, in babyhood, 't is rifted

A little, but mends, and closes-in the brain
To view the world through eye-holes, and no more
Through skull-cracks. Thus we value blood-stones
For what they bring in the market, not for what
They fetch in metaphor. Nevertheless,
Say—

MARCELLUS

Say, my liege?

KING HAMLET

To Voltimand, the closéd
Brain breedeth memories—and one of ours
Is of a frighted thrush-bird, in the Baltic,
Eager to soothe her mate, yet fond to sate
The appetite of an intruding Danish
Boar, bristling with battle-axes, with a dish
Of acorns for his breakfast, in good stead
Of goat's milk, lacking from her board, by death
O' the nanny, pilfer'd by the boar-king's battling
Followers, for their meat, at breakfast. So,
Bid Voltimand tell the charcoal-burner's wife
This blood-stone speaketh for a King, whose blood
Atoneth for the butchering of mothers—
Man-kin, or goat—and pray her buy with this
More goat's milk, in men's market. Thus, foot-haste,
Marcellus to Voltimand, and Voltimand
Post-speed to Poland!

MARCELLUS

Now, at once, my King.
[*Exit, left.*]

GERTRUDE
[*Who—at right—has re-entered, pale, on tiptoe.*]

Hamlet—

KING HAMLET
[*Not turning.*]

Gertrude—

GERTRUDE

What are you gazing after,
So intent?

KING HAMLET

The path to Poland. Nay, the intention 's
Not mine to follow it—only to follow
What follows after me.

GERTRUDE

What follows after—?

KING HAMLET

After. I see it through my back—i' the glass.

GERTRUDE
[*Catching her breath.*]

The glass!

KING HAMLET

As we beheld ourselves, together,
In sanctuary.

GERTRUDE

Ah!

KING HAMLET

"So let our souls
Stand mirror'd in our own serenity,
Reflecting what we are—eternal mates,"
I said.

GERTRUDE
[*Tensely.*]

Thank God!

KING HAMLET

Thank God for all. To Him
Alone our faith hath here its utterance,
Even as thou saidst to me.—Rememberest still?—
"Enter, O faithful, here this asylum of peace.
Here, speak we only of God, else let us cease."

GERTRUDE

Still I remember, love.

KING HAMLET
[*With intense quiet.*]

Else—*let us cease!*

[*They stand gazing in the glass.*]

CURTAIN.

ACT THIRD

Scene Four

ELSINORE. A ROOM IN THE CASTLE.

Enter, upper left, HORATIO, *accompanied by a* MAN *in Egyptian garb.*

HORATIO

[*Glancing at an open letter in his hand.*]

Yes, I have read the message. Come this way.

[*They move on, and exeunt, upper right.*]

After a moment, from lower left, enter KING HAMLET *and* CLAUDIUS.

CLAUDIUS

Are you return'd from war merely to answer
The call of Echo, whose reiterations
Lure our poor world to doomsday, ever repeating
Over and over the old word—*love?*

KING HAMLET

Even so:
That old word, *love.* I will new-say it still—
Love! Turn that word to dust, yet will it sing,
Like the cricket in the ashes: "Ember, remember!"
What else should burn me on the bloodied ice-trails
To goad me homewards? Yet—what is it?

CLAUDIUS

Is it?
Is what?

KING HAMLET

Love.

CLAUDIUS

Slowly, brother! Do you ask me
The question: *What is love?*

KING HAMLET

Aye; that enigma
Solved—answers all. Erosophy, insight
Of love: that wisdom doth unlock all doors
Of destiny—thy fate and mine and this
Poor world's, that hastes toward doomsday, as did Hamlet
Towards Elsinore from the embattled lists
In Poland—battling for what? For freedom: is 't not
So blazon'd on our shields and spears: *For Freedom!*
Freedom for whom—the victor, or the vanquish'd?
Freedom to build a world where vows are held
In veneration, and where mutual pacts
Are binding as heaven's law, which mateth lovers
In wedlock, and doth make of brother and brother
Keepers of each other's weal? That law of freedom:
Is *such* our goal of victory—for *both?*—
Lover and brother mutually strong
And free to will their vows? Or must they make them
By force, or cunning, under masterful
Compulsion?

CLAUDIUS

And who, pray, shall answer this?

KING HAMLET

Who?—None but him who knoweth to answer me
My question: *What is love?*

CLAUDIUS

And hast thou found
The answerer?

KING HAMLET

I seek him everywhere
Outside me, and receive a thousand answers,

All different; and then I seek him here
Within me, and receive one only answer
Ever the same.

CLAUDIUS

And him, within, what saith he?

KING HAMLET

He answers: *Love is freedom, freedom love.*
The lover is the freedman, who hath fought
To strike off his own shackles. The free man
Is he who serves no overlord but Love.
What other freedom sanctions any war?

CLAUDIUS

Amleto, I see, not even the blood and sweat
Of war have served to rinse thy virgin soul
Of honied metaphysic. Love, methinks,
Is sweatier, and freedom bloodier,
Than suits the delicate nostril of thy mentor
To smell; else hardly could it have been he
Who counselled thee to haste thy sweating war-horse
Home to our late carousal.

KING HAMLET

Why, thou art right.
The reek of that still festereth in my nose
Too noisomely, for me to hold the snot
From leakage to my lips; and, Claudio,
This is the spittal on 't: Henceforward, let
The cellarage of Elsinore be lock'd
'Gainst exodus of Rhenish—and of rats.

CLAUDIUS

Rats?

KING HAMLET

Rats and vats: they breed, together, vermin

Which spread the plague amongst us. Oh, I know:
Danskers be drinkers. *Wassail!* is our folk-word
Of fellowship; but let it lilt no tattle
For cuckoos' cries, nor mirth of liquor vaunt
The laugh of lechery.

CLAUDIUS
[*Smiling affectionately.*]

Is this the chapel
Sermon for morning-after, and *mon frère*
Become my friar?

KING HAMLET

Since thou turn'st it all
Into so fond a smile, 't is ended, now,
Save this, in epilogue: Thine honour, dear
My brother, is mine own, and mine is thine,
To hold in candour's trust 'gainst all the world.
Wise Caesar Julius, in the olden time,
Tempered the world to venerate his wife,
Calpurnia, unto so keen an edge
Of honour, that not only naught in whisper
Might scotch her virtue, but no *thought* of whisper.—
If Caesar's mate were pure as ice on Aetna,
Gertrude is snow upon Parnassus' peak.
And so my hand in thine, with benediction
On thy fraternal love to her and me!

CLAUDIUS
[*As they clasp hands.*]

The benison is more blessed than the sermon.
Since love is freedom, I will freely share
In the bestowal on 't.

[*Enter, right,* QUEEN GERTRUDE, *with* HORATIO, *who pauses.*]

HORATIO

And—and soon, Madam?

GERTRUDE

Yes; now, Horatio. I will tell the King.
[*Exit Horatio.*]

KING HAMLET

Ah, Gertrude! You were even on our lips.

GERTRUDE

I hope, not weightily.

CLAUDIUS

Oh, lightly, sister:
Less heft than song, though more than metaphor.

GERTRUDE

Methinks, your trope doth trip more light than I
Can follow it. I fear me, it doth need
A soothsayer. And haply one is found.
Hamlet, my dear, our good Horatio
Hath ask'd me bring you tidings, even now,
That one is at the door.

KING HAMLET

One, at the door?
One—what?

GERTRUDE

A soothsayer, and beggeth soon
Admittance to your presence, to impart
Some word of special import.

KING HAMLET

Word from whom?

GERTRUDE

The stars, he saith.

KING HAMLET

The stars! What manner beggar?

GERTRUDE

Nay, he 's not beggarish. I caught but hasty
Glimpse of him, on the stair. Egyptian
He looked to be, in mien and garb.

KING HAMLET

A gypsy?

GERTRUDE

More reverend in poise: an ancient figure.
Profiled against the dusky wall, his bronzéd
Face and his chalk-white beard, cut angular,
Gleamed motionless and rigid as an image
Of Pharaoh, charr'd on some cotta urn
Unearth'd from tomb of Nile.

KING HAMLET

Waits he without?

GERTRUDE

He doth, and asketh entrance here.

KING HAMLET

Myself
Shall glimpse him first, and so I will decide
Whether to fetch him here for conference.
Your pardons, and pray tarry my return.

[*He starts away, right.*]

GERTRUDE

Not long away?

KING HAMLET

A moment only. Ah,—

[*Pausing, he smiles wanly.*]

And by the by—you know, my dear, I trust—
There is no need of any repetition
For making silent gesture on your lip
To my avoidance, when my back is turn'd
A moment—as before.

GERTRUDE

[*Tensely.*]

As—as before?

KING HAMLET

Nor you, dear brother, to share sudden dread
Of my supposed resentment at such chance
Juncture of circumstance as your joint meeting,
Lest it should rouse the scampering of rats
To bob out of their holes, and prick their noses
For smells, to whet their livers.

CLAUDIUS

Share sudden dread?

KING HAMLET

Surely we now know better than to dread
Rats in the corridors, since here our hands
Have clasped in benediction, which shall cause
Our fingers to spread ratsbane through the Castle
Henceforth. Or was 't, perchance, some other reason
Of dread you shared, together?—What, my Gertrude?—
Claudio?—

GERTRUDE

We?

CLAUDIUS

Together?—When?—Where?——

KING HAMLET

Nay, then,
'T is sure, the glass was blurr'd—not crack'd. Adieu,
A moment—merely for a moment! [*Exit, quickly.*]

GERTRUDE
[*With stifled cry.*]

Ah!—
Moment, that shatters monuments of time!

CLAUDIUS

The glass—not crack'd!—What glass?

GERTRUDE

The glass, which mirrors
All agonies between the womb and tomb—
Glass of our walléd earth-life: would it were
A window—into Yorick's Nothingness!
He stood before it, when I signed to you
To turn back, and we left the room, together.

CLAUDIUS

Ah, so—and watched us in the mirror! Well,
May not a queen make sign unto her subject?

GERTRUDE

May not a queen-wife answer her king-husband,
Who questions why she signed? Or, must she stand
White as a ghost, and stutter like an idiot?—
Claudius, the glass hath crack'd, which shall reflect
All Elsinore in ruin, ere it shivers.

CLAUDIUS

Tush, 't is a king of childhood; 't is a lamb
Of metaphysic, sucking still the teat

Of innocence, for milk to make it gambol
To the Lord's Prayer. Espy us in a glass?
Why, if he spied us mirror'd lip-to-lip,
He 'd clap his palms and cry us: "Kiss, my dears!
Ben'dicite! 'Tis bedtime. Ere you snuff
Your candles, read St. Augustinus, his
De Civitate Dei."

GERTRUDE

Could I snuff
Those coals of satire in your devil eyes,
I 'd scratch mine own out, and go blind in peace!
But there 's no seer of magic to exorcize
These demons in your gaze and mine—unless . . .
Ah, when my son comes home from Wittenberg,
I 'll slant him as a sword 'twixt you and me
And grasp the hilt, to wield his singeing blade
Of intellect, to pierce thee—succubus!

CLAUDIUS

Methinks, you conjure cleverly without him,
Sibyllic sister!—But our "merely a moment"
Too soon, I see, is interrupted—

GERTRUDE

[*Glancing, right, where he is looking.*]

Ah!

CLAUDIUS

Nay, nay!—No fingered silence on the lip,
But genial salutation.

[*Enter* KING HAMLET, *followed by* HORATIO, *with* SOOTHSAYER.]

Well, Amleto,
And are the stars auspicious?

KING HAMLET

We shall learn.

[*He turns to the Soothsayer.*]
You ask of us an audience. 'Tis granted
Here, in the presence of our queen and brother
And this our friend, Horatio, who tells us
You are a soothsayer. Is such your calling?

SOOTHSAYER

Sooth is my calling, Sire, for such as call it
Forth from me. I am but an instrument
Whereon your majesties may play what sooth
You most do yearn for, to your souls' content.

GERTRUDE

What most we yearn for!

KING HAMLET

How can you know that?

SOOTHSAYER

Even by mine own response to it. Such is
Mine art.

KING HAMLET

What is your art?

SOOTHSAYER

Astrology,
The Logos of the Stars, who never yet,
Since the beginning was, have broken the vow
To Sooth, wherein their will and word are mates,
Whose scion is Destiny.

KING HAMLET

Whence did you learn
Your art?

SOOTHSAYER

First, from my need of it;
Thereafter, from the *Arcanum Magicum,*
In secret lore of heaven and hell, reveal'd
Within this volume: *Manual-Höllenzwang*
Doctoris Johannis Fausti.[9]

GERTRUDE

Ha, what is 't?
Is it a manual to exorcize spirits
Of hell, who plague us here? And can your art
Thus sate what most we yearn for, and so grant us
The dearest wish we will?

SOOTHSAYER

Madam, to wish
Is not to will. Though you have wished my coming,
You have not willed it. 'T is the stars who willed it,
To grant you opportunity to will
The thing you wish, and speak the master word
To evil, or good, not be the toy of both.

KING HAMLET

Nay, what are you, who stand between us here,
Uttering these enigmas of the stars?

SOOTHSAYER

'Twixt you and you, most gracious majesties,
I am the focus of a twinkling star
Whose name, although you have not spoken it,
I read now in those yearnings of your eyes
Which interblend with mine, unknowing yet
What eyes they are, who read your own so well.

KING HAMLET

What eyes? Whose eyes, then, are they? And what name

Of all the innumerable stars have we
Not spoken, yet revealed within our gaze?

SOOTHSAYER

One of the Seven Stars.

GERTRUDE

The Pleiades?

SOOTHSAYER

"The brightest of the seven," once you called him,
Who shows you here this little reliquary
Wherein he still doth shine.

[*He holds something out for the King to see.*]

KING HAMLET

Ha, what is here?—
Rosemary?

SOOTHSAYER

For remembrance! 'T is the sprig
Which Yorick gave him once, to give to you.

KING HAMLET

Yorick!

SOOTHSAYER

And you did give it back to the giver,
Thus saying: "From thy mother's heart and mine
That all thy thoughts of us, through future lights
And darks, may guard our love, take now this sprig
Of fragrant rosemary, my little son,
Nor part with it to any, save for love;
And when at last my presence says, *adieu!*
Hamlet, remember me!"[10]

KING HAMLET

Yea, God! But how—

GERTRUDE
[*To King Hamlet.*]

Our "little son"—Aye, so it was, you said—
On 's seventh birthday!

SOOTHSAYER

Good Horatio,
Unroll the Constellation, whilst I kneel,
And show the Seventh Star, till he be named.

[*Stepping back, he kneels where Horatio, standing before him, lifts high and unrolls in front of himself and the Soothsayer the scroll of a wide, blue banner-chart, whereon are emblazoned the* SEVEN STARS *of the Pleiades, six in silver, the Seventh in gold.*]

GERTRUDE
[*Pointing to the Seventh, with a cry.*]

Ah, Hamlet, look: he shineth there, in gold—
Alcyone!—our little princeling's star.

KING HAMLET

Brightest o' the pollen'd swarm—Alcyone!

[*For a moment, they stand gazing bewildered at the starry chart, shifting their eyes from it to each other, then back to the scroll, as—slowly stepping aside—Horatio removes it, revealing there—amid the crumpled garb and sloughed headgear of the Egyptian—the kneeling figure, garbed in gold and blue, of* PRINCE HAMLET, *his bronzed, beardless face and glowing eyes uplifted toward the King and Queen, in answer to their cry of* "Alcyone!"]

PRINCE HAMLET

Father!—Mother!

KING HAMLET

Hamlet, my son!

GERTRUDE

Our own
Alcyone!—How *can* it be?—Yet 't is!
But how?

PRINCE HAMLET

Magic!—*Arcanum Magicum!*

[*Leaping up, he springs forward to clasp and kiss their hands, where they embrace him.*]

Dear Sire—Mother, most dear!—Ha, good mine uncle—

CLAUDIUS

Our prince, return'd from Wittenberg—a gypsy,
With a mysterious tale!

PRINCE HAMLET

[*Laughing.*]

But not to step on,
Like *Serpens'* tail, in the old Mystery!—
Horatio, marshal of the heavenly chart,
My hand to thee, prompt-boy and property-bearer
To Egypt's "soothsayer!" What said I, lang syne,
How I should be a player, and learn kings
To know their roles! This here is but rehearsal.

KING HAMLET

How came you thus in secret?

GERTRUDE

Tell us—tell us
More of this marvel!

PRINCE HAMLET

More, indeed, I 'll tell you
Marvellous, but first of all must I confide it
Unto a cagéd amsel-bird. Where is he?
Elsinore, lead me there!

[*Gazing rapturously about him.*]

Ah, home, at last—
Home!—Elsinore!—Beautiful Elsinore!

CURTAIN.

ACT FOURTH

Scene One

ELSINORE. SHRUBBERY, NEAR THE CASTLE. LATE SPRING MORNING.

A leafy nook, sheltered by a hedge of honeysuckle.
Under boughs of a tree in pink blossom, close to another with clusters of yellow blooms, a wooden bench, on which OPHELIA *is seated. Near her stands* PRINCE HAMLET, *looking at her dreamily.*

PRINCE HAMLET

O, you are like a memory of young May
When the pink hawthorn bows her posied cheek
Deep in the droopt laburnum, where shy birds
Utter their honeyed vowellings of love
In plashing drops, like shooken dews from eaves,
On the daisy sod beneath.[11]

OPHELIA

A memory,
My lord? How am I so?

PRINCE HAMLET

A fantasy
More real than earthy fabrication, more
Component of all vision than these eyes
Are witness of elsewhere. Ophelia,
When I was far away in Wittenberg,
Your absence was the presence of a wonder
Which held me here, enspell'd. Now I am here
At last, and feel your breathly presence, you
Are a far faerydom—a flower-fragrance,
Wafted by winds that steal it. Nay, you are
Not made of time and touch, like others. You
Are thoughts of early morning violets
Blowing in brooky dells, where the green linnet
First pipes from dark, and we as lovers meet

To pluck their blossoms for our trothal vows
And kiss their dews away. Blue violets,
They are your eyes, their pupils, for heaven's truth
Outglowing gently there: white violets,
To rim them round with pureness: yellow ones,
To hide the others with the aureole
Of your ring'd locks, breeze-blown.

OPHELIA

I'm glad o' that,
For violets—they are of all wildflowers
Your favourites and mine. "Winter runaways,"
You named them once, because they peeped their faces
Out of a snowbank's runnel, winking to us
Their dewy eyes, till you did laugh to see them.
Do you remember?

PRINCE HAMLET
[*Moving to her.*]

Well. 'Twas on the morning—
That faery morning—when you first came back
To Elsinore, out of the nunnery
Wherein your budding-time too long had winter'd;
And here, beneath these very hawthorn boughs,
We first took hands—as now; but then I feared
To touch them with my lips—as now, unfearing.

OPHELIA

Why did you fear, my lord? They are willing hands
In yours.

PRINCE HAMLET

Ah, then they were not mine, as now,
In trothal.

OPHELIA

What is trothal?

PRINCE HAMLET

This, when hands
Utter to lips their vow of willingness
And lips seal here their own. For these, that clasp
Each other—these your hands, these lips of mine—
Are made of meditation, moulded not
Of mould, but spirit. Therefore they are wrought
Of stuff invisible, whereof alone
Vows can be made.

OPHELIA

Is spirit, then, a thing
Invisible? I would not gladly look
On you, sans lips, nor you on me, sans hands!
Spirit and mould—? Methinks, they 're one, not two.

PRINCE HAMLET

Why, you think right. One are they, both—but only
To eyes of them, whom Cupid blindfolds. Dear
My virgin university, I come
From Wittenberg to learn of you my classics
And all the occult lore, o'er which the powers
Of *Höllenzwang* hold no dominion.

OPHELIA

Oh,
My lord, I hope you will not cease to tell me
More of that secret learning, which your letters
Have stirr'd my heart to hear, in your kind voice
Rather than in your quill-script.

PRINCE HAMLET
[*Smiling, as he sits beside her.*]

Not so kind
And harder still to cipher?—Surely will

My poor tongue try to mend my poorer script.
Where did my quill leave off?

OPHELIA

You wrote me, last,
That you were interrupted by two friends
Who came to bear you company, just then,
Unto some master, but I could not scan
Their names aright, so strange they were. The first,
It seemed, began with *R*.

PRINCE HAMLET

Ah, Rosencrantz
And Guildenstern, my fellow students, there:
Yes, yes. We share a sort of friendship, such
As wildfowl by the same pond, ere they wade
Through mud to swimming-water, and arch necks
To prove which archéd curve is swan, which—goose;
But not such friendship, shared by two sky-larks
In the same welkin, as Horatio
And I plucked out of heaven's blue, when we
Erst went to Wittenberg. Then all of learning
Was but the half of friendship, and being friends
Was to be masters of our lore, more great
Than e'en the mighty *Magister Doctorum,*
Faustus, himself.

OPHELIA

Ah, Faustus: that 's the name
O' the master in your letter! It begins
With *F*. What did you learn from him, my lord?

PRINCE HAMLET

Scholars, my lady, from their masters learn
Only what first they 've taught themselves, yet fail
To know, till searching finds it in another

More skill'd to show them where it lies. I fear
I was not early versed in Elsinore
Deeply enough, to scan my Wittenberg
To mine own visioning. Yet Faustus showed me,
In sudden, unpremeditated moments,
Glimpses of far unknowns, of timeless valleys
And spaceless peaks of moonlight, whence I scanned
Wild swarms of monster beetles, silver-sharded,
Dropping swart eggs, which burst in thunderings
Darkly below on fiery lady-bugs,
Crawling strange seaweed, wefted of men's brains
And clotted blood, to seek their nutriment.

OPHELIA

Alas, what woeful vision!—But what were these?

PRINCE HAMLET

Offspring of an inter-elemental monster,
Aquaterraerial Man, metallicly geared
With gills, claws, wings, and guts of Phoebus Apollo,
Self-poised to explode and obliterate the world
By the collapsing vacuums of wisdom.—
All this to me Faustus foretold in dream.

OPHELIA

Oh, a dreadful dream!—Of what more did he tell?

PRINCE HAMLET

Of far-off isles he told, in western ocean,
Where the down-sinking sun, guléd with dawn,
Doth eastward rise from underneath the wheel
O' the whirling world, to stare on shapes, begotten
Not in Earth's womb, but Acheron's. On one such,
Amid the blue Bermouthes, vext with tempests—
An isle of flushing coral, whose dusk silence
Throbs with harp-music and the magical

Note o' the sea-nightingale—dark under
A salty cavern's archéd rock, lit only
By green stalactite jewels—

[*He pauses, with eyes fixed in gruesome expression.*]

OPHELIA

[*Gasping.*]

Oh! What 's there?

PRINCE HAMLET

There crawleth on his belly a man-fish
With scaly hairs, pearléd with barnacles,
And wriggleth one splay foot to claw the crab
He keepeth for a tooth-bit, to entice
The wonder-smile of a mute lady there.

OPHELIA

A lady?

PRINCE HAMLET

A lady, lovely as her wonder
And piteous as her smile. The crawling sea-brute
Knuckleth his oozy eyes, voiding a brackish
Spittal, with a hiss, and clambereth upward
From off his belly, to clutch her knees, when—sudden—
Even as the marvelling lady uttereth
A cry of sharper pity, lo!—

[*He pauses, gazing as at some noble apparition.*]

OPHELIA

What then?

PRINCE HAMLET

Dark, in the cave-rock door, against the sea-blue,
More deep in purple, standeth a tall form,
Majestical as twilight's brooding star,
And lifteth a wand—its glister of wild lightnings

Flashing the cavern. And the lady cryeth:
"Look, father!" And in awful thunder-peal—
All vanisheth."[12]

OPHELIA

What! Vanisheth? But how,
My lord? Nay, have you not beheld all this?

PRINCE HAMLET

In Faustus' magic, yes.

OPHELIA

How great a master
He must be!

PRINCE HAMLET

Some, indeed, account him so—
The mage of magic and of necromancy.
Such throng on him, to hear his conjurings,
And pore at midnight on his secret glyphs
Of Hanasai, Isasamuel,
Thezaylemach, Yoth, Mo, Zamariel,
Neyathor, Haylor, Geliorsion—

OPHELIA

How wondrous they do sound—like knolling bells
At twilight!

PRINCE HAMLET

So they do—to ears, that hark
Their overtones of wonder. Simplest among them
There is a *Seelen-Ruf,* a solacing call
To souls in sorrow, summoning the love
Of Mary, Christus' mother, to expel
Demons of fear. It is the magic word,
Marion, that inward spoken fills the heart

With silent bravery, to meet the world
Of wrong with ringing challenge.

OPHELIA

Marion:

Indeed, the tone rings true.

PRINCE HAMLET

The glyph is written
Thus:

[*Kneeling, he writes on the ground with his forefinger.*]

+O+ +O+

So the Cross unites the sundered world.[13]

OPHELIA

This Faustus must be good.

PRINCE HAMLET

To some he is.
To others he is the mage of mountebanks,
An ignoramus of old eruditions,
Who feeds the gulls and gudgeons of his lore
With the same stock of oats and gnawing-bones
He feeds his talking horse and laughing dog,
He kennels in his sanctum.[14]

OPHELIA

Nay! Hath he
A horse, that truly talks? And have you heard
His dog a-laughing?

PRINCE HAMLET

Verily have I,
And learned his deep art of ventriloquism,
A ducat a lesson.

OPHELIA

Is it so deep an art
And long to learn?

PRINCE HAMLET

As deep as his own belly
And long as his windpipe.
[*Rising, he paces slowly back and forth, with dreamy pausings.*]
But there is a third
School, form'd of his novitiates, who deem
They sense, within the mountebank, the man,
And in the great magician—the all-probing
Angel-spirit of man, who seeks to wrest
From mystic lore and mean chicanery,
From heavenly conscience and its counterfeits
Alike, the deep-throned power of knowledge, held
Prison'd too long by passionate ignorances—
Aye, yearns to crown the hidden king in the open,
Restored, in pristine faith and innocence,
To earth's allegiance, as of old in Eden.

[*As Prince Hamlet pauses, there appears—from behind the hedge, left, unseen by them—* KING HAMLET, *his head and shoulders only visible. Entering, he draws back a little, and looks on, listening.*]

OPHELIA

To which of these three schools do you adhere,
My lord?

PRINCE HAMLET

To all and each and none of them.
Of Faustus I am satirist, disciple,
Apologist—all. For I am errant son
Of a great father, whom to serve with knowledge
Wrested from good and evil, I did wander
Forth unto Wittenberg and Faustus, till—
Surfeited there—I homeward turned to him,

To fill whatever need of me he craves,
Be it nothing—or all.

OPHELIA

His need cannot be nothing,
With whom you share so great a love.

PRINCE HAMLET

I share
With him what he, through all the obscuring
Prismatic glooms and twilights of this world,
Hath shown me—fiercely glowing in his own heart—
The love of innocence. And that hath led me
Where now I tremble, peering in your eyes
To fathom the love-light there.

OPHELIA
[*Rising.*]

Why do you tremble?

PRINCE HAMLET

So deep the light is, and so dark the plunge!

OPHELIA

Dark?

PRINCE HAMLET

Under closed eyelids, diving inward
To explore the darkling mystery, beyond
This little day—this dear, this happy day!

OPHELIA

Can there be other day than this?—I think
There is none.

PRINCE HAMLET

Thought, alone, can make of it
Eternity.

OPHELIA

And is that why you tied
The verses to the bars of Amsel, telling
None there, but Thought, to enter?

PRINCE HAMLET

"Endearing damsel,"
Yes, that is why. And that is why, together,
Beyond this day, yet ever within it, we
Immortally shall live—so all which follows,
Whatever it may hold of dark mischance,
Shall meet eclipse in this our glowing hour
Of trothal, witness'd by the angel, Thought,[15]
Hid in this pink hawthorn, within whose bloom
Deeply the gold laburnum droops, to listen—
And weep.

OPHELIA

Weep?

PRINCE HAMLET

Even as our joy is weeping
For all who never knew it.

OPHELIA

There is one,
Who knows it, is not here.

PRINCE HAMLET

Who?

OPHELIA
[*Smiling.*]

Amsel.

PRINCE HAMLET

Ah,
Then, let us haste to Amsel. Come, sweet flower,
And we will make his cage our trothal bower!

[*They go off, together, right, as—through a slit in the hedge, left,—King Hamlet comes forward and stands, looking after them, then up toward the blossoming tree-boughs.*]

KING HAMLET

"Witness'd by the angel, Thought!"—Thou pensive
hawthorn,
What blesséd tidings hath thine interloper
Heard from thy listening heart, to tremble here
These tear-drops from thy blossoms! Thou and I
Are ancient in such overhearing, yet
Thou put'st forth bloom anew, as if no shudder
Of searing winds had ever taught thy prime
To shiver unto nakedness, and feel
The stings of withering memory. Instead,
Thou mak'st thyself the emulative symbol
Of mating lovers, mated in the faith
That all which blossoms does so in the knowledge
That withering breedeth blooming, and what withers
Is bred of nothing else. Thou—old, brave tree!—
Thou dost this by thy nature, being no other
Than the strong angel, Thought, at work, as witness
Unto this living truth. Shall I, then, I,
Thine ancient fellow, do less?—These eyes of mine
Have peer'd in other eyes, to fathom love-light,
And "dived to explore the darkling mystery
Beyond this little day." These lips have prest
Other lips, that uttered: "There is no other day
But this!" With such these loins have bred the loyal
Scion who, testing good and evil, hath turn'd
Homeward from alien masters, to effect
The "all, or nothing" of his father's need.

What need, then, brooding hawthorn, have we twain
For withering memories of eyes, hands, lips,
To warp us? There 's no valid memory
But breeds us resurrection, not regret.
All 's well, old tree of youth!—And yet
[*His voice breaking.*] . . and yet . . .

CURTAIN.

ACT FOURTH

Scene Two

ELSINORE. OPHELIA'S BEDCHAMBER, AS BEFORE.

For a moment, all is silent. Then, from within his barred cage, the Amsel-Bird is heard singing, with sweet dreaminess. Soon, it stops suddenly, at sound of a human voice, calling softly from without [*left*]*—the voice of* QUEEN GERTRUDE.

GERTRUDE

Ophelia! . . Darling Ophelia!
May I come in?—Thou need'st not hush thy bird.
His song is welcome-sweet.

[*Gertrude enters, glancing about the room, then moves toward the bird-cage.*]

Ah, none but you,
Sir Amsel? Are you sudden grown so still
At my intrusion on your rhapsody,
Wrought only for the ear of innocence
To listen? Or, is this your hush for dread
To hear the throbbings of a guilty heart,
That fears to hark its own? Or, are you, Sir,
No dark-plumed angel in a bird's disguise
But a mute priest, caged in confessional,
To absolve this heart's confiding of a sin,
Only your silence can convey aloft
To the heaven, your song hath enter'd? Or, of all
These, are you naught—nothing, except your beak
Golden with morning, left of heaven's light—
But are a Plutonian messenger in black,
Prison'd, to bear to earth the imprisoning
Word of a pagan passion: the dark vow
Of Venus Pandemos, to bind her coil
Of lewdness round Urania's breasts, and twist
Her sister lips to utter heavenly lures
Of morning-song unto the sons of Man
For her own pander-lust?—Still you are dumb.

O, sombre, silent mystery, your pardon,
Since still I lack your absolution. 'Tis
For you, not me, to question. I should be
The answerer; and yet you ask me—nothing.

[*She starts,—looking off.*]

Listen!—Ah, no, not *him!* Not *them!* I came
To question her of him, in loving hope
Of joy for both. No intervening love
Of mine must tinge their own my mottled hue
To blear that joy. I, too, will cage me, dumb,
Within this hanging curtain—this bed-curtain—meant
Only for hiding innocence.—Hush, Amsel!

[*She withdraws quickly, behind the curtains of Ophelia's bed, as* OPHELIA, *herself, enters, left, with* PRINCE HAMLET, *who pauses on the edge of the scene.*]

PRINCE HAMLET

And may I enter here?

OPHELIA

Why not, my lord?

PRINCE HAMLET

So once, perhaps, did overdaring Phoebus
Pause on the verge of Daphne's secret wood,
Inviolate to men and gods, still fearing
To reach and touch, lest the tree-bark enclose her
Within her fragrant closet.—Is this real?
What foot of man hath ever ventured here
Before?

OPHELIA

My father's, oft; and once, by chance,
The Chorister's, whose far-away sweet song
To "Lily of the Dell" preceded him
Unto your mother's welcome presence here.

PRINCE HAMLET

My mother's presence! That shall give me sacred
Sanction of love to enter, since as well
I claim precedence of a certain singer,
Whose voice, methinks, is husht, to let my own
Become my emissary, in his stead.
[*Approaching the cage.*]
How say you, my lord Amsel, far-exiléd
Chorister to your prince, no longer doom'd
To exile?

OPHELIA

Oh, he 'll answer soon, for he
Hath found his voice, and sung to me full many
Sweet antiphons of far-off memory,
During these happy weeks since your return.
But what doth make me wonder is, that one
Whose eye 's so bright with seeing, and whose throat 's
So thrill'd with singing's bliss, should guise himself
In sables, and wear this suit of solemn black.

PRINCE HAMLET

Ah, 't is the hue of thought. "In the beginning,
Darkness was over the face of the deep, and God
Said, 'Let there be light!' and there was light." And that
Light was the colour of His love, which hath
Emblending prism rays. I 've brought thee two,
Here—green and gold—coil'd in this tiny casket.
[*He takes from his poke, and hands to her, a little jewel-case.*]

OPHELIA

Why, what is this?

PRINCE HAMLET

Our trothal-chest. It holds
The secret of this ring-rhyme from my lips:

A darkling greenwood pool,
Set in a sunlight circlet,
Forever so deep and cool
And clear that naught can mirkle it.
Look in! Look in, O lady mine!
And thou shalt wondrous sights divine:

[*As she wonderingly begins to undo and open it, he bends over, with her, still speaking.*]

Where the dark wave curls,
The mermaid's greenish lightnings;
Where the wood-brook purls,
The faery's dusky bright'nings;
Mossy gnomes, that crawl the mountain,
And the gleam of Mimir's fountain.

Look in, sweet! and divine
Everything thou art,
And everything that 's thine,
Till thou shalt see—thy heart:
Spring—and all the greening of it,
Love—and all the meaning of it.[16]

[*She gazes spellbound, as he lifts out a gleaming circlet, which they pass to each other's fingers.*]

OPHELIA

A gold ring—ah!—with a green jewel-stone:
An emerald! And see: What are these forms,
With flowing tresses, chaséd in the gold?

PRINCE HAMLET

Shapes of our souls, forever circling there,
Link'd to each other by the bond which frees them.

OPHELIA

Oh! 'T is a naiad, darting through the billows—
Throwing herself on her side—clasping the waves

In her arms—she shoots through their depths
In furrows of silvery light, fused with the golden.

[*From behind the bed-curtains—unseen by them—the face of* QUEEN GERTRUDE *peers forth, gazing where Prince Hamlet gazes at Ophelia.*]

PRINCE HAMLET

Naiad and sylph blend in that elfin light.

[*Kneeling before her, he reaches upward the ring.*]

Ophelia, of faeries
Fairest symphony,
O filia Veneris
Pulcherrima, tibi—
To thee, of thee, my prayer is
Wrought in this ring-rhyme: Wear this
Orb of the eye of Aries,
To shine
In the signet divine
Of Venus' sign,
For thine
Alcyone!

[*Breathlessly, she reaches towards him her left hand, where he holds the ring, looking in her eyes.*]

OPHELIA

Alcyone!

GERTRUDE

[*In a whisper, staring with grief-struck smile.*]

Dear God,—my dream!—my dream
Of long ago![17]

[*Slowly Ophelia sinks to her knees beside Hamlet, where he puts the ring on her ring-finger.*]

PRINCE HAMLET

Ophelia, my own!

[*He kisses the ring.*
As he does so, from above them, rises a clear sweet bird-note.
They look upward, together, towards the cage.]

OPHELIA

O, hark, my lord!—Hark!—Amsel is singing!

The clear, pellucid notes of the bird are heard rising higher and higher, as the

CURTAIN FALLS.

ACT FIFTH

Scene One

THE ROYAL LIBRARY. ELSINORE.
KING HAMLET *and* PRINCE HAMLET *discovered, in conversation.*

KING HAMLET

How can we compass love in a library?—
As well wage battle in an armoury!
When love hath lost its savour, 't is a book-louse.
Love not God so—nor child, nor woman, nor man;
Else wilt thou worm in parchment, deeming thou eatest
Ambrosia. Such are God's pedants, not
His poets, gotten of his midnight passion
On the storm-riven hill-tree.

PRINCE HAMLET

Truly, Sire;
Yet under bark of books runs sap of life
Which feeds the fruit of Eden.

KING HAMLET

Hast thou never
Hearken'd a wild bird singing, high on a bough
Above that bitter fruit, and heard the sap
Grow voluble with ecstasy, beyond
The barkish rind his talons flaunt, to fly
Following the joy that lifts him?

PRINCE HAMLET

I have listen'd
Unto a cagéd bird, and heard a rapture—
More quiet—lift an inward ecstasy
To make his wooden bars a reachéd ladder
For clambering joys to clasp descending angels,
As faeries climb by briars unto roses
To quaff their honeyed bliss.

KING HAMLET

Still bred in vellum,
And bookish to the bone—and yet a poet,
Cagéd in faerydom! God guard thine issue,
True scion of thy father's soul, with her,
Whose joys of faery youth share thine, and may
The pink of hawthorn and laburnum's gold
Glow in your hearts, together.

PRINCE HAMLET

What! You heard?

KING HAMLET

I overheard. Forgive the *over!* The hedge
Grows tall i' the garden, but not over-tall,
Nor thick enough, to shelter lovers' tryst
From ear and eye-gleam of a father's love.
But had it been as tall as Pisa's tower,
Leaning to listen earthwards for heaven's word
Of love, I would have heard that word, without
Intrusion—even as I hear it now
Soft-pealing through thy silence, my dear son.

PRINCE HAMLET

Father, she is—

[*A long pause.*]

KING HAMLET

Is she as beautiful
As that doth tell?

PRINCE HAMLET

As all that fails to tell.
To love a flower is most natural.
The smiled-on flower smiles on. 'T is natured so.

The rose, living her loveliness, knows neither
Our love, nor heeds our praise of her. But when
The rose returns the love that 's given her,
Ah, then—

KING HAMLET

Then?—

PRINCE HAMLET

Silence doth succeed in telling
The all it failed to tell before, which is:
Ophelia is the loveliness, that loves.[18]

KING HAMLET

And Hamlet, son of Hamlet, is the eye
Of loyalty, which images the troth
Both of his trothéd lady and his king,
Who blesses it—as one who needs such blessing.

PRINCE HAMLET

As needs such blessing?

KING HAMLET

Son of mine, within
The garden hedge, I overheard also
Thy pledge of love to me—to serve my need,
"Nothing, or all," whatso it might be.

PRINCE HAMLET

Sir,
I am glad you overheard it. Such it is.

KING HAMLET

And being such, why, then—

PRINCE HAMLET

Then, Sir?

KING HAMLET
[*With sudden change.*]

Let us talk
Of books. For books—as thou didst truly say—
At least hold sap of Eden, till fruits rot.
But such is my great need, in Elsinore,
Of fruits, bitter or sweet, that I must talk
And talk, to taste 'em—else, gnaw my nails,
Or chew, and chew—rolling my twisted tongue
Like to a stalléd ox.

PRINCE HAMLET

Chew what, my father?

KING HAMLET

I chew the cud of memory. I gulp
To swallow, yet 't will not down, but rises
Again in my gorge. Therefore, talking of books,
Return we to our undigested muttons,
And speak of Gutenberg.

PRINCE HAMLET

Of Gutenberg?

KING HAMLET

That mage, who, with the semen of black ink,
Begot the Printer's Devil, on the hag
Of Memory, and so bepeopled Hell
With her accurséd offspring, cast in lead,
That in remorse he stamped the sacred scriptures,
Like a tattoo, into the very tissue
O' their vellum hide, and tossed 'em earthwards
In retribution, duplicated—not
Once, twice, thrice, but thousandfold—to scatter
Bibles on Holy Bibles over the world
To wipe away his sin.

PRINCE HAMLET

I learned of him
At Wittenberg, where Faustus lectured on
His secret art demonic, which hath now
So spread its benediction through all time
From Homer's day to ours.

KING HAMLET

And didst thou learn
He had, like thee, a mother—even as we all,
Demonic, or angelic, must have mothers—
And Else was her name—not Gertrude—that 's
Thy mother's name, but that 's beside the point. . .
His father was named Gensfleisch, so he took
His mother's—Gutenberg—and who shall blame him?
A father of gooseflesh smacketh not so good
On lips of fame, as a good mother, made
All goodness, even as a strong fortress, like
To God's.

PRINCE HAMLET

And was his mother—?

KING HAMLET

Pardon!—The point lags.
This same good printer, Gutenberg, who mixed
The Devil's work with God's, and had a mother,
Most narrowly just missed having a wife;
For 't is recorded that, at Strasburg, he
Was haléd into court, for breach of promise.—
Now, how should that be?—Was the almost-wife
Less strong in goodness than the mother?—What
Did the most learned Doctor Faustus teach thee
Upon that ticklish theme?

PRINCE HAMLET

Why, Sir, he harped
Only upon the theme, that those deep powers
Of magic, which conjured the printer's press,
Would, in the future's memory, hale him—not
Into a court of censure, but of honour,
To hail him: Father of the Great Unfetterer,
Literacy,—the goal of liberty.

KING HAMLET

Lord of illiterates, dungeon'd in letters!
Father of the Great Incubus, whose leaden
Body shall lie on the sleeping souls of men
Until his impress prints them, all alike,
To pattern of the myriad-pockéd monster
Whose metal corse deadens their dreams.

PRINCE HAMLET

While sleeping:
But not when they awake from dreams, courageous
And luminous enough, to heap their darkness
On their endarkener, and free their souls
To know the thing which warps them, and to will
Their own deliverance from it.

KING HAMLET

Aye, but what
If they enact the monstrous dreams wherewith
This incubus doth permeate their sleep?
The future of thy Faustus' visionings
Wavers far off, in cloudy, beckoning contours
Of magic unimaginable now,
Yet we may sense it, in our vision's eye
Focuss'd the other way—on Ilion, flaming
For the false lips of Helen; on the smoking
Scripts of the Alexandrian library

Crackling to char the pith of Plato's dreams
For Turkish nightmares; and the demoniac
Burning of books, under the red moon's glare,
At Paracelsus' Basel. All of which
Leads back our wandering theme to Elsinore—
Our estimation of this Gutenberg,
His almost-wife's and his good mother's goodness;
The inward singing of a cagéd bird;
The unbooking of two minds, his human brothers,
Caged in the library of Denmark's castle—
Hamlet, with Hamlet's ghost.

PRINCE HAMLET

Ghost, my lord father!

KING HAMLET

What said I? Nay, my ghost hath ridden forth
To Poland's border, and here stands my body
Talking—of naught: the nothing of my need
Of thee—Hamlet, my only son—mine own!
[*He embraces him, with sudden clutch, burying his face against the Prince's breast.*]

PRINCE HAMLET

Sire, dear Sire! The nothing of your need
Is eloquent—past talking. What 's of doing
Which I at once may act for 't?

KING HAMLET

Nothing, also.
Let thine own action be in loving all.
So wilt thou serve my need, in loving me
With others—doing the great will of love
For all of us, who need it.

PRINCE HAMLET

But this silence

Secreted in your speaking—let me ease it
To some good utterance, for your sake. Hint me
Some clue. What 's wrong, or loose, i' the Castle?

KING HAMLET

Rats.

Here now they patter to us, once again.
This time, a pair. They come in couples, now,
To keep each other warm. Coupling 's their art.
Observe it.

[*Enter* OSRIC *and* CORNELIUS.]

OSRIC

[*Bowing.*]

Ah, my gracious lord, the King,
Pardon! beseech your grace! May we—

KING HAMLET

Pardon,

My egregious lord, the king-beseecher,—well?

OSRIC

Polonius, my liege—

KING HAMLET

Polonius

Is *not* thy liege, but—Well, Cornelius?

CORNELIUS

Horatio, your Majesty— [*To Osric.*] *Excusez-moi, Monsieur!* [*To the King.*]
My liege, and if we may—

KING HAMLET

We may,

Or may not, choose between you, Sirs. But, well—
Speak on, together!

BOTH [*at once.*]

Sire, Polonius——
Sire, Horatio——

KING HAMLET

We choose Horatio, his herald, first.—
Well?

CORNELIUS

Sire, Horatio hath ask'd me bring
Your Majesty this word: A courier
From Norway waiteth in the antechamber,
Conjoinéd there with another, fresh from England—

OSRIC

Even as, my liege, Polonius hath bid me
Announce you a third messenger—a rider
From Poland, who attendeth him in—

KING HAMLET

In
His duty, doubtless. Therefore, thank you, both,
And bear our instructions—to Horatio,
That he report of Norway and of England
Himself to us, here—as, for Polonius,
The same to him of Poland. Then, Sirs, haste ye,
Both, to the kitchen larder, and instruct
Our Master Cook to place two pungent baits
Of vigour'd cheese—Limberger were the best—
Within the cellar exit; and beware,
My lords, not to incline your sentient noses
Too near the baitings, lest they snap too soon
For your deliverance from dalliance. So,
Hush this enigma of our warning, for
If it should sudden pop to knowledge—Adieu,
My lords!—

[*Lowering his voice almost to a whisper.*]
Silence! Sera notre parole!

OSRIC AND CORNELIUS
[*Imitating him.*]

Silence! . . . Silence! . . .
[*They bow themselves out.*]

KING HAMLET

Still coupling! They couple in whispers.

PRINCE HAMLET

But, Sire, do not you banter 'em with enigmas
Too subtly for their comfort and your own,
And also mine, who fail to catch your parable
O' the cheese-baiting?

KING HAMLET

True; let them bait themselves
And us be freed of 'em. I 've other need
For laying bait—and bantering myself,
Not them.

PRINCE HAMLET

But still you would withhold it
In secrecy from me?—Why, Sir?

KING HAMLET

Because,
Under a hawthorn tree, I overheard
The breathéd secret of a sacred vow,
Whose delicate opening flower I would not blast
By any beetle, making his escape
From cankering mine own quick. Yet this confiding
Of what I will not tell, urges us both

To this: that thou be free as summer wind
To seek thy goal, as I am winter-bound
To guard its source—renewal of the spring
Of manhood. As for statehood—here once more
It comes to plague us.—

[*Enter* POLONIUS, *agitated, followed by* HORATIO, CLAUDIUS *and Others. King Hamlet addresses Polonius.*]

Yes, my lord, you may.

POLONIUS

May what, O King?

KING HAMLET

Impart the news from Poland.

POLONIUS

'T is that, my liege, I come even now to bring you—
Most joyful news—wondrous, indeed, past telling!

KING HAMLET

We hope not.—Tell it.

POLONIUS

The Polacks flee our arms
Into the eastern wastes!

KING HAMLET

There let our joys
Follow them, and reclaim the wastes, to make
Their homeland safe and hold them there, in praise
Of God, whom here we pray to keep all homelands
Free from all pestilence of war—and peace.
Go, bid the bell-ringers proclaim our triumph!

[*Exit Polonius.*]

Horatio,—thy tidings.

HORATIO

None so glad
I bring you, Sire.

KING HAMLET

Then let the sad news make
Our gladness strong to welcome it with meekness.
Tell on. What word from Norway?

HORATIO

Fortinbras,
Making his oath beside the urn wherein
His father's ashes lie, hath sworn this vow:
Never to forget how Hamlet, King of Denmark,
In the olden time, tore out the kingly heart
Of Fortinbras, his father, from his breast
And sent the inurnéd ashes back to Norway
In mockery.

KING HAMLET

Remorse—not mockery!
Send back to him that word of ours.

HORATIO
[*Pointing to a Soldier.*]

My liege,
Here waits his courier, to take your word.

KING HAMLET
[*To the Soldier.*]

Herald of Norway, say to Fortinbras:
Hamlet of Denmark, too, hath sworn *his* vow,
Never to forget how, in the olden time,
He tore from out the breast of Fortinbras,
His father, that heart, which here in his own breast

Still throbs, to quicken yearning for forgiveness
And hatred of all hate, which cries for vengeance.

THE COURIER

O King, forgiveness is a lovely word
On victors' lips, but not upon avengers'.
All prettiness aside, force speaks to force
Straight out, when both weigh equal, but slantwise
When ounce of doubt doth tip the balance. So
Let us speak out forthright in frankness, now,
Assuming we are equals. Shall the assumption
Be granted?

KING HAMLET

Gladly granted.

CLAUDIUS

Stay! Think, Hamlet!
Think well, before the event.

KING HAMLET

We are thinking well
After the event—the event of old, to avoid
Renewal of its woe. [*To the Courier.*] Speak, for your lord!

COURIER

Denmark, the lands you wrested by the sword
Of old from Norway, Norway comes anew
To claim again. Stolen must be return'd
Ere peace can hold, else feud shall double feud.
For what our fathers fought we fight once more.
How saith the King, in answer to our lord?

KING HAMLET

Norway, the lands *you* wrested by the sword
Of old from Denmark, Denmark wrested back

And holds its own. Your stealing stands forgotten.
If you renew it, feud shall *treble* feud.
For what our fathers fought, we too fight on.—
Thus saith the King, in answer to your lord.

CLAUDIUS

And bravely answer'd!

KING HAMLET

To make Bravery
Dance in a circle round the altar of Death?

CLAUDIUS

What say you, brother? Prithee, do not jest
When great things hang in balance.

KING HAMLET

Did I jest?
Then why are you not smiling?

CLAUDIUS

Oh, I smile,
Of course, since you are jesting.

KING HAMLET

Dearest brother,
Sith we, as brothers dear, have only each other,
Draw nearer, pray!

[*Claudius draws near.*]

Now, will you smile at me?

CLAUDIUS

Why, see: am I not smiling?

KING HAMLET

Are you? Thanks.

’T is not great things are great, it is the little
When great things hang in balance. A wild oat,
Bending, will show which way the wind is blowing,
Better than a wild bull, who stamps upon it.
Grazie for your smiling, Claudio!

COURIER

Denmark, have you no other word for Norway?

KING HAMLET

None other. ’T is the word of statehood, utter’d
From kingdom unto kingdom down the ages
By them, to them, who dream it is themselves
Who speak it. So shall it be echoed on
Till there be no more states, but only—Man.
Yea, ’t is the selfsame word, Cain, in a day-dream,
Did put in Abel’s ear, asleep in the orchard.

CLAUDIUS
[*Murmurs.*]

Asleep in the orchard?—

KING HAMLET

’T is the only word
For sleepers, till they wake.

COURIER

Doth Denmark dream
Norway is sleeping?

KING HAMLET

No more than other kingdoms,
Nor less.

COURIER

This news shall gladden Fortinbras

To teach the Danes what sluggards Norsemen be.
We shall report to him the word of Denmark.

KING HAMLET

Report him, then, as well, this word of Hamlet,
Who speaks now for himself:
Hamlet, to King Hamlet's Lord,
Master of all marks of men,
Prayeth the world-sword
Shall be sheathéd, when
Folk of Norway and of Denmark
Brothers be in mighty Menmark.
Farewell!

COURIER

Farewell, King! [*Exit.*]

KING HAMLET

Now, Horatio!
What more of message for us?

HORATIO

This, from England:
Yon stands the messenger, to make it known.

KING HAMLET

Speak, Courier, your message.

ENGLISH COURIER

King of Denmark,
Heart's greeting from the King of England! First,
In ancient time, before the crown of Christ
Gleamed like the dawn through mists on Dover Cliff,
The Roman with his galleys landed there
To make of Britons slaves. Saxon and Norse
Followed, and Norman followed them, to do
The same.

KING HAMLET

But did not!

COURIER

No. Roman and Norse,
Saxon and Norman enslaved not Britons. They
Themselves became the British, and conquering
Were conquered by the unenslaveable
Will, whose enduring name is England.

KING HAMLET

That
Did Denmark also learn, in conquering
Your land sufficiently to levy tribute
In gold.

COURIER

Of that same tribute-gold I come
To speak now. Even as my fellow-courier
From Norway hath declared: Force equals force,
Or not. When not, the lesser force must needs
Pay penalty of weakness. Such are war
And war's peace. England pays that penalty,
Being less puissant in arms than Denmark is,
Though not in gold. Therefore, in gold we pay it:
Gold, fetcht by our industrious argosies
Of peace, in routes of farthest east and west
And shores o' the Middle Sea, plying their boon
Of trade.

KING HAMLET

Boon, yes, when fair and free, not plied
From undercover of high walls, to filch
Booty from neighbour gardens: trade, when *trade*
Means wealth of common good, not otherwise.
Pardon, brave England, our interpolation;

But this your keen addiction to gain sweets
From salty water-courses, oft hath gain'd you,
Invidiously, the slurring attribution
Of stocking bales, instead of beauty, and so keeping
Shop for yourselves, more bent on merchandising
Than ministrating unto others.

COURIER

True,
O King, 't is slurr'd of us, *not* true the slurring.
For trade lives not by hoarding, but expending;
By openness, not stealth; by friendly handing,
And not by hate's withholding. Gold is sown,
Like barley seed in spring, to reap us crop
Of golden harvest, big with Christmas cheer
For all to share in. So, in crypts of England,
Our storéd gold of tribute waits for Denmark
To fetch it home.

KING HAMLET

Waits!—Have you, then, not brought it
Here, with you?

COURIER

Nay, King. And for that, one favour
The King of England pleads your Majesty.

KING HAMLET

A favour? What?

COURIER

That you will send to fetch it
One, dearest to you, nearest in your grace,
That he, in coming to us, shall not leave us
Until, by sampling of ourselves, he learns
To appraise the gold he beareth back to you
For what it is: the coinage of our friendship,

Fresh minted from old metal, proved in ore,
Ere press'd through fire to that which shall endure,
Stampt with our kings and our folk-heritage,
For trade to stand for truth among the nations
And hold the world in balance. Such, O King,
The favour England asketh; and for envoy,
Lacking your own high person, only one
Who represents it highly shall, he hopes,
Become your choice, to claim the debt we owe,
Which, paid at home, shall bring you home—ourselves.

KING HAMLET

We would not be the King of Denmark, could we
Deny the King of England such a favour,
Which turns his debt to our indebtedness.

CLAUDIUS

Nor would I be the King of Denmark's brother,
Near in his grace to him, who hath of late,
In absence, made me regent of his crown,
Could I deny myself the honour now
Of craving his high favour, to become
His representative to England's king,
For claiming there the tribute.

KING HAMLET
[*With startled brusqueness.*]

Claiming it?
Who comes as claimant where the payment 's offer'd?

CLAUDIUS

Have I o'erstept myself? If so, your pardon!

KING HAMLET
[*Quietly.*]

Nay, thanks for this surprise—your askéd favour,
Which plumbs deep to our sources of affection.

For near to us you are, and ever have been,
Dear brother; so even dearer, ever nearer
We hope to hold you, and to have you *smile*
Closer to us. Wherefore, we trust the honour
You do yourself, shall be—to stay with us.

CLAUDIUS

Stay here?—Why, then, it is the same. Your deep
Confidence of me toucheth me, here, or there.

KING HAMLET

So, Courier, though lacking our own person,
As needs be, to companion you to England,
You shall not lack one, who doth represent us
Highly, as you request, and is our royal
Choice:—Hamlet, Prince of Denmark.

PRINCE HAMLET

Father!—I?

KING HAMLET

So name fits need.

PRINCE HAMLET

Is this your need of me—
To leave you now?

KING HAMLET

Nay, not to leave me, ever.
Bear me in your heart, where I am never absent;
So shall your going fill my greatest need—
The certitude of knowing all is well
Abroad, for Denmark, and at home—for Hamlet.

PRINCE HAMLET

Shall not my mother share in this your choice?

KING HAMLET

Thy mother? Yea, heaven! Thy mother shareth in all
Thy father's choosing—still, in sharing, keeping
Her own free will of choice. Such is our matehood,
Wherein no lightest thing earth lifts, but holds
Its heft of heavenly import. This, we trust,
Thou knowest as keenly as thine own dear uncle.

PRINCE HAMLET

Indeed, Sire, I have known it well, since childhood.

CLAUDIUS

And I, of course.

[*From outside,* THE CHIMING OF BELLS *is heard.*[19]]

KING HAMLET

Wherefore, we all await
The sanction of the Queen to this our choice
Touching this worldly matter, which itself
Is toucht by hands celestial—hands of friendship
And love—with victory in both,—for hark!
The bells beginning, telling our war is won—
Our war for freedom's choice to be ourselves.

CLAUDIUS

Indeed, Polonius hath aptly timed
The bell-ringers.

KING HAMLET

Go, then, my son! Be oracle
To the bells, and tell thy mother what they tide us—
The triumph of *our cause*—the cause of freedom
For man and woman. Haste! Thy mother knoweth,
Best of us all, the sacramental meaning
Of freedom's vow, the bells are sounding. Haste!
Bring here thy mother!

PRINCE HAMLET

Gladly. [*Exit.*]

KING HAMLET

Yea, my lords,
What are all mothers, sisters, wives, but Woman?
What are all fathers, brothers, husbands, else
Than Man? Each rules himself, herself, none other,
Where freedom rules. At home, then, let 's begin:
I—you—each—here, now let Love's will be done!
Freedom of millions rests upon each one.
The world itself must abdicate, till we,
By love's will, make one man and woman free.
So freedom gauges choice, and choice reveals
The scope of freedom. Lords and gentlemen—
The Queen!—

[*In the doorway, with* PRINCE HAMLET, *appears* QUEEN GERTRUDE, *who speaks with agitation, as she enters.*]

GERTRUDE

Hamlet! The bells! Is 't true, their wondrous
Tidings—the foe hath fled, the war is won?

KING HAMLET

Aye, on one battle-front—though others wait
In challenge.

GERTRUDE

Where?

KING HAMLET

I' the north, with Fortinbras,
And here, in strategies of peace.

GERTRUDE

Here?

KING HAMLET

England
Asks envoyage, to fetch her debt of tribute
Home to us, thus in friendcraft to outvie
The boasts of foecraft. In that gauge strategic
Hath Claudius, our noble brother, plead
To be our envoy; but, to parry his love,
And hold him to our hearts in Elsinore,
Have we—his king and brother and your husband—
Besought him stay, and in his stead made choice
Of this our dear son, Hamlet, who stands ready,
Sans doute, to sail for England, on the morrow.

GERTRUDE

Claudius stay—? Hamlet to leave us!

KING HAMLET

Which?
No choice of Hamlet's father but 't is shared
By Hamlet's mother. The Queen Mother's word
Of sanction, here in this assemblage, merely
Is lacking now, to seal the choice.

GERTRUDE

Is lacking?

KING HAMLET

We mean, of course, in utterance, not in thought.

GERTRUDE

How—how else can this mother think, but on
This boy of ours—for still 't is but a boy,
Forgive, dear Prince!—that our son, late so far,
So now-but-newly home—should will to leave us?

PRINCE HAMLET

'T was not my willing, Madam. 'T is alone
My willingness.

GERTRUDE

For what?

PRINCE HAMLET

To leave.

GERTRUDE

But why?

PRINCE HAMLET

To serve the affair of state. Nay, the command
Was not my father's. 'T is mine own, to me,
In whatsoever serves him best. The choice
Itself is free.

KING HAMLET

So is thy mother's, Hamlet,
Which now she makes.

GERTRUDE

Makes? Makes against thine own!

KING HAMLET

Against?

GERTRUDE

How far is England? Is it far
As Wittenberg?

KING HAMLET

Perchance, more far—or less.
Why do you question?

GERTRUDE

Why?

KING HAMLET

'T is what I asked.

GERTRUDE

The tides are treacherous in the Channel waters,
Methinks, I 've heard.

KING HAMLET

No more than in home waters,
Methinks—but I perhaps may be mistaken.

GERTRUDE

Is, then, the need so great, which takes away
Our son,—or, else, our brother?

KING HAMLET

If it prove
More than our sorrow in having to part with either.
The wrench of choice is hard. 'T was ours in choosing,
As now it racks your own.

GERTRUDE

Mine?—Nay, it draws
Less hard my breath now.—What, Horatio?

HORATIO

Madam.

GERTRUDE

Of old, you brothered our dear son,
At Wittenberg, as you were twins at heart,
Not casual fellow-students merely. So
You heartened him, and us—his far-away

Mother and father. All you steadfast were
You are still.—Will you fellow him again,
On this new voyage to England?

HORATIO

Madam, of course,
And if it be your wish, in common.

GERTRUDE

Mine
It is. [*To the King.*]
And thine, my lord and love?

KING HAMLET
[*Starting.*]

Yea, mine!

[*To Claudius.*]

And thine?

CLAUDIUS

Mine shares the "of course"—superfluously.

KING HAMLET

So freely rings our sharéd choice. The bells—
Again they ring it, oracular, for home
And victory afar. What said I, erst,
Hamlet, how—best of all—thy mother knoweth
Their sacramental meaning?—Courier,
Your envoyage is settled. For to-morrow
Have now our best farewell. And that you may
Bear unto England's king the publishment
How we in Denmark twine our victories
And sorrows with our hearts, be witness here
Now to our own farewells, commingled with
Our God-be-thankéd greetings, in this bosom
Of Elsinore.

[*Turning suddenly, he clutches Prince Hamlet close and kisses him.*]
Farewell, dear son!

PRINCE HAMLET
[*Startled.*]

My father!

KING HAMLET
[*To Claudius, grasping both his hands.*]

Brother, praise God, here do I hold thee fast!

CLAUDIUS
[*With a wincing smile.*]

But not in irons! Soft, pray, thy loving grip!

KING HAMLET
[*Turning as suddenly to the Queen, grasps her hand.*]

And now, Gertrude, my own—

GERTRUDE

Hamlet, what 's this?

KING HAMLET

This is to lead thee, love, unto the kiss:
[*He leads her to Prince Hamlet.*]
The farewell kiss.

GERTRUDE
[*Kissing the Prince.*]

Good-bye, sweet boy!

PRINCE HAMLET

All 's brief.

KING HAMLET

And now—the sister-brother kiss—joy's fief.
[*He leads her to Claudius, where he watches them keenly.*]

GERTRUDE

[*Extending to Claudius her hand.*]

Brother, I would thank God—

CLAUDIUS

[*Taking her hand, lifts it and moves his face to hers, as they kiss upon the cheek.*]

So, sister, He is thankéd!

KING HAMLET

[*Turning to the assemblage, speaks in harsh, searing tones, amid deeper swelling of the chimes.*]

Lords!—Now in love and peace our red-barb'd spears are rankéd.
Hark, from this barbéd peace, the pealing which foretells
Our destinies—the bells—the bells . . the bells . . the bells!

CURTAIN.

ACT FIFTH

Scene Two

ELSINORE. THE HALL OF THE SHRINES AND THE MIRROR. NIGHT.

Enter QUEEN GERTRUDE *and* CLAUDIUS *with lighted tapers.*
As they move, together, toward the left, Gertrude pauses abruptly, staring in the glass.

GERTRUDE

Why must we walk again into this mirror
Which shows us what we are? Cannot we hide
Even from ourselves? Let us turn back.

CLAUDIUS

Turn back?
What backward turn is there, but leads us forward
To find the thing we seek? Is it a bed
We seek? Then, whose? Is not the apple mellow
Which once you tossed away, as being too green
Still, to be toothsome?

GERTRUDE

Aye, 't is overripe
With will-less thought, and I must bite its core
Before it rots with rank anticipations
Which spottle me like a lazar.

CLAUDIUS

This way, then!—Yonder
He reads all night within his library
Where husband's bookishness is lovers' boon.

GERTRUDE

Lovers?—Ha, lepers!

CLAUDIUS

Still fickle?

GERTRUDE

Set them there—
The lights—beyond the mirror's dreadful glassing.
Sit here i' the shadow.

CLAUDIUS

Why?

GERTRUDE

To analyse
This obscure business of the pealing bells.
Could he have plann'd it all?—To weave a braid
Of vows, so subtly twined—of love and war,
Of victory and peace, of will and freedom,
Made sacramental with dear ties of home,—
That he might twist it round my mother's heart
Till the blood swelled my throat with the concealéd
Choice, which to utter clear would blast us all—
My yearning choice to hold thee here!

CLAUDIUS

Horatio—
Ho, excellent! Who else so well and fair
Could serve the double purpose—to conceal
Our secret joy and soothe the public sorrow?
And thou, O wit of mother woodcock-bird,
To lead the stealthy hunter the wrong trail
By flutters and waftings of thy broken wing
To hide thy home-nest with the cuckoo's egg!

GERTRUDE

Perdition have thee, thou—thou dearly vile
Invaluable thing—half death, half quick
Of livingness, turn'd lust! 'Twas not my wit
Of mother, but my pang of mother love,
Which turned my choice of evil to the good
And safety of my son. Horatio

Is more than friend to him, or public servant.
He is my princeling's father-brother-angel—
His tower of strong fidelity. Being such,
I know my darling safe from destruction, and
Myself—saved, to destroy myself with thee.

CLAUDIUS

Destroy thyself? Surely, thou mean'st—enjoy!

GERTRUDE

It is the same. All 's one, when joy doth feed
Itself on infidelity. What 's left us,
But ever to keep suspecting whether he
Suspects, whose soul was born blind to suspicion?

CLAUDIUS

If he suspects, 't is even as a child
Who make-believes the fear of his belief.
If he suspects not, 't was shrewd childishness
Wherewith he led thee to me—for the kiss
Of sister-brother love, amid the gazings
Of Elsinore and the English courier.
But so with him, or not so, now with us
'T is time for it to *be* so, in full, shameless
Gaze of ourselves, in gorgeousness of shame,
Even as there the glass beholds, and bids us
Go hence—to consummate it.

GERTRUDE

Do not point
There—not *there!* Not in the glass.—*That* hath beheld
Too much—too much of all, and bids us gaze
Within ourselves, and——

A VOICE
[*From outside—calling low, then louder.*]

Who is there?—Who 's there?

[*Gertrude and Claudius start away from each other, staring.*]

GERTRUDE

His voice!—*his!*

CLAUDIUS

His.

GERTRUDE

[*Drawing farther away.*]

No, not now—not tonight!

Don't follow me.

CLAUDIUS

What!—

GERTRUDE

[*Moaning.*]

Oh!—don't follow me!

[*Exit, upper left in the dark.*]

CLAUDIUS

Perdition hath me indeed—in the very apex-
Instant of success! Still—still, malicious mirror—
I will collaborate in thy reflections
To see mine image crown'd. What 's sown is sown
In a king's bed, to bourgeon in a throne.—
Another night!—To-night, I sleep alone.

[*Exit, left, with the taper-lights.*]

*Darkness—pierced soon, from the right, by an increasing glow and the sound of a man's voice—*KING HAMLET'S*—calling.*

KING HAMLET

Who 's there?

[*He enters, right, holding in one hand a brass candlestick, with lighted candle, in the other hand a book.*]

Who moaned? Could it be no one?

[*Approaching the mirror, he sets the lighted candle upon a table, near it.*]

Nay,

What 's in the mind must have its counterpart
In nature—and conversely—for all 's mind,
Glassing and glass'd. What 's beauty unto beauty
Without her mirror? Or horror—imageless?
Naught: nothing, that matters to itself. All 's nothing
Which does not know its likeness.—Know I mine
In yonder mirror—mateless? Here we stood,
Together, knowing each other there, and eyes
Of love without made echo-light for love
Within, to hear and see and know their oneness.—

[*Shuddering.*]

Now stand I here alone, where loneliness
Is all that 's left to glass. What 's broken here
Is splinter'd there, surely as crack in ice
Is cleft in frozen water. So, what matters it
To Hamlet, if his angel be a whore,
Or ministering mate, when seraph wings
Are turn'd to webs of bats, where his own eyes
Are sered to blacken'd cinders, blind as char,
Crackled from ever mirroring hers again
Sans doubt of her defection squeezing there
Its acid of suspicion, speckling with whoredom
Each lovely glance she glints from me to him,
My brother, and him to me, blasting them both
With concupiscence and me with infamy
Of ravishing faith with doubt.—It matters not.
I know. And failing proof of what I know
Cannot give death to it.—What know I, then?
That God is good and Caritas is strong.

[*Opening the book.*]

'T was written here, lang syne, to the Corinthians,
By Paulus, who by Caritas was snatcht,
In vision, even from the poison-fangs of hatred:

[*Reading from the book.*]

Caritas suffereth long—is kind—envieth not.
Caritas vaunteth not itself, is not puff'd up . . .
thinketh no evil, rejoiceth not in iniquity,
but rejoiceth in the truth; beareth all things,
believeth all things, hopeth all things, endureth
all things.—Caritas never faileth.[20]

[*Dropping the book on the table.*]

Ah, never faileth—*whom?* The loving. 'T is we,
Who, hating, are defaulters. What matter, then,
To Love, if I be infamous, and he,
My brother, bawdy, and she, my mated soul,
A harlot?—Caritas suffereth long—is kind—
Caritas never faileth.—Aye, but this
Also I know: He *smiled* at me, my brother;
My brother smiled and smiled and smiled—and loathed me.
Why so?—Is he, whom lately I did make vice-king
The King of Vice, himself, to turn himself
Now inside-out, and smile—like *that?*—yea, kiss
Even so, to curse me cuckold? Ha, but I,
Myself: do I, heart-pack'd with brother-love,
Now gape my mouth, to vomit—guts of vengeance?
Outside, turn in, again!—What matters it?
Ah, ah! All 's inside-out! What 's in the mind
Hath here its counterpart, and Elsinore
Shall mirror Hamlet for the ghost he is,
Haunting the cornice of a splinter'd glass,
Warp'd from the soul he was. About, about!
Love's candle be out! Cursèd be Caritas!

[*Lifting the brass candlestick, he holds the candle-flame high, glaring toward the mirror.*]

Revenge, behold thyself! Rend now thine image
And wreck all vows—but vengeance!

[*He hurls the brass candlestick, with its flame, towards the mirror. Black darkness, amid tinkling roar and crash of falling glass.*]

CURTAIN.

END OF "ODIN AGAINST CHRISTUS"

THIRD PORTICO

REVERE

THIRD PORTICO—On its lintel is blazoned, in clear blue, the word REVERE!

Once more the READER *re-enters. Turning his gaze toward the azure inscription, he speaks inwardly:* A moment's pause amid catastrophes!—Was it the Mirror of Truth—or Delusion—that shattered? Can curse of the unrevering affray the soul of Caritas?—Here's silence. Once more a niche discloses two hidden scrolls—brief mind-reflections: What of these reflections?—*Revere!*—How scant, or immense, is the scope of our reverence? Surely not less than our capacity to revere the awe-uplifting, cloudy vastness of

"OUR OWN MINDS" and "THE MYSTERY OF THINGS"

From SHADOWS OF OUR THOUGHT, *by* *ROBERT KEITH MACKAYE*

[I]

So man moves on, as foam that falls
In midnight dance, by rockbound walls
To gambol on the sculptured breast
Of thundrous rapids, unrepressed . . .
Till always, when our living tide
Has reached the turning, far and wide
There floats across the hollow sky
A tinnient whisper, or a sigh
Half heard, half shadowed in the mind
By wraiths of patient bones behind;
And wakened spectres, dimly wrought
Grope in the shadows of our thought . . .

Without the bitterest of life
Unknown we slumber in the strife
Of our own minds, and dying go
To learn what man must live to know:
The gifts of God to every man
Are free: all dream, some think, few plan;
But only sublime fools create
The grandeur of our future state.

From KING LEAR: *Act V, Scene III*

[II]

Lear: We two will sing like birds i' the cage.
When thou dost ask me blessings, I'll kneel down
And ask of thee forgiveness. So we'll live,
And pray, and sing, and tell old tales, and laugh
At gilded butterflies, and hear poor rogues . . .
And take upon 's the mystery of things
As if we were God's spies.

THE SERPENT IN THE ORCHARD

THE SERPENT IN THE ORCHARD

[TIME: IMMEDIATELY FOLLOWING THE THIRD PLAY]

BEING THE FOURTH PLAY OF THE TETRALOGY THE MYSTERY OF HAMLET KING OF DENMARK, OR WHAT WE WILL ✢ BY

PERCY MACKAYE

THE SERPENT IN THE ORCHARD

DRAMATIS PERSONAE

[*In the order of their appearance*]

QUICKSILVER, *orchard-keeper*
RICHARD, *shearer*
NICHOLAS, *shepherd*
CLAUDIUS, *brother of King Hamlet*
PRINCE HAMLET, *son of King Hamlet and Queen Gertrude*
HORATIO, *his friend and aide to King Hamlet*
COURIER *of England*
TOPAS, *grave-digger*
MOLL COWSLIP, *attendant to Queen Gertrude*
KING'S CHORISTER
GERTRUDE, *Queen of Denmark*
OPHELIA, *daughter of Polonius*
POLONIUS, *Lord Chamberlain*
HAMLET, *King of Denmark*
LAERTES, *son of Polonius*
CORNELIUS, *courtier*
YAUGHAN, *gardener*
HOSTLER
HERDSWOMAN
SMITH
CRIER
GUILDENSTERN
ROSENCRANTZ

English villagers; Choir-Boys; Castle-Folk; Children; Retainers; Priests, Lords, Courtiers and Ladies.

PERSONAE:— [*Of ACT I, SCENE II, of Shakespeare's "Hamlet, Prince of Denmark"*]:—*King* [*Claudius*], *Queen Gertrude, Prince Hamlet, Polonius, Laertes, Voltimand, Cornelius, and Lords Attendant.*

PRESENCES:—
GALLUCINIUS, *as Quicksilver; as King Hamlet's Daemon*
Voices of the Invisible
THE GHOST OF YORICK

SCENES

ACT FIRST:—*Scene One*

Elsinore. An Orchard, near the Castle. *Toward autumn.*

Scene Two

England. A craggy Eminence, near Dover.

ACT SECOND:—*Scene One*

Elsinore. Shrubbery, near the Castle.

Scene Two

A Footpath Way, near the Castle. A Cleft in the Path.
A few minutes later.

ACT THIRD:—*Scene One*

The Royal Library of Elsinore. *Later, same day.*

Scene Two

A Corridor in the Castle. *Night.*

Scene Three

The Royal Library. *The following afternoon.*

ACT FOURTH:—*Scene One*

Elsinore. Hall of the Double Throne.
Same time as Act Third, Scene Three.

Scene Two

The Cleft in the Path [*same as Act Second, Scene Two*].
Same afternoon, toward evening.

ACT FIFTH:—*Scene One*

Elsinore. A Courtyard of the Castle. *Next morning.*

Scene Two

An Arcade to the Chapel. *Several days later.*

Scene Three

Bedroom of Prince Hamlet. *A few days later.*

Scene Four

Ophelia's Bedroom.

Scene Five

A Balcony of the Castle.

Scene Six

A Room of State in the Castle.
[Shakespeare's *Hamlet, Act One, Scene Two.*]

ACT FIRST

Scene One

ELSINORE. AN ORCHARD, NEAR THE CASTLE.

Under an apple-tree—in a high crotch of which CLAUDIUS *sits, half concealed—the grassy turf rises to a low mound. Near it are seated, together, three Persons: an old* SHEPHERD, *with his crook; a middle-aged* SHEARER, *with shearing-iron; and the* ORCHARD-KEEPER, *a young-looking fellow, with a sickle slung from his shoulder, a snake-wound winged staff stuck in the earth beside him, and across his knees a stringed instrument, which he is strumming, to his own voice in a song [soon joined, in refrain, by the voices of the two others], pitched to an old folk-melody.*

SONG

[*Solo*] Sickle, Shepherd's Crook, and Shears,
All one shining summer's day,
Wrangled in a roundelay
What the Law said
As to which of them had causéd
Love the most of tears.

[*Solo*] Said the Sickle:
"I ha' gather'd mickle
Meadow-roses, for to garnish
Lover's grave,
Ere the ring of troth could tarnish."
[*Trio*] *What is Love,*
What is Love, by tears, to misbehave?

[*Solo*] Quoth the Crook: "Ah,
I ha' oft forsook a
Sorry black sheep, lonely bleating
On the trail
Where he 'd lost his snowy sweeting."
[*Trio*] *What is Love,*
O, what is Love, when lonely, to bewail?

[*Solo*] Sighed the Shears: "Oh,
I ha' clipt the spears o'
Barley o'er wild lovers, hidden
In the field,
Bare, by bold eyes to be chidden."

[*Trio*] *What is Love,*
What is Love, by loving, so to yield?

[*Solo*] Sickle, Shepherd's Crook, and Shears
Ceased, that shining summer's day,
All their wrangling roundelay,
When the Law said:
"None of these hath ever causéd
Love the least of tears—
For, O, Love—poor Love, brave Love!—
Was born of tears."

[*Trio*] *Why should Love,*
So, why should Love turn pale, for any fears?

THE ORCHARD-KEEPER

Thus, brethren, endeth our lesson, at the beginning.
Hence, let us turn our sickle, crook and shears
From askings of sweet song, on *What is Love?*
To taskings of summer sweat, on *Who be we*
To tackle 'em with clean tools and hearts devout?
Good fellow—thou, who swivellest thy grin
To ape thy gaping scissors—who art thou?

THE SHEARER

Short, I be Dick. Long, I be Richard Shearer.

ORCHARD-KEEPER

Long may thy shears enrich thee, nor short-cut
Time to Dick-dub thee richer for all shorn!—
Shepherd, what art thou call'd?

THE SHEPHERD

My christen-name
Is Nicholas, but I be calléd Nick.

ORCHARD-KEEPER

A nice nickname, at Christmas-tide, to nick
On holly crook, for guarding manger!—Shepherd,
Art thou religious?

SHEPHERD

Aye.

ORCHARD-KEEPER

Know'st thou thy Proverbs?

SHEPHERD

Aye.

ORCHARD-KEEPER

And thy Catechism?

SHEPHERD

Aye.

ORCHARD-KEEPER

Then answer me:
Why is 't as good to be killed for a sheep as a lamb?

SHEPHERD

'T isn't.

ORCHARD-KEEPER

Why isn't?

SHEPHERD

Because 't is 'gainst Commandment.

ORCHARD-KEEPER

Commandment!—Which?

SHEPHERD

The First: *Thou shalt not kill.*
For— sheep, or lamb— 't is certain, to be kill'd
Implyeth killing. Wherefore 't is far better
To butcher, than be butcher'd, and so keep
The First Commandment.

ORCHARD-KEEPER

How! Isn't butchering killing?

SHEPHERD

Why, Sir, how should it be? Thou knowest well,
Accordant to law and statute, every shepherd
Hath license to butcher, after the shearing season;
Else how shall gentry be served with mint and lamb?

ORCHARD-KEEPER

What hold'st thou, there?

SHEPHERD

My crook.

ORCHARD-KEEPER

And know'st thou not
How 't is the holy sign of the Good Shepherd,
Yet would'st thou butcher with 't?

SHEPHERD

Nay, verily.
This staff is wood, not steel. Steel is for butchers.
My crook is for to guard my lambs and sheep
From stealers, and to raise old ewes from ground
When they be weak and tottery, and guide
My flock in to the fold, when cometh dark
And only evening star for candle-shine
And wolves be prowling round, to do foul murder
Upon the silly innocents.

ORCHARD-KEEPER

Yet thou
Would'st emulate the wolves, and murder those
Same innocents, thyself?

SHEPHERD

What, what? Nay, nay!
I would but butcher them, when wool 's been shear'd
And stored for spinning baby-clouts and tabards.

ORCHARD-KEEPER

Then, is not butchery murder?

SHEPHERD

Nay, God fend us!
Murder is 'gainst man's life, but butchery 's
For livelihood, and lawfully commanded
By kings and stately councils.

ORCHARD-KEEPER

And who hath
Commanded kings and councils to command
The butchery of man, for livelihood
Of states?

SHEPHERD

Faith, thou must ask of them, not me.
I be a shepherd and a sheep-butcher,
And raise my staff to kill no living thing
Against commandment.

ORCHARD-KEEPER

Whose commandment?

SHEPHERD

Nay,
I 've answered thee enough. So prithee, Sir,
Answer me back: Who art thou?

ORCHARD-KEEPER

Why, I see,
We fence each other deft as politicians,

Sharp'ning their tongues blunt on Polonius'
Whetstones. Why not? You 're Nick and Dick. I 'm Quick—
That 's short for Quicksilver—and I am keeper
O' the King's orchard, where the King himself
Cometh for quiet slumber, from turmoil
Of war and stealthy whisperings of state.
I keep the law of the orchard, whose quick-changing
Dewfalls from off the ripening apples rise
In silvery mists to swiftly rosying clouds
Which, sudden dark'ning, fall in purple showers,
Turning to dews again. This, my caduceus,
Round which the Snake uptwines to the Dove's wings,
Hath been my staff of office since the hour
Erst I was errand-boy for Juno. Then,
Along the dawny trail of a Dorian stream,
Fronded with ferns and prankt with irises,
Together, we did lead the pristine gods
To Phoebus Apollo's bowl, to pour its golden
Libation on the roots of Eden Tree.—
Ha, Nick! Step on him, there! Strike with thy crook!

SHEPHERD

Step where? Strike what?

ORCHARD-KEEPER

The serpent.—See! Look down!
Look where he coils, to strike at thee. Thy staff—
Strike back at him!

SHEPHERD
[*Stepping away, crossing himself.*]

Maria sacra! Nay,
Strike with thine own. Let snake bite snake. My crook
Guards sheep.

ORCHARD-KEEPER
[*To the Shearer.*]

Swift, Dick! Thy steel! Cut off his head!

SHEARER
[*Squatting back.*]

My clip 's for hedges, not for heads.

ORCHARD-KEEPER
[*Leaping forward, strikes with his caduceus.*]

Occidi,
Serpente! Ha, 't is gone! 'T hath wriggled off
I' the grass, under the mound.

SHEARER
[*Rising and peering.*]

Aye. Yon 's his hole.

SHEPHERD

Orchard hideth its snake since Eden garden.
I 'll hie me to pasture. The ewes be bleating. Gi'e thee
Good day, Quicksilver!

SHEARER

Me along of thee!
I 'll go thee to the hedgerow stile. Farewell,
Good Master Quick!

ORCHARD-KEEPER

Fare better, Dick and Nick!

[*He gazes after them, for a moment, then—loosing from his shoulder his sickle—he begins carefully to trim the grass-tops about the low mound, as Claudius—swinging from his crotch in the apple-tree—drops to the turf beneath, and slowly approaches him.*]

CLAUDIUS

Good evening, Orchard-Keeper!

ORCHARD-KEEPER

God be with you,
My lord!

CLAUDIUS

What make you here?

ORCHARD-KEEPER

Nothing. The making
Is God's work, with his rain and mould and sunshine.
Mine 's but to trim and prune the residue.

CLAUDIUS

You mean, with that—your sickle?

ORCHARD-KEEPER

Aye, my sickle,
Being a baby scion of Time's scythe,
Trimmeth the eternal grass.

CLAUDIUS

Is that a grave,
You trim so close?

ORCHARD-KEEPER

It may be, Sir, dependent
Upon who lies upon it, and upon
The intentions of the asp, which hath his lair
Beneath it. 'Tis the pillow, where the King
Of Denmark rests his head from weariness,
Seeking cool sleep here, in the apple shade,
As is his custom, at warm afternoon
Towards twilight, when the breezes rise. The snake,
Too, seeketh his own seclusion, when he slides
Downward—from that same apple-bough, your lordship
Dropped down from, here—and slips into his hole
Under this mound.

CLAUDIUS

The snake! Is it an asp,
You say, and poisonous?

ORCHARD-KEEPER

Aye, poisonous
As wormwood, 't is, but not as lazar-like
In vilely leprous spume, as one that spitteth
Hebenon from his weasand.

CLAUDIUS
[*Starting.*]

Hebenon?

ORCHARD-KEEPER

Yet wormwood may be swapp'd for hebenon
To stipple nipples such as Angela's,
Or vials be swapp'd for serpents in the orchard,
When Adam dreams in Eden, ere the voice
Of God the Father calleth—like the cock
Of dawn, in porch of Peter's ear—"Where art thou?"

CLAUDIUS

Nay, then, I 'll ask, not *where,* but *what* art thou?
A witch,—or keeper of the orchard?

ORCHARD-KEEPER

Which—
Well may you ask, and—answer!

CLAUDIUS

Art thou not
He, whom I heard the Shearer name, but now,
As "Master Quick"?

ORCHARD-KEEPER

Quicksilver?—Aye. But he
Hides him in many headpieces, and one
Is *Maître Chantecler*.

[*Swiftly passing behind the tree, he emerges on the other side, accoutred in the red-combed headpiece of a* COCK, *as—from sudden twilight—there rises an eerie, crowing Cry.*]

CLAUDIUS

Gallucinius!
Still, as of old, crowest thou over me?

GALLUCINIUS

Again, thrice shall I crow, and then—no more.

CLAUDIUS

That cry! That lording voice! 'Tis vaunting now.
Ah, God! Thou mock'st me from the apple-bough.

GALLUCINIUS

The cry—am I. The mockery—art thou!

CURTAIN.

ACT FIRST

Scene Two

ENGLAND. A CRAGGY EMINENCE, NEAR DOVER.
PRINCE HAMLET *and* HORATIO, *discovered.*

PRINCE HAMLET

Here, on this Dover cliff, seascape and sky
Turn earth to dreamy vision. Reach to me
Thy hand, Horatio, whilst I peer downward
Over this clinging shrub.

HORATIO

Take care, my lord!
Keep from the edge. The chalky turf may crumble.
Lean not on the wind's shoulder, but on mine.

PRINCE HAMLET

Look down—far yonder, where the green tide crawls:
Yon tiny, tufted shell—is that our ship
With towering masts, wherein we shall embark
Homeward so soon for Denmark?

HORATIO

Aye; 't is she.

PRINCE HAMLET

Nay, sure, thou errest. 'Tis a silvery snail,
Lifting its dewy antennae in the dawn-shine
To feel the early breezes; or, perchance,
The crackled egg-shell of a hedge-sparrow
Gaping the cleft beak of its fuzzy nestling;
Or, else, an opening water-lily bud
Disclosing its gold stamens to our gaze.—
What, then, are we, of mortals or immortals,

To make therein our far sea-pilgrimage
From port to port of our deep-yearn'd desire?
Tell me, Horatio.

HORATIO

What should I tell?

PRINCE HAMLET

The secret of our earth-quest: Are we twain,
Who stand, together, on this dizzy verge,
Facing its windy mists of destiny
Pregnant with births of battling sea and clouds
Evolving tangled forms of future portents
Beyond our scan to fathom,—are we twain
Divinities, or fellows of the dust?
Sworn-brother demigods, Castor and Pollux,
Gazing from this dawn-height upon a realm
Where mighty-masted ships are turn'd to mind-toys—
Snails—sparrow-eggs—and water-lily buds—
For our play-mirth to shape, by beauty's law,
To infinite similitudes? Or, are we
Earth-urchins, staring at the mud-puddle
Whereof our clay is moulded?

HORATIO

Why, 't would seem
We 're both, since this same muddy matter can
Thus hold discourse of godhood.

PRINCE HAMLET

What is God
That He, of whom the Scripture calls us image,
Can thus agglomerate unto Himself
This mass of chalky cliff and mould from it
These slender pencils, pointing to the stars,—

These selves of ours—to write His scriptures down
On the black scroll of being, and annotate them
With self-reverement?

HORATIO

Point your gesturing thoughts
More near the ground, my lord, lest it cave, under
Our heft, and smooch us both from that black scroll.
Step back, a little, to this firmer earth.

PRINCE HAMLET

This earth of England—aye, it tugs me back
To a new homeland, ancient in my blood,
As if I 'd here re-enter'd the great womb
Of the Earth-Mother, to feel again her primal
Quickening of an olden heritage—
Mine own, from birth beyond the alien bourn
Of Denmark—dear though that is.—Ha! Look inland
Now, where the engulfing sea-mists swallow the hollies
In yonder burst of sun-glow, crimsoning
Their green thorns berry-bright—and listen, listen
From high the lark's epistle, chanting his lauds
Of heaven, to shame us sodden underlings
To emulate his trances, and pierce through
This grey veil to the blueness, ever beckoning
Above us. Hark! His vow hath no abatement
In God-forgetfulness. That word of a bird is grooved
In His great signet-ring, to press in our souls
The seal of certitude, that this indeed
Is He, the living God, who cannot lie,
Uttering His love of all.

[*Pausing, with a start.*]

My dearest friend,
Know you of whom, for whom, 'mongst all who live,
He poureth there his palpitating draught
Of love into my thirsting heart?

HORATIO

My lord,
I were not your dear friend, did I not know
What guileless lady shares your listening heart.

PRINCE HAMLET

Ophelia—no utterance of heaven,
Or earth, or underworld, but gives me clue
For thoughts of her, to worship, praise, or shield her.
So now yon ceasing sky-lark, by his silence,
Hath sudden sunk into my soul some barb
Of dread, that pains my listening with a hushéd
Sob, and the soft cry of an amsel-bird.
I would I were in Elsinore, to know
The meaning on 't.

HORATIO

Ere long, we shall be there.

PRINCE HAMLET

A smother hath closed round me, even as this
Swift chilliness of cloud-shadow.—My father!
Methinks, I see his face in yonder fog-twist
Scowl'd on the profile of that agéd cedar,
The gales have blasted. God shield 's! Is he weeping?
And this—his shower of tears, comes whipping towards us,
Frozen to pebbled hail, like tinkling glass?

HORATIO

'Tis but the quick gust of a passing rain-flaw
Out of the nor'east.

PRINCE HAMLET

And nor'easterly
Lies Denmark—and my father. Would I were with him!

All 's thick here in my throat. Now the old tree's face
Laughs in the fog-shine, and methinks it soundeth
Like to mine uncle's laughter. Listen!—What is 't?

HORATIO

Being what 't is—'t is like the wind, my lord.
Your hand is cold. Here, have my cloak!

PRINCE HAMLET

I thank thee.
Mine own sufficeth.—Ah!—the sun again,
And oh, the eye-bright blue! Such is dear England,
Who muffles our eyelids with her hoodman-blind
Only to kiss them open with her smile
Of winking roguery.

HORATIO

My lord, methinks,
Here comes the delegation from the village,
Headed by one who bears the royal standard,
Hard on our trail, to escort us to our ladings
On the beach below, and bid us *bon voyage.*

PRINCE HAMLET

'T is so, indeed. Yet one last gulping look
On this mine other homeland, ere good-bye!
Greet them, meanwhile, for me. I 'll come again
I' the moment.

[*He goes off, left.*
Enter, right, a group of ENGLISH VILLAGERS, *headed by a* COURIER, *bearing the royal standard.*]

COURIER
[*To Horatio.*]

Greetings, Sir! And gratefulness
That we have found you safe. Out of our midst

Sudden you were gone, and we have anxiously
Been seeking you, high-road and footpath way.

HORATIO

Prince Hamlet chose the footpath to this crag
Of lordly overlook, verging both worlds
Of wild shore and of woodland-nestled thatch,
His heart doth twinge to part withal. Your pardons,
He prayeth, for this seeming truancy
From your folk-circle to this lonely coign
Of contemplation on 't. But the breath catches
And lumps the throat, at the sharp instant, when
Sweet new-found friendships must, all sudden, turn
To memory, in mistings of the eyes.

COURIER

There were no sun of friendship, did it not
Gather such mists, to hide it from the world
Till fresh dewfalls reveal it, shining steadfast.
But where now lurks your prince? Safe as yourself,
We trust, since else you would not speak for him
Thus tranquilly.

HORATIO

See you yon giant beech-tree,
With her big coiléd roots, shank'd up like knee-bones?
There sits he in their gnarl, his arm-flung cloak
Blue-mottled 'gainst the grey; his slanted cheek
Dream-hidden, as he were being suckled there
By the great Earth-Mother, at her dryad dug
Smooth-noded to his thirsting quaff, grown vast
To sate his pang of parting. Let our scan
Turn elsewhere, from intrusion, till this moment
Passeth to littler passion.

COURIER

Feels he, indeed,
So great a wrench, to leave this land?

HORATIO

Indeed,
A mortal wrenching. He hath told me so.
Is our barque ready?

COURIER

All 's aboard of her.
The sails, mizzen to mast'ead, tilt their wings
Like butterflies aslant a hollyhock,
Quivering for quick flight. Squalls pelt their patter,
But sea-prophets avouch a steady voyage.
The mariners bawl chantey, and the boatswain
Waits in the beach-foam, with the cock well-oar'd
To pull your lordships out to deeper tide
Where the brave ship tugs anchor. Sad-of-heart
Sings oft the merriest, and we have fetcht
Along of us these village chapel-boys
To choir you beachward, to this shepherd's pipe.—
Fellows, catch here your pitch-note!

[*He blows a note on the pipe, echoed by* ah's *and* oh's *of the Boys and Villagers.*]

Shall we intrude
Upon your prince's tree-dream, if we stir
The woods to waken with our voices, Sir?
They rise even now into our throats, to pray
For both of you a fond return to us
Back from this parting-time, which strikes too soon.

HORATIO

Nay, Sir, I 'm sure your thoughts are all our own,
So cannot make intrusion on my prince's
Nor mine. Pray, lift your voices, as you will.

THE VILLAGERS
[*Singing, together.*]

Far, far from England,
When you are far away,
Hearken, in your dreaming,
What in English woodlands,
By night, by day,
The birds of Merry England say:

Pee-wee! Twit-tweet-tereu! Cuckoo!
You, you we greet, greet sweet, you, you!
Till when
You come again,
Come again, come again, come again
Home to England—
Home!—Amen! Amen!

Far, far
Far when you are
From Merry England and the footpath way,
Through the changing of strange sea-tides,
churning,
Dream on us, who dream of you returning
Home to England, home from far away.

[*Towards the close of their singing,* PRINCE HAMLET *has re-entered.*]

PRINCE HAMLET

Friends of dear England, dear my English friends,
Your heart-pitcht song would fetch the wild bird winging
Back to his home bough, were he treble-barr'd
In icy dungeon of the Boreal dawn.
So wild a bird am I, albeit a petrel
Who fain would be a house-wren, to abide
A sweet life-long beneath your thatchéd eaves
And, mated, hide away there. You have torn,
Unwittingly, this princely cloak of mine
To show the shepherd's heart, it holds within 't.
But I must lordly furbish up this clout

And pace to statelier measures.
[*To the Courier.*] Hail, good Sir,
Who bear the standard of your goodly king,
Which hath my father-king's salute of friendship
And mine of gratitude. Erstwhile, it was,
At Elsinore, you asked me come as envoy
To sample of your England, before bearing
Your English gold away.

COURIER

Speaking, my lord,
For England's king, we trust that you have found
The asking kindly and the coinage valid.

PRINCE HAMLET

The sample tells the substance. Less, far less,
That 's golden, can we bear away with us,
Than the ever-increasing good we leave behind.
So, richly laden, we do leave you richer.

COURIER

True, Sir,—by all you 've brought us in yourselves
In the bright ore of Denmark's manhood—you
And this your quiet comrade. Here, then, ere
The beach-roar drowns our word, we bid you now
God's home-speed and good-bye.

PRINCE HAMLET

Good-bye, sweet England!
I came to ask thee tribute, but instead
I 'll come again to pay it sevenfold.—
Heaven's kingdom of kindness in a little isle,
Thou spread'st thine embers o'er the world, to kindle
New Englands of thy heart in every land,
For fearless glowings of their own hearth-fires.
And here, on this white altar of Dover cliff,
Which rises chastlier from the sacred sea

Than rose of old the sunset-rubied Pillar
Of Hercules to awed Odysseus' eyes,
Thou lightest a dawn-candle, for brave men
To gauge their freedoms by, which shall outburn
The centuries, till slaveries turn cinder
'Neath its undying wick-flame.

COURIER

Praise, my lord,
From Galahad rings clean in Britons' ears,
And tells old truth of Faerie, for new times
To keep enduring chivalries untarnish'd.

PRINCE HAMLET

Old truth of Faerie is the all can save us
From modern dissolution, and pervades
The future with its fragrance. Here, this soil
Is leaven'd deep with 't. By yon Druid beech-tree,
E'en now it drew me into Faerydom,
Where, underneath mine eyelids, all a-sudden,
I waked to second sight, beyond this sharded
Glaucoma of our intellect, wherein
To-day is sense-imprison'd.—Lo, beside me,
I saw a gentle lad, his blue eyes beaming
Deeply within mine own. Golden as clouds
That lift from Helicon when Phoebus rises,
Livingly waved his locks of Saxon hair
Backward from his pure brow; and from his lips—
Bright as the quenchless spring, which wells from out
The heart of that wild mount of the early gods—
His rich voice smiled, in speaking. "Come!" quoth he:
"Jog on, jog on, the footpath way with me,
But erst, look there—the sea—the immortal sea!"
And there, with overdangling scan, he pointed
Where—airy-poiséd, like a drop of gum[1]
Clinging to silk of gossamer there swung,
Half-high the cliff, a samphire-gatherer,

Storing his pigmy basket.—"All for pickles!"—
Shrill sang the Puckish laughter of the lad:
"For briny pickles would he risk his span
Of life, spun out upon a spider-thread
Above the briny roar of Homer's sea—
Polyphloisboio thalasses! Hillyhoho!
Yet Simple Simon saith, only poets are mad!"
Thereat he drew from out his poke a pipe—
A shepherd's pipe, like yon within your hand—
Touching its fine stops with resilient fingers,
The while he blew upon it—such wild strains
As Pan doth improvise, when he doth brood
On Hecate and hoof-dancing of fauns
On blind Orestes' grave—strains, wherein mirth
Of heart's delight so mingled with bleak woe
Of mind's dilaceration, that the air
Whereof his breath was organ, swelled in vortex
Bepeopled all with spirits, faery-form'd,
Miming, in masks of tragi-comedy,
The myriad human roles we mortals feign
Between the womb and tomb. Then, sudden, all
Were suckt within his pipe, and from its node
There grew a rainbow bubble, waxing ever
In gleam of vast distending, till it shone
A globe, translucent, center'd by a theatre,
Wherein the vanisht spirits, reappearing,
Renewed their roles; and there, in suit of sables,
Black against scarlet glow, stood I, amidst them,
Holding a human skull.

COURIER

A skull?—Ah, me!

[*The Villagers murmur.*]

PRINCE HAMLET

Then, soft, the bubble—like a faery globe
Of dandelion seed, on summer wind—

Did loose its stem and waft into the air,
Scattering, in vanishment. All then was silence;
Till, gazing in the lad's star-sparkling eyes,
I asked: "Is this a dream, which thou hast made?
And have I dreamed thee, too?"—"Aye, verily,"
He answered: "We have dreamed it to each other,
For *I* have dreamed *thee,* too. We are such stuff
As dreams are made on, and our little life
Is rounded with a sleep." "What is thy name?"
I asked, again. "*Will* is my name," quoth he:
"All grows of what we will, for we *are* wills;
And so I like my name. What 's thine?"—"Alas!"
I said, "If so, I fear mine own is *Will-less;*
For, an thou dreamed me, why else didst thou dub me
Hamlet, who, being Prince of Denmark, yet
Would liever tog me in a hamlet shepherd's
Clout of white wool, than wear this castle cloak
Of purple fur, to dream mine empery?"
"I 'll tell thee why," said he, with his April smile.
"All empery of soul is beauty's realm,
And that is thine: all else is soul-Sahara.
Yea, I have proved it in a song, I 've made
To Sylvia, the holy, fair and wise,
To Sylvia, who excels each mortal thing
Upon the dull earth dwelling.—Look, now! Yonder
She greets us! Would'st thou other empery
Than her and her devotion? Gaze—serve—pray!"
And from the doorway of a faery cot,
Carved with the secret name of "Arvia,"
Lost in a twilight glade of fragrant pines,
Pure as the twilight's ever-deepening star,
The eyes of Sylvia smiled. The glow of her
Filled the still air with soundless melody,
As all of beauty awed the listening world;
Till soft the grave lad touched his shepherd's pipe
And sang of her to her:

Is she kind as she is fair,
For beauty lives with kindness?
To her eyes love doth repair
To help him of his blindness,
And, being helped, inhabits there.

Then, as two ripples on a star-lit pool
Glide to each other from its ferny shore,
The spirit lad and spirit maiden met
Within the center'd hush, transmuted there,
In hues of gold and white, to gleaming swans,
Like unto such as move on Avon stream,
And glided onward in the living dream.—

[*Prince Hamlet makes gesture to the Courier.*]

And now, good Sir, your shepherd's pipe, I pray you!

COURIER

[*Handing it.*]

Have here, my lord.

PRINCE HAMLET

My thanks! Hereon, I 'll play you
The very pitch-note which the golden lad
Did end upon, or ere the elvish-mad
Globe-bubble vanished; for, in sooth, it seem'd
He blew it from this same pipe, here, as we dream'd.—
Listen!

[*He blows a single, quivering note.*]

THE VILLAGERS

[*Muttering among themselves.*]

Whist! Hist ye!

PRINCE HAMLET

So is proved the spell!
Lo, I have brought, in bidding you farewell,
This strange tree-dream-tale out of Faerydom—
For unseen, spoke, spins more than seen, that 's mum—

And I would fain hold faith within my heart
That Hamlet, when he goes, shall not depart
From faery earth of England; but, on breath
Blown by elf-angels through the skull of death,
Shall float within that bubble theatre-globe,
Wherein the shadow of a sable robe
Shall cast his image on a spirit stage
To show the shape of destiny, which rage
Of warring kingdoms in the human mind
Sculptures in clay of passion, from the blind
Crepusculum of vision: aye, even this
Your parting-pilgrim Prince of Denmark, his
Image, for times e'en more than ours distraught
By turbid wills to ponder, till from thought
Shall rise the angel, peace: image of one,
Who 'd gladlier be a sitter in the sun,
World-bounded by a nutshell, with no toy
Else than a shepherd's pipe, for his heart's joy
To play upon, than be the princely heir
Of Alexander, lord of everywhere
But peace.—That hallow'd word let breathe the last
Upon his lips, dear friends, when he has pass'd
With doubts of all to be or not to be
Discarnated from darks of destiny:
Peace to the good; peace to the bravely kind;
Peace to the moral servants of the mind;
Peace to the serene masters of the soul;
Peace to the strong, who guard the mother's goal;
Peace to the child in the heart of man; surcease
Of suffering unto the Prince of Peace!

COURIER

Hamlet, His peace to thee! Till soon, or long,
Our last good-bye let be your homing-song,
And the Good Shepherd's pipe lead us, in throng,

To shore of the great sea, where homelands reach
Their hearts toward homelands.

[*Lifting the pipe, which Prince Hamlet hands to him, and turning to the others, he blows upon it the pitch-note, and then calls.*]

To the beach!

THE VILLAGERS

[*Echoing his call.*]

To the beach!—the beach!

[*Escorting Prince Hamlet and Horatio, the Courier leads them to the procession of Villagers, who lift their song, moving off, together, right, while the curtain is falling.*]

See page 673

CURTAIN.

ACT SECOND

Scene One

ELSINORE. SHRUBBERY, NEAR THE CASTLE.

Hedged nook, beside hawthorn and laburnum trees. Towards autumn.
TOPAS *and* MOLL COWSLIP, *discovered. Topas, standing, leans on his spade.*
Moll, seated on the bench, is plaiting a wreath of wild lilies.

TOPAS

Here, in the loam, under this hawthorn bough,
She bade me dig it neat—cut out the turf
In yon wee square, for to be squeezéd back,
Tight 's her thimble over thumb, after all 's
Been lower'd and tuckt in.

MOLL

Aye, so she would,
And have all clean, to lay the lily strewings:
Lilies, no bit but lilies will she have.
She hath sent, all winds and ways, to find and fetch 'em:
Lily o' the field; lily o' the valley; lilies,
Tube-blow and dangle-bell; and elfin-boys,
In blue and rose, to be his choristers
For *Lily o' the Dell.* She knoweth her mind
For her play-pretty bird, maid though she be,
Like any mother for her babe. Aye, babeling
Was he to her; and many 's the time I 's watch'd her
Feeding him crumbs in cream, as they were nipples
For him to suck, not peck. And "Amsie! Amsie!
Tweet, tweet, my Amsel sweet!" she 'd chuckle him,
Dearier than darling. Heigh, though, he was lordly
As any prince in black, preening his wing
Wi' his golden bill. And now—to lay him in grave
Here, under the hawberries! Nay, God gi'e me guts
To bide the heart-break o' the pretty lady,
Poor childless mother of an amsel-bird,
Must lay her chick in grass.—Stint whistling, Topas!

TOPAS

Moll, hast ne'er listen'd Master Blackbird whistling?

MOLL

So, have I.

TOPAS

What doth he whistle?

MOLL

Sweet is it! Sweet is 't! Sweetest!

TOPAS

Aye, doth he: [*Singing.*]

Sweet, sweet, springeth the hour
O' life, i' the blooming.
Sweeter, the flower
O' love, fro' the tombing!

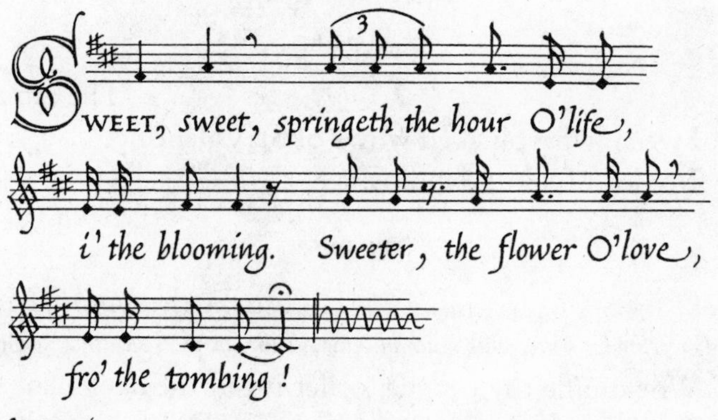

See page 673

So, smell o' thy lily flowers, there, thou plaitest
For Master Amsel's grave, and I will tune
My whistle-ditty to his.

[*He whistles again, looking up in the boughs, whence a musical whistling answers him.*]

Hark him, up yonder,
Wi' his yellow bill, mocking me o' my whistle.

'Tis Master Blackbird, himself. Black he weareth, to mourn
His brother, Amsel.

[*Laughing.*]

Ha, by Gismerry!
I ha' dug grave for richm'n, poorm'n, thief,
Beggarm'n, doctor, lawyer, merchant, chief,
And lock'd tomb-door on lord and chapel-master,
This more than twenty year; but here 's the day
Ever I first set foot for to spade a bed,
This less than twenty inch, to cozy an elf-king!

MOLL

Cock-robin, thou meanest! Aye, and who killed him? The hawk
Prowling the Castle!

TOPAS

Hawk? What hawk?

MOLL

The same,
I ween, who plucked wings of St. Valentine:
My lord Duke Claudius.

TOPAS

God strike thee mum, Moll.

[*Lowering his voice, with quick hushing gesture, he peers stealthily about.*]

Wilt muffle thy tongue, or let it call the hangman
To noose thy neck up?—Him—the Duke, sayst thou?
Why would 'a harm the bird?

MOLL

Why would n't 'a?

[*Speaking behind her hand at Topas' ear.*]

'A loveth Prince Hamlet like a thorn in 's thumb,

And pretty Amsel were the Prince's gift
To Lady Ophelia, who doth while away
From him the thoughts of another lady
He aimeth to cage for himself.

TOPAS

A lady!—Who, then?
What 's in thy noddle?

MOLL

[*Turning suddenly away.*]

Nay, my noddle 's crackt,
And leaketh nonsense. Hush me up! 'T is surer
Poor Amsie died hearing the horny-owl,
Home-sickness, hooting woe unto his master
Sent into England, leaving his lorn lady
Alone with him, in cage.—Home is he, now,
Prince Hamlet, at long last; but hasteth home
Too late for all but this—to be pall-bearer
Unto the lady Ophelia's purty bird,
He gave her, as valentine.—Hark, yon! 'T is them!
Hear'st thou the tinkle-bells? She hath 'em chiming
In tufty cap of every bluebird-boy,
Who beareth birdie's litter.

TOPAS

Puts she bells
In bird crests?

MOLL

Aye, bluebell blossoms. Every bell's
A silvery flower, with a golden tongue.
She teased the silversmith to cast 'em pretty
For to clap tune to the blue-wing'd choir-boys.—
"Moll, dear!" she saith to me. "They must be only
Bluebirds, wi' rosy breasts, shall bear my Amsel

Unto his bed, beside my trothal tree."—
Ha, Topas! God gi'e me pardon-grace for that!
She bade me never speak it, and I swore to 't.
So must thou never tell, how the sweet lady
Was trothéd to our prince, right where we be
Under this hawthorn bough. 'Tis secreter
Than tomb. Thou wilt not tell it: Swear me!

TOPAS

Spare me!
Tomb-secrets be my trade. I dig 'em in
Like yeast in kneading dough. They will ne'er rise
But to be swallow'd down.

MOLL

Nay, cross thy heart!

TOPAS
[*Crossing it.*]

My heart be criss-crosst to a patchy-quilt
O' women's secret tucks.

MOLL

Whisht, now! I spy 'em
Along the shrubbery. The King's Chorister
Walketh the first. He knoweth well the song.
She hath all plann'd so nice and purtily
As 't were a May-day, and no funeral
Of autumn tide, but she her Amsel's queen
To deck his death-bed all with blossoms. Come!
I 'll hang his lily-garland on the hedge.
Duck we behind it, here.

[*They go within the hedge, partly concealed there, as song of Choir-Boys and Chorister is heard, approaching near. Moll lifts her finger to Topas.*]

Hark!—Let us pray.

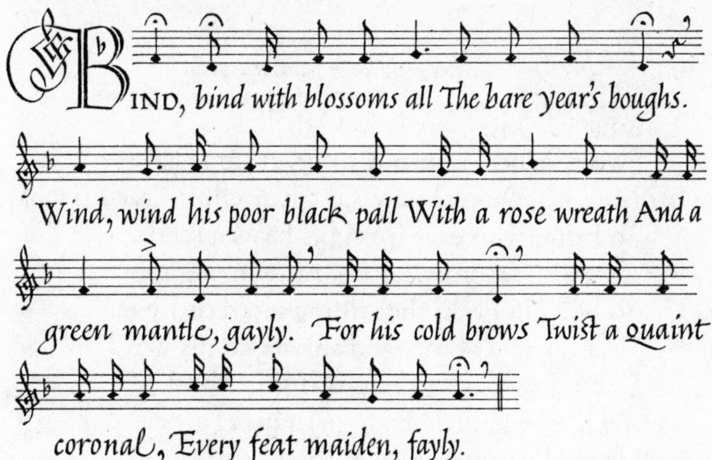

[*Enter, from the left,* AMSEL'S BURIAL PROCESSION:

First, the KING'S CHORISTER, *in blue and white vestments, followed by* eight Choir-Boys, *garbed as* Bluebirds, *with silver bluebells tinkling in their tufted caps, the first and last ones bearing—three, on each side, accompanying—a small lily-strewn Litter, upon which at centre lies a tiny Casket of wild roses, in shape like a heart.*

Following the Litter, come QUEEN GERTRUDE, *in purple, veiled with black, walking alone; then, two by two,* OPHELIA, *in soft white and pale green, her yellow hair braided with valley-lilies, accompanied by* POLONIUS, *in black, ruffed with white; then* PRINCE HAMLET, *all in black, with* CLAUDIUS, *in purple, striped with crimson; then* HORATIO, *alone, in grey. Behind him follow, in less formal groups,* YAUGHAN, *with* Children, Retainers of the Castle, *and* Folk of the Garth, *but no Courtiers or Ladies.*

Topas and Moll Cowslip peer over the hedge.

As the Chorister reaches the tiny, open grave, and pauses there, the Procession breaks up its form, and all gather near. Till then, the Song of the Bluebird Choir-Boys is continuing.]

THE CHORISTER
[*After gesture for pausing, speaks.*]

Your Majesty! My lady, Ophelia!
Sweet Prince, returnéd to us, from afar!
My lord, Duke; honour'd Chancellor; dear Friends!—
To Him, who ever from his heaven sends,
Across the stormy floods, his winging Dove
To bear, in beak, the stilling word of Love,
We bow our hearts, and answer to his word
By sending back to him this spirit bird,
Amsel, whose little body lieth here
Upon this wattled litter, for a bier.
The heart of rose, he lies in, is the heart
Of a gentle lady, whence he doth depart,
Uncaged, to that pure sky of gentleness
Whereto her yearning reacheth, to caress
Again her pet—now dartling, glad and freed
From bars of pining patience, fond to speed
Home to her call—through sky, so bright of glitter
It paints these brother birds, who bear his litter,
Blue with its brightness. Bright, then, be the prayer,
We offer here to Him, who everywhere
Bringeth breath to fallen sparrow. For the breeze, He
Once breathed through holy heart, in old Assisi,
Still wafts his love within the vellum'd book,
I hold;—this prayer of sweet St. Francis, who
So loved the dawny flowers, in their dew,
And fed the little birds, in a leafy nook
Of his hermitage. Our gracious lord and king,
Hamlet, whom illness, to our all regret,
Absenteth from this hour's remembering
Of Amsel, sendeth—as an amulet—
This ancient script, to shed afresh its glow
Of love: St. Francis, his *Precatio:*

[*Opening the book, he reads aloud from it.*]

Lord, make of me Thine instrument of peace.
Where hatred is, there let me sow love;
Where injury, pardon; where there is doubt, faith;
Where despair, hope; where darkness, light;
Where there is sadness, joy.

Master divine, O, grant that I may seek
Not so much to be consoled, as to console;
To be understood, as to understand;
To be loved, as to love.
For 't is in giving, that we receive;
In pardoning, that we are pardoned;
In dying, that we are born to eternal life.

THE BLUEBIRDS
[*In choir.*]

Sic dicit Deo
Francisci precatio.
Amen!

THE CHORISTER
[*Speaks—glancing from the book to those gathered about him.*]

In dying, when Francis saw this life was done,
Naked he lay, his grassy bed upon,
And listened the singing of the *Canticle of the Sun:*

[*Gazing upward to sky and tree-boughs, he chants—not in sing-song, but in deep and sweetly natural cadences.*]

Praised be my Lord for all his creatures,
And—highest over all—for our brother the Sun,
Who bringeth us the day,
Who bringeth us the light.
Fair is he, shining with exceeding splendour.
O Lord, to us he signifieth Thee.—
Praised be my Lord for our sister Moon,
And for the Stars, the which he hath set clear
And lovely in the heaven.

Praised be my Lord for our brother the Wind,
And for air and cloud and all weather;
By the which Thou upholdest life in all creatures.
Praised be my Lord for our sister Water,
And our brother Fire.
Praised be my Lord for our mother the Earth,
The which doth sustain us, and keep us,
And bringeth forth diverse fruits,
And flowers of many colours, and grass.

[*Turning again to those about him, he speaks to them with direct simplicity.*]

Praised be my Lord for all those who pardon one another
For His love's sake,
And who endure weakness and tribulation.
Blessed are they who peaceably shall endure,
For thou, O Most Exalted, shall crown them.—
Praised be my Lord for our sister the Death of the Body,
From whom no man escapeth.
Praise ye and bless the Lord, great thanks give unto Him,
In the greatness of humility.

THE BLUEBIRDS
[*In choir.*]

Sic dicit Deo
Solis Canticulum.
Amen!

[*At gesture of the Chorister, their leader lifts the tiny rose-casket from the litter and hands it to him, who holds it towards Ophelia.*]

THE CHORISTER

Lady, the bed of grass, wherein His light
Layeth all in dark, is ready. Meek is His might.

OPHELIA
[*Taking it, with a faint cry.*]

Amsie!—Good-bye, my pretty bird.

[*She nestles it to her. Then, kneeling with it beside the little grave, she puts it in, and bends over—for a long, still moment.*]

Good night!

[*Very softly, in tone of lullaby, she sings—looking down.*]

By low; by, dearie.
Lie low, from high.
Why didst thou die, dearie?
[*Looking up.*]
Come!
Fly low—home.

See page 673

[*Rising quickly, she turns with a sob to Polonius.*]

Father!

POLONIUS

[*Holds her to him, gently, patting her head.*]

Filly, dear.

THE CHORISTER

[*Speaking low.*]

Topas!

[*He makes sign for Topas to approach, from hedge, to the grave. Then, turning to the Choir-Boys, he lifts his right hand.*]

Bluebirds, our anthem!

[*They raise their voices in song—while Topas, stooping over, scoops in with his hands the tiny mound of earth beside the grave, smoothes it over, and fits back the square turf of grass.*]

SONG

Underneath, far underneath,
The dead year lies in funeral . . .
The dead year lies in funeral . . .
Far—far—far . . .

Lily of the dell,
Ring, O, ring his passing-bell—
His passing-bell . . .
Small birds, be his choir-boys—
His choir-boys . . .
And sing, O, sing!—
Far—far—far . . .

[*Topas has retired, as Queen Gertrude and Prince Hamlet have approached, with lilies from the litter, and begun to strew them over the turf, while the Song continues.*]

And ever, at their antheming,
Fly, fly, thou raven, Doubt!
For earth is fair, without.
Fie, fie, thou cypress, Death!
The primrose blossometh,
And Spring—hey-day, the Spring!—
To her sweet maids' gathering
Cometh on the kine's breath.

[*Ophelia, approaching, has taken from her hair her wreath of lilies, and drops it as a crown upon the strewings.*
With gentle smile to her, Prince Hamlet glances from the strewings to the boughs above them.]

PRINCE HAMLET

Lady, our springtide blooms, changed there to berries,
Turn here again to blossoms. All, which serries
Nature with darkness, turns for you to dawn.

OPHELIA

My lord, he had not died, had you not gone;
But your returning makes him live anew
Where nothing turns to darkness.

PRINCE HAMLET

Thanks to you!

QUEEN GERTRUDE
[*Approaching them.*]

How music doth unite what grief would sever—
Me with you both, this little moment, never
To be again, as now! The song—that song!
And him—the Chorister! Ah, memories throng
Too thick with pending portents.

PRINCE HAMLET

Mother!

QUEEN GERTRUDE

This
Only remember, if the great amiss
Survenes: In all we yearn for, wreck, or do,
We live not in one element, but two—
Where Amsel was, and is. So 't is with all:
Superterrestrial, subethereal
Creatures, we crawl to climb, and fly to fall.

PRINCE HAMLET
[*Drawing her aside.*]

Mother, share all with me. What are you hiding?

QUEEN GERTRUDE

What I share only with myself, dividing
My own from me, wrench'd by an inward birth-pang,
Which leaves me staring at the infant issue,
So feeble to help itself, amid this earth-pang—
Hamlet, your father, and his mortal tissue.

PRINCE HAMLET

Mother!—My father? What 's amiss?

QUEEN GERTRUDE

Ourselves.
Amsel is happy, guarded by good elves—
Heaven's Sun, Moon, Stars, to whom St. Francis prayed.

PRINCE HAMLET

But my lord, father?

QUEEN GERTRUDE

Since your voyage was made,
He walks once more in sleep—not once, but many
A night—yea, day. Do not we all—each, any?

PRINCE HAMLET

What do you mean?

QUEEN GERTRUDE

Not here, now!—I will tell
More in my closet. Come there—soon!
[*Turning quickly.*] Ah, well,
My sweet Ophelia! Take—not give me—this!
[*She kisses her on the cheek.*]

OPHELIA

Madam——

[*She seeks to kiss her hand, but the Queen has turned toward the Chorister, to whom she speaks.*]

QUEEN GERTRUDE

To you, Sir, all our thanks! What is
Here, sent from heaven, returns there in your song.
Renew it, as you go.
[*To Polonius.*] My lord, they are wrong,
Who deem this ritual of a pet bird
A fantasy of girlhood. The absurd
Of sentiment is in us elders, who
Outgrow our teens of tenderness.

POLONIUS

'Tis true,
Your Majesty.

QUEEN GERTRUDE

Your own Cornelia
Will vouch for that, in Amsel's heaven.

POLONIUS

Ah,
Perchance, indeed, she may.

QUEEN GERTRUDE
[*As Claudius approaches them.*]

What, Claudius?
You would attend me? Thanks. Polonius
Hath ask'd that office. The bluebirds lead us back.

CLAUDIUS
[*Aside.*]

To-night?

QUEEN GERTRUDE
[*Aside.*]

Or any night!

CLAUDIUS

This?

QUEEN GERTRUDE

All are black,
Lit with red lightnings. What 's already riven
Cannot be tatter'd—*Serpens,* dear. What 's given
In secret knowing—need n't be snatcht.

CLAUDIUS

Enough
Of blessing for me! Sure beggars seek rebuff.

[*Queen Gertrude moves quickly forward with Polonius. Claudius, lagging somewhat behind, encounters Horatio in his path, and accosts him.*]

Ah, greetings! Welcome home, Horatio.

HORATIO

Thanks, Sir.

CLAUDIUS

Tell me your tidings, as we go.

[*Following the Chorister and the Bluebirds, who begin softly to renew their song, in choir, all pass off the scene, leaving only Prince Hamlet, with Ophelia, who stands gazing at the little grave.*]

PRINCE HAMLET

O, filia Veneris, rememberest thou
Alcyone?

OPHELIA

His night-black bird is now
Gone home to him, among the Pleiades,
Perhaps, my lord.

PRINCE HAMLET

Still, here, amid these trees
Of hawthorn and laburnum, he may hide
More near, methinks; or, if he must abide
Still far away, he haunts this vicinage
Of Venus, in Denmark, and from his cage
Of fresh-strewn flowers, his home-alluréd spirit
Singeth a wandering tune.—Oh, can you hear it,
Close by us, throbbing nearer?

OPHELIA

Where?

PRINCE HAMLET

It sings,
Afar, of nearing home, as here it brings
Me near to you. Hush: now you hear it! Do you?

OPHELIA

My lord, I hear your voice.

PRINCE HAMLET

I 'd sing it to you.
But I 've no voice for that. The humming 's this:

[*He hums a snatch of melody.*]

OPHELIA

It soundeth an old folk-tune.

PRINCE HAMLET

And so it is,
From England, where I heard it, on a cliff
Which overlooks a world, where cloud and skiff
Of sea, and song of bird, are blended, all—
Clutcht in love's throat. The words, I half recall:

[*Humming, then speaking.*]

Far, far from England,
When you are far away,
Hearken, in your dreaming,
What in English woodlands,
By night, by day,
The birds of Merry England say:

Pee-wee! Twit-tweet-tereu! Cuckoo!
You, you we greet, greet sweet, you, you!

You see, 't is Amsel's song—and all of you.

OPHELIA

In sooth, 't is sweet.

PRINCE HAMLET

And we will make it true,
Together, for it goes on:

Till when
You come again,
Come again, come again, come again
Home to England—
Home.—Amen! Amen!

Amen doth mean
So let it be! Amsel shall change our scene:
As, first, from Wittenberg, then Elsinore,
And thence to England—on. There, ever more,
Shall folk hold Hamlet and Ophelia
Together, in heart. And there, together—ah,
What bliss to be!—beneath the thatchéd eaves,
Nested with Amsel, amid holly leaves,
We 'll make our home, as happy house-wrens, where
We 'll seek, like dear St. Francis in his prayer,
Not so much to be loved, as to love; and sweet
You, you I 'll greet, greet sweet, you, you! and meet
With Amsel's *benedicite.*

OPHELIA

Oh, my lord
It is a glint of bliss to gaze toward
From this green grave.

PRINCE HAMLET

Together, toward it, then,
Come, with me! We 've outtarried the *Amen,*
So Amsel bids you wear your crown again,
To bear it homeward to him.
[*He lifts her wreath of lilies, and reaches to place it back upon her head.*]

OPHELIA
[*With start of hesitation.*]

Ah, think you so?

PRINCE HAMLET

Dear love, why need I think it—when *I know!*

[*Gently as he offers it, she takes the wreath, and places it again in her hair.*]

And now—where hides our secret trothal-ring?

[*On the loop of a slender gold chain around her throat, Ophelia slips forth the ring, from folds of her breast-garment, and holds it toward him.*]

OPHELIA

Here—

PRINCE HAMLET

[*Kissing it.*]

Hark! Now—once again—dost hear him sing?

Listen, there—up, there—his *benedicite!*

OPHELIA

Ah!

[*She listens—where he points up into the hawthorn boughs.*]

PRINCE HAMLET

Yonder——!

[*From high in the hawthorn, the musical* WHISTLING OF A BLACKBIRD *is heard, floating down to them.*]

OPHELIA

Ah!—Amsel!—again!—'Tis he! 'Tis he!

CURTAIN.

ACT SECOND

Scene Two

ELSINORE. A FOOTPATH WAY, NEAR THE CASTLE. A CLEFT IN THE PATH.

The path, through a wooded glade, divides—near the left middleground—at the hollow trunk of a great oak tree, turning left [soon concealed behind shrubs and foliage] towards the Orchard beyond, but continuing in the foreground towards the Castle, off scene, left.

Along this path, walking towards the Castle, the last of AMSEL'S BURIAL PROCESSION *are straggling, among them* MOLL COWSLIP *and* TOPAS, *who pause in the path, before following the others off, foreground left.*

MOLL

[*Looking back, fiercely.*]

I tell thee, Topas, I 'll gi'e him a good piece o' mind!

TOPAS

Mind thou gi'e 't a good chawing, first, and gulp it down.
Mouthing ne'er mended a broken egg, nor better'd
A bad un.

MOLL

True, for that! But Molly Cowslip
Can spit as far as any rotten duke,
And land the spit-ball—*sping!*—between his eyes,
As pretty as him, who sang the Psalms o' David
And smacked Goliath.

TOPAS

Take care to plug thy spit-balls
Pretty with psalms, then. Here 's one, David, he sang:

[*Intoning.*]

Set a watch, O Lord, before my mouth; keep the door of my lips!

[*Tugging her, by the arm.*]

Along! Come along!

MOLL

[*Holding back.*]

I 'll bide, I say, and face him.

TOPAS

Here 's another, then:

[*Intoning.*]

Our bones are scattered at the grave's mouth, as when one cutteth and cleaveth upon the earth.

Come along!

MOLL

Stint! Stint! I 'll bide,

And lay a trap in his path.

TOPAS

Hearken the Psalmist!—

[*Lilting.*]

Let the wicked fall into their own nets, whilst that I withal escape!

[*He pulls her, with him, off the scene, left.*
After a moment, from the right, enter CLAUDIUS *and* HORATIO.]

CLAUDIUS

And so the gold from England is safe stored
In vaults of Elsinore. Have you made sure on 't?

HORATIO

Myself did oversee the stowing, my lord.

CLAUDIUS

Well stow'd!—A cheery bit of golden bullion
To exchange for purple wines, and store the vats
For glorious rouses!

HORATIO

That were heavy cheer, Sir,
For Elsinore. Your pardon, my lord, Duke:
Methinks, the Prince awaits me. I 'll go back
This footpath, and waylay him. [*Exit, right.*]

CLAUDIUS

Lay him away,

Were better!

[*He moves onward to the crotch in the footpath, at the oak tree, where he pauses, looking along its partly concealed turning in the middleground, so that he does not observe the re-entrance, in left foreground, of* MOLL COWSLIP, *who approaches him from behind and touches him on the shoulder. Turning, he gives a startled ejaculation.*]

Ha!

MOLL

[*Tensely.*]

Who killed cock-robin?

CLAUDIUS

Who?—

[*Raising his eyebrows, with a searchingly amused smile.*]

Why, the sparrow, with his bow and arrow.

MOLL

Who dug his grave?

CLAUDIUS

His grave?

MOLL

Across the shrubbery-hedge—from Angela's.

CLAUDIUS

[*Bites his lip; then, after a moment's stare.*]

What 's this?—Molly Cowslip's catechism for kiddies?

MOLL

Nay: Molly Regent's catechism for kinglets—
As would be kings.

CLAUDIUS

[*About to strike her.*]

God's death, woman!

MOLL

Aye, His death
Was on his cross. The thief, to his left hand,
Fared worser than this castle's hen-hawk—yet.

CLAUDIUS
[*Glares, then suddenly bursts out laughing.*]

Hoho, Molly! Still art thou flapping wings
To warn St. Valentine against that rouse
We roistered, i' the Castle?

MOLL

Hoho, no, Claudio,
My lord, Duke, ducky-ducker under the sheets!

CLAUDIUS

'Swounds!

MOLL

Hold thy fist! Who 's Regent—thee, or me?
Of all between us and the dearie queen,
I 'd cut my throat, to swab thy kisses off!
Aye, us—me, with thee! Damn me first, Lord God,
For to 've been a witless pimp, without the wotting
What heaven's flesh is made on.

CLAUDIUS

Heaven's flesh?

MOLL

Aye;
Man's flesh is Eden-made, and woman's sliced
Outen the ribs o't. Were my wits turn'd whey,
Or churn'd to butter, to blot my eyes from seein' 't
Ere Angie's grave was digg'd, for wormwood bitters
Laid on the Queen's dug?—Wormwood!—If thou didst
Feed Amsel crumbs, dipt in that wormy daubing—

CLAUDIUS

And if I hadn't, would the pretty bird
Have had so pretty a funeral?

MOLL

Ha, God,
I guessed it!—Yea, so feddest thou apple to Eva
When thou didst play *Serpent* i' the Garden.

CLAUDIUS

Play—
Surely! And why not—*play* him?

MOLL

Me, I watched thee,
And spied no more than a play-foolery,
And eggéd on my queen to plague my king
Wi' jealousy—and all for fun-play. Fie on 't!
This dance o' jealousy 's a jig for fleas
To hop—not man and woman, born o' grace.
Fools ha'e more heaven-sense. Moll, she 's lost, for all
The dying grace o' poor fool Yorick's kiss,
Afore he slipped to God. But Moll be still
Regent in Elsinore behind the scenes;
And when again thou playest *Serpent*—

CLAUDIUS

Hearken,
A moment, Molly Eloquent, and thou
Shalt judge, if I be only player, or
The thing I play.—Look yonder!
[*He points along the path's turning to the middleground.*]
Knowest thou
That footpath?

MOLL

Know it? Aye.

CLAUDIUS

Where doth it lead?

MOLL

To the orchard.

CLAUDIUS

Knowest thou Dick Shearer?

MOLL

Aye.

CLAUDIUS

Ask of him whether, in the orchard, under
A mound, beneath the tallest apple-tree,
There hides a hole, leading to a serpent's nest.

MOLL

Why axe him such a question?

CLAUDIUS

To learn whether
Thou knowest a real serpent from a false one,
Merely a serpent-*player*. Only, beware:
Be sure thou first ask Dick. Go not, thyself,
Alone, to find the hole, before thou askest
Dick Shearer, where it hides; for he will tell thee
The serpent is an asp, and poisonous.
So, be most careful not to go alone
To investigate the mound, lest thou be bitten
And suffer mortal hurt.—When thou hast been there,
With Dick, and spied a real serpent, then
Come back to me, and I will tell thee more

To ease thy great aspersion of thine old friend,
Who *playeth* the serpent and the hen-hawk, but
Is neither one, nor t' other. So, good-bye!
Or, wilt thou accompany me, to the Castle?

MOLL

Nay,
I 'll bide, and go my own way.

CLAUDIUS
[*With smile, and a wave of his hand to her.*]

Till we meet, then!

[*Exit, left.*
Moll stands, for a moment, in the crotch of the path, looking bewilderedly after him.]

MOLL

Serpent—true snake, or false snake?—me, find out!
What for? What would he make o' me—fool, or friend?
Or both the two? He lieth. That is sure.
I 'll trust him, like a flea in my flannel, never
To bite for blood. I 'll stomach him, like vinegar.
Dick Shearer—him, forsooth! I know mine orchard
Better than Dick. Well ken I the apple-tree,
And the wee mound under it. 'T is faery mound—
A holy mountain for the little folk
O' Hallowe'en, to dance up. Nary serpent
Durst make his hole there. And this honest sweet lord
Commandeth me, I must not go alone
To find out whether he lie, but take the word
O' Richard Shearer, first, for fear I 'll be
Bit by an asp, and poison'd. Bonny Duke,
Thou hast more poison, in thy smiling cheek,
Than ninety nests of adders.—Fool, or friend?
Neither I 'll be to thee. What trick soe'er
It be, I 'll not be whistled off thy trail
By twist o' thy tongue. Nay, lie thy spittleful,

Thou shalt not make *me* lie where Angie lieth—
Not till I lay *thee* there, by truth, spoke out
Before all Elsinore. Then, "till we meet!"
It is. Meantime, this path, I 'll go my lone,
And learn if be, there hideth hole in the mound,
Or here, in Molly's noddle, where the serpent,
Claudius, he coileth—for to *play* at serpent!

[*Turning up the middleground footpath, she disappears behind the foliage.*]

CURTAIN.

ACT THIRD

Scene One

ELSINORE. THE ROYAL LIBRARY.

KING HAMLET, *discovered, standing beside a table, placing books upon it, absorbed in arranging them.*

A KNOCK *sounds, from the door, left. He pays no attention. The knock is repeated.*

KING HAMLET

[*Still absorbed.*]

Come in. Enter.

[*Enter the* KING'S CHORISTER, *with a book in his hand.*]

CHORISTER

Your Majesty——

KING HAMLET

Come in.

Enter.

CHORISTER

My liege——

KING HAMLET

Enter—enter!

CHORISTER

Here am I, Sir.

KING HAMLET

Enter, O faithful, here, this asylum of peace—

CHORISTER

Your gracious pardon, Sire. Here, I return
The book, you sent to bless the ritual.

KING HAMLET

Here, speak we only of God—else let us cease.—

Cease!—Come in, Celestino. Welcome, sweet Padre!
Enter.

CHORISTER

My liege, this is no padre.

KING HAMLET

[*Starting, looks at him for the first time.*]

Not?

CHORISTER

Nay, Sire. 'T is I, your Chorister. I bring
St. Francis' prayer—this book.

[*He lays it on the table.*]

KING HAMLET

A book 's a block
To build with. A door 's a block whereon to knock.
Go. Go. Knock, and it shall be open'd.—Enter!

CHORISTER

O, King——

KING HAMLET

Into thy kingdom—enter! Go—
Go, go! Enter! Knock no more—knock no more!

[*He points to the door, commandingly. Exit the Chorister. The King turns again to the table. Intently arranging the books, he begins to lilt softly to himself.*]

Our Father dear, which art
In every foolish heart,
To make it heaven,
Whenas—

[*Pausing, he turns.*]

Come in, Yorick.
[*Listening.*] Yes, yes. Come in, dear fool!

[*He turns to the table, lilting again, low.*]

Let no man's foot trespass
Thy kingdom in the grass
His fellow's to gain,
But haste, on every hill—
[*Pausing, listens.*]

Yea, yea—in very deed.
[*He lilts on.*]

To do Thy holy will——
[*Pausing, speaks, with emphasis.*]

In every deed!

[*He turns again to the books, selecting from among them and measuring some, which he arranges carefully, in four separate, straight-upright piles, like pillars, equal in height, and equidistant from one another.*

After a moment, enter, at left, furtively, QUEEN GERTRUDE *and* PRINCE HAMLET, *who hesitate in the doorway.*]

QUEEN GERTRUDE
[*Speaking low.*]

Wait! He is there. Now I must leave you with him,
If it be him, indeed. Oh, he is not
Himself, that was. Remember all I 've told thee,
And keep this close, in case—
[*She hands him something, which he slips into his pocket.*]
You understand?—
And will?

PRINCE HAMLET

I will, dear mother.

QUEEN GERTRUDE

God be with us,
All—all!

[*Exit. Prince Hamlet slowly approaches the King, waits a moment, then speaks, softly.*]

PRINCE HAMLET

Father.

[*The King remains absorbed. The Prince speaks more loud.*]

My lord, father!

KING HAMLET

[*Turning.*]

Ah!—so far?

Still farther and farther and farther—

PRINCE HAMLET

[*Gently.*]

Nay, very near thee.

See.

KING HAMLET

So? Art thou the Carpenter, come now
To watch my building?

PRINCE HAMLET

Are you building, Sire?

KING HAMLET

Rebuilding—even as thou. Thou wentest away
To walk upon the waters, and to climb
Into a mountain in the wilderness—
All for to meet *him,* and say, "*Retro me!*"
But now, thou comest back, through a dark garden
Behind a hill—and we must work, together,
Again, my dear son—thou, with thy Lord, Father.

PRINCE HAMLET

Together, always. Will you show me the task?

KING HAMLET

Look! Here 's our work-bench. We will build it anew—
All Elsinore. Books! We are at it again;
But this time—Ha, thou wert right! For under bark
Of books runs sap of life, to feed the roots

Of Eden—and bells shall ring another tune
Than free choice—for a kiss. I 've planned it well,
Based on the four corners of the world.
See you these four?—They are the pillar-columns;
The rest fit in, for walls.

PRINCE HAMLET

These books?

KING HAMLET

These, here:
Aristotle—pole-star—his *Organon.* Plato,
Broad-shoulder'd bearer of soul-planets, his
Symposium. Sanctus Augustinus, his
City of God. Saint of the Little Flowers,
Franciscus, his *Precatio.*—These four:
Mind—Stellar Spirit—Seerhood—Peace of Heart.
Now—dost thou mark me well?

PRINCE HAMLET

Indeed, Sir.

KING HAMLET

Look, then.
On these strong pillars do I place the roof—
Invisible, as yet—tetrahedral four-
Arrow-pointed: its triangles upslanting here
Unto the apex, hollow at the peak,
Through which, from underneath, a slender stalk,
Rooted in Eden earth, doth upward pass,
Even as a center'd pole, to petal above,
Over all, in the heavenly flower of Caritas.
Midway her stem, as 't were a fallen halo,
Circleth a thorny wreath—the garland of Christus,
Upheld by its own bleeding spikes, sharp-grooved
In the roof's slantings, whence the eternal ooze

Of blood slides off the eaves, to dribble the earth
Which nourisheth the flower, leaving within
Our Castle of Elsinore, all innocent
Of scathe—save for one nettle-vine.—Ha! I 've forgot
To name to you the tetrahedral roof-sides,
The four, down which blood floweth eternally.
Here are the books, which form the slants and sluices.
Perchance, though, thou hast guess'd their titles?

PRINCE HAMLET

Nay, Sire.

KING HAMLET

Among the myriad suzerains of world woe,
Whose roofbeams blaze the bloodiest, to be upheld
By these white pillars of peace—four have I chosen,
And here their histories, in scarlet vellum:
Alexander, Caesar, Attila, Ghengis Khan.—
Hark, how they beat their bleeding storms in vain
Along the slimy slants and glutted sluices.
Ha, overhead, now rage, ye wars and havocs!
For, like the Esquimau, in his igloo,
Here sitteth Hamlet, snug in his library.

PRINCE HAMLET

Is this our Castle of Elsinore, you are building?

KING HAMLET

*Re*building, I told thee: bottom to top. But wait:
Now, to our nettle-vine! You see, he springeth
From the eaves' drippings; and, underneath the Castle,
He coils himself around the straight, upsoaring
Stalk of the blossoming Caritas, and twists
Upward, to poise himself, at last,—aha!—
Here, opposite her petall'd lips, and sudden
As death,—ha!—deep here, in the calyx heart—
Stings the pure quick, and blasts it—hilly-ho, heigh!

Ha, ha!—And the stalk shrivels, and the Castle
Cometh crumbling down—down—down, in blood—to the rubbage.

[*Wildly.*]

Clean away—clean away the rubbage! Off—off! In—in!
Up, up! Into chimney—up flue—out to heaven again,
In fire—pure fire!—Cremate her,—Caritas!

[*Scuffing and flinging the books from the table, onto floor and into fireplace, amid the burning logs there, he sinks to his knees before it, bowed over, shaken with moaning sobs.*]

PRINCE HAMLET
[*Aghast.*]

Forbid this, heaven! O, God!
[*Springing to his side.*] Father!—My father!

KING HAMLET
[*Looking up, slowly.*]

The little plum-tree sobs in the wind. The winter
Flakes are her snow-blossoms. These are not *my* sobbings.

PRINCE HAMLET

Father—dear Sire! Do not you know your son?

KING HAMLET

Know?—Know—who knows himself?—or, himself to be
A father—aye, of any son?—On that
Was builded the world, which now hath crash'd. Poor son—
Of whom?—Do not you know your father?
[*With giggling laugh.*] Agh!—List!
It was the vicious louse, who bit the lady.
Vice versa, methinks, might have been better for
The lady, though worser for the vice of lice.
How think you?

PRINCE HAMLET
[*Bending over, to help him up.*]

Rise, Sir. So is better.—So!

KING HAMLET

And better so 's better *so* than *not* so!—Not so?

"Don't prick me so deep,"
Quoth to Needle the Pillow,
"For feather-tick doth sleep
Sounder than willow
Can weep."
Yet the Pillow made never a peep
While Needle, he
Sang: *"Fiddle-dee!"*

PRINCE HAMLET

Sir, fling away those words with the rubbage.

KING HAMLET
[*With coarse laughter.*]

And these?

Once it was, upon a time,
A punster, picking for a rhyme,
Pinned a pun-upon-a-pun
Upon a pack-ass—
Humm!—
The bum
Rotten rhyme for *pun*, he pick'd,
Never even prick'd
The dumb
Jack-ass.

PRINCE HAMLET

Oh, I must go for succour!

KING HAMLET

Nay, *I* must go
For to suck a splinter out of this finger, here,
Under where the ring is. Fare you—Well, fair Sir,
We soon must seek our welfare in farewell!

PRINCE HAMLET

I pray you, wait a moment.

KING HAMLET

Forever, Sir,
Is but a moment; yet, in all books of time,
'T is strange, one poet only hath recorded
How the clean sheep baas at the scurvy shepherd.

PRINCE HAMLET

A moment, Sir!

[*He starts for the door. The King stops him, by a commanding gesture.*]

KING HAMLET

Stand, stand! Stay put! The King
Goeth foremost. Follow thine own tail—not ours!

[*He goes majestically out. The Prince stares after him.*]

PRINCE HAMLET

What shall I do? God, shall I choose to tell
The world, my father 's mad, and let the welkin
Peal with it? Do, or not do—nothing, or all?
Dally—decide! Silence, or speech? King—kingdom—
Elsinore—hangs it on me? Perhaps, this moment.—Ah,
Who is there lives, who deems he can evade
The indictment and the judgement of himself?
Or, shuffling on the floor of indecision,
Thinks: "Nay, I 'll not face the court!"—when, even thus,
Not to decide, itself 's to make decision
To ignore the encircling event?—We are all will-wheels,
And each of us on his own axle turns
The hub of choice, wherefrom the flanging spokes
Ray to the infinite's rim.

[*Gazing off, with sudden cry.*]

Ha! Thou, my pillar—

My buttress, in the sands!—Horatio!

[*Enter* HORATIO.]

HORATIO

My lord, I met the King in the corridor.

PRINCE HAMLET

How looked he,—frowning?

HORATIO

Nay, majestical,
But gentle. He bowed to me, as I myself
Were kingly.

PRINCE HAMLET

Oh, methinks he 's mad.

HORATIO

My lord!

PRINCE HAMLET

What said I? Ah, forget those words, but be
My sounding-board to heaven, for our souls' pang.—
To measure ourselves with the highest, 't is to gauge
The scale of our humility, and plumb
The nadir of our courage to its zenith,
Inversely, against the pull of scorn. For such,
The cubits of Goliath are assay'd
By David's pebble.—Then to work, to work!
In Elsinore, though I may pace as prince
In puissance, I 'm but a crawling ant to bear
My dream-bales through the desert world. Yet ants
May climb the Pyramids more sure of foot
Than camels can; and on this castle's top
Poises a crown, to be kept from tottering
Into the moat of madness.—First, to creep
Within the fever'd brain, throbbing beneath

The noble skull, which holds the crown, and suck
The venom from its fetid thoughts. For strangely,
Horatio, my father's thoughts seem poison'd
Even at the source. The change is rank and sudden
From all I 've ever known him—gently kind,
Loving to overtolerance—all, now
Wrench'd to a syzygy of sizzling hates,
Hanging unhing'd, yet clamp'd in dislocation.
Have you observed it?

HORATIO

Why, my lord, I 've noted
Something, 't is true.

PRINCE HAMLET

Some fetor from within
Exhales, to taint his discourse; for—even while
He ranges Plato's heavenly reason'd world,
Lord of sweet words, fit for an angel's lips—
All sudden, he turneth boor, laughs jokes of peasant,
Rank from the dung-heap, mix'd with rhymes and quirks
Of punning quibbles.—All converse reeks its food.
Who eats dirt, talks it, till his coated tongue
Fouls the fresh air, and fills his silent pausings;
But the clean speaker dainties the room around him
With fragrant savours, which pervade his thinking.—
What spirit excrement, then, hath he eaten
To utter this raw spew? What 's at the bottom?—
Thought.—He, himself, hath taught me, still as child,
This little world of ours is large as thought,
No less, no more; and from that mere "no less"
Rises the self-raising, all-transglorifying
Superbness of our own infinitude.
Yet now he mocks his teaching.—What 's the cause?
The cause—the cause! Give me some clue, for God's sake!

[*In the doorway, right, appears* CLAUDIUS, *who draws back, unobserved by them.*]

HORATIO

My lord, I hesitate. Perhaps, your mother—

PRINCE HAMLET

What of my mother? Why, she knows as little
As we. Yet she hath given me this hint
Of her own guessing: his old malady
Of walking in his sleep,—dost thou remember?

HORATIO

I do remember.

PRINCE HAMLET

Well, his malady
Again hath come upon him; aye, indeed,
So oft recurrent, that my mother feareth
It preys upon his dread—as on her dread—
Lest he, in sleep, meet with mischance. If so,
'T would seem his malady is its own cause,
And mounts upon itself, the more he falls
Asleep, to walk—and so moves on toward madness.

HORATIO

Alas, my lord—

PRINCE HAMLET

Yet there 's one recompense
In this.

HORATIO

How so?

PRINCE HAMLET

Why, see you not? 'T is thus
I 'll creep into his brain, and find the cause
Of this deep soul-infection: whether it be

Merely his dread of sleep-walking, or else
Some thing more dreadful, which he will not tell
While waking. Such, from all I 've noted, seems
Far likelier. So, Horatio, next time
He walks, watch with me, and we 'll follow him,
And you shall hear me question him, in sleep,
And note with me his answers.

HORATIO

Hath the Queen—?

PRINCE HAMLET

My mother gave me this—her kerchief, soak'd
In aromatic salts, and bade me press it
Close underneath his nostrils, should I thus
Encounter him, asleep.

HORATIO

Would not that wake him?

PRINCE HAMLET

Yes, yes, of course; but not till after I
Have put my questions, and obtain'd his answers;
Though, to be sure, my mother bade me use it
Upon the instant of encounter, lest
Mishap befall him.

HORATIO

So.

PRINCE HAMLET

But, sure, methinks,
I need not this to wake him.

[*He tosses the kerchief away.*]

Once I 've pried
His hidden secret from his slumbering brain,

Together, in close confidence, we 'll keep it,
Except to impart it to my poor, distraught
Mother; and so, with her assiduous help,
We 'll form a trio of mediciners
To heal his mind, and save the noble crown
Of Elsinore.

[*Laughing, in glad relief.*]

Ought that not win me honours
Among the doctorates of Wittenberg?

HORATIO

Perhaps, my lord, already your queen-mother
Hath tried this test of questioning.

PRINCE HAMLET

No, no.
I 'm sure not; for she never mentioned it
In all our anxious conference. 'T is now
Mine own bright inspiration, in this moment;
And, in the next of opportunity,
I 'll engine it, myself, with thee, for witness.
Come! Let us pray, together, for the chance.

[*They go out, left.*

From the doorway, right, Claudius comes forward.]

CLAUDIUS

First chance is his, who chooses to be first.
God holds the winner's stakes, for best or worst.
[*Stooping, he picks up the kerchief, tossed away by Prince Hamlet, and smells of it.*]
This will I use, or not, myself, to wake him.
Tangled in mad thoughts, 't is in his sleep, I 'll take him.

CURTAIN.

ACT THIRD

Scene Two

ELSINORE. A CORRIDOR OF THE CASTLE. *Night.*
Enter, simultaneously, at left and at right, CLAUDIUS, *holding a lighted candle, and* KING HAMLET, *holding one, unlighted. They meet at the centre of scene.*

CLAUDIUS

Good morrow, your Majesty!

KING HAMLET
[*In low monotone.*]

Good morrow—good morrow—

CLAUDIUS
[*Aside.*]

Ha, the time clicks! He follows his snuft-out candle.
[*To the King.*]
What make you here, Sir, in this bright noon-time?
Hunting, perhaps? Are you hunting?

KING HAMLET

Hunting—hunting—

CLAUDIUS

What for, my liege? What are you hunting for?

KING HAMLET

Hunting for—hunting for poi —

CLAUDIUS

Aye, so?—for poison?

KING HAMLET

For poison, aye so: for poison—

CLAUDIUS

Whom for, I pray?
For whom, my own dear brother?

KING HAMLET

My own dear brother—
For whom—I pray—he may be damned—

CLAUDIUS

Why, damned?
Hath he offended thee?

KING HAMLET

Offended thee?—
Me—me!

CLAUDIUS

Aye, Sir? Can it be Claudius,
You mean?

KING HAMLET

Aye, Claudius, you mean—you mean—
Mean, mean, adulterous, incestuous beast—
"Vengeance is mine," saith the Lord—vengeance—revenge—

CLAUDIUS

Why, then, here is a good fellow, come to help.

KING HAMLET

Good fellow—here, come help—

CLAUDIUS

To find the poison—
Yes?

KING HAMLET

Find the poison, yes.

CLAUDIUS

And when 't is found,
How will you portion it?

KING HAMLET

Por —

CLAUDIUS

Pour? Pour in what?

KING HAMLET

Pour in the porches of his ears.

CLAUDIUS

Aye?—When?
Asleep? Is 't best, while sleeping?

KING HAMLET

Best while sleeping—
Aye, asleep.

CLAUDIUS

And here 's a good fellow, cometh to help!
So, rest your searching mind, and hunt no more.
"Vengeance is mine!" saith the Lord.

KING HAMLET

Mine!

CLAUDIUS

All 's secure.
The poison hath been found. It hath been found.

KING HAMLET
[*Sighing, as with great relief.*]

It hath been found.

CLAUDIUS

So, rest. Tell no one.

KING HAMLET

No one.

CLAUDIUS

Sleep is best. Rest well. Sleep on, in peace.

KING HAMLET

In peace.

CLAUDIUS
[*Laughing, cheerily.*]

A ducat, in hand, to drink the health of Denmark?
Coin in the hand, Sir?
[*Claudius reaches out his hand, obliquely, as for a* pourboire.]

KING HAMLET
[*Cheerfully, feeling in his wallet.*]

Coin in the hand—here 's a
Good fellow—help—help drink the health of Denmark.
[*Holds out a coin, which Claudius takes, with a low bow.*]

CLAUDIUS
[*Aside.*]

Now am I tipt, to tip him into hell.
[*To the King, exchanging their candles.*]
Have here your candle, my liege. Whilst we 've conversed,
Fair noon hath waned, and dark hath fallen—deep.
[*Then, putting the kerchief in the King's other hand, he lifts the hand, to press the kerchief under the King's nose.*]
This to your nostrils, Sire! 'T is water of Cologne,
And wafts remembering perfume.—Cologne water!
[*He steals slowly off, left, with the unlighted candle, leaving the King holding the lighted one, with the kerchief pressed to his face.*]

KING HAMLET
[*After a moment, coughing.*]

Cologne——

THE VOICE OF PRINCE HAMLET
[*Outside, right.*]

This way, Horatio!

[*Enter, with lit candle,* PRINCE HAMLET, *accompanied by* HORATIO.
They pause, gazing at the King.
Drawing back a little, the Prince half-whispers to Horatio.]

His candle 's lighted!—
Strange; for my mother said, he walketh in dark.

KING HAMLET
[*Coughs again, dropping the kerchief.*]

Cologne—Cologne water—

HORATIO

What! Listen. Look.

PRINCE HAMLET

The kerchief! Why, but how could he have found it?

KING HAMLET

Cologne—

PRINCE HAMLET
[*Approaching.*]

Father!

KING HAMLET
[*Quietly.*]

Cologne is far away,
Is 't not, my son? Fare you along that route,
On journey to Wittenberg?——Ah!—Hold the candle!

[*Horatio snatches it, as the King staggers, and leans heavily against the Prince, whom Horatio relieves of his own candle, as he holds his father.*]

PRINCE HAMLET

Lean on me, Sire. You 're very tired.—Horatio,
Lead us ahead.—Give light. I 'll help him onward.

[*Led by Horatio, holding both candles, the King, leaning on the Prince, moves slowly off, towards the right, speaking with weary cheerfulness.*]

KING HAMLET

Methinks, I dreamed. It was a right good fellow,
Who came to help me—hunting—in the noon-time.
Some help themselves to kindness. Others hunt kelp
To eat. We all need help—we all need help—

CURTAIN.

ACT THIRD

Scene Three

ELSINORE. THE ROYAL LIBRARY.
QUEEN GERTRUDE *and* PRINCE HAMLET, *discovered.*

PRINCE HAMLET

Dear mother, rest! He 'll be here presently.
Together, we 'll work this out to some good end
For our beloved one. I bade Horatio
Conduct him momently to Horatio's bed,
Where our true friend attends him. For my father
Seemed deeply wearied—though he did not sleep
After we found him, with his candle lighted.
How came he by it, and your kerchief there
Held in his hand, I cannot even conjecture.

QUEEN GERTRUDE

His wandering wit eludes all our conjectures
When this his malady seizes him. 'Tis true,
Though rarely, I have known him trim his candle
By daylight, and walk forth with it, as 't were,
Seeking for something.

PRINCE HAMLET

Seeking for what? That *what,*
It is, we seek, to aid his hunt. The anise—
Give me some anise scent to follow.

QUEEN GERTRUDE

O Hamlet,
It is no anise, but a ranker scent.
I dread to think the reek of it is near.

PRINCE HAMLET

What mean you? Where?

QUEEN GERTRUDE

Here, in the Castle.

PRINCE HAMLET

Here?
Unriddle me this!

QUEEN GERTRUDE

These latter months, even years,
While you have been far off—in Wittenberg,
Earlier; and more recently, in England—
You have been spared, thank God, what I, your mother,
Your noble uncle and your nobler father
Have had to fend away from us, of odours
Leaking from crannies through the corridors
O' the Castle.

PRINCE HAMLET

Odours! Odours of what?

QUEEN GERTRUDE

Of filth
In dirty minds; of stench, from scandal breath;
Of blight, from perfumed lips and oiléd tongues,
Especially during absence of the King,
Linking the royal names of Elsinore
In wedlock calumny.

PRINCE HAMLET

Ha, 't is the thing
Which I did half make guess on, to Horatio!
So, *that* 's the excrement.—No more, sweet mother!
Spare thy dear self. Thy son deduces all,
And snuffs the scent, at last!
[*With rising vehemence.*] Myself shall be
The scavenger of Elsinore, triple-beak'd

For nabbing lecherous lies: thy calumny's Nemesis;
Thy lesser Hamlet, to defend thy greater;
Thy brother—my hurt uncle—his exonerator,
To blast their defamation. Rest you merry,
All three of you, for I will merrily
Mount to the hunt, and scatter fifty foxes—
Yea, fiftyfold of varmints—into their holes,
And bung their secret burrows, at the top,
Where we shall breathe sweet air, and blow the death-horn
For villainy, in Denmark.

QUEEN GERTRUDE

[*Gasping.*]

Hamlet dear!
Ride not too rash into the nettles. Subtly
Sprangle the twists of tongues, the coils of lips,
To snare their venom's avenger.

PRINCE HAMLET

Ho, I 'm subtle
As syrup in porringer. They shall not swallow me,
Though, when I 'm tasted. Now, for the swabbing up!
Mother, wilt leave it to me, and our devout
Horatio, to clean the Castle? He is
Sound to the secret core.

QUEEN GERTRUDE

I know. I know.
Of course, and if 't be not too late to heal
The stricken—Ah!—Dear son, see! Look!

PRINCE HAMLET

Where?

QUEEN GERTRUDE

[*Draws back, pointing downward toward the doorway.*]

There!

PRINCE HAMLET
[*Turning, draws quickly back.*]

Dear God!
[*Before their gaze, in the doorway,* KING HAMLET, *on his knees, is reaching one arm towards the Queen.*]

QUEEN GERTRUDE
[*Fearfully, to the King.*]

Hamlet—

KING HAMLET
[*Stumbling to his feet, enters, gazing at her as he calls out.*]

Monica—sancta!

[*Sinking again to his knees, he begins to move towards the fireplace, bent over, searching the ash-strewn floor of stone, with his eyes and hands.*]

PRINCE HAMLET
[*Going to him.*]

Sire!
Father, what is it? What are you searching for?

KING HAMLET

The City of God—
[*He gropes onward, feeling with his hands.*]
ashes—

QUEEN GERTRUDE
[*To the Prince.*]

Oh, succour him!

KING HAMLET

Even though it vanish, still there be beacons o't
Beyond our burnings—ah, a piece of one
In this book's charnel!
[*He lifts, from out the ashes, a* SMALL VOLUME, *charred and blackened.*]

PRINCE HAMLET

Sire!

KING HAMLET

What 's in a book
But what 's behind it?—and beyond it?

QUEEN GERTRUDE

Help him!

PRINCE HAMLET

[*Assisting the King to a chair, by the table.*]

Rest here, Sir.

KING HAMLET

[*Examining the volume.*]

Smooch'd black by the smouldering.
'Twas when the nettle kissed the calyx—*then*—!
Charr'd on the edges only—not the *City;*
That 's gone.—*Confessioni*—but the script 's
In our own tongue. Confession surviveth fire.
He wrote it—Augustinus. He should know,
Having a mother, who taught him. Hearken, son—
And mother!

[*From the open, partly burned volume, he reads aloud, huskily, with interpolations.*]

"*She*"—*she* meaneth Monica, Saint Augustine, *his* mother—"*She and I stood alone*"—alone—"*leaning in a certain window*"—certain window—"*which looked into the garden of the house where we now lay, at Ostia*"—or, was it Elsinore?—"*We were discoursing together very sweetly . . . of what sort the eternal life was to be, which eye hath not seen, nor ear heard*"—nor ear heard—"*when we came to that point, that the very highest delight of the earthly senses was, in respect of the sweetness of that life, not only not worthy of comparison, but not even of mention: we, raising up ourselves with a more glowing affection towards the Self Same, did by degrees pass through all things bodily, even the very heaven, whence Sun and Moon and Stars shine upon the earth; yea, we were soaring higher yet, by inward musing . . . and we came to our own minds*"—minds—

[*He looks up at Prince Hamlet and Queen Gertrude, beckoning with his finger.*]
Come nearer. Is the door latcht?

PRINCE HAMLET

What door, dear Sire?

KING HAMLET

To our own minds. Knock—knock! The latch will lift;
The hinges are rusted deep, but they shall swing
When—

[*He reads on, while Prince Hamlet grows more absorbed in listening.*]

—*"to our own minds, and went beyond them, that we might arrive where life is the Wisdom by whom all these things are made, but is, as she hath been, and so shall she be ever; yea, rather, to 'have been,' and 'hereafter to be' are not in her, but only 'to be,' seeing she is eternal. For to 'have been' and 'to be hereafter' are not eternal"*—not eternal—!

[*He looks up, piercingly, at the Queen.*]

Monica-Gertrude!—*not* eternal.

QUEEN GERTRUDE
[*Breathlessly.*]

Not—

KING HAMLET
[*Reads on.*]

"And while we were discoursing and panting after her, we slightly touched on her with the whole effort of our wills,"—our wills—*"with the whole effort of our wills, and we sighed . . . We were saying, then: If to any the tumult of the flesh were hushed"*—tumult of the flesh—*"hushed the images of earth, and waters, and air . . . hushed the poles of heaven, yea the very soul be hushed to herself, and by not thinking on self surmount self"*—surmount, surmount, SURMOUNT SELF! —*"hushed all dreams and imaginary revelations, every tongue and every sign—whatsoever exists only in transition . . . having roused only our ears to Him, who made them, and He alone speak . . . not through any tongue of flesh, nor Angel's voice, nor sound of thunder, nor in the dark riddle of a similitude, but might hear whom in these things we love"*—

whom in these things we love—WE LOVE!——*"and this one vision ravish, and absorb, and wrap up its beholder amid these inward joys, so that life might be forever like that one moment of understanding which now we sighed after"*—that one moment--ONE MOMENT! —of UNDERSTANDING—sighed after——*"were not this: Enter into thy Master's joy!"*

[*He rises, with the book, looking upward.*]

Thy Master's joy—joy! Have it, again! Take it!
Enter into thine own, O Master of the damn'd—
The damn'd, who drag thee down! Have it back—Thine
own!

[*He hurls the book into the embered fireplace.*]

PRINCE HAMLET

O Father, great sire! From where you have lifted us
By this radiant script, yourself, cast us not down
From that immense Impersonal!

KING HAMLET

Impersonal?—Aye,
Poor son, poor mother, poor tortured fools that we are—
Afflicted with personality ourselves,
We would inflict it on all things else. Are we not
The very nothingness of finity?
The vast unfathomable nature of the Impersonal
Feeds us. Our personality, in all its pettiness
Is but the product of that inevitable law
Of opposition, which reigns all-supreme
In the universe. Our grief and vehemence
Are merely foils, which render us more apparent
To such Godlike eyes as are the engulfing calm
Of the immutable.—Am I a fool? Verily,
Such gods as are sustain us—in these hours
Of passion, which steal upon us, when we dare
To ponder on what we are, have been—and must be!

[*He sinks into the chair, as Prince Hamlet turns to the Queen, with fond, glad gesture, speaking low.*]

PRINCE HAMLET

Mother! This is not madness. This is the torrent
Of meditation, loos'd in passion. Here 's
No malady, but gust of health, in tempest.
The storm-vane wheels sou'west, and the whirlwind's sun
Glistens the rainbow. [*Turning to the King.*]
Father, such gods as are
Indeed sustain us, in your passionate
Pondering. Look up! The draggled cap of Fortune
Sits jaunty again.

KING HAMLET

Ah, son of inexperience,
When Fortune sets her cap, bid her good-bye!
Her rouge is dyed in danger, when the tinct
Is ruddiest. But trap her in the sallow,
Untrimm'd and raw, peevish as autumn wind,
With scrannel throat and sparsy locks unkempt,
Then catch her against your heart, and she will yield
Her hoarded jewels to her charmer's touch
Like the warted toad's spewed gold.

PRINCE HAMLET

If so it be,
Dear father; if the warted toad—your malady
Of walking in your sleep—hath spewed this gold
Of contemplation from your heart, then verily
Is Fortune less fair in rouge than "trapp'd i' the sallow."

KING HAMLET

Walking in my sleep! Aye, there,—what was my dream?
Hunting, I was—hunting for it, and an Angel—
Was he an Angel?—*found* it!

PRINCE HAMLET

Found what?

KING HAMLET

A thought—
A sparkling, quartz-sharp dream-word—crimson in colour,
Matching my heart—my very heart. So now
My heart beats peacefully—very peacefully.
Feel o' my pulse!—Crimson, crimson as blood
Fresh from the artery: single—shining—clear!

QUEEN GERTRUDE

Oh, Hamlet, what thought?

KING HAMLET

You ask it,—Monica?
First, let us exchange eyes, then part our lips;
For what we have to say is the way we say it,
Far deeper than wording delves.—Dost thou love Hamlet?

QUEEN GERTRUDE

Yes, Hamlet.

KING HAMLET

Which?

QUEEN GERTRUDE

Which?

KING HAMLET

Monica's, or Gertrude's?

QUEEN GERTRUDE

Both.

KING HAMLET

Thou didst glance at Monica's. My blessing
Upon thy mother love!

[*To the Prince.*] Hamlet, *filius*
Monicae sanctae, faustum fatum tuum!
My breastplate—gird me it on, my comrades dear,
Will you?
[*He points to his suit of armour, hung against the wall, near them.*]

PRINCE HAMLET

Your breastplate, Sire?

KING HAMLET

I 'm in need of it—
Sore need—lacking underleather. But loins, too,
And thighs, need steely splints.—Will you help me on?
Aye, heels to headpiece—all the appurtenances:
Helmet and gorget, épaulière and pallette,
Brassart, cubitière, taces and tuille,
Cuisse, genouillère, jamb, solleret;
Smithy metal, to encase soul mettle.—Between you both,
I should be fettled quickly for it.

PRINCE HAMLET

Sir,
For what?

KING HAMLET

My nap.
[*Looking out the window.*]
The afternoon is fair,
And the breeze warm, for autumn. 'Tis my nap-time.
[*Removing his crown, he turns where the armour hangs and, reaching, takes down the helmet, replacing it by the crown.*]
Hang there, my crown,—in stately interchange
Of crafty war and statecraft!

PRINCE HAMLET

But, dear Sire,
In armour—for your nap?

KING HAMLET

'Tis not so much
Against the hornets, as the snakes in the grass,
Who breed with fecund spawn, I have observed,
In royal orchards, when the King 's at home.

QUEEN GERTRUDE
[*Aside, to Prince Hamlet.*]

You see, 't is as I told you. Still he broods
Upon our scandallers.

PRINCE HAMLET
[*To the King.*]

Nay, rest your mind, Sir,
For I am self-appointed to grub out
All vermin from Elsinore.

KING HAMLET

You hesitate,
I see, to gear me—being dubious
About my reasons for this arming? Well, then,
In secret, thus it is: my reasons are
State reasons. Help me on, and I will show you.
Thanks!

[*Assisted, in anxious bewilderment, by Prince Hamlet, he vests himself in the armour, while he continues speaking.*]

Pondering on what we are—such was
Our discourse, was it not? What are we, then?
Metal?—or mind?—or something airier?

PRINCE HAMLET

Airier, methinks.

KING HAMLET

Ah, that depends upon
Our trappings. Clamp the breastplate—closer, prithee.

So—am not I swoll'n to lustier dimensions?
On—on—the brassart! What is bravery?
Now, steel me over the leggings.—Stouter still!
Skirt me, like Mars a-wooing. Greave me 'gainst shin-grief!
Nothing so airy, now,—except this windpipe
Pumping my reasons mouthward. Come, the helmet,
But leave the visor open, for my flow
Of reason still to drip. So, now, what have we?

PRINCE HAMLET

Hamlet, King of Denmark, arm'd.

KING HAMLET

Not yet completely
Denmark: not till the visor is tight closed.
Till then, there 's still a leak of Hamlet, the Man;
And he informs thee, scion, in his last gasp
Of this our airy communion, 't is the encaséd
Manhood forgeth the metal; but 't is the metal
Which the *un*caséd man-fear of this world
Holdeth in awe and worship. In a moment,
This visor shall clamp over. Then gaze on this
Which stalketh away into the orchard grass:
This thing of might—this mastodon of statehood
Icéd in steel, to tread the hearts of men
Into the ooze of time.—Good-bye, prince-son
Of mastodon! Farewell, mate-mother of Hamlets!
This one—behold him now in arms, embracing
His heart's mate, his *one* thought, all others effacing:
Wish him bright crimson dreams—inside his casing!

[*Closing down his visor, he stalks toward the door, as*

THE CURTAIN FALLS.

In a moment, it rises again, disclosing Prince Hamlet bending over the Queen, in the chair by the table.]

PRINCE HAMLET

'T will pass. Poor mother, 't will pass!—I 'll seek him soon
I' the orchard.—It will pass.

QUEEN GERTRUDE

I fear me, never.
You saw, how deeply he broodeth on our wrongs
Of calumny, till his dark thoughts turn crimson
In roils of madness, mingling turbid streams
Of sweet and gallish bitter. 'T will not pass,
Such madness. What to do, then?—That must devolve
On thee, dear son.

PRINCE HAMLET

On me—how?

QUEEN GERTRUDE

On thy status
As next in heritage unto the crown.

PRINCE HAMLET

In heritage—while still my father liveth?

QUEEN GERTRUDE

In regency—while still thy father liveth
In madness.

PRINCE HAMLET

Nay, at first, I also thought
He 's mad; but now my heart says—'t is not so.

QUEEN GERTRUDE

Alas, our minds must contradict our hearts
And tell us, *'t is* so. For to hold one thought,
One single crimsoning dream, whatso it may be,

Blighting all others to its hue of blood,
How else than madness can it be construed?
As very surely 't will be gauged, and weigh'd
In great scales of the state.

PRINCE HAMLET

Oh, do not utter
Those damning, damnéd words, "the state," whereof
I do most deeply hold my father's concept,
That 't is as loveless, lifeless, and metallic
As the clinking coins it minteth. I was not
Born o' the state, but of love. Thou, Mother, thou
Knowest that best of any, save him through whom
I live the heir of both of you, to be
Love's servant and yours to the end. Make me naught else!

QUEEN GERTRUDE

What else are we—who did not make ourselves
King, Queen and Prince—save minions of the state?
The baubles of its baubles—prismatic puppets
Of its crown-jewels?—Nay, my darling son,
Princeling of my breast! We must, ourselves, submit
To the submission we compel of our subjects—
Our common slavery to that thing of armour,
Toning thy father's voice, which stalked, but now,
Hence—out through yonder doorway.

PRINCE HAMLET

Ah, then! Haha, then,
He was *not* mad, in his parting utterance,
That 't is man-fear debases manhood to metal!
Where, then, is courage? Are our thews and hearts
And craniums clamp'd in steel to simulate
The thing they forge, or break it? Are we cowards,
Who gule our crests of arms with valiant rubrics
And mottoes of bravery, so we may slink

Snugly within them, thumbing our noses there
At courage, stabb'd, and cast in a ditch of slag
Sluiced from our own entrails?—Nay, valiant mother,
Who bore me, bid me not be of lesser breed
Than thee, and so account my valorous father—
Thy loving husband—sane.

QUEEN GERTRUDE

I must repeat,
Dear son, 't is not as *I* account him; 't is
Even as he is accounted by the state
That we must act, in his own interest
And ours. Before he went to the Polish war—
Thou being distant then, in Wittenberg—
Himself, as head of state, for interim
Of his absence, here appointed his dear brother
To serve as regent, and thine Uncle Claudius
Did kindly acquiesce.

PRINCE HAMLET

Let my kind uncle,
Then, kindly acquiesce again, should need
Ever again arise. No regency
For me, in God's name, Mother! Promise me that,
Whatever may betide. These moils of state,
These fears of madness threat'ning, all enmesh me
With doubts and dread responsibilities,
Which hold me far—too far—from near compassion
For one most dear to me—more dear than all
The empty splendours of my heritage—
For one, who may even now, in lonely hush,
Be telling her still rosary of prayers
For her dead amsel-bird.

QUEEN GERTRUDE

Ophelia—

PRINCE HAMLET

Aye, but her bird hath got him angel wings
To lure us both away—my love and me—
From thorny tanglements and thimblerigs
Of court and castle—lure us far away
Unto the tiny heaven of a cottage nest,
Hid under thatch of mistletoe and holly,
For mated pair, who—even before the pairing—
Prevision now their bliss of matehood.

QUEEN GERTRUDE

No more,
Sweet son, to whelm me, and us all, with vain
Flutterings against those thorny tangles! Caught—
Caught are we all in the clutching thicket.—Quiet:
Let us be quiet, and pray.

PRINCE HAMLET

Promise me, Mother,
Whatso befall, that you will leave me free
From vow of regency, or royal heirdom,
To serve—first, last—as son; and in some happy
Sequel, as lover of my trusting mate,
Heavenly Ophelia!

QUEEN GERTRUDE

As far, and as deep,
As in my own heart lies my love of thee
And of thy love, I promise thee, my son.

PRINCE HAMLET

That promise I know thou 'lt keep. I need no other
Than thine all-faithful word.—Heaven bless thee, Mother!
[*Pressing her hands, he gazes into her eyes.*]

CURTAIN.

ACT FOURTH

Scene One

ELSINORE. HALL OF THE DOUBLE-THRONE.

CLAUDIUS, POLONIUS *and* LAERTES, *discovered, the two former listening to Laertes.*

LAERTES

In brief, my lords, if I might make summation
O' the graces, arts and grandeurs of brave France
In one swift rapier phrase of praise, 't would be:
Neat to occasion, noble to eternity.
So endeth my humble epic. *Seigneurs, voilà tout!*
[*He bows low, with a flourish of his sword.*]

CLAUDIUS

Too brief, Laertes! It hath pleased us well—
Your father and myself—to hearken from you
This telling of your soldierly exploits
And merriments in Paris. Since our parting,
That wild night o' St. Valentine, just ere
You sailed for France, we are the all more eager
To gauge your prowess in new fencing feats,
Learn'd of those martial craftsmen, not to mention
Your mastery in bouts of foamy bibbing,
Wherein, we trust, your skill is equal.

LAERTES

Sir,
In both I 'm still apprentice, but apostle
Of something keener to come, for sword and cup.

CLAUDIUS

Welcome, then, heartily home! I 'll not detain you
From your own quarters, for I must request

Some further moments of your father's presence
On matters urgent between us.

POLONIUS

Briefly, son.
I 'll join you, after a little.

LAERTES
[*Bowing to them both.*]

So, your pardons! [*Exit.*]

CLAUDIUS

Your boy hath bloom'd. He hath a wild-grape tang,
Still in the blossom savouring of the wine.
Felicitations!

POLONIUS

His wine of headiness
Springeth from the heart, my lord.

CLAUDIUS

The need is waxing
For such a vintage, here at Elsinore,
Where bubbles in the blood grow flat, and swords
Are turn'd to goosequills. Speaking painfully,
Polonius, and from my prick of conscience,
The immediate emergency, wherewith
We are confronted here, within the Castle,
Is exceeding serious.

POLONIUS

Your lordship meaneth—?

CLAUDIUS

My brother's madness.

POLONIUS

That! So much as that?

CLAUDIUS

Madness: That was my word, and 't is my meaning,
Alas!—Would God 't were not so. But to say
Woe 's me! is not enough to cure the woe.
We must speak plain between us.

POLONIUS

Plain, my lord,
Is honour's garnish, when the serving-platter
Is nobly crested—as your own.

CLAUDIUS

The crest
Is *Elsinore,* whereof I am the servant.
My royal brother 's mad. Brooding upon
His malady of many years, return'd now
Newly to plague him in his age, hath wrought
This grievous change, which you, 'mongst many others
His liegemen in the Castle, must of late
Increasingly have noted.

POLONIUS

'Tis my virtue,
If any I possess, to make notation
Of virtue and of vice, in this mystery
O' the world, and more especially of Denmark,
How vice and virtue dramatise themselves
And make their heroes, each, in his own image,
Their villains, in the other's—forging the plot
Accordantly.

CLAUDIUS

Here is no plot of villains,
Nor of heroes, but of actors, prompt at cue
In this emergency.

POLONIUS

Bearing, perchance,
Some likeness to another, enacted here,
After another royal return from war?—
Then Nemo bore your Highness' viewless train
Unto the dais of yonder double-throne,
Whereto you mounted, suddenly descending
To fit a millstone round your servant's neck,
Bidding him spit all knowledge on 't.—Or, doth
The newer emergency blot the older one
From memory?

CLAUDIUS
[*With quiet keenness.*]

Unless 't is blotted out,
It may be more emergent for your neck,
Sans head, than for mine own, Polonius.

POLONIUS
[*Bowing.*]

'T is blotted,—Sire.

CLAUDIUS

Methinks you do misdub me.
And spell me with an *S* instead of *R:*
Claudius, *Regent.* For, if the choice—which duly
Requires your vote, as Chancellor—unless,
I say, such choice should fall too sheer upon
The Prince of Denmark, it must fall obliquely
Upon the Duke, as Regent.

POLONIUS

Sheer is too short
A cut to regency. Experience
Is longer, being oblique, and the road already
Trod smooth with practicality. The Prince,
'Tis true, doth peer forth from the glass of graces
More prettily bedight—a scholar, preening
His plumage of Wittenberg—a courtier, quick
In all the alluring arts of courtesy.—
Who doth not love and venerate our Prince
To peak of admiration—*as our Prince?*
But as the regent of our monarch—his own
Father, in sore affliction—'t were too much
To claim his filial services, in such
Son-racking emergency. No, no! Such task
Is in itself *fraternal,* and demandeth
A brother's intimate care; a brother's fund
Of loving loyalty, already tested
In this same function, regency, perform'd
So ably, sanction'd by the double joyance
Of castle and garth, of lords and populace.—
To all this must the Chancellor give note
In dutiful obedience, alike
To conscience, and to sacred interests
Of state, surpassing even conscience' crown:
Wherefore, Polonius doth cast his vote
Of perfect confidence in our good Duke,
Brother of our stricken King, for Denmark's *Regent.*

CLAUDIUS
[*Tapping his hands together.*]

These diffident palms of the said loyal brother
Are stricken dumb, to clap sufficient plaudit
Of the dutiful Chancellor's vote. The registry

Thereof, in black and white, shall move him even more
Deeply, with conscience of the *quid pro quo*.

POLONIUS

For the *pro quo*, your Highness, this neck, provided
With undisjoinéd headpiece, shall provide him
Peaceful contentedness, whatever content
The *quid* may hold.

CLAUDIUS
[*Laughing.*]

Be sure, it shall hold humour,
Howsoever its quiddity may fail of holding
Water, in weight of something less transparent.

POLONIUS

All that can wait the event.

CLAUDIUS

That promises
To be no light one. The King's madness hangs
Heavily on all and each of us. It calleth
For some quick edict of the lords in council,
Before too rumour'd gabble of it, beyond
The Castle, may cause us such confusion of choice
As may impede the vote, and trouble the ears
O' the pretty Prince, dazing his filial sense,
Perhaps, to deem himself of prime importance
In this emergency.

[*Enter* CORNELIUS, *who stands as if to speak.*]

Yes, yes: what now,
Cornelius?

CORNELIUS

My lord, a cloddish lout,
Who calleth himself Yaughan, hath come in haste,

Desiring to speak only with Polonius
And with none other.

CLAUDIUS

Doubtless, Polonius
Shall bid you tell him to convey his haste
Hither, and sate his desire.
[*To Polonius.*] Is 't so, my lord?

POLONIUS

Bid him come here to me, Cornelius.

CORNELIUS

Sirs, thank you, both.
[*He turns and beckons.*]
Fellow, this way—and thy manners!
[*Exit Cornelius, as enter* YAUGHAN, *who bows, cap in hand.*]

CLAUDIUS
[*To Polonius, with a gesture towards Yaughan.*]

As 't were, now *I* am *Nemo,* and none other—
All made of *No One* and of empty air.
[*He retires a few steps, and looks on, faintly smiling.*]

POLONIUS

Well, Yaughan! Com'st thou in haste? Speak out: what is it?
We are alone.

YAUGHAN
[*Staring at Claudius.*]

Ah—Ah—

POLONIUS

Alone, I said.

YAUGHAN

Ah—Gramercy!—Ah!—

POLONIUS

Chew not thy cap, but speak.

YAUGHAN

'A 's bit.

POLONIUS

What, what? Speak out.

YAUGHAN

'A 's bitten—aye,
Sore bitten.

POLONIUS

Bitten! Who 's bitten?

YAUGHAN

'A 'erself.

[*Gulping and staring at Claudius.*]

Ooh!—Gramercy!

POLONIUS

Stop thy gaping! None is here,
But us. God's name, who is 't, is bitten?

YAUGHAN

Moll,
Erself—Moll Cowslip. Aye, bit nigh to death.

[*Claudius' smile has vanished, and his eyes are riveted upon Yaughan.*]

POLONIUS

Moll Cowslip! Moll? What meanest thou, she 's bitten?
Who bit her?

YAUGHAN

Nary who.

POLONIUS

Then why this haste
To tell me naught hath bit her?

YAUGHAN
[*Confusedly.*]

Said I *naught?*
Nay, *nary who,* I said. Aye, but 'a 's bit,
And no mistake about. I ha' seen the bites—
Double, they be, twice double. The red puckers
Be prickt, like wee worm-holes, in her right hand,
Nigh betwixt thumb and forefinger; and all
Her arm be bloated like a sausage-meat.
Na, no mistake. I wot an adder's bite,
Sith I were so high.

POLONIUS

Adder's bite! What 's this,
Thou tellest me? A poisonous snake hath bitten
Poor Molly?

YAUGHAN

Poison-fang'd, it were, and scotcht 'er
Twice, under skin. The purple scum hath spread
Up in her neck and face—red as boiled crab.
But ere she could n't speak, she bade me run
And tell it nobody but you, my lord—
I know not wherefore—but to hasten a leech.

POLONIUS

Where happened this?

YAUGHAN

In the orchard, by yon agedest
Apple-tree, where the pixies ripe the reddest
For bobbings i' the bowls, to Hallowe'en tide.

POLONIUS

Is Moll there now?

YAUGHAN

Nay, nay; 'a hurried off
To Dick the Shearer's, where 'a lieth abed,
Her breath a-whistling, like a bumpy lid
On a boiling pot—if be 'a breatheth yet
At all. Prithee, my lord, send fast the leech
To spare her life.

POLONIUS

I will, good Yaughan, straightway.
Go, tell her so.

CLAUDIUS
[*Stepping forward.*]

A moment!

YAUGHAN
[*Shrinking back.*]

Ah, by Gis—
Gramercy!

CLAUDIUS

When you tell her, ask of her:
Who warned her not to venture near the mound
Under the apple boughs?

YAUGHAN

Aye, but 'a said it.
I all forgot to tell. 'A said it, afore
Her mouth it bloated. 'A said it were yourself,
My lord, as warned her keep away, and bade me
Tell it to him. Sorry I am, I all
Forgot to tell it.

CLAUDIUS

Don't forget to tell her
The leech is on his way to Dick the Shearer's.
Hasten ahead of him. Go, now!

YAUGHAN

Gramercy, lordings!

[*Exit Yaughan.*]

CLAUDIUS

These tidings of poor Moll serve to increase
The tension of our problem.

POLONIUS

Increase it—how?

CLAUDIUS

Why, know you not the old apple-tree, in the orchard?
'T is there his majesty doth oft retire
To take his nap, of afternoons. The serpent
Which poisoned Moll is doubtless still in lair
And doth endanger royalty, asleep
In the same spot, unwarned o' the dire menace.
He must be warned, the King, by you and me
And others, in good time, but most of all
By one of us.

POLONIUS

Why us, your Highness?

CLAUDIUS

Why?
Because we both are stanchions of the state,
High in his kingly favour—I more, you less.
Well, have you spent your life in Elsinore
And still must learn what tattling means? To swerve
The pricking-points of tattle—tattle quicker
Than your opponent. That 's keen foil, in fencing,
And we are fencers, though as yet we use
But foils.

POLONIUS

As yet?

CLAUDIUS

Well, call it *as ever,* if
It liketh you better. Should mischance befall
The King in the orchard, innocently sleeping,
And snake should bite him mortally, towards whom,
Think you, would then the venom'd points of tattle
Be pointed?—To ourselves, as most of all
Responsible to have fully warned the King
Against such fearful hazard of his life—
And me, the first of all, as being—or soon
To be—his guardian, in my stately capacity
Of regent.

POLONIUS
[*Nervously.*]

Fearfully, indeed, it might
Be so; and so, be fearfully a thing
Too fearsome, for our fearings to be afraid
To try prevention of. I know not, as 't were.

CLAUDIUS

Oh, bosh to fears and fearings! Now is time
For clearances and clearings of all words
But our clear warnings to the King, to avoid
The orchard. Go you, now, and hasten the leech
To Moll, in her death-danger. I will go
And guard the orchard path against such woe.

CURTAIN.

ACT FOURTH

Scene Two

THE CLEFT IN THE PATH, AT THE HOLLOW OAK TREE.

Same as Act Second, Scene Two. Afternoon, towards evening.
Enter, left, CLAUDIUS. *He pauses, beside the oak.*

CLAUDIUS

Early! In time. Here is the cleft in the path.
The cleavage turns the road—but not the wrath.

[*He sits down, on a flanging root, and takes from his pocket a gleaming object.*]

The vial stopple still keeps the hebenon
From spilling out, and Yorick's will undone.

[*An obscuring mist begins to infiltrate the scene, partly concealing Claudius, where he sits pondering. With the mist comes an eerie music of* FEMALE VOICES, *as from within, or amid, or behind the oak, singing in trio a song.*]

THE SONG

Lithe and nimble, blithe and nimble,
Spinner's wheel and stitcher's thimble
Ply the thread for time's untwisting.
Block the shuttle! Break the spindle!
Dream shall wane and deed shall dwindle
Where the Mist-Mothers hold their trysting.
What Norna knit,
Pluck, bit by bit!
Piecemeal, tatter and scatter it!
All of triumph—all of travail—
Ravel, Mother, ravel![2]

CLAUDIUS

Waiting, again!—"To wait is not to win:
Nay, first we learn to card, and then—to spin!"
So, of old, I said it, and I learned to card.
Angela—Molly—Amsel—spin the reward!
Shall the reward avail?—Avail, or not,
Murder is made of what the murderer wrought,

Imagining it; else were it merely killing,
As beast killeth beast. Reward is in the willing
Before the event, whatever follows after.
If God be humorous, He 'll share my laughter,
As He shared Cain's. To nurse this nap of Abel,
An orchard 's neater than an ass's stable.

[*He rises, laughing, but stops, as he looks off, left, listening.*]

Whist, now! Methinks, I hear the tread of hooves.
Ass's, or imp's, the ground they tread hath grooves
To the orchard and old Eden's apple-tree.

[*He moves away, right, to the edge of the scene, standing a moment there, in the shrubbery path; then backs off, disappearing just before* KING HAMLET *enters, from the left, in armour, with helmet slung at his side, accompanied by* PRINCE HAMLET, *who touches the King's arm, as he speaks gently.*]

PRINCE HAMLET

Prithee, dear father! Will not you return with me,
Now, to the Castle? The airs grow raw and chill,
And dampy mists are rising.

KING HAMLET

A happy will
Makes its own weather, and mine is wondrous happy,
Hugging its inward heart-fire. 'T is my nappy
Hour, long grown habitual, and the pleasure
Of habit exceeds its pain, by the kindly measure
Nature extends to age. Thy blood of youth
Tingles to ruthlessness, but mine to ruth,
For 't is God's pity giveth me this peace
Sunk from all grappling-hooks, save only His
Who keepeth its cause plunged in submersities
Carmine and deep and calm.

PRINCE HAMLET

If thou art, then,
Peaceful at heart, ah, bring that peace again

Back to my mother; for her heart is sore
With anxious fear, lest all of Elsinore
Should rue your suffer'd health, if you lie down
In armour, on damp earth.

KING HAMLET

Damp earth 's a gown
For May-Day queens to wear, compared with that
Of ice and snow, whereon I 've laid me flat
In this mine armour, many a black midnight,
Lit only by the eerie northern-light,
On Poland's bleeding borders, in our war.
Tell her, if that be all she worrieth for,
To laugh at it, and lay her down abed
On hen-hawk feathers, and feel her husband's head
Cuddle to hers, incising with his teeth
The speckled feather-lining of their sheath
Of dreamy slumbers.

[*Putting on his helmet.*]

Tell her, too, that same
Head holdeth this helmet, filling it with flame
Of a crimson dream of her—a ruddy fleece,
Wrapping him round with peace—peace—glad, sure peace.

PRINCE HAMLET

Devoutly I trust, your message shall abate
Her fears. Sweet rest, Sir! Pray, sleep not too late.
I will await you, at the western gate. [*Exit.*]

[*The King moves onward to the cleft in the path, where he pauses, looking back towards the Castle.*]

KING HAMLET

Revenge—*thou* art my dream!—my crimson dream,
Sparkling thy crystal mica, all agleam
With raspy, pricking spike-sand, trickling blood
Of poison—lymph of peace, engulfing flood

Of peace—revenge, revenge, revenge, secure
In reciprocity of evil!—Sure?
[*Removing his helmet, he sits on the flanging root.*]
What else on earth can be more sure than death?
And this is death, I plan, for one whose breath
Itself is poison. Thus I 'll manage: She,
Not I, shall do 't. The enigma of iniquity,
Herself, shall innocently murder him,
Who murdered good in her.—A leg for a limb,
A Roland for an Oliver of lust!—
The poison 's in my brain, which soon shall thrust
Itself in a vial, labell'd: *Sleeping-draught:*
Pour in the porches of the ears, abaft
Below the temples. Avoid the mouth and lips.
So will I be confederate, when he slips
Between our sheets—oh, brotherly, unwitting,
Of course, why he might wish to, thus acquitting
Evil with innocence, making double test.
And so, some afternoon, when needing rest
From overwork, or overnight carouse,
He frowns and yawns, I will observe his brows
And gapéd mouth, and most fraternally
Myself invite him to my bed, that he
May nap there, till 't is supper-time.—Oho!
But ere 't is time for supper, he shall know
In hell, what time it is, and how to sup
By ear, not mouth, and drain the nasty cup
Of his own soul-poison. For the Hebe server
Of the ravisher shall be the ravisht! I 'll nerve her—
My unsuspecting queen of guilelessness—
When he is deep in nap, to do no less
Than minister—she, she!—the sleeping-draught,
Marked, *porches of the ears;* to soothe, by craft
Of sisterly devotion, her overtired
Brother—dead-asleep, in the royal bed, he hired

From his majesty, to perform, *ex officio,*
His kingly offices—ah-ha! hoho!—
On earlier occasions.

[*He leaps up, groaning.*]

Am I madman, thus
To think, she 'd do 't?—The pseudo-virtuous
Feign deepest virtue, to deflect all doubt
Thereof, back on the doubter. "Murder will out"—
Only where lust comes in. Aye, but in this
Psycho-autopsy of death, what leaves me amiss?
What else but Death, himself, *his* doubt thereof.
I hear him murmuring: "Hamlet, what are love
And lust, that thou, by loveless strategy,
And lusty-loving ambidexterity,
Wouldst exculpate thyself? Come: Canst thou cure
Unvirtuousness by vice? Pest—by the impure?
If murder be not vice, what else is murder?
To extol thine own vice—what could be absurder?"

[*He sits again.*]

Death—death, the only evaluator of life,
Lust's bane, love's vision, strangler of all strife—
Asks, but 't is I, must answer. What if I die,
Before this thing is done? What if 't be I—
Dead, by some accident, or error—dead,
With all my imperfections on my head,
These murderous thoughts I coddle—still unforgiven!—
And he, to suck my honey, whilst from heaven
I reach in vain to blast my blossom, even
In his very sucking on 't!—From heaven? From hell,
'T would be. There is no otherwhere to dwell
For Hamlet evermore, and naught can hurt him
More *on* this earth than off it.—Peace! Desert him
No more, sweet peace,—Revenge! Once—once, in days
Long gone, I had a will, that wandered many ways.
"The stars will guide," I said. But 't is ourselves
Who are our stars, and steadfast. So the elves

Of my bewitchéd will, in sudden rush—
Like errant autumn leaves, after summer hush—
Guided me nowhere. Now I have one thought
In place of many—*one still thought,* undistraught,
Which never moves, nor turns aside—intent
Upon itself; and so, I am unbent
By others, because I *am* that thought—that, *that!*—
And nothing else—
[*He blinks.*] still as a Persian cat,
Purring, before he pounces—

A VOICE
[*In cock-call.*]

—upon *me?*

[*Starting out of sudden darkness, he beholds beside him* A GLEAMING FIGURE, *garbed like himself in full armour, save that the helmet, with visor open, is crested above by a crimson Cock's Comb, quivering with spikéd flames.*]

KING HAMLET
[*Looking at the Figure.*]

A cat is very wareful, before he
Pounceth upon a cock,—Gallucinius.

GALLUCINIUS

The cock likewise is wary, ere he thus
Presumeth to interrupt the cat, in purring
Revenge—revenge—revenge—still, never stirring
To wreak it.

KING HAMLET

I will wreak it, never fear.

GALLUCINIUS

In quick reversal, let us hope. Seeing clear
Is love. Revenge is love reversed. Love's course
Flows ever upward to its springing source
Of deeper passion, not downward, where 't is damm'd
From every egress, save to push what 's cramm'd
Around it, even to bursting.

KING HAMLET

Let all burst!
I 'll do this thing. I 've willed it to do.

GALLUCINIUS

What first
We will, is done already. What followeth
Is to reverse the doing, if the lens of death,
Which makes life clear, reveals a choice more wise.
'T is simple: heaven's law. Thyself hath said where lies
The true appraiser. 'T is death. But thy blurr'd vision
Of death, mistook the source of all decision

Which judges true. 'T is love. And death *does* answer,
Not merely ask. To extirpate this cancer
Of vengeance' hatred—*I* am Death in thee,
Waiting thy choice, in the Eternity
Of Now, to *live*—by loving—and let live.

KING HAMLET

I know,
I know!—What of it?—I see him, all aglow,
Between the sweaty sheets!—You lie, you lie!
There *is* heaven's law for sticking pigs in sty.
The sticking-knife 's *Revenge,* and he shall die!

GALLUCINIUS

Knife? knife?—Methought, 't was *poison,* thou didst purr.

KING HAMLET

Aye, poison—true! Knife's blood would spatter her
With public shame—her, my sweet love!—and him,
My darling son—both my adoréds!—and dim
Their glorious lives to blackness. Only unespied
Revenge can save their being crucified
By taunting scorn. From such abhorrent fate
I 'll succour them, before it be too late
And I be tempted to *knife.*

GALLUCINIUS

Will telleth destiny
What to command us. Ah, my Hamlet! See—
Imagine clear—thy murder's sequel, and be
Not ghost before thou diest, having slain
Thy brother with thy thought. Else, ever again,
Murder shall cry, through Elsinore, upon
Thyself—all thou lovest, and most of all—thy son:
"Revenge! Remember me!"—*me,* self-accuser!
Abuse of love upbraideth the abuser.

KING HAMLET

I 've known—I know—I know—I said!

GALLUCINIUS

To know
Is not enough. Imagine!

KING HAMLET

So, or not so,
I know my plague's solution. Secret must
This murder be. 'T is poison, I can trust
To put him softly away.—Ah, grief!

[*Suddenly staggering, he leans against the trunk of the oak tree, clutching the bark with his fingers, and looking up toward its boughs.*]

Old oak!
I 'm grey as thou, and hollow, and rotted with choke.
Why bendest thou over me, like weeping willow?—
I 'll to the orchard, and my grassy pillow,
And nap my woes in night.

[*He turns up the orchard path. As he is moving slowly along it,* CLAUDIUS *emerges from the shrubbery, right, and peers after him.*]

GALLUCINIUS

[*Calls to King Hamlet, as he is disappearing.*]

Whatever woe,
Forever, unseen, beside thee—*I* will go!

[*He vanishes within the oak's hollow, from which the eerie* VOICES *are heard again, in trio, singing, as the mist draws more darkly across the scene.*]

THE SONG

Out of smother and darkness, Mother,
Tell us, who shall shape another
Woof, like the one that we 're unweaving?
Many and many a nobler weaver
Shall toil anew, but none can ever
Recapture the soul's conceiving.

Whirl a skein
Of joy and pain—
Then wind it on the world again!
All of triumph—all of travail—
Ravel, Mother, ravel!

[*During this, Claudius has moved forward to the cleft in the path, pausing there.*]

CLAUDIUS

Now is the moment when all moments cease
And mingle in the tide of destinies.
Toward this did he and I, on Trojan shore,
As boys, build Troy with blocks of Elsinore,
And I was Agamemnon, he King Priam.
His towers of triumph crumble, and now *I* am
The imminent lord of his scorch'd earth, for bliss
To crown my conquering with a stolen kiss.

[*He takes forth and holds upward the crystal vial of hebenon, gazing at it.*]

My thanks to thee, fool Yorick, for that foison,
In yielding back to me this vial of poison!

[*Turning his gaze to the orchard path, he starts back, with choked cry, at beholding there, coming towards him,* THE GHOST OF YORICK, *his head and right side partly wound with torn bands of blood-stained wool.*[3]]

THE GHOST OF YORICK

Hail, Claudio! The hand of God, you eased
In pushing the heavy rock, hath gently seized
Mine own, to lead me hither.

CLAUDIUS

Yorick!—Art
Thou—ghost out of hell, or God-sent?

YORICK

Both—in part:
Through hell I 'm come *with* God, not *from* Him, now;
And on this orchard path, by the hill's brow,

We left Moll Cowslip with my Angie, while here
God leadeth me to lead you back, this near
Path, towards home.

CLAUDIUS

Back!—Back?—There *is* no path
Backward.

YORICK

Oh, yes. The backward road from wrath
Leadeth through hell unto our childhood home
Where you and Hamlet and I were children. Come
Back with me to the castle garden, where
The broken wall was being mended.

CLAUDIUS

There!
There, where the blood from the fallen stone's crash still
Clotteth those wool strips, soakéd with its spill,
Which bind thy head and rib?

YORICK
[*Feeling of his bandages, with a smile.*]

'T is Topas' shirt,
He tore for me. He could not cover, with dirt
O' my grave, his own good thoughts o' me. Come! We 'll mend
The crack in the broken wall, together, and end
This tug-o'-war of two worlds. Our world is one,
Not two, nor tatters of two. His will be done,
Who made us to mend walls and open gates,
Not bang in each other's faces, and crush pates.
Come, Claudio,—thy hand!

[*He extends his right hand, with a winsome gesture and droll uplifting of his eyebrows.*]

CLAUDIUS

How can I take
Hand of thy spirit?

YORICK

What other hand to shake
Is there, between friends?

CLAUDIUS

No hand: a shake of head.
[*He moves away, frowning.*]
There is no friendship between quick and dead.

YORICK
[*With a laughing eye-wink.*]

There quickly can be, if the dead wake up
To know a live eye's wink, from the crackt skull-cup
Of a dead one!

CLAUDIUS

Still fool-quibbling in thy grave!

YORICK
[*Quietly.*]

'T is a still, grave hour for fools to misbehave.
A noble mind is napping, in strange trance,
Which holds, within the will-less hand of chance,
The choosing of a world, yet to be will'd.
The cock-crow hath warned twice. The moment is still'd,
When moments melt, to flow beneath time frozen.

CLAUDIUS

You overheard me think it. I have chosen.—
Poison of his poison'd thought shall be his dosage.

Now, lying in sleep, he walketh to the close edge
Of hell's pit, where the gulf of his despair
Is my abyss of hope, which openeth there
In Hamlet's grave.

YORICK

In Hamlet's heart, you mean.
All graves are empty, when they 're clearly seen.

CLAUDIUS

Then I will fill *one* up, till all between
His ghost and me, shall be a mound of green!

[*Holding the crystal-bright vial, lifted before him like a lighted candle, he glides away, up the orchard path, followed by the Ghost of Yorick, lilting softly, as he goes—his voice still audible after he has disappeared.*]

YORICK

Our Father dear, which art
In every foolish heart,
To make it heaven,
Whenas Thy living bread
Riseth from heart, in head,
On hallow'd leaven!

Let no man's foot trespass
Thy kingdom in the grass
His fellow's to gain,
But haste, on every hill,
To do Thy holy will.
Amen!—Amen!

[*As the sound of Yorick's voice is dying away, and the mists are gathering even darker than earlier, the* VOICES OF THE MIST-MOTHERS, *from within the hollow oak, begin again, in trio, the eerie melody of their Song.*]

THE SONG

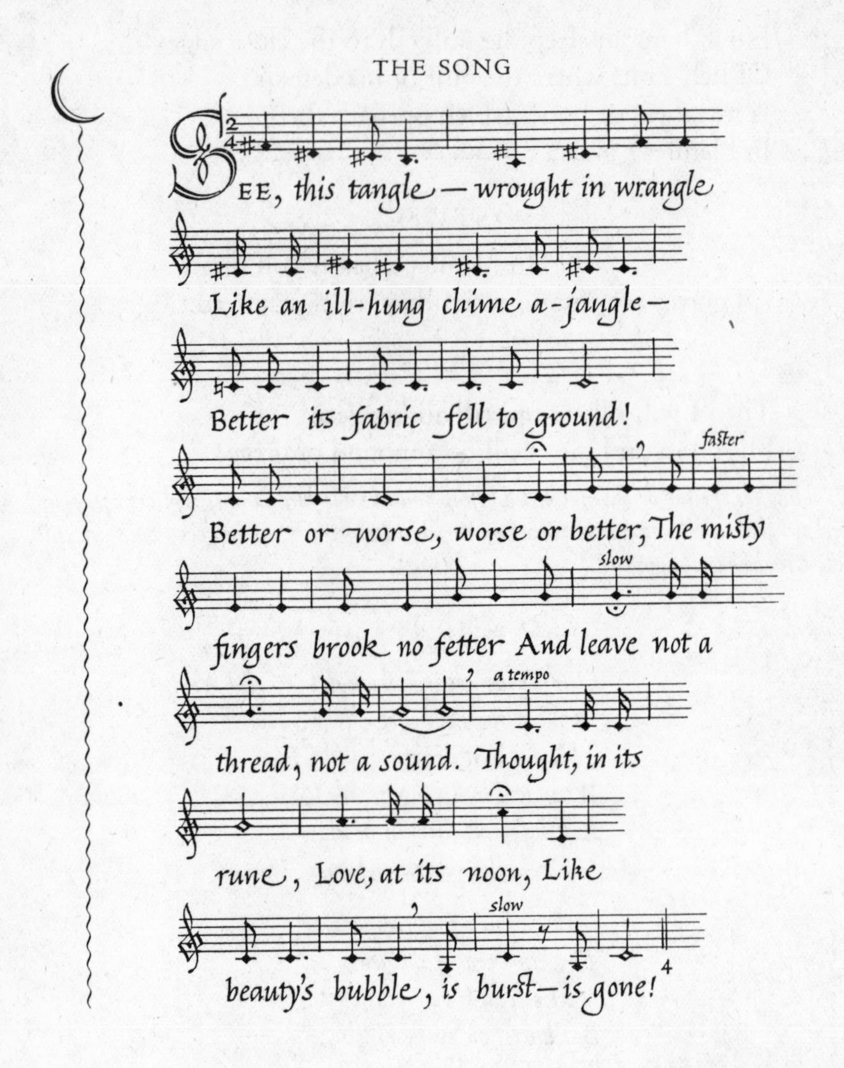

[*Piercing the mists, rises the long, lingering call of a* COCK'S CRY, *followed by the reappearance of* CLAUDIUS, *rushing down the orchard path, as he glances fearfully backward over his shoulder.*

Stopping, with sharp abruptness, beside the oak tree, stealthily he reaches his hand, with the hebenon vial, over the opening of the hollow in its trunk, and drops the vial within, pausing an instant to peer after it.]

CLAUDIUS

Empty!—Hide there, i' the hollow! Down—where his ghost goeth down!

[*Turning then, he clutches at an overbent spray of the purple-turning oak-leaves, as he utters a passionate cry of relief and triumph.*]

To-night—I hold the Queen! To-morrow, the crown—the crown!

With his cry, through the mists, there bursts A SUDDEN GLEAM OF BLOOD-HUED SUNLIGHT, *spreading quickly to streak their moisty greyness with blotches of raw, bluish crimson, as*

THE CURTAIN FALLS.

ACT FIFTH

Scene One

ELSINORE. A COURTYARD OF THE CASTLE.

A CROWD OF RETAINERS,—*Hostlers, Smiths, Ploughmen, Herdsmen, Servants, Men and Women with a few Children—are gathered in great commotion, their bursts of noisy excitement stilled, at moments, by awed sorrow and wonder. In their midst stands* DICK, THE SHEARER, *holding up a dead serpent.*

A HOSTLER

Hah, see, see, see! 'T is fearsome big, the varmint!

SHOUTS

Room!—Away!—Let us look!—Hush!—Still!—Let him tell!

A HERDSWOMAN

Dick Shearer, tell! Go on! Is yon itself?

DICK SHEARER

Aye, 't is the very snake that killed the King.

MURMURS

Ooh! Ah! Oh!

A SMITH

How camest *thou* by it?

DICK SHEARER

Nay, will ye let me tell?—
Myself, I killed the snake, yonside the mound
By the old apple-tree. Nigh to his hole
'T were lying, in a wriggly coil. Ah, *Sacra!*
Awful a sight were his poor majesty,
His head still laid asleep, and helmet off;

But hardly could I spy his eyes and ears,
So bloated were they, wi' a lazary scum
Crusted all over.—Bid ye me tell no more on 't!

MURMURS

Ah, aye—the adder-poison. 'T is an asp.
Poor King! Woe for him! Woe to our land! Woe!

A HERDSWOMAN

Dick! Dick, how came ye there?

DICK SHEARER

I told it afore.
Eke it were this same sarpent bit Moll Cowslip
To death. 'A died to my house, did poor Moll.
There Thekky, my wife, e'en now, doth strew her corse
Wi' cowslip greens and mallows fro' the brook
I fetched for strewings. But afore she passed,
Moll catched her breath again, a minute more
To lilt a blithe snatch of a ballet ditty
And babble about babies.—"Babes and sucklings!"
Quoth 'a. "Bull-sucklings and ram-lamblings!
This world hath never weaned 'em, and old Moll
Be weary o' the borndin' and the duggin'.
God bide with 'em, for I 'll be off and away
To Yorick and Angie. Babes and sucklings—all!"
They be her last spoke words. And so she passed—
As good a soul as ever were a midwife.

MURMURS

'A were! 'A were, poor Moll!

SHOUTS

Here 's Yaughan, wi' Topas!
Speak up, Yaughan! Hark to Yaughan!

YAUGHAN
[*Who has entered, with Topas.*]

Here 's more to that!
An earlier word Moll Cowslip spake to me.
"Yaughan, Yaughan," quoth 'a, "fetch fast to me a leech,
And tell the Castle 't was him, the great lord duke,
Himself, bewared me 'gainst the sarpent's bite
And bade me shun his hole i' the mound."

MURMURS

Hark that!
Lord Claudius!—The good duke warned her well.

TOPAS

And well she warned the Castle, wi' her word
How good he be, the Duke.

MURMURS

Aye, so! How so?
What sayest, Topas?

THE HERDSWOMAN

But the King—the King!
How came ye to the King, and found him dead?

DICK SHEARER

When Moll she 'd passed, Thekky, my goodwife, "Dick!"
Quoth 'a, "go fetch me strewings fro' the brook
By-under the orchard hill. There groweth the greenest
O' mallows and cowslips. Run, now!" So I ran;
But whiles I went, thinketh I; I ken yon hole
I' the mound, and I 'll go find the snake, bit Moll,
And cleave his head off wi' my shearing knife,
Afore I fetch the mallows. So I hurried,
And so I did, and whanged him sharp, as ye all
Can see it now, his devil-head still dangling.

VOICES

Aye, aye! A purty whang, Dick Shearer! Hail!
Spike up the poison-varmint on the wall!

SHOUTS

Hail, hail our Dick! Heave him up! Shoulder him high—
Killer o' the killer o' the King! Dick Shearer, ho!
He whanged the sarpent! Shearer—Shearer—Shearer!

[Raising Dick from the ground, the Crowd begin passing him along from shoulder to shoulder towards the courtyard wall, to fasten up the dead snake there, when they are brought to pause by the deep-toned clanging of a bell, swung at his left arm's length by the CASTLE CRIER, *who enters, with his right hand raised to quiet them, as he paces slowly past across the courtyard, followed at a distance by* POLONIUS *and* PRINCE HAMLET, *the latter with his eyes fixed on the ground.]*

THE CRIER
[Intoning.]

The King is dead! The King is dead! The King
Is dead! Hamlet, our lord and king, is dead!
Mourn ye the King! Mourn ye the dead! Mourn—mourn...
[He goes off, right, the deep clang of his bell still continuing distantly.]

VOICES FROM THE CROWD
[As Dick Shearer is lowered to his feet again.]

Down! Let him off! Set him down!

POLONIUS
[Pausing, with shocked expression.]

Silence—and sorrow!
Have ye not hearkened the dreadful tidings? Hush!
[Pointing towards Prince Hamlet.]
Behold your sorrowing lord! Do reverence.

MURMURS FROM THE CROWD

'T is him, the Prince—young Hamlet—Bless him, poor soul!

LOUDER VOICES

God save the King! Hail our new King of Denmark!

PRINCE HAMLET

[*With appalled look and gesture.*]

Oh, silence them, Polonius!

[*He rushes off.*]

POLONIUS

Silence! Silence
And prayers to be forgiven! Are ye Danes
Of Elsinore, or are ye quackling ducks
O' the garth-pond? Heard ye not? Our royal lord,
Our great and gracious and beloved liege,
King Hamlet, hath been poison'd by a serpent,
And lieth dead, on awful catafalque,
E'en now, in the Castle throne-hall. Still your voices,
And scatter homeward to your kneeling-stools
And lift your hearts to him, in heaven. Hush!
Ope not your lips in hail of the new king
Till our great stately Council doth proclaim him:
They, at the nod of heaven, alone can name him!

The Crowd gape dumbly at Polonius, who faces them, with arm uplifted in stern admonishment, as

THE CURTAIN FALLS.

ACT FIFTH

Scene Two

Just before and during the slow rise of the curtain again, deep tones of a heavily tolling bell are heard, as from above and beyond, continuing at slow, steady intervals throughout the disclosed scene:

AN ARCADE, *leading from the Castle [right] to the doorway of the Chapel, approached [in left foreground] by low steps, leading up, onward to the door beyond view.*

On the lowest step, HORATIO *is standing, quiet, his face toward the chapel doorway. Behind him, opposite, across the arcade, near the edge of the scene, right, grouped in soft-toned conversation, stand three young men:* LAERTES *and* TWO OTHERS. *All are garbed in dark raiment.*

LAERTES

Your ship hath brought you barely in time.

THE FIRST OF THE OTHER TWO

This bell
Doth toll as lonesome as the harbour buoy
That warned us from the rocks.

LAERTES

The rocks still hold
Their peril in shallows, ashore, under our feet.
The waiting was awesome while, in frozen chamber,
The King lay still upon his catafalque,
Biding his burial, whereto we now
Move on, as soon as chapel-rites are over.

THE SECOND YOUNG MAN

We left immediately upon the message,
We jointly received, from the Duke Claudius.

LAERTES

The funeral feast is busily preparing
For rouses, from the cellarage and the kitchen
Wherein the hospitable duke, our host,

Is lordly expert. After the feasting lulleth
A fitting space for judgement's brain to cool,
We shall have knowledge how the solemn Council
Of State hath voted, for the realm of Denmark
Thereafter to be ruled in majesty.

THE FIRST

His majesty will be—?

THE SECOND

His majesty,
Methinks—

LAERTES

To think what will be, is to be
Too deep in shallows, nigh the grating rocks
Of greatness, as aforesaid, under keel
Of this arcade, whereon the treading feet
Of our procession is already, now,
Almost at starting-point. The moment waiteth
Only our Prince's reappearance. He
Is gone within, to make his last adieu
Unto the majesty of death. Nay, lo,—hush, friends!
He comes, now.—Softly!

[*Enter* PRINCE HAMLET, *left, from the chapel, where he pauses on the bottom step, beside Horatio.*]

PRINCE HAMLET

Thanks, Horatio,
For your good patience! What I looked upon
Was in my soul's eye—beautiful in manhood
And living memory: not there—not there
In fleshly sight.

HORATIO
[*Gently.*]

My dear lord!

PRINCE HAMLET

I did leave
A tiny token, there, but vast of import.

HORATIO

A token?

PRINCE HAMLET

Aye: the sprig of rosemary
He gave me, as a child. So shall he know
How, as a man, forever I remember.—
Now, to my mother. I am sorry, very,
To have kept all waiting.

[*Followed by Horatio, he hastens toward the right, where, meeting the group, he greets them, half absently, half in surprise.*]

What, Laertes!
And you!—you, my good mates of Wittenberg!
Your hands, my Guildenstern and Rosencrantz!

GUILDENSTERN

Our hearts in them, my lord!

ROSENCRANTZ

My lord, our souls!

PRINCE HAMLET

What, sans your brains, which all of us so cudgelled
To keep in hand, as scholars, coddled for scribes?
Ah, those dear coddling days! Our heads are bludgeon'd
To keep our hearts in order, now. But how
Came ye hither?

GUILDENSTERN

By ship, my lord.

PRINCE HAMLET

Of course, of course!

But I 'm far out of course—and on my way
I know not whither. Sadly, gladly, be welcome—
Both of you—all of you! Horatio,
Better my greetings for me. Friend Laertes,
Thy hand, too!

LAERTES

Hamlet, thine!

PRINCE HAMLET

And so, my mother
Waits—and my father, also.—Fare you well!
[*He hurries off.*]

HORATIO

The bell, dear friends! It tolls a quicker cadence.
We, too, must follow him.

LAERTES
[*Looking off, right.*]

The Queen hath ta'en
Her place. But what is there, Horatio?
Behind her, next to follow, there 's my sister,
Ophelia. Wherefore so—next to the Queen?

HORATIO

The Queen would have it so. At least, Prince Hamlet
Did so inform me of it.

LAERTES
[*Raising his brows.*]

He informed you!

[*They go off, together, right.*
The bell has begun to strike its tolling tones at shorter intervals. While it does so, there emerges from the chapel the KING'S CHORISTER, *who comes down a step or two; pauses to make a solemn, signalling gesture; watches, a moment; then returns within, as the* FUNERAL

PROCESSION *begins to enter, from the right, headed by* PRIESTS *and* CHOIR-BOYS, *in their chapel vestments. At their entrance, the deep music of an* ORGAN *sounds from within.*

Following the silent Choir, comes QUEEN GERTRUDE, *her solitary figure hidden in long veil of deep black.*

Behind her follow OPHELIA, *alone;* PRINCE HAMLET, *with* CLAUDIUS; POLONIUS, *with* LAERTES; ROSENCRANTZ, *with* GUILDENSTERN; OSRIC, *with* CORNELIUS; HORATIO; *other Lords and Courtiers, with Ladies, two by two, coming into view, until the Procession halts for a moment, as Queen Gertrude pauses, on the lowest step of the chapel.*

There, lifting partly aside her veil, she half reveals her haggard face, looking fixedly down at the step, then upward toward the chapel doorway, as she murmurs to herself.]

QUEEN GERTRUDE

Good-bye, sweet long-ago!
[*Half turning quickly, she whispers.*]
Ophelia dear!

OPHELIA
[*Drawing close to her.*]

Madam—

QUEEN GERTRUDE
[*In low, swift tones.*]

This step!—'Twas here he lifted me
Down from the pommel, in my bridal veil.
All white, all virgin white, I was—and now
All black.

OPHELIA

Dear Madam—

QUEEN GERTRUDE

Child, though he be black,
Thine amsel-bird, he hath in heaven a beak
Golden with dawn. Believe him, dear! Believe him,
When in thy heart thou hear'st him singing—singing!
But oh, believe *not* what our earthy breath
Goes chanting, where Hamlet doth *not* lie in death!

[Closing quickly her black veil, she moves on—to tones of the unseen organ, within—upward to the chapel doorway, disappearing there, as the Priests and Choir-Boys of the on-following Procession break into choral chant, while the Curtain is slowly falling, to the tonal marching cadence of the words in Latin.]

Vita nostra brevis est,
Breve finietur,
Vita nostra brevis est,
Breve finietur.

Post jocundum, jenectutem,
Post molestam, senectutem,
Nos habebit humus—
Nos ha-be-bit hu-u-mus!

CURTAIN.

ACT FIFTH

Scene Three

ELSINORE. THE BEDROOM OF PRINCE HAMLET.
PRINCE HAMLET, *discovered, alone, in meditation, during which at times he paces back and forth, with pausings.*

PRINCE HAMLET

O, sepulchre of marble, devourer
Of manhood! Shall thy clutchéd jaws no more
Disclose his splendour to me?—his strong beams
Of glowing gentleness, irradiant
With martial lightnings? Doth thy frozen silence
Secrete no murmurous runnel, to betray
Some flow of heavenly tricklings from beyond,
Sprung of these falling tears? Hath nature form'd
No effigy of spirit, adumbrating
Its analogue in clay, which sculptural art,
Impregning fleshly hand, itself betokens
When clay is alter'd to entombing marble
In portrait images, for weeping eyes
Of clay to gaze upon? Hath brain of God
Conceived no corollaries to His own
Concepts of man, when even puny man
Is able to picture his immortality
By musing on 't, and people universes
With gods and angels of himself? Ah, God
Of terrible silences, be vocal—speak!
Aye, even in whisper, answer: Is my father
My father no more—forever?—Hushing . . only hushing!

[*With desperate gesture, he throws himself beside the bed, in kneeling posture, and buries his face in the coverlids, for a moment; then lifts it, clasping his hands, like a child.*]

"Our Father, which art in heaven!"——
No, no! *My* father—*my* father, which art there,
Else heaven for me is fatherless! For what
Art thou, *our* Father, couldst thou so bereave

Us both, of fatherhood and sonhood, here,
Even by a serpent's bite?—Silence! . . Thy silence—
It doth not even hiss!

[*A low knocking at the door.*]

Ha, but thou hearest!
Enter, O answer!

[*Enter* HORATIO, *who stands hesitant.*]

Brother!—'T is Thy word,
Made flesh, and needeth no other answering
To foist this serpent-poison from my heart.

[*Rising.*]

Come in, brother!

HORATIO

My lord—

PRINCE HAMLET

Bringing with thee
Thy brotherhood, in place of what is lost!

[*He takes Horatio's hands, pressing them to his heart.*]

HORATIO

[*Speaking with willed effort.*]

My lord and friend, I bring—

PRINCE HAMLET

What thou alone
Canst, and dost ever, bring me—thine own courage
To brave whatever comes.

HORATIO

To fend the brunt
Of this world-staggering blow, from off your breast
Of anguish, to mine—I would I were
Hercules, and not Horatio, to ward it.
But this is beyond fending. 'T is for standing.

PRINCE HAMLET

And that, for me—my very self—might be.
With you beside me, I could bear this woe,
Not smiling, merely withstanding. Yes, for me,
My father's son, Ophelia's lover, *me*,
Hamlet, of Hamlet's loins. But this *mock*-me,
This pseudo-self, this Prince of Denmark, this
Regarded idol of all I least regard;
This mimic mask, a tenth of a tithe of me:
How could I accept the adulating hail
To *me*-less *him*, from Castle and from courtyard,
Out of mobbish mouths, calling, "God save the King!"
Even while their *un*saved monarch, succourless
In death, lay stretchéd for the tomb! Was I—
Am I—to doff my cap of sorrow, and mince smiles
To lure the vote of such unfeeling mass-love
For a picture-prince, and scare the solemn Council
To make them cry the same to him? Fie on 't!
Love?—Love!—'T is lubbery of loyalty,
Fit for a court of urchins!

HORATIO

My dear lord,
You need not fear your sentiency again
Must shrink from such bold hailing. The Council—

PRINCE HAMLET

Why,
I tell thee, 't is manner'd even as in a play,
At curtain fall, just as it lifts, a moment,
To show the grief-struck hero of the scene,
With hand obsequiously bent to breast,
Bowing his obedient smiles of player-triumph
To the hoarse-throated groundlings, where their upgrunting
Huzzays, o'ertopping his thanks, outdrown the still

Speech in the censuring eye of the only *one*
In the theatre, whose praise is valid, because he loves
The aim of its art, not merely its artistry—
The aim of truth to nature. We, who share
In life that gauge of art, are life's true players,
Learning from unvalid praise our own self-censure.

HORATIO

My lord, in coming here, I passed, but now,
By the feast-hall, towards—

PRINCE HAMLET

Ah, yes, the feast!
How long shall men make feasts of funerals
To drown the source of sorrow, which should quicken
Their grief to glorious acts of self-restraint,
Selfless onmoving to mend the offending cause
Of agony, not increase it, by hugger-mugger
Of belly-worship! But 't is as I did say:
Drowning 's the dream of groundlings—their frog-choir,
Soused in their natural element, 'mid smell
Of bog-mud.—Well, in coming by the feast-hall,
You were saying—this death-feast of Elsinore—
How long, by the way, hath it lasted?—A week, a fortnight,
A month? What 's time to topers? Are they still
Flound'ring and drowning, ere they rouse for the crowning—
God's woe!—the crowning of *my* brows?

HORATIO

Nay, not . . A lull
Hath fallen, deep, and the Council—

PRINCE HAMLET

Ah! And our duke,
The all-imbibing Claudius, mine uncle,
Hath he, then, kept his legs, to stagger thence
To the solemnity of the Council?

HORATIO

Yea, my lord,
And nay. He hath kept his legs astutely spry—

PRINCE HAMLET

As they are stout to lug him there, yes?

HORATIO

No,
To remain in the feast-hall.

PRINCE HAMLET

Reeking too much, perhaps,
In hose and doublet, not to mention unmentionables,
Yes?

HORATIO

No. He abstaineth to go to the Council, because—

PRINCE HAMLET

Reeking, Horatio! Let me give thee a piece
Of philosophy—not piecemeal, but profound
In fathoming. Which of all our senses five—
Sight, hearing, smell, touch, taste—which one of all
Hath most empiercing sensitivity?

HORATIO

Why, as you list them, my lord, methinks—the first.

PRINCE HAMLET

Sight?—Ah, indeed, what other mortal sense
May compensate us for being blind? Sans vision,
What were the eyes of love, to be gazed upon
As well as to enlure the gazer? Or, what were it,
Being deaf, never to hear the loving gazer's voice?
Or, paralysed, never to taste the keener-
Than-wine-cup fragrance of the breathing lips,

Nor feel the tender touch o' the tendrilling hands
Of them, who love us? Aye, the senses, all,
Are their own advocates; and to their pleas
Of ardent service to us, who is there, that 's wise,
Can render judgement against any of them?

HORATIO

Have you not omitted one?

PRINCE HAMLET

Have I? Which one?

HORATIO

The third.

PRINCE HAMLET

Ah, true!—the heart of 'em all, at centre,
Quickening the other four so pregnantly
And silently, that I did even forget
To mention it.

HORATIO

Smell! Would you appraise smell
To be the quickener of what we sense?

PRINCE HAMLET

Aye, smell, the avatar of all the senses,
Their incarnator, quintuple-crown'd, to each
Outreaching a cuppéd hand—invisible,
Unhearable, impalpable, yet half,
As 't were with dream-touch, tastable—each cup
Of losséd softness, holding the viewless wellspring
From which all vision, music, flavour, feeling
Rise, intermingling, as *fragrance,* or—as *stench.*
So, by a sentient brotherhood with man,
Dipping their noses in smell's ambient world,

The sniffing rabbit and the bloodhound vie
With Raphael's and Buonarroti's sense,
By palette-craft and chisel-twinge of nostril
To scent the sources of their Sistine arts.

HORATIO

My lord, a strange piece of philosophy!

PRINCE HAMLET

Of poesie, which holdeth all philosophy
As lily-cups hold perfume, or as skunk-weeds
The reeking of bog-mire. Who hath not been
Translated to heaven by fresh rose-buds' smell?
Or suckt to the underworld by the rank odour
Of petals dung-polluted—dropt, wind-rended,
From briars of rose-vines, climbing to their bloom?

HORATIO

Duke Claudius, my lord,—the Council—

PRINCE HAMLET

Oh, I 've kept
Counsel with myself, in this epitome
Of reeks and rose-bud smells and stench of bogs.
Your nostril is your only arbiter
Of nature, in its quick. Indeed, I 'd trust
My unpowder'd nose, rather than eyes, or ears,
As spirit-detector, to plumb the various
Reekings and fragrances of literature,
Wherein, by following it, I 'd point the moral
Perpendicular, or aslant, by one deep snuffing—
As, let us say, of Erasmus, by the smell
Of his buck-chamois vellum, acrid still
Of the Alp-rock leaps of his expanding vision;
Or, of Rabelais, mingled of juices, gather'd
From nectar-horns and stink-pots of the gods.

Even so, Horatio, have I smelled—mine uncle,
And sensed him nearer to Rabelais, than Erasmus,
In his exhalings. How think you?

HORATIO

Dear my lord,
What I have now to utter of your uncle
I would that I could swallow, if to do so
Could hide your ever knowing it.

[*Prince Hamlet fixes upon him a quick look of apprehension; then speaks, in low voice.*]

PRINCE HAMLET

Horatio!

HORATIO

Yea, though I winced to death, and so saved thee
And Denmark and the world the dooming throes.
But bitten lips must open. Now, at once,
Is destiny, and no procrastination
Can alter doom. In, must out.—This very hour,
The Council hath proclaimed Duke Claudius—King.

PRINCE HAMLET

Mine uncle, King? What,—*King?*—Oh, glorious!

HORATIO
[*Breathlessly.*]

Glorious?

PRINCE HAMLET

Ah, Ophelia!—We are free!

[*He bursts into joyous laughter; then leaps toward the bed, kneeling beside it.*]

"Our Father, which *art* in heaven!"—Oh, heaven of *earth!*

[*Springing up, he tosses the bed-pillows in air—stretches his arms upward, clutching and unclutching his hands.*]

Kiss thy ring, love!—thy ring! Out from under thy breast,

Our ring—kiss our ring! Amsel, our Amsel! Sing—
Sing, O, sing an anthem to dear Spring
And our joys!

[*He dances toward Horatio.*]

King—King! Mine uncle is King—not I!
Horatio, our herald-deliverer!

[*He hugs him, patting his shoulders; then weeps, clinging to him.*]

Ah, joy,
That cracks with forgetfulness! Father, forgive me!
Forgive me, also, brother!

HORATIO

[*Disengaging himself.*]

Brother, my friend!
If this be thy deliverance from evil,
Heaven's will be done! But ah, my lord and prince,
What waits for Denmark—and your mother?

PRINCE HAMLET

My mother!
The Queen? Why, now—why, now, my mother—she
Must be—Queen Dowager.

HORATIO

Now. And to-morrow?

PRINCE HAMLET

To-morrow?

[*A low knocking sounds on the door, left.*]

Hark!—a rap? Is someone knocking? Is it—To-morrow?
Ha, is 't another answer of destiny?
Come in!

[*Enter* QUEEN GERTRUDE.]

QUEEN GERTRUDE

Hamlet, my son—

PRINCE HAMLET

[*Goes towards her, with tender deference.*]

Mother—my blessing!

QUEEN GERTRUDE

Ah, would it were so! Let it so be, I pray!
Call me—thy blest-in-thee! That shall suffice,
I hope, for both of us.

PRINCE HAMLET

Aye, *'t is,* Horatio,
To-morrow's self, come now to give us answer
In dear, great person!

[*Stooping on one knee, he kisses the Queen's hand.*]

QUEEN GERTRUDE

To give answer?

PRINCE HAMLET

Mother,
Is not it as Queen Dowager that you
Receive your son, letting him kiss your hand
In homage to the solemn Council's vote—
The glad, unfettering vote!—which doth relieve
Your brow and heart of all the weight of years
To greet your boy again?—albeit now
Fatherless, yet twice mother'd by one love!

QUEEN GERTRUDE

Ah, you have heard? Horatio hath told?—
I came to tell it thee.

PRINCE HAMLET

[*Rising.*]

Mine uncle receives

The crown—and we the *benedicite*
Of its being lifted from our brows to his!

QUEEN GERTRUDE

Dear son, it lifts, only to fall again,
Doubly, on a great grief and a great duty.

PRINCE HAMLET
[*Staring.*]

What new enigma 's this?

QUEEN GERTRUDE

A pending knowledge,
Which I must be the first to lay upon
Thy heart, to be transforméd there, I trust,
By love, to different benediction than
Being relieved of duty.

PRINCE HAMLET

Duty?

QUEEN GERTRUDE

Duty
And obedience to the State.

PRINCE HAMLET
[*Gropingly.*]

Obedience
To the——?

QUEEN GERTRUDE

State of Denmark, by whose august Council
The Queen of Denmark hath been solemnly
Adjured to share the double-throne of Denmark
Once more—with him on whom the impelling sanction
Of the great vote hath fallen.

PRINCE HAMLET
[*In stupefaction.*]

Share the throne!

QUEEN GERTRUDE

The twin-crown and the double-throne of Denmark.

PRINCE HAMLET

Share! Share them with him—with *him*—Duke Claudius?

QUEEN GERTRUDE

With Claudius, *King* of Denmark.

PRINCE HAMLET

Oh, my dear
Poor mother! And thou camest to bring me here
This answer of destiny for our to-morrow?
Adjure!—Adjure?—The solemn Council doth
Adjure my father's wife—their prince's mother—
To—to—to *what?*—To share the throne of Denmark
With—with a brother—a pseudo-brother?—'Swounds!
This adjuration shall have answer. I,
Methinks, am still sufficiently the Prince
Of Denmark to *ab*jure their adjurings!

QUEEN GERTRUDE

Patience,
Hot heart! Plunge not in our still-wounded breasts
The knife of this decision, but let it glance
To sever the obstacles, which otherwise
Might stand between you and your happiness.

PRINCE HAMLET

Happiness! *My* happiness? O, heaven,
What 's this?

QUEEN GERTRUDE

The implication of my promise,
Which I have surely not forgotten, Hamlet,
As far as lies within my love, to free thee
From the immense responsibilities
Of state, and loose thee to thy dearest aim—
Thy quest of quiet with Ophelia.

PRINCE HAMLET

'T is that I now rejoice in. But, O say not,
At *thy* expense, sweet mother!

QUEEN GERTRUDE

I said not
Expense. I might have said, my *privilege.*

PRINCE HAMLET

Privilege!

QUEEN GERTRUDE

To smooth away all obstacles
Between you and your longing's consummation—
Your marriage with Ophelia.

PRINCE HAMLET

What hath that
To do with this?

QUEEN GERTRUDE

Is not it reasonable,
Aye, even logical, to—

PRINCE HAMLET

O love, relieve us
From blight of logic and the blear of reasoning!

They 're made of obstacle. So, Mother, I pray you,
Intrude not needlessly Ophelia's name
Into the moil of this most vile request—
Term'd, "solemn adjuration"—of the Council.

QUEEN GERTRUDE

Vile? Needless?—These are words that leap too sudden
And thoughtlessly, my son, from thy hot youth.

PRINCE HAMLET

I am not old, yet.—Nay, Horatio,
You need not steal away. We 're both young, yet,
And brothers, ever, all the more blest for not
Being legalized in our fraternity
By solemn councils.

QUEEN GERTRUDE

Gentle son!

PRINCE HAMLET

Gentler mother!

QUEEN GERTRUDE

Was it in me, then, *needless,* I should fail not
To keep my promise to thee?

PRINCE HAMLET

Nay, most kindly
Needful.

QUEEN GERTRUDE

Is it, then, *vile* of the great Council
To adjure me—call it, *ask* me—to do the thing
Which, incidentally, may best enable me
To further that promise?

PRINCE HAMLET

Incidentally:
There gleams the quick of its vileness! Was this ask'd you
By the Council, to further *my* sincerest love,
Or their own sincerest desire to serve themselves?

QUEEN GERTRUDE

To serve the State.

PRINCE HAMLET

The State—the State! O, stately
God of us all! What is this State, we foster
In Thy great name, to make us puppets of it
To serve our purposes of self-love—gross
Or glorious, petty, grand, chicane, superb,
Greedy, or sublime—call them by what officious
Titles and terms we will—invented, forged
Of our own flesh and brains, to satisfy
The means, and sate the ends, of our self-loving
Fear of our non-survival—when we ourselves
Selflessly lay us on the altar of sacrifice
To send our sons and brothers to their deaths
In pomp and agony of sacrifice
To oppose our very purpose of sacrifice—
Service to Thee, our Father!—and so crush
Our hearts in doing so? How long, how far,
Till what eternal hour, must we still wait
To learn what secret purpose of Thine own
Ignites these acts with motive?

QUEEN GERTRUDE

Until we learn it,
We must obey the—

PRINCE HAMLET

Must?—Must!—Must we, indeed!

QUEEN GERTRUDE

We must obey the mandates of that power,
Our brains have forged.

PRINCE HAMLET

Our brains, but not our wills.
Forging is done with fire. Power is not smithied.
Power is the smith, himself, whose will must forge
His instruments of brain to shape the illuming
Vision of their use, which gilds the impassion'd hour
Of forging love, hailed by the cocks of dawn
When they salute the Sun-God, and revere
The burning angel of all lovers.

QUEEN GERTRUDE

Ah,
Hamlet, my Hamlet, princeling of my breast!
I must not stay, to falter. I must go,
To veil myself in an obscurer vision
Of that relentless hailing of the dawn,
And close my eyes to the other. But ere I go,
I leave with thee this little coil of gold,
Forged in that dawning hour of rubiate dreams
That slips now from my clutch, like a falling star
Vanishing in darkness, whence—I pray the God
Of sun-gods!—some other dawn shall bear to me,
On wild-dove-wings, a more enduring glimpse
Of that other vision, which doth now illume
Thy dear eyes, lost in Ophelia's. Take it, and after
You open its casing, read this letter, writ
In love, and fore-imagining, and hope
That what its brief lines tell, and fail to tell,
May not obliterate the boyhood trust,
Thy heart still holds, of me—thy mother—thy mother.

PRINCE HAMLET

[*Takes wonderingly from her hand a tiny parcel and a letter.*]

These—mysteries?—dear mother, with thy love,
I accept, whatever, open'd, they let fall.

QUEEN GERTRUDE

Acceptance is the suffering of us all.

[*She kisses him gently; then, moving swiftly to the doorway, pauses an instant to look back at him, before she goes.*
Prince Hamlet stands, for a moment, looking at the little packet in his hand; then unwraps it, opening a tiny case, and peers within, while Horatio watches him, during a breathless pause.]

PRINCE HAMLET

Horatio,—a ring. Great heaven,—*her* ring!
Her wedding ring, with the glowing opal-stone:
My mother's wedding ring!—A score of times,
I 've seen my father kiss it, on her finger:
Their wedding vow, in gold and opal-stone.—
What said she?—"Acceptance is the suffering"—
What mystery of suffering is here?
For what acceptance?—and by whom?—wherefore?
And why thus offer'd to me, now?—Mystery?
Aye, mystery more obscure than is the meaning
Of what we are: inexplicable—beyond
All meditation!

HORATIO

My lord, why meditate
Upon it? The letter in your hand—

PRINCE HAMLET

Aye, so—
Her letter!

[*Thrusting the ring-case in his breast, he unfolds the letter, and stands reading it, held in one hand; passes his other hand across his eyes; reads again; stands silent; tries to read the letter again;—drops it, with closed eyes and a half-audible cry.*]

Ah—ah—ah—ah!—No!

HORATIO

[*Approaching him, anxiously.*]

My lord, Hamlet!

PRINCE HAMLET

Acceptance—suffering—

HORATIO

[*Picking up the letter, reaches to restore it to him.*]

'T is here. You dropped it.

PRINCE HAMLET

Read it. Mine eyes are sered. Aloud, to me—
Very slowly—read it.

HORATIO

[*After a moment's hesitation, reads.*]

My son—my Hamlet—
I hope to tell thee this—but may not, all. In such case, here is the rest. I have accepted the Council's adjuration. After the feast is quieted, I wed thine Uncle Claudius.

Thy mother—still, thy mother.

[*Horatio stops, and speaks with solicitude.*]

My lord—

PRINCE HAMLET

The feast—my father's funeral feast—
After it is quieted—I wed—she weds—she—after
It is quieted—the feast—weds—weds . . weds . . *weds*
Him!

HORATIO

There 's a postscript. Have you read it, my lord?

PRINCE HAMLET

Postscript?—No. Read it.

HORATIO

Must I read—?

PRINCE HAMLET

What? Read what?
Acceptance—she accepts—him, him—*him!*—What!
A postscript to—to *that?*

HORATIO

Methinks, 't is brief.

PRINCE HAMLET

As memory—but not as *mine!* Read on.

HORATIO

I see, though, now, 't is longer than the letter.
[*He reads.*]

The ring. There is a morning time and an evening time. This ring is of the morning time. I am of the night. I pray thee, give it to her, who is of the morning, still, as token for her to remember, never to leave the morning behind, when the evening appeareth, for both are one day. I am night. May thou and thy Ophelia be ever of the morning!

PRINCE HAMLET
[*With moaning cry.*]

Ophelia—Ophelia—Ophelia!

HORATIO

My dear lord—

PRINCE HAMLET

Suffering—acceptance—yes.
But why accept more?
[*Taking it from his breast.*]
Here 's the ring, Horatio.

Take it. Keep it. Bury it in *thy* bosom,
Where passion of the morning never turneth
To night's satiety, because for thee
The stars are lit at noon. But let no ray
Of the heart's-blood hue of its opal-stone ever pierce
The soul of my Ophelia!
[*Giving Horatio the ring, he sinks upon a chair, where Horatio bends over him, tenderly.*]

HORATIO

I 'll keep it safe.

PRINCE HAMLET

My father in heaven, dost thou behold my mother
In hell? My mother, there, dost thou behold my father
In the hell of beholding thee on earth? Do ye both
Perceive your son, conceiving the woe of each—
Woe, woven of memory and forgetfulness!—
Horatio, methinks, I see thee bending
O'er me, to gaze on me—and me, myself,
Gazing on my father's and my mother's gazes,
Drifting into darkness.—Hark!—Is it thee, God-Father?—
Silence . . . only Thy silence!

DARKNESS.

ACT FIFTH

Scene Four

The darkness turns to pale, evening twilight, revealing a glimpse of OPHELIA'S BEDROOM *—the vine-clambered frame of a Gothic window, against which is silhouetted the hung bird-cage of Amsel, empty, and beside it* OPHELIA, *seated, telling the beads of her rosary.*

OPHELIA

Pater noster, qui es in cœlis,
Sanctificétur nomen tuum!

[*She drops the rosary in her lap, and spreads out there a crushed script, reading it aloud in low, soft tones, stifled by faint sobbings.*]

Lady, loveliest of the lost—
Return to thy nunnery!

Wherefore didst thou emerge, to freshen this desert world? The wells are dried up, here. In the sered oases, the song of our love-bird hath ceased. Dumbness reigneth over all. The deaf are the blessed. The blind possess their salvation.

Oh, turn again to thy nunnery—to thy convent walls return! And in thy casement window there, plant in one pot two sprays: the slip of a valley-lily, the sprig of a rose-hawthorn. And, while the Pleiads are rising in the east, tend the sprays to bloom again for us—my once Ophelia—thine erstwhile

Alcyone.

[*She reaches toward the open-swung door of the bird-cage.*]

O, Amsel dear! Come back—come back to me!

She weeps beside the empty cage, while the pale light is deepening into darkness, as

THE CURTAIN FALLS.

ACT FIFTH

Scene Five

Out of the silent darkness, rises sound of far-off
TRUMPETS,
increasing slowly in nearness and in volume till their brazen tones burst in a climactic blaring of sonorous triumph, intermingled with deep and shrill
VOICES,
hailing in wildly excited acclamation the suddenly-illumined contours of
A BALCONY OF THE CASTLE,
where KING CLAUDIUS *and* QUEEN GERTRUDE, *standing aloft, smiling, in their splendid crowns, sparkling with prismatic jewels, are receiving the homage of the* Lords, Courtiers, *and armoured* Liegemen *of the Castle, hemmed round by the thronging* Retainers, *in the obscurity below—from which their lifted Spears, raised Shield-tops and tossing Caps emerge upwards into the Radiance, accompanied by the Clamour of* Shaken Shields, Beaten Drums, *and the* Hoarse Shoutings *of the Multitude.*

SHOUTS
[*In rhythmic wave-tones of the Voices and the Trumpetings.*]

Huzzah! Huzzah! Huzzah! Huzzah! Huzzah!
God save the King and Queen—the King and Queen!
Claudius and Gertrude! Claudius and Gertrude! The Crown!
The Double-Crown of Gertrude and Claudius!
Queen and King, together! King and Queen!
Denmark for the Danes! Elsinore forever! Elsinore!
Huzzah! Huzzah! Elsinore! ELSINORE!! ELSINORE!!!

DARKNESS.

[*The Clamour slowly diminishes into Silence.*]

ACT FIFTH

*Scene Six**

To a marching tune, Music of Hautboys, Flutes *and* Harps *is heard, preceding the curtain's rise, which reveals another scene in Elsinore:*

WS

A ROOM OF STATE IN THE CASTLE.

Enter the KING [Claudius], QUEEN [Gertrude], [Prince] HAMLET, POLONIUS, LAERTES, VOLTIMAND, CORNELIUS, *and Lords Attendant.*

King. Though yet of Hamlet our dear brother's death
The memory be green; and that it us befitted
To bear our hearts in grief, and our whole kingdom
To be contracted in one brow of woe;
Yet so far hath discretion fought with nature,
That we with wisest sorrow think on him,
Together with remembrance of ourselves.
Therefore our sometime sister, now our queen,
The imperial jointress of this warlike state,
Have we, as 't were, with a defeated joy,
With one auspicious and one dropping eye;
With mirth in funeral, and with dirge in marriage
In equal scale, weighing delight and dole,
Taken to wife: nor have we herein barr'd
Your better wisdoms, which have freely gone
With this affair along:—For all, our thanks . . . .
But now, my cousin Hamlet, and my son,—
Hamlet. [*Aside.*] A little more than kin, and less than kind.
King. How is it that the clouds still hang on you?
Hamlet. Not so, my lord, I am too much i' the sun.
Queen. Good Hamlet, cast thy nightly colour off,
And let thine eye look like a friend on Denmark.

*Shakespeare's *Hamlet,* Act I, Scene II: The "Room of State" is the "Hall of the Double-Throne."

Do not, for ever, with thy veiled lids
Seek for thy noble father in the dust:
Thou know'st, 't is common; all that lives must die,
Passing through nature to eternity.
Hamlet. Ay, madam, it is common.
Queen. If it be,
Why seems it so particular with thee?
Hamlet. Seems, madam! nay, it is; I know not seems.
'T is not alone my inky cloak, good mother,
Nor customary suits of solemn black,
Nor windy suspiration of forc'd breath,
No, nor the fruitful river in the eye,
Nor the dejected haviour of the visage,
Together with all forms, moods, shows of grief,
That can denote me truly: These, indeed, seem,
For they are actions that a man might play:
But I have that within which passeth show;
These, but the trappings and the suits of woe.
King. 'T is sweet and commendable in your nature, Hamlet,
To give these mourning duties to your father:
But, you must know, your father lost a father;
That father lost, lost his; and the survivor bound
In filial obligation, for some term
To do obsequious sorrow: But to persever
In obstinate condolement, is a course
Of impious stubbornness; 't is unmanly grief . . . .
For what, we know, must be, and is as common
As any the most vulgar thing to sense,
Why should we, in our peevish opposition,
Take it to heart? Fie! 't is a fault to heaven,
A fault against the dead, a fault to nature,
To reason most absurd; whose common theme
Is death of fathers, and who still hath cried,
From the first corse, till he that died to-day,
This must be so. We pray you, throw to earth

This unprevailing woe; and think of us
As of a father: for let the world take note
You are the most immediate to our throne . . . .
Our chiefest courtier, cousin, and our son.

Queen. Let not thy mother lose her prayers, Hamlet . . . .

Hamlet. I shall in all my best obey you, madam.

King. Why, 't is a loving and a fair reply;
Be as ourself in Denmark.—Madam, come;
This gentle and unforc'd accord of Hamlet
Sits smiling to my heart: in grace whereof,
No jocund health that Denmark drinks to-day,
But the great cannon to the clouds shall tell;
And the king's rouse the heaven shall bruit again,
Re-speaking earthly thunder. Come away.

[*Exeunt King, Queen, Lords, &c., Polonius, and Laertes.*]

Hamlet. O, that this too too solid flesh would melt,
Thaw, and resolve itself into a dew!
Or that the Everlasting had not fix'd
His canon 'gainst self-slaughter! O God! O God!
How weary, stale, flat, and unprofitable
Seem to me all the uses of this world!
Fie on 't! O fie! 't is an unweeded garden,
That grows to seed; things rank, and gross in nature,
Possess it merely. That it should come to this!
But two months dead!—nay, not so much, not two;
So excellent a king; that was, to this,
Hyperion to a satyr: so loving to my mother,
That he might not beteem the winds of heaven
Visit her face too roughly. Heaven and earth!
Must I remember? why, she would hang on him,
As if increase of appetite had grown
By what it fed on: And yet, within a month— . . . .
Ere yet the salt of most unrighteous tears
Had left the flushing of her gallèd eyes,
She married;—O most wicked speed, to post

With such dexterity to incestuous sheets;
It is not, nor it cannot come to, good;
But break, my heart; for I must hold my tongue!

——— WS

[*He presses his clutched hand over his eyes.*]

DARKNESS.

out of which, in deep tones of his father's voice, is heard a heart-moaned cry:[5]

Hamlet! . . Remember me! . . .

POSTLUDE

VOICES OF THE INVISIBLE

Vox Sola [Tenor.]

CHORUS

CURTAIN.

Finis.

SUPPLEMENT

PREFACE AS AFTERWORD

THIS WORK was experienced rather than "written," and is concerned chiefly with realities of experience. The writing of it was incidental to the revealing of it. For it was not planned beforehand by me. It was compelled—with exacting, disciplinary gentleness—by powers within and beyond this material scene: powers to obey whose creative will became my agonizing and inspiring mandate. Those powers are no rhetorical allusions, no poetic allegories, no literary apostrophes. They are immortal realities, akin to our highest selves: transcendent powers of that mysterious "bourn" from which [despite a poignant phrase of the great soliloquy] some travellers may return. I know, because I am one—doubtless one amongst unnumbered others throughout the ages—who briefly has crossed over that bourn, and has lived to return with living records from beyond it—contained in this volume.

> *"There 's a divinity that shapes our ends,*
> *Rough-hew them how we will."*

I did much arduous rough-hewing of this work. It was the "divinity" who silently and easily shaped its ends. By its nature, then, imitation has had no part in producing it. Inwardly and outwardly it grew as a tree grows—as a flower grows—from mysterious seed.

Its seed was planted more than half a century ago; grew—during the years 1896-99 and 1916—into two other branching works, less in stature [*A Garland to Sylvia* and *Caliban*], and—during the years of World War II and thereafter, 1939-44—matured into this Tetralogy, which comprises the third, fourth, fifth, and sixth parts of a Heptalogy, the seventh part of which—sequential to Shakespeare's *Hamlet* —is still in the making.

The total making has been a subtle kind of collaboration between two sensitive human beings in touch with supersensible beings: a kind of collaboration having in no sense anything whatever to do with so-called practical affairs. The names of the two human beings are Marion Morse and Percy MacKaye, who were wedded, in 1898, and are, in this work, the aliases of *Sylvia* and *Felix*. In a way, they are to each other nameless: it suffices they are woman and man, conscious beings who are mated. But the use of names is a convenience and here is needful. So with truth I say here of Marion this: Without her, this work would not be. With her, it is what it is, thus far, because the years-long needful opportunity for communion with her in solitude was forthcoming. If similar opportunity shall again be granted, hopefully the completion of the whole work may with her always-continuing help be attained before I die.

In a sentence of his profound Commentary on this work, my dear friend, Erlo van Waveren, writes: "One might conclude that MacKaye's development of the Hamlet myth reveals the unfolding of a pattern of doom." Such apparent conclusion as to doom is sufficiently clarified away by him in his comprehensive essay. For myself, I would add, simply for double clearness: Personally, I have all faith in the surpassing powers for good in the universe. In that faith of poetry—which is the theme of my own essay, *Poesia Religio*—I might indeed, as poet, term myself a serene pessimist, who harbours in his heart no refuge of optimism for the ultimate triumph of evil.

Concerning the structure of this Tetralogy, the planning art of play-writing has had much, yet almost nothing to do with it: much, because I am a playwright; *almost nothing,* because almost no portion of it was consciously foreplanned. Having been born in and of the theatre, the craft of making plays for professional actors and productions became early familiar to me. My interest in the craft was always a poet's interest, wherein making money, though often very important to a poet's existence, is wholly unimportant to his reason for being a poet. Having to deal with theatrical managers I had need for making scenarios of my plays, and I made them, both for the managers and for myself. In the case of this work, however, there was no such need and no such possibility. I made no scenario of it, and could not have made one, for myself or anybody, because from the start I did not know its outcome, except in cloudiest outlines.

Living alone, during most of the time, for nearly four years, while writing it, I had no thought of theatre managers, or of book publishers. I had thought only of fulfilling a sacred task imposed on me—not against my will, but conforming my will to the will of powers far greater than my own, as *Felix* in the "Prelude" of this work has expressed it to *Sylvia*—in their dialogue concerning Shakespeare—the challenging task:

"for the soul of man
To measure himself with the mightiest, and earn
The privilege of reverence to serve
The imagining powers of poesie, who wrought
Through him his masterwork.

SYLVIA

And you have dared,
Felix, to answer the challenge!

FELIX

No, not dared
But obeyed the powers. I have obeyed their law:
To listen, intensely listen, only to them—
To them alone—none else. The rest is theirs,
Who *are* the poem—not mine, their instrument.

SYLVIA

Their instrument attuned to them.

FELIX

So only
Could it convey their modulating voices.
If I have lapsed, 't is where I did not listen
Keen enough, not where I dared, or feared to dare
Anything. For to love demands no daring,
And all this garland is a love token."

This work is thus a blending of two creative sequences: the outward dramatic sequence of four Plays with a Prelude, and the inward lyric sequence of a single Story: the story of Sylvia and Felix, who—in communion with the mystery of what God wills—are the makers of the "fourfold wreath" of this Tetralogy—woven by them as an enduring love-token for all who will to put their trust in love.

PERCY MACKAYE

The Players, 16 Gramercy Park, New York, The First of June, 1949:
Tenth Anniversary of the Death of Marion Morse MacKaye
at St. Germain-en-Laye, France

COMMENTARY

An Interpretation of the Hamlet Tetralogy

by ERLO VAN WAVEREN

IN writing a commentary on a profound work of poetry such as Percy MacKaye's Tetralogy of plays on Hamlet, King of Denmark, I am fully aware of the many difficulties involved. It is therefore with great humility that I approach the task of writing about MacKaye, the mythmaker, and his development of the Hamlet Saga.

In the years to come there may well be other commentaries written on these plays, from their theatrical, literary, or other aspects. My opinions and statements are the result of many searching discussions with the author. Years of concentrated work on symbols, legends, and myths made me realize the unusual quality of this work. Mr. MacKaye handles primitive forces and Christian principles in such a straightforward and pithy manner, that it is refreshing in our time—as it will be in times to come—to read or see these plays.

My great personal interest is in the fact that Percy MacKaye translated his life-experience into the timelessness of a myth. It is a rare thing to find an individual who has been able to transform the experiences of his deepest inner being into a product which can serve as a mirror for himself and those around him. It takes perception, genius, and the capacity to suffer, in order to extract out of our daily life those eternal patterns which are the very essence of our being.

Rembrandt, Spinoza, Shakespeare, St. Augustine, Beethoven, da Vinci, and others like them have achieved this. They are great lights who stand out through their unique accomplishments. In their time, many would have raised their eyebrows, had one mentioned their existence as being of triumphant and everlasting fame, or considered them pillars of help to our society and centers of inspiration for ages to come.

On the other hand, Frans Snyders, Fénelon, St. Wilfred, Tycho Brahe, who in their time were regarded as great lights, now have faded into the vast cavalcade of the gifted. In their struggle with life they added a smaller contribution to the alchemical work of our evolution.

Where Percy MacKaye belongs we do not know and we cannot judge; the generations to come will judge for us. Life itself will deal with his wondrous eventful plays. But at all times these plays will have a place in the development of the myth for there is history in this book. It is the history of the development of the Hamlet Saga.

Hamlet was brought to our modern civilization in Shakespeare's immortal play, a play based on an ancient myth. Like most myths, it is a story shared by many peoples. Its original source is hidden in the annals of the development of the human psyche. The earliest historians to write about this legend were the Romans, Livy and Valerius Maximus, and the Greek, Dionysius of Halicarnassus. Their Hamlet was called Lucius Junius Brutus, who feigned insanity to escape the persecution of his uncle, who had usurped the ruling power. This was part of the mythological history of the Roman Empire.

Nine centuries later, when the great Persian historian and poet Firdausi wrote his epic poem, he recorded the same legend from papers which were gathered for centuries by the Persian Shahs. Then among the ancient myths we also have the tales of Bellerophon, Heracles, and Servius Tullius, as well as the story of Orestes—all closely related to the Hamlet Saga.

The Danish historian and poet, Saxo Grammaticus, might well have known about the existence of some of these myths. However, the lost Skjoldungar Saga was said to have contained the Amleth myth, and that Saga would be closer to his Scandinavian background. His Amleth was a royal prince in the mythological history of Denmark. The English counterpart was also more mythological than historical. Part of the Amleth myth, including his travels in England, belonged so typically to the hero pattern that it was often taken as a separate tale altogether.

It is an interesting fact that in so many countries early historians took up the myth as part of the history of their own country. It is of no great importance whether they copied from each other or not; the main thing is that the Hamlet story seemed to belong naturally to their own mythological history. It was accepted by the peoples of the different countries as part of their own background, an integral part of their folklore and folk-soul.

It was in the sixteenth century that this old, old story, accepted by the peoples and belonging to them for centuries, was developed by the greatest of all dramatists, William Shakespeare. He succeeded in bringing this legendary tale to life for us, making it the greatest drama for centuries to come. The ancient Amleth became our Hamlet, a hero of modern time.

In 1559, approximately forty years previous to this great event, the story had been recorded anew by François de Belleforest in his *Histoire Tragique.* The Elizabethan intellectual knew this book well. However, the mere recording of a myth does not give it new life. Any myth goes to sleep when it can no longer carry our projections. It loses its power and ceases to function as history advances. It comes to life again when a new myth writer can project into the prototype of the tale the problems, achievements, and sufferings of his age. By this recreating process he enlivens the sleeping myth.

Shakespeare selected the prototype of the Amleth Myth, the royal usurper-uncle in conflict with the nephew, who feigned madness. All other characters recreated or created anew by Shakespeare must have appeared as of necessity to bring his Hamlet version about. The old characters received a new cloak, and new characters took their places to become in their turn familiar to us all. The eternal question of "to be or not to be," with all its complexities, was brought into new light.

Under Shakespeare's hands the ancient folk tale became a play. Its function can best be likened to that of the ancient mystery plays. Like them, it enacts our inner drama, and we easily recognize the voices speaking through the various characters. For three hundred and fifty years this play has kept vitality and vigour. Through all these years it has served as a vehicle for many actor-creators. Many new Hamlets were created on the stage, but no new Hamlet was created in writing; for as long as there is such power and vitality in the characters drawn by Shakespeare there is no necessity for a new expression.

However, the myth develops as the psyche of the people develops. Its life depends upon the psychic need of the owners of the myth, the people. The fact that Percy MacKaye was forced from within to continue this saga-play might well suggest the possibility that our need has helped to bring this development about. It is quite in keeping with the present-day search for greater clarity within, that this development is achieved by going to the roots of the Hamlet tragedy. Seldom do we have the opportunity of witnessing the growth of a myth; but now it is possible for us to speak and commune with the author and the source within him.

Percy MacKaye has distinguished himself with his plays and masques; he has been an outstanding poet for the last fifty years. It is a great privilege for us to be present at the birth of his life-poem, a tetralogy of plays on Hamlet, "King—Father—Royal Dane,"—King of Denmark.

The father-ghost of Prince Hamlet has come out of darkness and with him, his devoted court jester Yorick. The ghost and the skull have come to life as full-fledged characters.

The development of the Tetralogy is intimately related to the life story of Percy MacKaye. In *Annals of an Era* we read about the accomplishments of the MacKaye family. It shows a true American background of cultural achievements. However, it tells only half the story; the rich inner life, the marvellous worlds of make-believe and fantasy, cannot be put into annals. They live on in poetry, in the imaginative plays, masques, and Kentucky legends, created and recreated by Percy MacKaye. His youth was fancy free and highly coloured, alive with the happy glows and with the tragic events of an acutely sensitive nature. At times the top layers of daily life were fearful burdens, threatening to dampen the colourful riches of the archaic forces within. Throughout his life this struggle has endlessly continued. Buona Fortuna and Mother Disaster become prominent factors in such a nature.

MacKaye's famous actor-father, Steele MacKaye, did not provide an ideal setting in the conventional sense. There were ups and downs, riches and poverty; but at all times an enormous vitality supported the vivid imagination of the boy.

The first great change and shock in MacKaye's life came when he was nearly fourteen. It was the death of his brother Will, six and a half years his senior. It had been Will who had introduced him at an early age to the worlds of foreign gods, gnomes, and the entire galaxy of the mythological world. Through him had come the contact with the "green world." "Poog's Pasture," a Vermont meadow, became the setting of many of their magic tales. There it was that young MacKaye experienced the very nature of the "kingdom in the grass," which was to become such an important part of Yorick's prayer:

"Let no man's foot trespass
Thy kingdom in the grass
His fellow's to gain."

Or, to put it less lyrically; let no man go against that green chthonic world, abode of all nature spirits, for self-gain. In modern times we see a striking example in the Irish, who recognize a power in the "green folk" and still use this symbology in their daily life. The snake and the frog, redeeming and "gold-spewing" symbols, both belong to this world. These nature spirits can work positively or negatively. A recognition of their powers has existed in all primitive societies, and many gods have been created in their honour. Since ancient times we have been advised to respect the nature spirits. A Yorick is well aware of their powers and, because of that, is in close contact with nature's wisdom.

Will MacKaye, who had a close affiliation with this green world, died as a young man. For a year Percy did not attend school, in order to compile and edit all the writings of his brother, amounting to about one hundred thousand words. By the end of that year, he looked so much like his brother that an intimate friend of Will's was quite overcome by the striking resemblance.

Will is a powerful spirit behind the scenes in the Tetralogy. His life was not to be lost; that which could be carried on by the younger brother went on as his spiritual burden and asset.

At eighteen MacKaye entered Harvard, and three years later the greatest event in his life took place. This was the introduction to Marion Morse on the village green. About two years later they were married. The sensitivity of Mrs. MacKaye was extraordinary and carried a truly prophetic sense. She could always follow the flights of her husband, but at times her feminine intuition would take the lead. There is little need to write much about her here, for her life is woven into the Tetralogy. She is part of it. For what is this myth but a tale of human souls struggling with the powers of good and evil, a tragic song of love for creation, and the life-myth of Percy and Marion MacKaye?

On June 1st, 1939, Mrs. MacKaye died. It was just before her sudden death that her husband wrote the first lines of their life-poem.

> "O, you are like a memory of young May
> When the pink hawthorn bows her posied cheek
> Deep in the droopt laburnum, where shy birds
> Utter their honeyed vowellings of love
> In plashing drops, like shooken dews from eaves,
> On the daisy sod beneath."

These words are spoken by Prince Hamlet to Ophelia. They describe the beautiful garden in France, at St. Germain-en-Laye, where Marion spent her last days. There she wrote in her diary about her deep satisfaction that her husband was writing again. The great work, which they both knew had to be written, had been a long time in coming. MacKaye's poet-daemon had been silent for some time. Only lesser works had been accomplished. As we contemplate the long years in which his prolific pen was less active, we might venture an explanation of their necessity. Those years were full of difficulties and personal tragedy.

The distillation of life's process is a fearfully cruel experience. It takes us far from this world into the unknown and unseen. During that time we can only pray God for His mercy and grace, that we may survive the darkness and come again into light and understanding. The outer world is far away and cannot be reached. Faith is tested many times, until in the end a new understanding rises from within, purified and strengthened, bringing with it a rebirth.

On that long lonely path the love and companionship of his wife was MacKaye's greatest solace. But he came back with the work they had waited for. The seeds were sown, harvest would be later. The last entry in Marion MacKaye's diary—the last words she ever wrote—

were written on May 27th, 1939. She wrote of him there: "His acts and thoughts now envisage a great cosmic work of life-creation." Those words were prophetic indeed: "the work of life-creation" was forthcoming. However, preliminary to it and directly springing from his personal sorrow, a small book of songs and sonnets was created, expressing the deepest experiences and feelings of their forty years of marriage. These lines from *My Lady Dear, Arise!* convey perhaps the quintessence of that lyric volume:

> "All *that* was ours, and not the world's affair.
> But now, the Immortal rises beyond rhyme . . .
> . . . .
> For Death is all the difference. Death makes share
> Of life and all of love—the world's affair."

Switzerland provided the shelter and haven for that poignant piece of writing. In 1940 MacKaye returned from war-torn Europe. The quiet town of Littleton, very near his boyhood home of Shirley Center, Massachusetts—scene of so many happy memories—provided the seclusion needed for his work. Again an inward journey had to be made into the vast spaces of the unknown, but this time the record was kept. Thoughts took shape and could be put into words. The entire life-experience was recreated, always with an awareness of his wife as leading spirit and mentor. Powerful forces from the collective unconscious forced their way, and used the instrument forged through sorrow, suffering, and love.

There was no direct knowledge of the shape the poem would eventually take. The clearest statement that could possibly be made about the creative source from which this myth developed, was given to me by Percy MacKaye himself. Slowly and after long concentration, he answered my query with the following words:

> "Utter loneliness—the pang of sorrow—the bliss of concentration—physical illness—the glory and wonder and livingness of English words—the anticipation of oncoming creative images—from these ceaselessly unfolded the scenes and acts and characters of the expanding work, the ultimate, final outlines of which were still but cloudily envisioned."

It is a beautiful and true statement. Thus the Hamlet Myth received its new life-blood. With MacKaye it grew into its new phase, which brought with it the wise Gallucinius, the primitive Yorick, and the saintly Father Celestino as three different aspects of our Christian faith.

MacKaye's life-experience of the green world, the kingdom of the grass, was given to Yorick; all that which wrestled fervently to attain the accomplishment of purpose belonged to Claudius. All that which was spirit and strove for purification was for Hamlet the King. Thus every character was created in its own way.

The development of the Hamlet Saga has as its main theme the strife between two brothers: one searching for spiritual values; the other for earthy realizations. It is the primitive fight between spirit and matter which, in their endless striving, creates our possibility for development. We are constantly drawn into that fight, which is part of our creation. Within it is our struggle for individual consciousness. In the East it has been recognized as the struggle within us to become creators in our own right.* It is the story of "What We Will."

A new and powerful character was created in Gallucinius, towering in consciousness, never interfering, but teaching and providing that wisdom which can lead to greater consciousness. He is the all-knowing spirit. The fact that he plays such an important role in the lives of King Hamlet and Claudius shows that both have achieved a high level of consciousness, in which the voice of the Wise Man is listened to. Neither can take advantage of his counsel, as the primitive forces in them are too powerful. The Christian virtues—of love, humility, sacrifice—although recognized, are not sufficiently developed in the characters of Hamlet and Claudius to counterbalance their instinctive impulses. This is the chief reason for their ultimate doom. Both have first to experience what St. John of the Cross has termed "the dark night" before they can handle their primitivity and succeed in this world with a Christian consciousness as their main strength.

I would like to regard the Castle of Elsinore as the castle of our mind, where we find present, as in their natural abode, Gallucinius,

*See: *The Secret of the Golden Flower* (a Chinese book of life) tr. from Chinese, and explained by Richard Wilhelm (New York: Harcourt Brace, 1932).

the Queen, Moll Cowslip and Topas, as well as a host of other people, who are there by virtue of their inherent nature. As we develop our minds, the intensity of the archaic values recedes and is assimilated. Primitive outlines grow constantly dimmer, and we think we have overcome nature and its law. We imagine ourselves to be living in a world of our own willing. Our insight in life, and our experience with it, has made us apparently masters of our fate. At that moment we experience victory and a man-made life. For some that is a worthy achievement. For others the powers of the inner being are too strong to be overruled by the mind. Their psyche demands a greater expansion and must experience a life that stems from the greater source within us. To those individuals Mother Disaster seems to lend a helpful hand, overthrowing all that has been created by intellect and power, which is not true to their inner nature. The old world of the mind and brain is taken away and recognized as insufficient. This experience, which can be regarded as the dark night, offers great opportunities. In that darkness a spark of the divine inner being may be experienced, which becomes the center of the new life. Neither King Hamlet nor Claudius were capable of achieving this.

Thus in an endless chain of events we go through the doing and undoing, and learn a way of living true to our own individual natures. It is an enormous task to take these cycles of life and put them into myth form. Daily living and our identifications with it prevent us from seeing and recognizing the patterns and powers of everlasting life. We are too engrossed in our likes and dislikes, too embedded in our routine, to recognize in our daily life the powers of eternally enduring laws. The myth contains these laws as well as daily life.

It is the transcendent quality of genius that it can lift daily happenings into the timeless realm of the myth. In it, we are profoundly attracted to the story, for we experience our own natures through the characters and recognize our struggles, past and present.

In the experience of the human race, there are endless struggles for survival in the physical, emotional, and spiritual worlds. The myth-writer takes these three worlds and moulds them into one. From within the psyche rises that co-ordinator of life which can blend every experience lived, understood or not understood, and shape it in an everlasting form. This work is not done by the mind or heart alone. It is done by a force which works with the mind and heart, purifying both until they can become the tools of that which is timeless in us.

When we compare the differences between Shakespeare and MacKaye and their Hamlets, we are confronted with a startling literary kinship. There must be some similarity between the characters of these poet-dramatists. Both were profoundly attracted to the same tale, which provided the vehicle for their deepest life philosophy. In the case of MacKaye, the primitive quality of the characters is drawn with such force and clarity that to me it is inconceivable that these plays should be considered imitative. Wherever Shakespeare's themes are employed, we must look for a deeper purpose than mere quotation. In the second play we find mention of the theme "to be or not to be." Yorick, educating young Hamlet, brings up that fundamental question. In the last play we come to the very root of that query. King Hamlet reads St. Augustine's *Confessions* in a desperate attempt to solve his dilemma. His search brings him to the lines in which the saint experienced Oneness with God and the great state of To Be. Percy MacKaye quotes these very words of Augustine and was impelled to do so by the nature of his writing. In like manner words and themes of Shakespeare are sometimes used. In some instances the words of Shakespeare are employed to integrate or tie the plays together. However, to the perceptive reader it will be obvious that there is no attempt to imitate Shakespeare or to produce an illusion of Shakespearean writing.

Many will have a sense of being familiar with themes or passages here and there throughout the Tetralogy. This is a phenomenon that often happens with writings which come from a source we all share. However, it is the genius of the author which makes this possible. By his words and writings he puts the reader in contact with the archetypes and thus connects him with his own roots. All truly inspirational writing has that power. It has that power regardless of whether we understand the full meaning or not. We never know the full meaning of our life, and still it is familiar to us.

The myth is a story which belongs *a priori* to the human race. The development of the myth is intimately connected with the development of the psyche of the people to whom the myth belongs. One might conclude from this that MacKaye's development of the Hamlet Myth reveals the unfolding of a pattern of doom. These plays show the dimming of the Christian voice of Father Celestino, the undoing of the loving devotion and wisdom of Yorick—willing to turn the other cheek and in so doing, being killed. The great Gallucinius who wakens "all drowsy earth-dwellers to insight" is not heeded.

Indeed it seems prophetic that this tale has been written now.

One might almost say that writing of this kind was forced upon the author. The persistence of the creative source was kindled by more than just a personal desire. The very scope of conception, which grew slowly to its present stage, to me shows a design beyond MacKaye's conscious purpose. This "larger-than-I" pattern, familiar to all creative individuals, might well have been set into motion by the demand of a collective need. The pattern seeks expression and so forces itself through the channel of an individual sensitive enough to receive it and cope with its demands.

The times create great men, and great men help to mould their times. It is the interlocking of an inner and an outer world, a duality of existence. Many writers have voiced ideas apparently dormant in mankind or their country. It is as if they were called upon by their times and surroundings to voice a request of the collective psyche. Sorrow, love, turmoil—all the emotions that make up our human experience—desire a channel in which to perpetuate the moment, and force their way into a record. It is on the common level of mankind that they find their greatest meaning and ultimate goal. There they are born and begin their mortal round. This law is beautifully illustrated by Shakespeare. Prince Hamlet, dying, makes a last request of his friend Horatio:

> "If thou didst ever hold me in thy heart,
> Absent thee from felicity a while,
> And in this harsh world draw thy breath in pain,
> To tell my story."

It was the Horatio in Shakespeare who wrote the story of Hamlet. Horatio—strong, loyal, simple, apparently not outstanding or recognized by the world. It is that simple element which, because of its love and devotion to the greater, can achieve a profound record. It is the Horatios in mankind who participate at the feast of the gods, watch their game, and devoutly help that which is greater than themselves. It is in this great love for human endeavour that we place ourselves in direct contact with the highest within.

Shakespeare pays tribute to Horatio and describes him as a man who takes fortune's buffets and rewards with equal thanks; and whose "blood and judgement are so well commingled that they are not a pipe for fortune's finger to sound what stop she please."

Only when the Horatian qualities of serenity and balance can be achieved do we come to the place from which an impartial record is written. All is transposed to an impersonal stage. We participate in a drama of life which has been transformed into the timelessness of the myth. Thus it becomes a record which belongs to all of us. Although many powerful forces might have run through the author of this Tetralogy, it is only the Horatio in Percy MacKaye who could bring it to us in this form.

So we find in Percy MacKaye a friend who has given us a story of the gods and heroes of our time. He shows a downfall of love and wisdom and faith, but in the very way he presents this disintegration there is recognition of a continuing spirit. This is implied by the very last lines of Gallucinius, addressed to King Hamlet on his way to doom and death:

"Whatever woe,
Forever, unseen, beside thee—*I* will go!"

Gallucinius—"the echo-call of that immortal Cock of Morn, who wakes to vision of thine own eternity, the God within thyself, being thy Daemon"—that guiding spirit, is forever with us. It is our eternally integrating source.

Without this great spirit the development of Horatio would not be possible. It is Gallucinius, forever—unseen—beside us, who leads us on to the goal of

TO BE.

REFERENCE NOTES

THE GHOST OF ELSINORE

1. Entire passage, beginning p. 14, with "The air bites shrewdly," is from *Hamlet*, Act I, sc. 4. The accents which do not appear in Knight's edition are my own, which I have found, from rehearsals, are of help to actors.

2. Entire passage, beginning p. 19 with "Where wilt thou lead me?" is from *Hamlet*, Act I, sc. 5.

3. The actor who takes the part of Yorick should never utter his songs or lilts in a manner resembling operatic or music-hall singing. He should utter them with the natural spontaneity of a folk singer, in a manner resembling the "poeters" of the Kentucky Mountains and of regions in Scotland and England still unspoiled by the radio. In both of these regions my wife and I have had personal experience and know that such natural folk-singing emanates from a special genius on the part of the singer, or lilter. In Scotland, for example, at the Globe Inn at Dumfries, in 1937, we joined in an informal get-together of local bards. One of them, a young genius named Thompson, lilted to melodies of his own improvising, some 15 or 20 rhymed snatches, directly and humorously hitting off the characteristics of each of his fellow bards [including ourselves] in succession, while he half-danced from one to the other, toasting each in a pewter can of ale. At the conclusion, he had totally forgotten the words he had uttered.

Such instances were fairly common in the days of Robert Burns; they are rare but existent today. They characterize the qualities of Yorick as court-fool at Elsinore. They also seem to characterize the "possel o' poeters" [once so termed by Uncle John Fiddler, of Pine Mountain, Harlan County, Kentucky], who are responsible for the existence of this Tetralogy, i.e., Sylvia and Felix.

Though I have sometimes used the word "song" and sometimes "lilt" the qualities above described pertain equally to both.

See also Note on Music, p. 673. Those interested in obtaining musical notation for these lilts and songs should address me, in care of the publisher.

4. *The maiden's milkpath* is an ancient folk name for the Milky Way.

5. Cf. pp. 65-66 of the "Prelude."

6. This allusion to crows that "caw in parliament for stolen corn" was written in my hermitage solitude at the very moment when the forces of Hitler had taken over "the breed of Norse" in Norway, where at the moment they were "kingless," while in Denmark the Danes of "their own breed" were still "king'd, praise God!" This is but one instance of many contemporary overtones and undertones which permeate the Tetralogy. The same is true of the allusions on p. 69 to the *V* of Victory, so often expressed by Winston Churchill's eloquent forefinger and middle finger.

7. Saxo Grammaticus states concerning the legendary Hamlet [Amleth]: "As they passed the sand-hills, and bade him look at the meal, meaning the sand, he replied that it had been ground small by the hoary tempests of the ocean."

8. Cf. *Hamlet*, Act I, sc. 1.

THE FOOL IN EDEN GARDEN

1. Padre Celestino da Alatri, with whom I read Dante's *Divine Comedy* at the Cappucin Convent near Frascati-Rome, is the prototype of the play's Padre Celestino. The couplet with which he greets Hamlet and Gertrude was inscribed over the gate of the convent.

2. The passages quoted in italics, beginning with "Give me the cups," are from *Hamlet*, Act V, sc. 2.

3. *Hamlet, ibid.*

4. For this and song on p. 177, use the music of the old song: "The boar's head in hand bring I."

5. From John Mathews Manly, *Specimens of Pre-Shakespearean Drama* (New York: Ginn & Co., 1897), I, 1-12: "The Story of the Creacion of Eve, with the Expellyng of Adam and Eve Out of Paradyce"; my adaptation of the two versions of *The Grocers' Play of Norwich:* [first version composed before June 16, 1533; the other in 1565]. The words, here spelled as in the original, are pronounced with European sounding vowels, especially the French *u*; *ee* for *I* [but slurred so that the audience knows one means "I"]; a trilling *r* and sibilant *s*; and spoken with an archaic Irish flavour, so that "sweet" is pronounced "swate"; "leave" is "lave"; and so forth. Where such pronunciation would sacrifice the meaning to modern ears, it is wise to modify this rule slightly.

6. Entire passage from Dante's *Divine Comedy*, beginning "And then the ghost of the great-hearted answered" is from "Inferno," Canto 2 [ll. 43–72]. The translation is mine.

7. *Hamlet*, Act III, sc. 3.

8. Cf. *My Lady Dear, Arise!* pp. 25, 39, 175.

9. Gertrude's dream, pp. 217ff:—cf. Queen Gertrude's description of Ophelia's drowning

[*Hamlet,* Act IV, sc. 7].

10. *Hamlet,* Act IV, sc. 5

11. "So runs," says Rudolf Steiner, founder of the Goetheanum, Switzerland, "the complete title of that Faust who lived in the 16th century, as a representative of the moribund clairvoyance, that Faust who still had a vision into the spiritual worlds even though the vision was chaotic."

12. The careful use and selection of bells, wherever bell ringing occurs throughout the Tetralogy, is a very important factor in rightly producing the work. For example, in this play, an old bell with an iron clang to it is preferable to a modern bell. It must ring slowly and softly in this scene, so that Yorick's song is heard clearly above it.

13. *Hamlet,* Act V, sc. 1.

14. *Ibid.* Topas' lines are sung to the same traditional tune that was sung by the First Grave-Digger in Shakespeare's drama, and handed down ever since Shakespeare's time.

15. Cf. *Hamlet,* Act IV, sc. 5.

16. A "nicker" is an Anglo-Saxon term for a water-monster of the bogs and marshes. Cf. Grendel scene in my drama *Beowulf.*

17. A "horse-heel-hoof" is a term, coined by me, for the shallow, icy-snow replica of the concave hollow within the hind-foot, iron-shod heel of a horse, imprinted by the pressure of his weight —especially when climbing a steep, snowy, country hill-road—and cast off on the wintry track behind him, where it lies as a solid entity, icy hard, or semi-hard dependent upon the freezing-slush condition of the snow. In Cornish, New Hampshire, about 1907, my little son and daughter, Robin and Arvia, used to discover and treasure such mysterious horse-heel-hooves on the wintry hill-road near our home "The Wayside" [where later their sister Christy was born], and often I would chant to them—in high-and-low, hollow tones—the heavily aspirated couplet, which Yorick here intones to the children of Elsinore.

18. Cf. My Masque, *Caliban.*

19. Cf. "The Meadow Lark," by M.M.M. [Leaflet.]

20. Cf. "Facing Infinitude," *ibid.*

21. Cf. *My Lady Dear, Arise!* p. 35.

22. *See* Note 14, above.

ODIN AGAINST CHRISTUS

1. Cf. *Hamlet,* Act I, sc. 1.

2. Cf. *The Fool in Eden Garden,* p. 149. *See also* p. 147 for the passage "The Book of *Amor* hath as many leaves . . ." quoted herein in part.

3. Cf. *Hamlet,* Act IV, sc. 5.

4. *Ibid.*

5. Cf. *The Ghost of Elsinore,* pp. 42–43.

6. Gertrude's dance should be done in the spirit of the cellarage scene. The actress should study what Gallucinius has said about Tiberius' wine. No dance of a particular period, but of delirious imagination: no formal steps, and in contrast to the drunken folk dance which precedes it.

7. Cf. *King Lear,* Act IV, sc. 3.

8. Cf. *Fool in Eden Garden,* p. 194.

9. The full title-page of "this volume" reads as follows: "DOCTORIS JOHANNIS FAUSTI *sogenannter Manual-Höllenzwang, Wittenberg, 1524. Inhalt: Entdeckte höhere Kenntniss des Geheimnisses, aus der Karte sich zukünftige Dinge vorherzusagen. Die Salomonische Conjuration. Claviculae Salomonis et Theosophia Pneumatica. Cabulaischer Schlüssel. Die Länge unseres lieben Herrn und Heilandes Jesu Christi. Gewisse und wahrhafte Länge unserer lieben Frau, der gebenedeiten Himmelskönigin Maria. Englisches Glücks-Gebet.* ARCANUM MAGICUM, *der magische Metallspiegel. Theophrastus Paracelsus. Pius Quintus, Pontificis Maximi. Seelen-Ruf. Der gerechte Kornreutter.*"

10. Cf. *Fool in Eden Garden,* pp. 117 and 152.

11. Cf. *My Lady Dear, Arise!* p. 240.

12. Cf. *Caliban.*

13. The actor should actually trace this glyph with his forefinger, showing it to Ophelia. It is taken from the Faustus volume [p. 198] of which the title is quoted above.

14. It was Johann Gast [died 1572] a protestant pastor of Basel, who in his *Sermones Convivia-les* [Basel, 1543] first credited the magician with genuine supernatural gifts. Gast believed Faust to be in league with the devil, by whom, about 1525, he was ultimately carried off, and declared the performing horse and dog by which he was accompanied to be familiar and evil spirits.

15. Cf. *My Lady Dear, Arise!*

16. Cf. Marion's Ring Rhymes, Vol. I. *See also* Gertrude's dream, *Fool in Eden Garden,* pp. 208–209; and Note 9 for that play. *Also* Marion's Journal, June 15, 1898 and September 15, 1898.

17. *Fool in Eden Garden,* pp. 208–209.

18. Cf. "What Is She?" [A Sonnet of Sonnets, by P.M.]

19. Cf. Note 12 for *Fool in Eden Garden.* It is especially important here that the mounting climax of bells be achieved with the clang of *iron* bells.

20. II Cor., chap. 13.

THE SERPENT IN THE ORCHARD

1. Cf. *King Lear,* Act IV, sc. 6.

2. Following this song there has been omitted a very brief episode which may appear in a future edition.

For further information concerning the music for this song [as well as for "My sorrow is gone," pp. 24–25; "Give me thy heart," p. 187; "Sing, Sorrow, Sorrow," p. 235; "Come, come, come, come," pp. 263–264; "Night will glower," p. 323; "Who's king," pp. 363 and 377; "Sickle, Shepherd's Crook and Shears," pp. 499–500] write the author, in care of the publisher. The Mist-Mothers' singing first occurs in the "Prelude" [p. 27]. For those who do not see the "Prelude," the significance of the Mist-Mothers, in connection with the Heptalogy of which these plays are a portion, will be found in *A Garland to Sylvia* (New York: Macmillan Co., 1910), pp. 160–171. When practicable, a chorus of three voices should sing the first three lines, and a solo chant the remainder of the song: for the words are important to the play.

3. *See* pp. 254, 273, 276; *also* final scene of *The Fool in Eden Garden.*

4. *See* Note 2 above, and general Note on Music, below.

5. The "deep tones" of King Hamlet's voice in any production should be amplified with a deep, soft reverberation such as shall fill the whole scene; but mystically, not noisily—in a way that leads directly, uninterruptedly, but dwindlingly on to the opening voice of the "Postlude." That voice should be like that of an angel who has witnessed the whole struggle of these mortal beings and sums up the story. The last verse is taken up by a chorus which should be heard while the curtain is falling and briefly afterward. Thus there is no fall of the curtain between the ending of the Tetralogy and the "Postlude," but the two are blended orally.

6. The verse beginning "Then let the strucken deer go weep," is from *Hamlet,* Act III, sc. 2. *See also,* general Note on Music, below.

MUSIC

THROUGHOUT this Tetralogy and its Prelude, the music of all songs, lilts, chants, and choruses [except those which are traditional] originated in the mind of the author simultaneously with the words. He hardly realized this consciously until the first occasion arose for him to read the plays aloud. Then the outward sound became consonant with the inward, and it was as simply natural for him to sing, lilt or chant the words in accord with their melodies and rhythms as it was to speak the lines of verse-dialogue in accord with their metric and rhythmic structure. All being structural elements of one continuous lyric-dramatic reverie, directly related to human life and human insight of the superhuman, the total work is naturally integrated with the art of the theatre, which by its fusion of all the arts is concerned with the full scale of human consciousness. In that scale, of course, music is peculiarly an element, inseparable from the art of the singer and of the symphonist. Potentially the author of this work is both, whatever be his defects as such in accomplishment. So he finds, somewhat to his surprise, that he is both the author and the composer of it: "composer," however, in no usually accepted musical sense, for he is almost totally ignorant of the technique of music and cannot easily read a bar of music script.

It may, therefore, appear strange that, in the premiere production of the Tetralogy, the musical items of it were sung, lilted, or chanted, in strict accordance with the author's "composing." This occurred because of the invaluable assistance in their transcription which he secured from Professor Child Lathrop and Marion Nugent Lathrop, who caught, from repeated hearings of his wire recordings, the folksong quality of these melodies which the author has heard for so long in his head.

Both members of the Brooklyn College faculty, the Lathrops are musicians of catholic tastes and interests. The author owes them his profound gratitude for transcribing the quality of these melodies; for they have been as *un*academic in their transcriptions of the material as the music actually is, thus keeping the informal nature of the melodies, which should be sung almost as though they were improvisations by the actors—as mountaineer folk-singers render the Elizabethan ballads which are still handed down from generation to generation in the Appalachian regions of America.

When it was decided to insert the music for these songs in the text, it seemed more fitting to leave out the usual directive concerning how the song should be sung. In general the melodies should be sung slowly, with great freedom, especially those in which it was considered best to use no bars at all. However, "Gaze there where the moon's white beams," should be sung very slowly; "And all the world were a green cheese," briskly; "Far, far from England," vigorously; and "The stag that bells at break of day" should be sung at moderate tempo.

Aside from its value as a foil to the rigidity of type, calligraphy offers a more personalized interpretation of the author's meaning, which, in the case of the songs and lilts, is still further enhanced by writing out the melodic line. Raymond F. Da Boll, designer of this book, derived the style of his musical notation from early manuscripts where the diamond-shaped note was prevalent. The style of the calligraphy is based on the chancery cursive hand of a 16th century scribe, Ludovico degli Arrighi, whose work has been given special study by the designer for the past twelve years. Thus, it is related to Frederic Warde's italic type, *Arrighi,* derived from the same source and used throughout this book in combination with the noblest roman of them all—the Centaur of Bruce Rogers.

Not only through the use of freehand calligraphy for the music and for other decorative features at the front and the back, has Mr. Da Boll enlivened the text of this book: The marginal symbols and the device which marks the beginning and end of direct quotations from Shakespeare were worked out in conference with the author. They are closely related to calligraphy and, aside from their decorative value, indicate to the reader different planes of action which in actual performance would be accomplished by lighting or other theatrical effects. In regard to the solid black bleed pages, the designer and the author are aware that they are a radical departure from tradition in a book dealing with as traditional a character as Hamlet. They feel, however, that these provide a necessary element of surprise, and that, since illustrations as such have been avoided, this powerful graphic device is consistent with the symbolism used throughout the book and is justified by its dramatic impact.

INDEX OF SONGS AND MUSIC

---

*Sung by Voices of the Invisible.

†Information concerning music for this may be obtained by writin to the author in care of the publisher. The same is true for all the lilts of Yorick.

ENVOI

For Sylvia from Felix

What was nowhere now is here!
What was not for seeing-
eyes, but all-exceeding near
to being
nigh
for the outward-blinded eye
that listens,
and the inward ear
whose vision glistens
ever keenlier, calmlier clear
with the onward coming
of beauty, like the far, moon-wafted humming
of lunar-moth wings o'er
death's arbutus-scented shore:

What from out that unseen, magic bourn
back we brought
in thought
{whose silence more excels
than the thrilling
bringing
of its singing},
Sylvia, now't is here, and I
with you am eager-willing
to return.
So—to all else
at all
but that All-Magical—
. . . . goodbye . . !